A Historical and Contemporary Look at Psychological Systems

Joseph J. Pear

University of Manitoba

LEA LAWRENCE ERLBAUM ASSOCIATES, PUBLISHERS
2007 Mahwah, New Jersey   London

Senior Acquisitions Editor: Debra Riegert
Editorial Assistant: Rebecca Larsen
Cover Design: Tomai Maridou
Full-Service Compositor: MidAtlantic Books and Journals, Inc.

The cover design was inspired by a suggestion from Frances Falzarano.

Lawrence Erlbaum Associates, Inc., Publishers
10 Industrial Avenue
Mahwah, New Jersey 07430
www.erlbaum.com

Library of Congress Cataloging-in-Publication Data

Pear, Joseph, 1938–
A historical and contemporary look at psychological systems / Joseph J. Pear.
    p. cm.
Includes bibliographical references.
ISBN 0-8058-5078-3 (case : alk. paper) — ISBN 0-8058-5079-1 (pbk. : alk. paper)
1. Psychology—History. I.Title.
BF81.P43 2007
150.9—dc22

        2006030181

Books published by Lawrence Erlbaum Associates are printed on
acid-free paper, and their bindings are chosen for strength and durability.

Printed in the United States of America

10 9 8 7 6 5 4 3 2 1

To My Brother, Bill

Contents

Foreword

Exposure to the history and systems of psychology has long been the "capstone" requirement for the major in many, perhaps most, undergraduate psychology programs in colleges and universities throughout the Western world. A comparable course has also often been required in curricula for master's and doctoral degrees, typically during the first or second year of graduate study. These requirements are appropriate. Psychology is now such a diverse discipline that there often is little overlap in subject matter among the various specialized courses that make up the typical psychology curriculum. Immersion in the history of the discipline, including examination of the various perspectives ("schools" or "systems") that have emerged for study of the variegated aspects of psychology's many facets, can help provide an at least somewhat integrative overview of the now fractionated field of psychology.

Several textbooks are currently available for both undergraduate and graduate courses on the history and systems of psychology, most of them well suited to the task. But almost all of them use the same basic strategy. After a brief (typically quite cursory) examination of ancient, medieval, and Renaissance precursors to later thought about what are now considered to be psychological issues, there are chapters on eighteenth and nineteenth century developments in philosophy and natural science that led to the emergence of psychology as a distinct discipline aspiring to become an experimental science. Discussion of the late nineteenth century founding of psychological laboratories is typically followed by a detailed account of the major "schools" of psychology that flourished primarily during the first half of the twentieth century: structuralism, functionalism, psychoanalysis, Gestalt theory, behaviorism, and sometimes a few others as well. Most available texts end with a chapter or two on developments after the "age of schools" waned during the second half of the twentieth century, and many of them deal at least briefly with the emergence of such newer orientations as cognitive psychology, neuroscience, evolutionary psychology, behavioral genetics, and other currently prominent perspectives.

This strategy which, to repeat, is typical of almost all history and systems textbooks now in print, appears to work reasonably well—but it also is becoming a bit stale. The "schools" of the first half of the twentieth century no longer dominate the field and no longer structure the research activities and scholarly endeavors of today's psychologists. Perhaps it is time for an alternative strategy for teaching "history and systems."

Professor Pear offers an intriguing one. In this boldly original book he invites the reader to develop a sophisticated overview of the fragmented discipline of psychology in an entirely new and creative way. Instead of focusing on the mostly moribund classical "schools" of psychology, he proposes that there are now four distinct "systems" identifiable on the psychological scene. While they have their roots, of course, in the preceding classical "schools" and systems, they are, he claims, the dominant approaches being used de facto during the early twenty-first century. He calls these approaches respectively the humanistic, psychodynamic, cognitive, and behavioral. He does identify two other major recent trends, evolutionary psychology and neuroscience, but decided that these two in a sense inform all the other four, so that they need not be treated as separate "systems" or "approaches" in themselves.

Professor Pear's innovations do not end with his analysis of the four primary contemporary "systems" of psychological thought. He also came up with the device of identifying a set of what he calls "issues that have been fundamental to psychology throughout its history": consciousness, the "divisions of the whole person," teleology, free will, values, spirituality, therapy, and the nature of psychological research. Then he discusses in some detail how each of the four "systems" deals with each of these "issues" in a unique manner that no other textbook has ever attempted in quite this way before.

Part I of this book considers the historical background that led to the emergence of the four "systems." It does so in a manner that is similar to the strategy of most other history of psychology textbooks, but differs from the "traditional" treatment in several ways. It aptly devotes more detail to very early psychological thought than most other textbooks do. It also provides a somewhat idiosyncratic account of the usual topics— giving shorter shrift, for example, to some of the classical "schools" (such as Gestalt psychology) than most other texts, and often includes critical or controversial—but refreshing—original comments that should be intriguing, even challenging, to those readers who have already been introduced to the history of psychology by more traditional texts.

How Professor Pear decided upon the eight "issues" he analyzes in Part II from the orientation of each of his four "approaches" is not revealed. It is an interesting, original, but inevitably highly idiosyncratic set, and other scholars would almost certainly come up with a different list of issues (in fact, I generated what turned out to be a very different set of "fundamental issues in psychology" that was published in a book with that title many years ago—a book that is long out of print), and might wish to discuss them in a different order. But they work. Most of the issues are ones that pique the curiosity of any thinking human being (at least in the Western world), and Professor Pear does a thorough job of showing how each of his four "approaches" deals with each of his "issues." (While he tries valiantly to do justice to each of the four "approaches," he does not quite succeed in hiding his preference for the behavioral orientation.)

To repeat, other scholars might wish to discuss Professor Pear's "issues" in a different sequence, might want to present the four "systems'" perspectives on them in a different order, might choose a different set of "approaches" than the humanistic, psychodynamic, cognitive, and behavioral and, most likely, would select a set of "issues" different from those chosen by the author. And the perspective of other scholars on the more traditional history and systems of psychology would also frequently differ from Professor Pear's orientation to and conclusions about this history and these systems.

But that is largely what makes this volume such a valuable contribution. This is a refreshing, original, highly creative and most welcome addition to the scholarly literature on the history and current systems of psychology.

Not only undergraduate and graduate students of psychology, faculty members given the task of teaching the course on the history and systems of psychology, and other intellectuals interested in the historical and philosophical underpinnings of psychology and of contemporary approaches to it will find this fascinating book innovative, controversial, and thoughtful. It will also be of interest to historians of science and to lay readers who would like to explore a lively new perspective over a fast-evolving, fragmented, but always inherently intriguing field. It does a fine job of describing four current major approaches to psychology, how they came into being, and how they differ from—and are similar to—each other, and how they all deal with some venerable psychological issues. The intellectual community owes Professor Pear thanks for having made available to the public a work that may not only sharpen further interest in psychology but is likely to challenge others to develop their own new and different perspectives both on the history of psychology and on the variety of approaches that now are available to deal with the myriad issues that should be addressed by the psychological community. It is to be hoped that this thought-provoking book will turn out to be a path-breaking pioneer and will spark additional innovative efforts to provide comprehensive overviews over the venerable yet ever-new discipline of psychology.

Michael Wertheimer, PhD
University of Colorado, Boulder

Preface

The writing of this book began with a question that students of psychology often ask: Why is psychology so diverse in its subject matter and theoretical approaches? Students are curious about what differentiates the different systems or approaches, how and why these differences came about, and what prospects may exist for reconciling them. The purpose of this book is twofold: (1) to help provide answers to these questions by examining the systems of psychology in a systematic way; and, (2) to provide a view of the interconnectedness as well as the distinctiveness of the diverse theoretical approaches to psychology. By going back to the roots of psychology and tracing them to where psychology is now, theoretically and methodologically, it is hoped that students and other readers will gain a clearer understanding of the foundational differences and similarities that currently exist between psychologists with various theoretical allegiances.

"Psyche" is the ancient Greek word for soul, and hence "psychology" literally means "the study or science of the soul." This book begins with the concept of soul in ancient times. The ancient Greek philosophers' concept of soul was perhaps closest to a modern scientific view, for they regarded the soul as part of the natural world and thus something that could be theorized about and studied. This concept eventually became tied up with early Christianity, culminating in Descartes' dualistic separation of the soul and body, which promoted the scientific study of the material body but left a large question mark regarding how to study the soul. Rechristening the "soul" as the "mind," the British Empiricists initiated its study as an association mechanism. Eventually the experimental method that had produced impressive advances in other sciences began to be applied to psychology. But the question of exactly *how* to apply the experimental method to psychology became a matter of many tensions between various competing approaches.

This book shows how four broad systems (each containing many factions) emerged out of these tensions: behavioral, cognitive, humanistic, and psychodynamic psychology. Although they may disagree on the specifics, all four systems acknowledge the dependence of psychology on neurological and evolutionary underpinnings. Hence, evolutionary psychology and neuro-psychology (neuroscience) are here considered to be supplementary approaches, their findings informing the four broad psychological systems. Having thus provided a conceptual framework for the major contemporary approaches to psychology, this book then explores the differences and similarities of the four broad systems with respect to issues that were the primary focus of early philosophers and psychologists: consciousness, reductionism, teleology, determinism, values, spirituality, therapy, and how scientific research in psychology should be done. These are topics that throughout the ages have been seen as central by philosophers and scientists interested in the soul or mind. Each of the four systems has addressed these problems in a characteristic manner, and their differing and often opposing approaches to these topics are among the most important differentiators of the four systems. In order for students and other readers to appreciate the differences between the four systems and their similarities and interconnectedness at a deep level, it is vital to understand their respective approaches to these topics.

The book is written at the undergraduate level. Supplemented with other readings, it is also appropriate for graduate courses. To facilitate the use of this book as a text in courses, I have placed discussion questions at the end of each chapter.

The divisions of the book are as follows:

Part I focuses on the history of psychology leading to the development of the four broad systems. It contains seven chapters.

Chapter 1 traces the concept of the soul from the ancient Egyptians to the rise of Christianity and Islam.

Chapter 2 details how the heritage of the Greeks and Romans gave rise to Western science, culminating in two opposing philosophical positions: British Empiricism and German Idealism.

Chapter 3 discusses the rise of psychology as a scientific field, the first psychological experiments, neurological advances, applications in psychiatry, and the impact on psychology of Darwin's theory of evolution.

Chapter 4 examines the emergence of three major schools of psychology: Wundt's voluntarism in Germany, the Brentano school in Austria, and the functionalists in America. The rise of psychoanalysis is also detailed. Particular attention is given to the conflict between functionalism and structuralism, an offshoot of Wundt's introspective approach.

Chapter 5 details how functionalism gave rise to behaviorism, which led to the demise of the introspective approach of structuralism, leaving Freudian psychoanalysis and Gestalt psychology as the major forces in psychology opposing behaviorism. Although Gestalt psychology as a separate approach eventually became marginalized, it contributed strongly to the four contemporary systems that emerged.

Chapter 6 details how humanistic psychology arose as a reaction to the deterministic and reductive approaches of behaviorism and psychoanalysis, and how cognitive psychology arose as a reaction to the restrictions of behaviorists on talking about the mind. With psychoanalysis branching into a number of subsystems, collectively referred to a psychodynamic psychology, the four broad systems and the two supplementary approaches are clearly delineated.

Chapter 7 gives an in-depth look at the formation of each broad system, focusing on the similarities and differences within them.

Part II deals with the four broad systems as they exist today, pointing out both similarities and differences. Eight of the nine chapters in this second part are each organized around a topic that has been of major interest in the history of psychology. Systematically examining how each of the four systems approaches these time-honored (and perhaps timeless) topics today is, I believe, the key to a deep understanding of the four systems in relation to one another. Thus, Chapters 8 to 15 examine consciousness, reductionism, teleology, determinism, values, spirituality, psychotherapy, and approaches to psychological research. Chapter 16 provides a summing up and some tentative conclusions, particularly with regard to whether the systems appear to be converging.

I am grateful to the following colleagues, students, and friends for their help in formulating my thoughts as I wrote this book: Wayne Chan, Darlene Crone-Todd, Daniela Fazzio, Jim Forest, Tammy Ivanco, David Martin, Toby Martin, Jim Nickels, and Fran Silva. Special thanks go to Fran Falzarano and Tim Schroeder for the many detailed comments they made on drafts of the manuscript. I also thank the two reviewers whose feedback and comments were extremely helpful: Dr. Bernard Beins (Ithaca College) and Dr. Michael Wertheimer (University of Colorado). Further, I greatly appreciate the excellent foreword that the latter wrote for this book. Finally, I am grateful for the feedback I received from the students who used various versions of the text in my graduate and undergraduate courses in the history and systems of psychology. With all the generous and helpful feedback I have received on multiple drafts of this book, there should be no errors remaining in it. Any that do remain are mine alone.

PART I

A Historical Look

The psychological concepts that often may seem self-evident did not spring full blown into the heads of recent psychologists. The path to reach modern psychological concepts was long and often meandering. To understand psychological concepts and how they fit into contemporary psychological systems, it is helpful to look at the path that led to them. Part I of this book therefore provides an overview of the history of psychology.

The word *psychology* is a combination of the Greek words *psyche* and *logos*. *Psyche* (or *psuchè*), which originally meant *breath*, eventually came to mean *soul*. *Logos* has various meanings related to language, including *word*, *logic*, *study*, and *science*. Hence, psychology literally means the study or science of the soul. The word *psychology* is actually a fairly new word (coined about 500 years ago). The study of the soul, however, dates back a great deal earlier. But what is a soul?

The word that has been translated from other languages as *soul* often has shades of meaning that can only be approximately captured in English. There seem, however, to be three major meanings:

1. The soul is a life principle or life force—it is whatever it is that gives the individual the attribute of being alive. This may or may not be something inside of the individual that survives death and achieves an afterlife.
2. The soul is the part of the individual that senses, perceives, remembers, thinks, feels, and controls the individual's behavior.

3.   Rather than being an entity or thing (as it would have to be if it were a part of the individual), the soul is the overall functioning of the individual, including sensing, thinking, feeling, and behaving.

Every culture has developed something that might fall under the general label of science—the *logy* part of *psychology*. Clearly, even a cursory review of the history of science in every culture would be a monumental undertaking. Fortunately, this is not necessary for our purpose. The science whose origins are dealt with in this part of the book is that which today is taught as modern science all over the world independent of any particular culture. In a sequence of what in hindsight appears to be instances of human brilliance interspersed with amazing historical accidents, a particular group of cultures participated in the evolution of modern science, and therefore of modern psychological science.

CHAPTER 1

The Beginnings of Science and the Concepts of Soul

A natomically modern humans, people whom paleontology indicates were physically identical to us, evolved about 200,000 years ago in Africa (McDougall, Brown, & Fleagle, 2005). *Homo sapiens sapiens* (the commonly accepted scientific name for our species) showed remarkable ingenuity, which enabled them to spread out gradually to every habitable part of the world. The tools they made—stone knives and axes, spear throwers, bows and arrows, needles and thread—clearly involved scientific principles. However, they did not possess an understanding of these principles as a science.

PRECONDITIONS FOR THE DEVELOPMENT OF SCIENCE

Science could develop only after people had begun to live in cities supported by a surrounding agriculture. This provided a small proportion of individuals with the time needed to devote to science and a community of like-minded individuals with whom to share its development. Agriculture, however, developed very slowly for a number of reasons. The world that humans evolved into was very different from what it had become at the time that history began to be recorded. For hundreds of thousands of years, the earth's climate fluctuated erratically between long periods of extreme heat and ice ages. Then, for reasons that are not well understood, the earth's climate became stable enough to sustain agriculture and has remained relatively stable so far (Wright, 2004, pp. 51–52). Initially only a few plants that people could eat were suitable for cultivation (Diamond, 1997). Similarly, only a few animals were suitable for domestication, and suitable foods had to be available for them.

In addition to suitable climatic and soil conditions, a great deal of genetic selection of plants and animals by people had to occur before the first primitive farmlands could come into being. This genetic selection undoubtedly was accidental at first. Trade among different groups was also important in order to spread the seeds, tools, and animals necessary for agriculture. Moreover, population densities had to be sufficient for the specialized occupations that support an agricultural community. Furthermore, given the hard work agriculture requires, food from other sources had to be relatively sparse. Agriculture, therefore, developed gradually and, at least at first, largely by accident.

Thus, although anatomically modern humans evolved about 200,000 years ago, it was not until about 10,000 years ago that agriculture appeared in several extremely fertile locations in far-flung regions of the world. With agriculture came writing and mathematics, which originated for keeping inventories of livestock and agricultural products, but were also essential for the development of science.

EGYPT AND MESOPOTAMIA

The story of science and psychology begins in the fertile regions of Egypt and Mesopotamia about 1550 to 1250 BCE,[1] or about 8,500 years after the development of agriculture in these regions. By this time the Egyptians had invented a form of writing, called hieroglyphics, which they used to record their knowledge and beliefs. These included astronomical knowledge and a detailed description of their beliefs concerning the soul, which they saw as an entity that was much like a glorified version of the body. Their soul concept was tied in with their view of an afterlife, about which they had an extremely detailed description (Budge, 1997).

To the northeast of Egypt was Mesopotamia, which is the region of present-day Iraq. One of the earliest people in this area, the Sumerians, had devised a form of writing called cuneiform by about 3200 BCE (Maisels, 2001, p. 180). A later group of people who absorbed Sumerian culture, the Babylonians, had, like the Egyptians, a concept of the soul bound up with an afterlife. For the Babylonians, however, the afterlife was not considered a pleasant reward for good behavior, nor was it necessarily permanent. Babylonia was absorbed by Assyria, an empire that lasted from about 911 BCE to its defeat by Persia around 612 BCE.

---

1. BCE ("before the Common Era") replaces BC ("before Christ") and CE ("the Common Era") replaces AD ("Anno Domini") in most modern scholarly writings on antiquity.

THE ISRAELITES

Between Egypt and Mesopotamia was a region that was inhabited largely by the Hebrews or Israelites. Assyria conquered a large portion of the land of the Hebrews and exiled a number of them to Babylon (near present-day Baghdad) where they remained until the defeat of Assyria by Persia. The Hebrews appear to have been strongly influenced by the Egyptians and Babylonians in their mythology and the development of writing. The Hebrew myths, based on Egyptian and Babylonian myths, were recorded in their Sacred Scriptures (the Hebrew Bible, which is essentially the same as the Old Testament of the Christian Bible) soon after the return of many of them from Babylon. In several respects, however, the Hebrews were different from other peoples in the region. Although at first they believed in many gods and an afterlife, this had changed by the time they started recording their Bible (McDannell & Lang, 1988).

Instead of many gods, they believed in only one deity. Their efforts were concentrated on attempting to obey what they perceived to be the will of their deity. Despite their close contacts with the Egyptians and Babylonians, they appear not to have had a concept of a soul that persisted independent of the body or a belief in an afterlife. Instead, they believed that people and animals alike are made of dust and at death return to dust (e.g., see van Uchelen, 1994).

The Hebrew word *nephesh* is the word that has been translated into *psyche* or *soul*. As used in the Hebrew Bible, however, *nephesh* has various meanings, including life, living creature, person, and self. Like *psyche* it originally meant *breath*, but it seems not to have referred to something that survives the death of the body. The most by way of personal reward that the ancient Hebrews expected for pleasing their deity was a long life and other earthly amenities, although these were by no means guaranteed. Constantly subjected to domination by more powerful nations, they developed the belief that their deity would provide a future leader or *Messiah*—the word comes from the Hebrew for anointed—who would establish them as a great nation. Thus, rather than personal survival, the ancient Hebrews directed their aspirations toward their survival as a people.

PERSIA

The main religion of Persia, which is present-day Iran, was Zoroastrianism, so called because the Greek name for the prophet of this religion, Zarathustra or Zarathushtra (628? BCE–551? BCE), was Zoroaster. Zarathustra taught that there are two opposing forces in the cosmos—a force for good, led by an uncreated good spirit, and a force for evil, led by an evil spirit. He further taught that there would be a final judgment in which the souls of the dead would be reunited with their bodies and they would be rewarded in a pleasant hereafter on earth if they aligned themselves with the good spirit and performed good acts. However, they would be punished eternally in an unpleasant place if they aligned themselves with the evil spirit. Zoroastrianism may have had a strong influence on certain resurrection beliefs of the ancient Hebrews (McDannell & Lang, 1988), and on the soul beliefs of the Greeks.

GREECE: BIRTHPLACE OF SCIENCE

The attempt of the Persian Empire to expand westward was blocked by the growing power of Greece. Through Persia, the Greeks absorbed Babylonian influences, including astronomy and mathematics. Like most peoples in the region, the Greeks had multiple deities and concepts of a soul and an afterlife. They developed a rich mythology concerning their gods, their heroes, the soul, and an afterlife.

The afterlife envisioned by the Greeks in their early mythology was not optimistic. The soul was the life force of the body; without it, the body was an inanimate corpse. However, the soul also needed the body in order to be fully functioning. The Greek epic poet Homer (who lived sometime between 900 and 700 BCE) described the souls of the dead as *shades*—that is, mere shadows of their former embodied selves. Having no vocal chords, they were not even able to speak in a normal voice, but instead were described as making high-pitched or squeaking sounds. The sensing, perceptual, intellectual, emotional, and feeling functions apparently were not functions of the soul, but of the body, and died with it.

However, we must make a sharp distinction between Greek mythology or religion and a much more remarkable development that took place in Greece. This was the widespread acceptance and fostering of the view that knowledge can be obtained through thinking and questioning as opposed to blind acceptance of authority. It is not completely clear why this attitude developed in Greece to a much greater extent than elsewhere, but geography was probably a critical factor. In the hills and mountains of Greece there were many potential hiding places, making it possible to escape from any ruler who might take offense at an expressed opinion. Also, ancient Greece consisted of independent city-states; if a person offended the authorities in one state, that person could flee to or be rescued by another state. This is not to say that individuals did not sometimes pay dearly, even with their lives, for expressing opinions that a ruler might consider subversive. Greek culture, however, was more accepting of questioning and free expression than other contemporary cultures. Also helpful to the development of science is the fact the Greeks invented a cursive form of writing. While hieroglyphics and cuneiform were adapted for keeping lists of items, cursive writing is ideal for relating and discussing, and hence more conducive to scientific communication.

Because of its relative openness to questioning and debate, Greece became the cradle of democracy and of science. With regard to science, Greek thinkers questioned and theorized about all aspects of nature. The Greeks called this *philosophy*—from the Greek words *phil*, meaning love, and *sophia*, meaning wisdom or knowledge: love of wisdom.

Thales of Miletus

Philosophy seems to have begun in the Greek-colonized city of Miletus, located on the west coast of Turkey, with the philosopher Thales (624?–547? BCE). Thales may be said to be the first scientist that we know of. He made many astute astronomical observations and mathematical contributions. He also tried to explain all phenomena on the basis of a single principle, namely, that everything is made of water. Thales' reasons for this theory are open to speculation; however, it may have been prompted by observations such as that water is prevalent on the earth, that many things contain water, that living things require water, and that water can change its state (e.g., from a liquid to ice or steam). Another thing that Thales speculated about was the soul, which he regarded to be self-moving and immortal.

Later Greek philosophers, as we shall see, expanded the number of elements from one (water) to four: earth, air, fire, and water. However, the idea that everything is composed of just one or a few basic things followed directly from Thales. In addition, also following the lead of Thales, later Greek philosophers speculated about the soul.

In general, the early Greek philosophers held that the soul has three constituents or parts: *nous*, *phren*, and *thumos*. Although the functions of these parts varied somewhat among philosophers, nous was generally the thinking part, phren the perceiving part, and thumos the passionate or feeling part. Animals were said to have only the latter two parts, but humans were believed to have all three. Nous was usually the only part of the soul that was said to survive after death. Nous and phren are typically translated into English as mind.

The Pythagoreans

A highly influential school of philosophical thought was founded by the Greek mathematician Pythagoras (580?–500? BCE), who is best known today for the theorem that bears his name—although that particular mathematical fact was well known to the Babylonians in 1850 BCE, long before Pythagoras was born. The Pythagoreans' philosophy was based loosely on mathematics, and they were especially fascinated by ratios. They had discovered that the sounds produced by certain ratios of, for example, the strings of a lyre are more pleasing than the sounds produced by other ratios. In the spirit of generalization that was promoted by Thales and eventually came to characterize science, Pythagoreans extended this principle to everything.

The Music of the Spheres

The Pythagoreans saw a relationship between mathematics and music, and regarded both to be fundamental to the cosmos or universe. They believed that in the cycles of the moon, planets, sun, and stars, the heavenly bodies were generating a form of music—the music of the spheres—that was too lofty for mere mortals to hear.

The Pythagorean Concept of the Soul

For the Pythagoreans, music was also connected to their belief in the soul and the afterlife. According to them, the soul is a "harmony" and each star contains a soul that enters a human body, goes through a number of reincarnations, and finally reenters a star. The likely influence of this teaching on astrology is apparent, since the star one was born under would determine which soul would enter one's body. The Pythagorean belief in a soul entering a heavenly body when the human body it inhabits dies may be, in part, the source of the belief that after death the souls of the good go to heaven, which, it is believed, is located somewhere above us. The Pythagorean concept of the stars containing souls enjoined in the music of the spheres could be the source of the belief that heaven is populated by harp-playing angels.

In contrast to the Greek view of the soul in Homer's time, Pythagoras attributed psychological functions such as thinking and feeling to souls. A story told about Pythagoras coming across a man beating a dog illustrates his belief that many of a person's attributes—not just the life force—resided in the person's soul. According to the story, Pythagoras claimed that he recognized the voice of a deceased friend in the dog's yelps and pleaded for the man to stop beating the dog. Apparently Pythagoras believed that he was hearing the voice of his friend's reincarnated soul in the dog's body and that his friend was suffering from the beating.

A Possible Connection to the Religions of India

There may have been cross influences between the Pythagorean and Indian concepts of reincarnation through direct and indirect contacts between the peoples of Greece and India (e.g., see McEvilley, 2002; Vassiliades, 2004). Two major religions have their origin in India: Hinduism and

Buddhism. The latter in particular was eventually to have an important influence on psychology. The founder of Buddhism, Siddhartha Gautama (586?–? BCE), was a contemporary of Pythagoras. Focusing on obtaining enlightenment through meditation, Buddhism maintains that the soul is an illusory concept while at the same time retaining a version of the Hindu concept of reincarnation. Since there is no soul to be reincarnated, Buddhists speak of rebirth rather than reincarnation.

The Four Elements and Pneuma (The Soul Substance)

While the Pythagoreans emphasized the idea of the soul as a harmony among elements of the body, other philosophers tried to identify the soul with some type of material substance. They held that it might be composed of one or more of three of the four basic elements: earth, water, air, and fire. By considering the human body, one can appreciate how they arrived at these elements of which everything is supposedly composed. The human body is clearly composed of earth because upon death the flesh turns to dirt. It is also clear that the human body contains water, in the form of blood and other bodily fluids. A live human body also takes in and expels air, and therefore contains air. A live human body is also warm, and so contains either fire or something like it.

Some Greek thinkers hypothesized that because a live body breathes and is warm, whereas a dead body does not breathe and is cold, the soul must be composed of air and fire. The material of which the soul was supposed to be composed was called *pneuma*. Rather than contradictory of the Pythagorean view, this view could be seen as compatible with it. Perhaps the stars, for example, were composed of bright air or brilliant fire—that is, pneuma—and hence contained souls as the Pythagoreans claimed. The combination of air and fire was not the only candidate for the composition of the soul in Greek philosophy. Cases were made for the soul being composed of each of the elements except earth, separately or in combination with other elements.

Empedocles

Empedocles (490?–430 BCE) is the first Greek philosopher on record who postulated earth, water, air, and fire as the four basic elements. He postulated that these elements interact through two forces: one of attraction, called love, and one of repulsion, called strife. It was natural for philosophers of that time to think of things important to humans as being important to nature as a whole. As was typical of the ancient Greek thinkers, Empedocles designed his theory to attain complete generality: any happening, including human relationships, was an instance of these elements interacting through these forces. A physician who saw the universe as a process forever in a state of flux or change, like the body, Empedocles also came up with a crude theory of evolution. He conceived the idea of body parts springing forth and eventually joining together in a haphazard manner with those forms that were the most stable surviving. Empedocles believed that pneuma (the soul substance) consisted of air (note that breath and soul were originally synonymous), although he knew from his anatomical research that the fetus was surrounded by a fluid and could not be breathing. He postulated that through the placenta the mother provided the air that constituted the soul of the fetus.

Empedocles also held a form of what today is known as the *copy theory*, which purposes to explain how we know the world external to ourselves and are able to remember events that we have experienced and things that we have encountered. According to this theory, objects in the world give off images or copies of themselves that enter the senses and are transmitted to the soul. Thinking consists of agitation of these images. In one form or another, the copy theory has persisted to the present day in a number of psychological theories. For example, in a good deal of contemporary cognitive theory there are internal symbols that are considered to be representations or copies of objects and events in the external world.

Democritus

Democritus (460?–360? BCE) went beyond the four elements in his quest to understand the basic composition of everything. Inspired by his teacher, Leucippus of Miletus (480?–420? BCE), Democritus postulated that all matter is composed of atoms, which are particles that would be arrived at if one were to keep dividing a piece of material until it could not be subdivided further (hence the name atom: *a* for *not* and *tomus* for *to cut*). In other words, according to Democritus, atoms are indivisible constituents of matter.

According to Democritus, atoms come in different shapes and sizes. The soul, according to Democritus, is composed of very small, perfectly round atoms, which explains how it can move so rapidly throughout the body to sense stimuli and respond. If the body is the instrument through which the soul perceives the world, atoms explain how this occurs. For example, acidic foods have a sharp taste because, according to Democritus, their atoms are triangular (i.e., they have sharp points). Democritus had a version of the copy theory that was similar to that of Empedocles. According to Democritus, atoms emanating from objects enter the senses and cause copies of the objects they emanate from to be created out of the highly mobile fire atoms in the body.

Hippocrates

Around this same time period, the Greek physician Hippocrates (460?–377? BCE) was advancing medical science. In fact, he is considered to be the Father of Medicine and is known for the Hippocratic Oath, which even today many physicians swear to (although a modern version, not the original). Little is actually known about Hippocrates. In fact, many of the writings previously attributed to him have turned out to be written by unknown others who considered themselves his followers. Therefore, the body of works originally attributed to him is termed the Hippocratic corpus. The major advance Hippocrates and his followers made was to classify and treat diseases as having natural, not supernatural, causes. They based their treatments on the study of anatomy and the reaction of diseases to the treatments.

Remarkably, Hippocrates extended his view of disease to what are now recognized as psychological or psychiatric disorders. Hippocrates attributed physical and psychiatric diseases or disorders to imbalances of various fluids or humors, specifically blood, phlegm, black bile, and yellow bile. This idea may have come from the observation that people who are sick often expel or discharge blood, phlegm, or black, or yellow bitter-tasting fluids. It would have seemed reasonable (although incorrect) to infer that the body was eliminating excesses of these fluids, and that, therefore, improper proportions of those fluids in the body caused illnesses. Moreover, the idea that there were exactly four humors was supported by a perceived correspondence with the four elements.

We know now that this theory was wrong. However, it was based on detailed observations, and the records that were kept resulted in classifications that were often valid. For example, with regard to psychological disorders, Hippocrates distinguished mania (wild or violent insanity), melancholia (extreme depression), and phrenitis (inflammation of the brain with fever and delirium). Hippocrates also associated different proportions of the humors with different temperaments or personality types. For example, a phlegmatic person was one who was calm and unemotional. It was thought that the balance of humors in the body also affected mood. Originally derived from Latin for moisture or liquid, the English word *humor* has given rise to expressions such as *good (or bad) humor* and *sense of humor*.

Socrates

We turn now to the three giants of Greek philosophy: Socrates, Plato, and Aristotle. Socrates (469?–399 BCE) proclaimed his views orally and left no writings. From what we know of him, which is mainly from his student

Plato, Socrates believed that truth could be arrived at through rational contemplation and dialogue with other individuals who were seeking truth. The truth that Socrates was most interested in was not knowledge of the cosmos and the composition of the soul. The knowledge he was seeking was what makes a person good and how one leads a good life (Grayling, 2003). He believed that the completely rational person would naturally be good, and that a good life was one of contemplation. Doing wrong, in other words, was due to the error of irrational thinking. Socrates was tried by his city-state, Athens, and condemned to death for the crime of disbelief in the gods of Athens and for corrupting the youth, showing that acceptance of radical views was not universally characteristic of Greece. Socrates could have escaped but chose not to, believing that the more rational and noble course was to accept the sentence of his peers.

Plato

It is difficult to separate the views of Plato (427–347 BCE) from those of his mentor, Socrates, because Plato's writings consist of dialogues in which Socrates is the main interlocutor. It is generally, believed, however, that the more theoretical views expressed by Socrates in the later dialogues belong to Plato. Socrates was more concerned with rational thinking and goodness than in theoretical matters. Like his mentor, Plato was concerned with rationality and what makes a person good. Both of these characteristics, he believed, had to do with a person's soul.

In Plato we see the concept of the soul developed to a greater extent than it had been by previous philosophers. In particular, the soul took on a moral function. It no longer was merely the life principle or force. It was what enabled a person to be rational and good—which were equated by Socrates and Plato, both of whom held that it was rational to be good. In addition, Plato believed that a person could improve his or her soul by being rational and good. By adding a moral feature to the soul, Plato made a major advance toward what was to become the Christian and Muslim concept of the soul. It is to Plato, more than to any other individual, that we owe our current concept of the soul and—most important from the standpoint of psychology—of mind, as we shall see.

Plato viewed the soul as being organized like a state, with a good soul being organized along the lines of a well-ordered state. According to Plato, there are three parts or aspects of the soul: a rational part, an emotional part, and an appetitive part. These three come into conflict; but the ideal soul is ruled by the rational part, just as a wise king rules a well-ordered state. Each part of the soul has particular functions, and has particular virtues associated with it (e.g., the virtue of courage stems from the emotional part of the soul). Because the soul is self-moving (and therefore, presumably, cannot be stopped), according to Plato, it, or at least the rational part (Plato sometimes used the word *soul* to refer to just the rational part), is immortal. The Greek for the rational part of the soul or "rational soul" is often translated into English as *mind*.

One of Plato's most important ideas is his theory of forms, which has had a strong impact on all subsequent philosophy and religion. According to this theory, behind everything there is an unseen but ideal form of that thing. Thus, although no one has seen a perfect circle, for example, a perfect circle exists in an abstract universe of forms. All circles, according to Plato, partake in some measure of that perfect circle. Likewise, there is an ideal form of the soul. The ideal form of the soul is God, which is either Zeus (the ruler of the gods) or a higher god altogether. Unlike the Jews and, later, the Christians and Muslims, Plato did not have the concept of a God who created all things out of nothing. In addition, unlike the God of the three major monotheistic religions, Plato's God was impersonal.

When a person is striving to be good, according to Plato, the rational part of that person's soul is striving toward the ideal form of the soul. The irrational parts of the soul, however, seek fulfillment of their own desires. The good person lets the rational part of the soul rule the other parts, but some conflict is unavoidable.

To a large extent Plato accepted Pythagorean teachings. For example, he believed that knowledge is not arrived at through our senses, but rather is something we are born with through previous reincarnations. Learning thus is more like a process of remembering than of acquiring something new.

Plato taught in a park called the Academy, which therefore is often regarded as the first university and whose name has given rise to *academic* and related words. Students at the Academy probably used wax tablets to write notes, because these (unlike clay tablets that became hard) could be erased when what was written on them was no longer needed. These wax tablets provided a metaphor for a theory of memory, whereby Plato postulated that the brain—which Plato, agreeing with Hippocrates, thought to be the seat of thinking or the rational part of the soul—is like a wax tablet on which we stamp or impress things that we wish to remember (Draaisma, 2000, pp. 24–25). He attributed the supposed fact that individuals who learn quickly forget quickly, whereas individuals who learn slowly retain what they have learned longer, to the moistness of the brain. A more moist brain (like a wax tablet) receives impressions more readily but loses them faster, whereas a less moist brain (like a hard clay tablet) takes impressions less rapidly but keeps them longer. Note that this is a rather elaborate view of the copy theory such as held by Empedocles and Democritus, as described earlier.

This theory, like many other ideas of the Greek philosophers, would have been interesting to test experimentally. However, there was a bias against empirical research. Knowledge was to be obtained by rational contemplation, which was considered more worthy of philosophers than research that involved dirtying one's hands. That was work more fit for a slave or common laborer than for high-minded rational thinkers. There were individuals who went against this bias, one of whom we consider next.

Aristotle

Aristotle (384–322 BCE) was Plato's student, but disagreed with him in a number of respects. One of Aristotle's most notable sayings is, "Plato is my friend but truth is my greater friend." In particular, he vehemently disagreed with Plato's theory of forms. In addition, Aristotle carried out empirical research, mainly in the field known today as biology.

Aristotle's Theory of Forms: Hylomorphism

For Aristotle there is no universe of ideal forms that exists independently of the universe of things. Forms can exist only in some material substrate. Thus, a statue of Pericles consists of some material in the form of Pericles. There are many types of material that a sculptor could give the form of Pericles—for example, bronze or marble—but in no case can the form of Pericles exist independently of some material medium. In this example, one might think that form is shape. But the concept is broader than that, for it can also refer to function. For example, according to Aristotle, the form of the eye is sight. An eye that does not have the function of sight would not be an eye just as a piece of bronze that does not have the shape of Pericles would not be a statue of Pericles.

Thus, by the form of a thing, Aristotle meant those qualities and properties that cause us to place it in a particular category, which Aristotle considered to be its essence. This view that things consist of a material base combined with a form that depends on the material base is called *hylomorphism* (from the Greek *hyle* meaning *matter* and *morph* meaning *form*).

The Soul

Aristotle defined the soul as the form of the body. Thus, he did not regard the soul to be something in the body or in any way an independent part of it. He thought it as ridiculous to say, for example, that the soul feels an emotion as it is to say that the soul weaves or builds (Gallop, 1999, pp. 91–92). It is the person who feels just as it is the person who weaves.

According to Aristotle, the soul is the functioning of the body in the performance of its various activities. Similar to the way in which a piece of bronze cannot be a statue of Pericles without the shape of Pericles, a body without a soul is not a living body. It is relevant to note that the Greeks had separate words for living body (*soma*) and dead body or corpse (*nekros*).

Aspects of the Soul

Similar to Plato, Aristotle held that there are three aspects of the soul, which are sometimes called types of souls: a vegetative soul, a sentient soul, and a rational soul. Plants have the first, animals the first and second, and humans have all three. Like Socrates and Plato, Aristotle considered a well-ordered soul to be a goal that a rational person seeks. The way to achieve this, according to Aristotle, is to order one's functions and interactions in a harmonious manner. Consistent with his view that the soul cannot exist apart from the body any more than a statue can exist apart from the material of which it is made, Aristotle did not believe in personal survival after death (e.g., see Poortman, 1994, pp. 200–201).

The Four Causes

Aristotle identified four types of explanations that should be considered in accounting for any phenomenon: the efficient, the material, the formal, and the final. The term *cause*, however, is somewhat misleading because of our modern tendency to identify cause with Aristotle's efficient cause. Rather than Aristotle's four causes, it might be better to speak of his four *becauses*.

The efficient cause is, as indicated above, what we usually think of as a cause. It is an immediately preceding event that produces the outcome in question. For example, one stone striking another will cause the second stone to move. The material cause is the nature of the material that results in the outcome. For example, glass being hit by a stone will break because glass is the kind of material that breaks when struck with something hard. The formal cause is the plan, design, or shape of a thing. For example, the shape of a bowl causes it to hold water. Final cause refers to the end-state toward which things move or strive. For example, the natural state of heavy objects is to be at or near the center of the world. Another name for final cause is the *principle of teleology* or simply *teleology*.

Aristotle's emphasis on teleology or final cause led him to disagree with much theorizing that had gone on before. For example, he opposed the notions of evolution and of atoms, because these views imply random motion, which contradicts his view that things move inexorably toward their natural place or position. He also rejected atomic theory because it required the existence of nothingness, also called the void, for atoms to move in. The existence of nothingness seemed to Aristotle, as to many other Greek philosophers, to be a contradiction. Aristotle also opposed any suggestion that the earth revolves around the sun, rather than that all the heavenly bodies revolve around the earth, because the center of the earth was the natural place for all heavy objects and, therefore, had to be stationary.

Scientific Observation

Aristotle's work in science was prodigious. For example, he studied and described the development of chicks in fertilized eggs, and his work on embryology was highly sophisticated. He described, classified, and studied the behavior of numerous animals. This endeavor may have been aided by the fact that as the former tutor of Alexander the Great he had access to exotic animal specimens from regions that Alexander conquered. He was also interested in accounting for sensation and perception.

Theory of the Heart as the Seat of Feeling and Thinking

He theorized that the heart is the center of feeling and thinking, and that sense impressions are conveyed from the sense organs to the heart through the blood vessels. It is from this theory that we get expressions such as to take something *to heart* and to learning something *by heart*. The theory was reasonable at that time. Observation showed that the blood vessels connect to the heart, the vessels contain a fluid (blood) that clearly is vital to life (hence, might well contain the soul substance, pneuma), and the heart beats constantly in life and ceases to beat in death. Moreover, the heart varies its beating according to one's emotional state. There were other philosophers, however, who believed that the nerves conveyed sense impressions into the interior of the body, and that the brain—not the heart—was the center of feeling and thinking. Hippocrates, for example, may have held this view on the basis of studies involving dissection of nerves and the brain. Aristotle's teacher, Plato, also regarded the brain as the seat of thought and feeling.

Philosophers of the Good Life

As mentioned earlier, the focus of Socrates was on how one can live a good life. Three other Greek philosophers who were concerned with this were Diogenes, Epicurus, and Zeno of Citium (Grayling, 2003).

Diogenes

Diogenes (412?–323 BCE) founded a movement called Cynicism. He believed that the source of unhappiness is ambition and desire for material goods. He advocated forgoing such pleasures and living as simply as possible, as animals do. Because he practiced his belief to the point of never washing and living a hand-to-mouth existence, he was nicknamed the *Divine Dog*.

Epicurus

At first glance, it appears that Epicurus (342?–270 BCE) taught just the opposite. He taught that one should live for pleasure. However, he was not referring just to the pleasures of the senses or hedonism, as has sometimes been thought. He regarded the virtuous or moral life to be the most pleasant, and included philosophical contemplation and discussion to be among the greatest pleasures.

Epicurus was impressed with Democritus' arguments in favor of atomism—e.g., that if everything were infinitely divisible, matter would eventually divide into vanishingly tiny portions, and hence material things would cease to exist. Rather than moving randomly in all directions, as Democritus believed, Epicurus maintained that atoms had weight and therefore tended to move straight downward. Recognizing that this would prevent atoms from interacting, and hence coming together to produce larger pieces of material, Epicurus proposed that occasionally atoms swerve from their downward trajectory and collide with other atoms.

In developing his atomic theory, Epicurus may have been the first philosopher to clearly recognize a problem that would plague philosophers to this day—namely, the problem of free will. If people are composed entirely of atoms, and the movements of atoms are determined by lawful principles, then it seems to follow that people's actions are determined by events beyond their control. But if this is the case, then it seems (at least from a certain perspective) to follow that people do not have the ability to freely choose how they will act. This is a problem for two reasons: (a) it goes counter to our strong intuition that we can and do act freely in many situations; (b) it seems to make us not morally accountable for our actions. It appears that Epicurus attempted to resolve this problem by proposing that the swerves of the atoms are not determined but instead are random. Unfortunately, very little of Epicurus' writings survive, so it is unclear exactly how he thought this solved the problem. It has been pointed out many times since Epicurus that randomness is not the same as free will; or, as the philosopher Daniel Dennett (1984, p. 2) put it, "if such random swerves happen, they don't seem to be able to give us the sort of free will we want."

Zeno of Citium

Zeno of Citium (340?–256? BCE) founded a school called Stoicism (the name is derived from the porch where Zeno taught). According to the Stoics, the universe possesses a soul, which has ordered the universe in a rational way. The good life involves living according to the natural order of things. This involves not reacting with strong emotion or passion to anything that happens.

The Stoics called the ordering principle of the universe *logos*—which, as indicated earlier, has meaning in Greek ranging from logic to word. According to the Stoics, the universe is unfolding as it should according to logos. Belief in a universe ruled by logic is not easily reconciled with a belief in free will. Stoics tended to be fatalistic, that is, they tended to believe that everything that happens is determined beforehand by logos and could not be prevented or altered. The best one can do is to submit willingly to the overriding logos of the universe.

Stoicism appears to have had an influence on Christianity. The opening statement of the Gospel of John—"In the beginning was the Word [Logos]" (John.1, Bible, RSV)—and the Christian belief in God's rationality and the rationality of unquestioning acceptance of God's will, seem to reflect the influence of Stoicism. In addition, at least some versions of Christianity, like Stoicism, tend to look askance at the passions. Moreover, the Stoics saw the world as a great city and stressed the brotherhood of man, which may be reflected in the Christian emphasis on love.

THE ROMAN EMPIRE

Around 264 BCE the Roman Empire began its expansion, and by 133 BCE it had conquered Greece and made it a Roman province. Acknowledging the advanced state of Greek culture compared to their own, the Romans adopted much of what the Greeks had developed, including (with modifications) their alphabet, religion, philosophy, and science. The Romans also adopted Greek views of the psyche or soul. The Latin word that corresponds to *psyche* is *spiritus*, which like *psyche* also originally meant breath or air. Hence today the English words *soul* and *spirit* are roughly synonymous, although there are shades of difference between them.

While the Romans generally were more oriented toward technology than philosophy, the Greeks along with interested Romans continued to develop scientific knowledge (which, at that time, was still part of philosophy).

Science Under the Romans

The Greek mathematician and astronomer Ptolemy (100–170 CE) developed a highly predictive system of astronomy based largely on Aristotle's cosmology, with the earth at the center of the universe. The physician Claudius Galen (129–216 CE) continued in the Hippocratic tradition, building on the considerable amount of knowledge that had been accumulated in the intervening 600 years since the time of Hippocrates. It appears that some of this knowledge had, unfortunately, been obtained through experiments on prisoners at the museum in Alexandria.

Galen followed Hippocrates in stressing that diseases have natural causes and the importance of knowledge of anatomy in the treatment of diseases. Among Galen's accomplishments was a highly influential medical textbook, *On the Use of the Parts of the Human Body*. Like others before him, Galen theorized that inhaling involves taking in pneuma that the body converts into vital spirits that nourish the soul. To this he added that exhaling involves getting rid of something harmful (called fuliginous vapor), which makes his theory of breathing somewhat like the modern scientific view of respiration (although still quite different from it). Of special interest from a psychological point of view is that, like Hippocrates, Galen considered diseases of the soul (i.e., psychological disorders) to be due to natural causes. Interestingly, he regarded self-examination and talking about one's psychological problems and shortcomings with trusted others to be beneficial. Although the experimental method was not a notable feature of Greco-Roman science, Galen and others did perform some experiments. For example, Galen experimented by making incisions at different levels of the spinal cord of animals and observing the corresponding effects on vocal sounds and muscle movements.

Neoplatonism

The philosophers thus far mentioned considered the soul to be physical— either a physical object or, in the case of Aristotle, certain functions or behavior patterns (i.e., what Aristotle called the *form*) of the body. However, Plotinus (205?–270? CE) revived Plato's theory of forms and gave it a twist that Plato may not have envisioned. Plotinus appears to have thought that he was simply following Plato, but scholars today refer to Plotinus' views as Neoplatonism because of apparent differences with what is today regarded as Plato's views. According to Plotinus, beyond the material world that we interact with through our senses there is a transcendental or spiritual world of forms that is more real than the material world of our senses. The soul belongs to this nonmaterial world. Moreover, beyond the transcendental world of forms and material substances is what Plotinus called the One, which he believed was the source of all forms and matter. Neoplatonism complemented and influenced the developing Christian religion (Emilsson, 1999).

Christianity Under the Romans

Around 4 BCE, a Jew named Joshua ben Joseph (or Joshua son of Joseph) was born in the Roman-controlled territory of Palestine. Known today by the Greek rendition of his name (from the Greek form of the Hebrew name

Joshua[2] and Greek for anointed or Messiah), Jesus Christ had acquired a devout following by the time of his crucifixion by the Romans around 29 CE. Promulgated throughout important centers of the Roman Empire by the apostle Paul (?–67 CE), Christianity had broad appeal and spread rapidly.

The closest the New Testament of the Christian Bible comes to describing something resembling a soul, as conceptualized by the Greeks and Romans, is in Paul's letters to various communities of gentile Christians. Paul (whose original non-Roman name was Saul of Tarsus) was Jewish and, in accordance with Jewish tradition, viewed the body as necessary for life. The idea of a soul that survives the death of the body was not, as we have seen earlier, a feature of Judaism. But Paul was also a Roman citizen and was undoubtedly influenced by Greek and Roman views of the soul.

According to Paul, there are two historical kinds of men. Adam (the first man) represented the first kind. He was a "man of dust." Christ (the "second Adam") represented the second kind, one with a spiritual body. Those who follow Christ, according to Paul, will, upon the resurrection of the dead at the end of the world, also receive immortal spiritual bodies (1Cor.15, Bible, RSV). The idea of a spiritual body housing a soul (or what may be interpreted as such, for Paul did not use the word *soul* in that context) may have been Paul's way of combining the Jewish belief in the necessity of a body for life with the Greco-Roman, or Hellenic (i.e., pertaining to the ancient Greeks), concept of a soul (see 2 Cor. 5:1–9, Bible, RSV). If so, this may have been because Paul was appealing to people (i.e., Greeks and Romans) whose traditions involved belief in an immortal soul. The issue of whether or not Paul, as recorded in the New Testament, was alluding to a Hellenic-type soul did not receive a great deal of attention until the twentieth century when it became a matter of controversy among theologians (e.g., Cullmann, 1958; also see N. Murphy, 1998, pp. 20–23).

From Persecution to State Sponsorship

Regarded as atheists because they disbelieved in the Roman gods, Christians were seen as a serious threat. Christianity was outlawed and its practitioners persecuted by the Roman government. Nonetheless, Christianity continued to gain converts in ever increasing numbers. Then, as its influence grew, its fortunes remarkably improved when the Emperor Constantine I (288?–337 CE) showed increasing favoritism toward it.

Constantine's predecessor had divided the Roman Empire into a western half and an eastern half. Originally ruler of the Western Empire, which had Rome as its capital, Constantine suspended the persecutions of Chris-

---

2. This is not quite accurate because the letter J did not exist until centuries later. A more accurate rendering of Jesus' Hebrew name is Yeshua, and the Greek name eventually given to him is more accurately written Iesous (Harpur, 2004, p. 219).

tians in 310 CE and in 312 CE he converted to Christianity. In 324 CE, in a military campaign, Constantine reunited the two parts of the Empire under his rule. In 325 CE, he commanded a meeting of bishops, called the First Council of Nicaea after the city where the meeting was held, to hammer out some tenets of Christianity. The main tenet to be established at this council was the divinity of Jesus, which was affirmed through the doctrine that God and Christ were of the same substance or essence.

In 330 CE, Constantine established in the eastern part of the Empire a new capital, Constantinople, which was designed to be a purely Christian city. After Constantine's death, the Roman Empire again tottered between unity and an east-west division.

Competitors to Christianity

Christianity was not the only religion gaining in popularity in the Roman Empire. A leading competitor was Manicheanism, which was preached by the Persian prophet Manes (216?–276? CE). This religion was based largely on the Persian religion Zoroastrianism (which, as mentioned earlier, was founded in the fifth century BCE by Zoroaster or Zarathustra) although it also contained elements of Hinduism, Buddhism, and Christianity. The core belief of Manicheanism involved a conflict between the forces of light, which were considered good and identified with the spiritual world, and the forces of dark, which were considered evil and identified with matter. Manicheanism continued as an alternative to Christianity until well after the latter was established as the official religion of Rome.

Augustine

Two seemingly incompatible approaches to truth had emerged: the rationalism of philosophers and the faith of true believers. The Christian philosopher Augustine (354–430 CE) brilliantly merged these two approaches (O'Daly, 1999, pp. 393–396). Reason alone is not sufficient for perfect understanding, according to Augustine. This can only be obtained by introspection—literally, looking inward—and through faith in Christ, and even then it may not be obtainable in this lifetime. While insufficient for obtaining perfect understanding, reason is important as a check on our understanding. In addition, reason can lead people to Christ, for Christianity is compatible with reason. Augustine maintained, for example, that if Plato were alive he would have recognized the truth of Christianity.

Non-Christian Influences on Augustine

Augustine's philosophy was strongly influenced by Neoplatonism, Stoicism, and Manicheanism. He believed in an immaterial soul that survives death (O'Daly, 1999, pp. 405–409). The soul is self-moving and causes the body to move. Although it has no spatial dimensions, the soul is present over the extent of the body, and therefore is able to perceive in more than one body part simultaneously. In maintaining that the soul is an actual thing, Augustine's view was more in accord with Plato's theory than Aristotle's. However, he followed Aristotle in proposing that there are degrees or aspects of soul: vegetative, sentient, and rational. Only humans have all three.

Similar to Plato, Augustine maintained that the function of the rational aspect of the soul is to control the irrational aspects. The soul, according to Augustine, is indivisible but mutable; hence, learning, change in affections, moral deterioration, and moral progress can take place. Note that, following Plato, through Augustine the soul enters into Christianity as the agent of morality.

Functions of the Soul According to Augustine

Among the functions of the soul, according to Augustine, are the mental powers of perception, concentration, cognition, will, memory, and imagination. Of these functions, will is special because it can freely choose to be good or to sin, which is to freely do evil.

As we have seen, except for the Epicureans, the Greeks gave little attention to the issue of freedom of the will. Plato had emphasized the importance of morality, but had seen this as a problem pertaining to rationality rather than to the will. Wrongdoing was simply error. According to Plato, a completely rational person would be good automatically. Augustine, however, believed in free will, which he felt was required in order for reward in heaven and punishment in hell—both of which as a Christian he believed in—to be justified. But will alone, he maintained, was not sufficient for salvation; that required divine grace.

Choosing to sin is an enslavement of the will to evil, according to Augustine, whereas obedient slavery to the will of God is true freedom. Especially in need of control by the will, Augustine maintained, is sexual desire. Like Paul, Augustine believed that, although marriage is good, abstinence from sex is preferable. This is because, according to Augustine, sex—presumably unlike the other appetites—overwhelms the person emotionally, physically, and mentally.

Augustine's Theory of Sense Perception

Augustine had a physiological theory of sense perception, based on earlier theories regarding the function of the nerves. According to Augustine, as for many Greek philosophers (e.g., Hippocrates, Plato), the nerves contain the soul material, pneuma. Movement in the senses causes movement in the pneuma in the nerves, and this movement is transmitted to the brain. The movement in the brain results in the sensation corresponding to the stimulation in the sense organ.

Decline and Fall of the Roman Empire

The Roman Empire became Christianized at the height of its power. By 370 CE it was in decline, coming under increasing pressure from the migration of nomadic tribes. Recalled Roman legions, now consisting mainly of soldiers from conquered territories, could or would do little or nothing to stem the invaders. In 410 CE, the Visigoths sacked Rome; in 455 CE, the Vandals pillaged it. Finally, in 476 CE, the western portion of the Roman Empire fell, leaving only the eastern portion, which is called the Byzantine Empire or Byzantium.

With the severing of the two halves of the Roman Empire, Christianity took a very different course in each half. In Byzantium, Christianity was institutionalized in the form of what is today the Eastern Orthodox Church, which includes the Greek Orthodox Church and offshoots such as the Russian Orthodox Church. Christianity in the east took an increasingly mystical approach that shunned logic and reason as the paths to knowledge and wisdom. God, it was believed, could not be understood intellectually. God could be known, it was held, only by turning one's focus inward. It is not known why this inward-looking orientation occurred. Perhaps it was fostered by the relative security of the surrounding mountains. In any case, the works of Plato, Aristotle, Augustine, and other Greek and Roman philosophers and scientists lost their influence and fell into neglect in Greece and Eastern Europe.

In Western Europe, Christianity was institutionalized in what is today the Roman Catholic Church. With the fall of Rome, most of the philosophy and science that had been built up over centuries of Greek and Roman domination was lost to Western Europe. This is largely because the superstructure needed to maintain and transmit intellectual progress was in ruins. In addition, in the western as in the eastern portion of the former Roman Empire, there was distrust of pagan science and an emphasis on looking inward to the soul. Some writings of Plato and Aristotle were preserved in some West European monasteries, where they were particularly valued for their discourses on the soul, but there was no overall effort to systematize or build on these works at that time.

Although the advance of science thus was halted in both Eastern and Western Europe, there was a crucial difference between the approaches to Christianity in these two regions that was to have an enormous impact on the future development of science. While in Byzantium there was a turning away from intellectual understanding in favor of mysticism, Augustine's influence remained strong in the Roman Catholic Church. Recall that Augustine had taught that there are two compatible approaches to truth: faith and reason. Following Augustine, the Roman Church maintained that God had decreed a set of laws that may be known through faith or reason. These laws were moral and religious—for example, sin must be cleansed by suffering—rather than scientific. Nevertheless, the doctrine that there are universal laws that can be comprehended through reason was eventually to have a profound influence on the development of science. Gradually thinkers in Western Europe began struggling to understand God's laws intellectually, even though these thinkers were largely ignorant of the earlier related accomplishments of Greek and Roman philosophers and scientists.

THE RISE OF ISLAM

Our focus now shifts to Arabia, where the inhabitants worshipped a variety of gods, the chief of which was Allah. The prophet Muhammad (570–632 CE) asserted that there is only one god, Allah, who is also the God of the Jews and the Christians. Allah, Muhammad proclaimed, chose him to be the last prophet among a series that includes all the Hebrew patriarchs and Jesus. The essence of the religion that Muhammad taught was submission to the will of Allah; hence, the religion is called Islam (the submission or obedience), and an adherent of Islam is called a Muslim (one who submits). The appeal of Muhammad's message was so great that, after some military struggle with opposing forces, much of Arabia became united under his leadership.

Muhammad was followed by a succession of leaders (caliphs) who continued expanding Islam through conversion and warfare. By 850 CE, Islam was the prevalent religion in a vast region that included Afghanistan, Persia (present-day Iran), North Africa, and the southern half of Spain.

Islamic Scientific Advances

Through conquest of formerly held Roman territories, Arabs and other inhabitants of the expanding Islamic territories, which included Jews, Christians, and people of other faiths, came into contact with the collection of Greek and Roman writings that had not been lost or destroyed. Many of these works were found in libraries of formerly Roman-held cities, such as Alexandria in Egypt; and, many were obtained through trade with Byzantium. Translating these works into Arabic, cataloging them in an encyclopedic manner, combining them with technology and knowledge imported from India and China, and conducting their own scientific and scholarly research, Muslims and others of the Islamic world developed an impressive body of science and philosophy. Areas in which they made major advances included chemistry, medicine, astronomy, optics, and mathematics. Many of the scientific and technological developments of the Islamic peoples built on Chinese science and technology, which included the development of the compass, paper, woodblock printing, gunpowder, and movable type.

Islamic Philosophical Developments

Islamic peoples contributed importantly to philosophy. Two Muslim philosophers of particular note are Ibn Sina (980–1037 CE) and Ibn Rushd (1126–1198 CE), who are known by their respective Latinized names, Avicenna and Averroës.

Avicenna

A physician born in Persia, Avicenna made important contributions to medicine as well as philosophy. He based his philosophy on an interpretation of Aristotle that was tinged with Neoplatonism. He saw God as emanating the universe from himself in an involved process that transmits to all things their appropriate forms.

Averroës

A Spanish-Arab lawyer and physician who wrote extensively on religion and philosophy, Averroës is most noted for his commentaries on Aristotle. He contended that philosophic truth is derived from reason and not from faith, and developed a philosophy that denies personal immortality and asserts that all humans share in an active intellect (essentially, a universal consciousness).

THE RISE OF CHRISTIANITY IN WESTERN EUROPE

While science flourished in the East, Western Europeans' misdirected efforts to follow the Islamic scientific lead focused on the pseudoscience of alchemy, which, interestingly, comes from the Arab word al-kimiya, from which the English word chemistry also stems. The basic idea behind alchemy came in part from Aristotle's teaching that all things tend toward perfection. Since gold was thought to be the most perfect metal, alchemists believed that deep within the earth the less perfect metals were gradually turning into gold. They reasoned that with sufficient technological knowledge they could speed up the process and turn base metals into gold. On the whole, it was a futile enterprise, although it may have helped start the development toward chemistry in Western Europe. Astrology and magic were also widely practiced by Europeans.

While the development of science languished in Europe, by the 1200s theology had become the supreme area of scholarship, and those who studied it were called *scholastics* (or *Schoolmen*). There were increasing contacts between European and Islamic cultures through their intermingling in Spain, through the Crusades, and through trade. Largely lost to Western Europe after the fall of Rome, the works of Aristotle in Arabic translations returned, along with commentaries and interpretations by Avicenna and Averroës. Although Aristotle was particularly impressive to the scholastics because of the extent of his writings in science and other areas, Europeans also gradually came into contact with works by other ancient Greek philosophers, especially Plato. Translated from the Arabic into—or in many cases, back into—Latin (the language of the Romans and therefore of West European Christian worship and scholarship), these works had an enormous impact on Christian thought—although at first the Roman Church officials banned the study of some of Aristotle's writings, perhaps because they suspected (correctly) that he did not regard the soul as an entity separate from the body.

Thomas Aquinas

Church acceptance of Aristotle eventually came about through the writings of Thomas Aquinas (1225–1274), who argued that the teachings of Aristotle were consistent with Christian faith. While acknowledging his debt to Avicenna and Averroës, Aquinas took serious issue with their religious interpretations. However, he developed a psychological philosophy based largely on Aristotle as extended by Avicenna. Following the teachings of this Islamic philosopher, Aquinas distinguished among the vegetative soul, the sensitive soul, and the rational soul. Each of these has functions specific to it. For example, nutrition, growth, and reproduction are assigned to the vegetative soul. The five external senses, the internal senses such as intuition, the appetites that give rise to internal sensations, and a sense that unifies and locates the origin of sensations from the other senses are assigned to the sensitive soul. Memory, imagination, and intellect are assigned to the rational soul. According to Aquinas there are two intellects. One, called the *possible intellect*, is responsible for understanding, judgment, and reasoning about matters pertaining to that which comes in from the senses. The other, derived from it, is called the *agent intellect*. This intellect was postulated by Avicenna to enable us to comprehend such truths as the existence of ideal forms (which, actually, is more consistent with Plato than Aristotle) and our essential union with the universe. To Aquinas, however, the agent intellect enables us to comprehend the mysteries of Christianity, for example, the Dogma of the Trinity, which is the doctrine that God is simultaneously both one and three separate persons (Father, Son, and Holy Spirit).

The Roman Catholic Church and Aristotle

Through the writings of Aquinas and other scholastics, the Catholic Church came to accept the scientific teachings of Aristotle essentially as Church doctrine, and questioning those teachings became tantamount to heresy. Questioning did however come—slowly at first, then more rapidly. The rediscovery of Aristotle was only the beginning of a torrent of old and new knowledge that began to flood into Western Europe. Although this knowledge initially came from Arabic-Islamic sources, much of it also came from Greek sources (preserved in Greece and other parts of Byzantium) as Western European scholars began to realize the importance of studying ancient Greek as well as Latin. Through these ancient texts Christian scholars began to learn that opinions other than those of Plato and Aristotle existed in the Greco-Roman world, and that controversy and free expression were the norm.

The Influence of Islamic Science and Mathematics on Europe

Christian scholars also learned about advances Islamic thinkers had made in fields such as chemistry, medicine, astronomy, optics, and mathematics. For example, algebra (which, not coincidentally, comes from the Arabic word *al-jabr*) was known to the Greeks but developed further by Islamic mathematicians. Although algebra is primarily a method for solving problems by letting symbols stand for unknown quantities, it also provides for the development of mathematical concepts (e.g., irrational numbers, negative numbers) far beyond those that can be expressed in geometry (the mathematics used by the ancient Greeks). In addition, European scholars learned about and adopted Arabic numerals, which actually originated in India (and therefore are often called Hindu- or Indian-Arabic numerals) but were applied to science and technology by Islamic scholars. These numerals, which contain a zero and use position to indicate multiples of ten, are much less cumbersome for performing arithmetical operations than Roman numerals are. Algebra and Indian-Arabic numerals were crucial to the development of science. Indeed, the contributions of Islamic scientists to the development of science in Western Europe may have been much greater than is commonly thought, for it is known that the early European scientists discussed in the next chapter were avid readers of the works of Islamic scientists and mathematicians as well as those of Greek philosophers (e.g., see Khaleel, 2003). However, citing previous literature was not practiced as rigorously then as it is today.

Contributions of Universities and Technology

Other factors in the scholastic period that were important to the development of modern science were the establishment of universities and the beginnings of significant technological advances. The University of Bologna was established in 1088, and others soon followed. Universities were originally established primarily to promulgate religious teachings (theology), but they also began to transmit scientific and other secular knowledge. Technology was important to science in providing models for scientific study (e.g., projectiles impelled by gunpowder) and scientific instruments (e.g., lenses, which eventually led to the developments of the telescope and microscope; cog-wheel gearing, which was important for the construction of clocks and watches). Paper and the invention of the printing press were extremely important for scientific communication, which contributes importantly to the cumulative aspect of science. Many of these technological products were imported from China and India, often through contacts with Arab traders. Without the influence of the Islamic world, modern science, as we know it, may never have emerged.

SUMMARY

Science could develop only after people had begun to live in cities supported by a surrounding agriculture. The Sumerians had devised a form of writing called cuneiform and had a highly developed science of astronomy and mathematics. Like the Egyptians, the Babylonians had a concept of the soul bound up with an afterlife. The Hebrew concept of soul was indistinguishable from the concept of self or person. Through Persia, the Greeks absorbed Babylonian influences, including astronomy and mathematics. With regard to science, Greek thinkers, called philosophers (lovers of wisdom or knowledge), questioned and theorized about all aspects of nature.

For the Pythagoreans, music was connected to their belief in the soul and the afterlife. The idea of the soul as a harmony was too intangible for many Greek thinkers. These philosophers tried to identify soul with some type of material substance. The material of which the soul was supposed to be composed was called pneuma.

The early Greek physician Hippocrates emphasized the natural causes of diseases, including mental illnesses.

The three giants of Greek philosophy were Socrates, Plato, and Aristotle. The truth that Socrates was most interested in was what makes a person good, and how does one lead a good life, that is, a life that is both moral and satisfying or worth living.

Unlike his mentor, Socrates' student, Plato, theorized about the nature of the cosmos. He developed a "theory of forms." For every category of objects, there must be an ideal form that the objects depend on. While a person is striving to be good, that person's soul is striving toward the ideal form of the soul. Where the soul and body tend in different directions, the perfectly rational person will give the reins to the soul, although this is often difficult.

Aristotle was Plato's student but disagreed with him on certain points including his theory of forms. In fact, Aristotle stood Plato's theory on its head by asserting that in order to have categories (i.e., forms) one must have objects to categorize, whereas Plato thought that forms were necessary to objects.

Aristotle did not regard the soul to be something in the body. Instead, Aristotle applied his theory of forms, called hylomorphism, to the soul. He asserted that the soul is the form—by which he seems to have meant the functioning and behavior—of the body. Aristotle held that there are three aspects of the soul, which are sometimes called types of souls: a vegetative soul, a sentient soul, and a rational soul. In addition to his theoretical work, Aristotle's work in science, especially biology, was prodigious.

With modifications, the Romans adopted much of what the Greeks had developed, including their alphabet, religion, philosophy, and science. While the Romans generally were more oriented toward technology than philosophy, Greeks along with interested Romans continued to develop scientific knowledge (which, at that time, was still called philosophy).

Galen, like Hippocrates, stressed that diseases have natural causes and that knowledge of anatomy is important in the treatment of diseases.

Plotinus revived Plato's theory of forms and gave it a twist that Plato had probably not envisioned: The soul belongs to the nonmaterial world. Neoplatonism complemented and perhaps influenced or was influenced by the developing Christian religion.

Regarded as atheists because they disbelieved in the Roman gods, Christians were at first seen as a serious threat to the Roman Empire. Under Emperor Constantine, Christianity became the favored religion of Rome.

The Christian philosopher Augustine was strongly influenced by Neoplatonism, Stoicism, and Manicheanism. He believed in an immaterial soul that survives death. Memory and imagination, according to Augustine, are functions of the soul, and not subject to physical laws. According to Augustine, as for certain Greek thinkers during the time of Aristotle, the nerves contain the soul material, pneuma.

With the fall of Rome, the scientific knowledge and theories that had been built up over centuries of Greek and Roman domination were lost to Western Europe. Gradually much of this knowledge was restored and new knowledge came in through contacts with the Islamic world. Through the writings of Aquinas and other scholastics, the Roman Catholic Church, which was dominant in Western Europe, came to accept the teaching of Aristotle essentially as Church doctrine, and the questioning of Aristotle became tantamount to heresy.

Discussion Questions

1. Discuss the importance of writing in the development of science.

2. Is *soul* a universal concept; that is, did all ancient peoples have the same or similar concepts of the soul? Discuss the differences between the ancient Egyptians' concept of soul, the Israelites' concept of soul, and the ancient Greek concept of soul.

3. Discuss how the concept of soul relates to psychology.

4. Discuss why science developed in Greece rather than in other regions of the world.

5. Discuss how Aristotle's concept of the soul differed from Plato's.

6. Discuss the influence Plato had on the Christian concept of soul.

7. Briefly discuss the different views of the early Roman Catholic Church, Byzantium, and Islam toward the writings of the Greek and Roman philosophers and scientists.

8. How did Western Europeans initially attempt to emulate people of the Islamic world?

9. Briefly what was Thomas Aquinas' psychological theory, and how did he influence Church doctrine?

10. Discuss the contributions the Chinese, East Indians, and peoples of the Islamic world (from about 800 to 1300 CE) made to the development of science.

CHAPTER 2

The Beginnings of Modern Science and the Modern Concept of Mind

A ccording to Aristotle, the natural place of heavy objects is at the center of the earth. This position therefore cannot be in motion, and hence the earth must be stationary. Thus, Aristotle taught that the planets and other heavenly bodies rotate around the earth attached to crystalline spheres, which are of a higher and purer form than any earthly objects. This was the official view of the Roman Church, which also endorsed Ptolemy's mathematical formulation of Aristotle's cosmology. The Church also used Biblical references to support the view that the earth does not move, for example, the fact that Joshua of the Old Testament commanded the sun, not the earth, to stand still prior to the battle of Jericho. The view that the heavenly objects are more perfect, being closer to heaven, also accorded with Church doctrine—as well it might, since this was a view that came into Christianity through the Greeks dating back to Pythagoras.

THE HELIOCENTRIC THEORY

In 1543, the Polish astronomer Mikołaj Kopernik (1473–1543)—better known by the Latinized version of his name, Nicholaus Copernicus—published his life's work, in which he provided a simpler mathematical system of the movements of the planets. Copernicus' system is called heliocentric because it places the sun at the center of our solar system.

It is known that Copernicus studied Neoplatonism. In formulating his heliocentric theory, he may have been influenced by the analogy of planets aligning themselves around the sun with souls aligning themselves around the One. Copernicus' theory was not at first seen as a great challenge to the Catholic Church, which at that time respected Neoplatonism because of an identification of the One with the Christian God. In addition, Copernicus presented his system merely as a supposition, not as fact, so it did not seem to directly contradict Christianity. However, the Church later banned his book until the late twentieth century.

THE DECLINE OF ARISTOTLE

While Copernicus was not initially seen by the Church as a threat, systematic observation using technology and the development of the experimental method to a powerful means of scientific inquiry eventually led to the decline of Aristotle's stranglehold on European thought.

Galileo

Galileo Galilei (1564–1642) was widely acknowledged as one of the most brilliant thinkers of his time. However, he was a continuing annoyance to the Church for his insistent refutations of official Church doctrine.

Arguments in Favor of Copernicus

Galileo argued vehemently that the earth revolves around the sun. He constructed telescopes, pointed them toward heavenly bodies, and observed sunspots, mountains on the moon, and moons revolving around the planet Jupiter. These observations indicated that the heavenly bodies are not unblemished objects of a higher form, and that not all objects in the heavens rotate directly around the earth because at least one object, Jupiter, has objects rotating around it. Observations such as these proved to Galileo's satisfaction, although not to that of the Church authorities, that the earth is a planet orbiting the sun. Accused of heresy and threatened with torture, Galileo recanted his belief in the motion of the earth.

Galileo's Experiments on Motion

In addition to his observations of the heavenly bodies that got him into trouble with the Church, Galileo collected data on falling bodies. He did this by rolling pellets down inclined planes and measuring their rate of descent by using a water clock. Eventually, he worked out a law that described the acceleration of falling bodies. From a psychological point of view, we should note that Galileo focused on quantities that were relatively easy to measure, such as weight, amount of material, distance moved, and time to move a specific distance (or velocity). Galileo distinguished these properties, which he called primary qualities, from what he called secondary qualities. The latter included things such as color, heat or cold, and sound. Primary qualities, according to Galileo, exist in the objects themselves, whereas secondary qualities exist in the individual rather than in the object. Presumably they exist in the individual's soul.

Francis Bacon

While Galileo's ingenious examples of the experimental method influenced subsequent generations of scientists, Francis Bacon (1561–1626) was the prophet of the experimental method. He provided influential philosophical arguments supporting the development of science, or natural philosophy as it was called at that time.[1] He argued passionately for the application of the inductive method, which involves collecting sufficient data before constructing theories. He believed that this approach would enable humanity to gain the powerful control over nature that philosophers and magicians had aspired to with little success for centuries. He wrote approvingly of Galileo's experimental methods and the large amount of data he had collected. Bacon was critical, however, of Galileo's theorizing and mathematical formulations.

William Harvey

In addition to Aristotle's views about the heavens, his theory on the functions of the heart and blood vessels came under severe challenge, as did those of Galen whose works formed the foundation and better part of medical teachings. Through skillful dissection, ingenious experiments, and rational argument, William Harvey (1578–1657) overturned these teachings (Butterfield, 1957). Aristotle believed that the heart is the seat of thinking and feeling. The blood vessels should therefore contain *pneuma*, perhaps produced or brought in from air through the lungs. Harvey showed, however, that the blood vessels contain not a trace of air, but

---

1. The word science, from the Latin scientia, meaning knowledge, did not come into general use until the nineteenth century. The word scientist did not replace the term natural philosopher until the twentieth century.

only blood. Galen had theorized that blood from the left side of the heart somehow passes through the septum to the right side (even though there is no passage through the septum). Harvey showed that, in fact, blood follows the route of going from the right side of the heart to the left side by way of the lungs. In addition, and most importantly, Harvey established as a scientific fact the circulation of the blood through the body. His work therefore contributed immensely toward the modern understanding of both the circulatory and respiratory systems, and opened the way for the scientific study of the other systems of the body. It should be noted that under the influence of Galileo's work, Harvey took a strong mechanistic view toward the heart, basically thinking of it as functioning much like a pump within a system of wheels and cogs. No doubt advances in the technology of mechanical pumps were important in enabling Harvey to conceptualize the heart as a pump.

Robert Burton

Not everything that was written during this time period went against the views of the ancient thinkers. In 1621, Robert Burton (1577–1640) published a book entitled *The Anatomy of Melancholy*, in which he incorporated or discussed the teachings of practically every major thinker who preceded him. This work, which was the first book completely on depression, is based largely on the views of Galen concerning the humors and spirits. According to Burton the humors produce spirits, which are very subtle forms of matter that affect the soul. Melancholy was held to be due to an excess of black bile (*melancholy* comes from *melaina chole*, which means black bile). The view that various physical and mental disturbances were due to imbalances in the humors persisted well into the latter part of the nineteenth century.

DECLINE OF THE ROMAN CATHOLIC CHURCH

Although the Catholic Church had asserted its authority over Galileo and forced him to recant his view that the earth circles the sun, the Church's political power was on the decline. It faced not only scientific challenges but also religious ones as Protestantism began to sweep through many parts of Europe. Geography may again have played an important role in this, similar to the role it had played in promoting democracy and philosophical inquiry in ancient Greece. As a result of its terrain, Europe was divided into many kingdoms and principalities. People whose views were seen as subversive to one power could therefore potentially find protection and support from another.

MATERIALISTIC TENDENCIES

Contributing to the decline of the Roman Catholic Church was the tendency toward materialism—the view that everything (including human behavior) can be explained in material terms without reference to spiritual concepts—that was inherent in the work of experimenters such as Galileo and Harvey. Two philosophers who developed important views regarding materialism were Thomas Hobbes and René Descartes.

Thomas Hobbes

On at least two occasions, Thomas Hobbes (1588–1679) was forced to flee from one state to another due to his views. He fled first from England to France, and then fled back to England just when a change in the government favorable to him occurred there. It is not difficult to see how Hobbes' views got him into trouble with certain governments of that time period. First, he did not accept the proposition that monarchs rule by divine right. He regarded the state to be a giant creature—a leviathan—created by a social contract in which individuals agree to being ruled by a sovereign in order to avoid anarchy and receive protection. Second, he seemed to some to be an atheist. Although he did not deny the existence of God, Hobbes did develop a materialistic philosophy. According to Hobbes, sensations are movements in the brain or heart caused by pressures of material objects, including sound and light, on the sense organs and transmitted through the nerves to the brain and heart. Images are movements in the brain that persist after the external sensory stimulation ceases. Hobbes was a determinist: will exists but what it chooses is determined by prior events; it is not free. Hobbes was a strong believer that most philosophical issues can be resolved if terms are carefully defined. For example, he regarded the soul simply as a metaphor for life, and focused on activity in the nerves and brain to explain phenomena usually attributed to the soul.

René Descartes

René Descartes (1596–1650) was another philosopher who took refuge in one state, Holland, to avoid persecution in another, his native France, for views that church authorities in that country might find offensive. France was still Catholic at that time, and Descartes' philosophy involved arriving at truth by doubting. Actually, Descartes' method was similar to an approach Augustine took, although Descartes made it the centerpiece of his philosophy.

Descartes' Philosophy

Descartes wanted to develop a system of the universe that was as certain as a mathematical proof. He began by doubting everything that it was possible to doubt. The one thing that he found that he could not doubt was the fact that in doubting he was thinking. This led to his famous dictum, *Cogito ergo sum*: "I think therefore I am." Having proved his own existence, he next proved (to his satisfaction) the existence of God. He did this by using several proofs that were similar or identical to those used earlier by scholastics. For example, he found that among his thoughts was the idea of perfection. However, it could not come from himself because he was imperfect—as proved by the fact that he could doubt—and the idea of perfection, he reasoned, must come from something that is perfect. This, by definition, could only be God. Because God is perfect, he must be good, and he cannot be a deceiver. Therefore, the errors we make are due to faulty reasoning or imperfect information. In both cases, Descartes maintained that errors are the fault of our will, due to our being lazy or overhasty in drawing conclusions. This is important because Descartes wanted to avoid attributing deceptive tendencies to God. Intellectual error is always the fault of the human will, in Descartes' view.

Dualism

Having established the existence and goodness of God, Descartes found that other proofs and conclusions followed quite naturally. Descartes concluded that he had a soul and a body. The body is composed of matter, which has the property of extension in space, whereas the soul is not extended in space. Thus, there are two types of substances in the universe, material and spiritual; the former has the property of extension, whereas the latter does not. It should be noted that by identifying the soul with thinking, Descartes was restricting himself to what Plato and Aristotle called the rational or intellective soul. As pointed out earlier, this has been translated into English as *mind*.

Thus, according to Descartes, each human body has a soul, which is immortal. Although it is made of an entirely different substance from the body and has no spatial extension, the soul can influence the body. It exerts its influence through the pineal gland. Descartes guessed that the pineal gland was the point of influence of the soul over the body partly because that gland is the only structure in the brain that is not bilateral and the soul is regarded as a unitary entity. In addition, it was believed that animals do not have a pineal gland, and Descartes believed that animals do not have souls, that is, they are simply machines, or what today we would call robots.

Contributions to Physiology

According to Descartes, the body, being made of matter, is basically a machine. When the person wants to move a limb, the soul operates on the pineal gland, which causes a subtle fluid or very fine air (called animal spirits) to move through the nerves to the appropriate muscles in that limb, causing them to expand and move the limb in the appropriate direction. However, the soul is not always involved in bodily movements— only in those that involve volition or free will. Descartes proposed that other movements occur as a result of an external stimulus forcing animal spirits through nerves to the spinal cord and brain, and back again to an appropriate muscle. Thus, according to Descartes, the nerves function by a sort of hydraulic or pneumatic action that is similar to automatic moving figures that were popular in the courtyards of Descartes' time.

Given that the fact that nerves actually function by means of an electrochemical process was not yet known, Descartes' crude description of the reflex arc was remarkably accurate—so much so, in fact, that he is typically given credit as the originator of the concept of the reflex. Because according to Descartes animals have no soul, their behavior consists simply of reflexes.

Descartes also studied the eyes and explained, in terms that are reasonably close to our modern understanding, how light entering an eye is projected as an image onto the retina and is converted to energy that results in an image in the brain. He also explained the stereoscopic principle whereby the fact that we have two eyes enables us to see in three dimensions.

Contributions to Psychology

Two important trends culminated in Descartes. One is a trend toward the complete distinctness, called dualism, between body and soul. To most of the ancient Greeks the soul is made of more refined material than the rest of the body, but it is still made of matter. Aristotle was a notable exception, believing that the soul is the "form" of the living body (as we have seen). With the Neoplatonists and later the Christians, the soul acquired an idealized or otherworldly aspect. Descartes took the next step by concluding that a person consists of two completely different substances: one that has spatial extension (i.e., it takes up or occupies space) and one that does not. The other trend that culminated in Descartes is the idea, which as we have seen was fostered by Harvey and Hobbes, that the body is a machine. From the culmination of these two trends, we obtain the somewhat paradoxical views that we can study the body objectively, like a machine, but not the soul. These views were to have strong implications, both positive and negative, for the development of psychology in later centuries.

Contributions to Astronomy and Geology

Two other scientific fields Descartes contributed to were astronomy and geology, although his contributions here were more negative than positive. By Descartes' time, it was abundantly clear to most educated people that the earth is a planet, orbiting the sun like other planets. But what keeps the planets in their orbits was not known. Descartes postulated that space is filled with a very fine, invisible substance, and that beams from the sun produce vortices, or whirlwinds, in this substance, which, in turn, carry the planets about in their orbits. This vortex theory did not explain, however, why, as the astronomer Johannes Kepler (1571–1630) had shown, the planetary orbits are elliptical rather than circular.

With regard to geology, Descartes speculated on the formation of the earth, holding that it developed from the nonuniform collapse of concentric shells composed of various materials. Perhaps the most that can be said for Descartes' geological theory is that it held that the earth formed from natural processes (a view about which he had to be circumspect to avoid antagonizing the Roman Catholic Church).

Contributions to Mathematics

Although most of Descartes' scientific contributions were dubious, his contributions to mathematics were of immense importance. His greatest mathematical contribution was his uniting of geometry and algebra. He did this by showing how points on any geometrical figure can be specified by their distances from intersecting—specifically, perpendicular—lines. This greatly increased the generality of geometry, for Descartes showed that any algebraic equation can be expressed in geometrical form by plotting it on what we now call a Cartesian coordinate system. The lines or curves formed by the equation express the possible solutions to the unknowns, which, alternatively, can be considered as quantities that vary (i.e., as variables) over the range of their solutions. This graphical method has become so much a part of science today that it is virtually impossible to imagine where science would be without it.

THE ROYAL SOCIETY

Thus far, we have followed the gradual development of science, with relevant references to psychology. This is because issues that were later to become important to psychologists were not seen as separate from the rest of science. In fact, clear distinctions had not yet been made among any of the sciences. Thus, we see individuals such as Descartes making contributions to a number of what today would be considered distinct areas of science. In addition, up to the seventeenth century, experimentation had not played a major role in the development of scientific thinking. The writings of Francis Bacon, which stressed the systematic collection of data and the use of the inductive method, had their major impact on a later generation.

In 1660, a group of natural philosophers founded, and in 1662 incorporated, the Royal Society of London for Improving Natural Knowledge. Following Baconian principles, the Royal Society sought to provide a forum for members to share their methods and findings through meetings and, as this was a time when paper was becoming more available, through publications. In 1665, the Royal Society began publishing its *Philosophical Transactions*, one of the earliest scientific journals. Early members of the Royal Society included Robert Boyle (1627–1691), Robert Hooke (1635–1703), and Isaac Newton (1642–1727).

Robert Boyle and Robert Hooke

Both Robert Boyle and his assistant Robert Hooke were master experimentalists who made a number of important discoveries. Boyle is best known for his work using a vacuum pump (or "Pneumatick Engine" as he called it) that he invented to study the effect of pressure on gases. He is the originator of Boyle's law, which states that the pressure of a given amount of gas is inversely proportional to its volume. Hooke made many improvements in astronomical instruments, watches, and clocks. He studied the effects of stress on solids and formulated Hooke's law, which describes elasticity in solids. He also made microscopic observations of a wide variety of organic and inorganic things. Among his most important observations was the cell, a name that he coined (based on its resemblance to cells in a honeycomb) for what turned out to be the basic unit of complex life.

A versatile scientist, Hooke made an excursion into psychology with a treatise on memory that he wrote and presented to the Royal Society. Fascinated with the property of phosphorus to store and emit light, he postulated that there might be a phosphorus-like substance in the brain that could account for visual memory (Draaisma, 2000, pp. 50–53).

Isaac Newton

Although we usually regard Isaac Newton as a great contributor to the science of physics, like other scientists of his time he also delved into psychology.

Newton's Contributions to Psychology

Newton's early experiments were on the nature of light. One of his interests was in whether colors are present in light or added by the soul. His curiosity about this led him to perform dangerous experiments that nearly blinded him. For example, in one experiment, he inserted a long, needle-shaped instrument into an eye socket and pressed it against the eyeball, and noted that this produced the experience of seeing colors. In another he stared for a long time at the sun reflected in a mirror and noted that this also produced the experience of seeing colors. From these experiments he concluded, in agreement with Galileo, that the experience of color is a secondary quality.

He also conducted experiments with prisms to determine what properties of light are associated with the sensation of color. It was well known that directing a beam of light from the sun through a prism resulted in a rainbow of colors. A widely accepted theory was that the prism somehow added colors to the light. Directing colored light from one prism to a second prism, Newton found that a single color (or, as he preferred to say, sensation of color) from the first prism was refracted (bent), but that no new colors were added to it. From this experiment, Newton concluded correctly that sunlight is composed of light that corresponds to what he discerned as pure colors, but that each pure color is refracted differently.

Newton's Contribution to the Physics of Motion

Newton once said that if he had seen farther than others it was because he stood on the shoulders of giants. Those giants included Copernicus, Galileo, Kepler, and Descartes. Newton's law of inertia, which Galileo had also suspected, contradicted Aristotle's teaching that the natural state of objects is rest. According to the law of inertia, an object at rest will tend to stay at rest and an object in motion will tend to stay in motion, and these tendencies will be in proportion to the mass of the objects. In addition, in a theory of universal gravitation, he proposed that any two objects attract each other in direct proportion to the product of their masses and in inverse proportion to the square of the distance between them. This effectively overthrew Aristotle's view that the natural place of heavy objects is at the center of the earth and that they move toward it. In Newton's formulation, any object tends to move toward the earth because of the mutual gravitational attraction between the object and the earth. Orbits of one object around another are due to the balancing of inertial and gravitational forces. Further, Newton showed that his inverse-square law of gravitational attraction accounts for the elliptical orbits of planets around the sun, whereas Descartes' theory of vortices cannot explain this. In 1687, Newton published his classic work entitled *Mathematical Principles of Natural Philosophy*.

Newton's Contribution to Theory

Newton's theory of motion not only established physics as a precisely predictive science, but also provided a model that other sciences, including modern psychology, have attempted in some measure to emulate. The current emphasis on theory in psychology, for example, stems to a large extent from Newton's highly successful theory.

Cartesians and others criticized Newton's concept of gravity because it involved action at a distance. Natural philosophers at that time were trying to eliminate explanations that appealed to occult or mystical forces, and action at a distance seemed quite mystical. Newton countered that he did not know the cause of gravity, and that although he could make hypotheses that did not involve action at a distance, he was not inclined to do so. In modern terms, we would say that for Newton gravity was a descriptive concept, not an explanatory one.

Newton presented his theory in the form of a set of principles or axioms, which came to be known as Newton's laws, from which motions of physical objects can be deduced mathematically. In developing his theory, Newton invented a new mathematics, called the infinitesimal and integral calculus, which allowed velocity, acceleration, etc., to be calculated at any arbitrary point. Initially, however, he presented his theory in traditional mathematical terms, as he did not want it to be criticized because of its unfamiliar mathematics.

Gottfried Leibniz

Being German, the philosopher-mathematician Gottfried Leibniz (1646–1716) was not a member of the Royal Society. He is relevant here, however, because he was a contemporary of the members mentioned above (Boyle, Hooke, and Newton) and in frequent correspondence with them.

Leibniz's Contributions to Mathematics and Logic

Leibniz invented calculus independently of Newton, which led to an unfortunate dispute over the assignment of credit for it. Today both men receive equal credit, although Leibniz's notation is the one that has been adopted. Calculus is important not only for calculating rates of change at arbitrary points, but also for finding maximum and minimum points and for computing areas under curves. It is essential for all advanced mathematical and scientific study. In addition to calculus, Leibniz made other important contributions to mathematics and potentially to the area of mathematical logic. Unfortunately, he did not publish his contributions to this field in part because he kept finding contradictions between his results and Aristotle's writings on the subject. Because Aristotle's reputation was so strong, Leibniz incorrectly assumed the error was his; this delayed the development of mathematical logic by about one-and-a-half centuries (Russell, 1946, p. 572).

Leibniz's Contributions to Philosophy and Psychology

Another important concept Leibniz developed is that of parallelism, which answers a criticism of Descartes' philosophy. The criticism is that the body and soul cannot interact as Descartes asserted if they are composed of completely different substances—one extended, the other not. The concept of parallelism states that the body and soul do not interact, but only appear to do so because each follows a set of laws that correspond exactly to the set of laws followed by the other. At the moment of birth, or earlier, God synchronized the two entities—body and soul—the same way that a clockmaker might synchronize two clocks so that they always keep the same time even though they do not interact.

Although parallelism solved the Cartesian problem (at the apparent expense of free will), Leibniz's psychological philosophy was quite different from Descartes'. In essence, he maintained that there are not just two substances, but an infinite number, called monads. These are single indivisible points somewhat like atoms in early atomic theories. Leibniz postulated that each monad is a separate substance, that the universe is composed entirely of monads, and that monads (being of zero dimension) do not interact. Each monad perceives the whole universe from its own vantage point and moves in synchrony with all the other monads in a harmony that God predetermined.

Each individual person, according to Leibniz, is composed of many monads. Within each person there is a dominant monad, which is called *the* soul of that person. The dominant monad perceives more clearly, hence is more conscious, than the person's other monads. Whether an individual becomes conscious of a particular object or event is a function of the number of monads reacting to it, which in turn is a function of the number or intensity of the sensations produced by that object or event. This accounts for how we become consciously aware of a perception, or, in other words, how we apperceive something.

In his writings for public consumption, although not in his private writings, Leibniz tried to reconcile a belief in free will with his view that monads do not interact. He did this by assuming that monads strive to perfect themselves and in doing this they are self-determining; that is, in striving for perfection, they determine their own development.

BRITISH EMPIRICISM

In England the success of the experimental method in natural philosophy had an enormous impact on philosophical speculations about the soul, which in England facilitated the replacement in philosophy of the word *soul* with the word *mind*. Originally the English word *mind* was a verb pertaining to memory (e.g., to remind someone of something), thought (e.g., to mind your manners), or attention (e.g., to mind the store). English philosophers increasingly came to prefer the noun *mind* over *soul* because it did not have the latter's religious, supernatural, or spiritual connotations and hence seemed more objective or scientific. Notably, there is no separate word for the English noun *mind* in many languages, including French, German, and Russian, the national languages of three countries that have contributed greatly to psychology. In those languages the words for soul, spirit, or ghost are the closest corresponding to the English noun *mind*.

The success of the experimental method in physics did not yet suggest to anyone (so far as we know) that it could be successful in psychology. However, the fact that knowledge of the world depends heavily on experiment suggested to many in England—where due largely to Newton and other members of the Royal Society, the experimental method had acquired a strong foothold—that our knowledge, ideas, and concepts are not largely inborn, innate, or implanted in our souls or minds from birth, as many philosophers (e.g., Plato, Descartes, Leibniz) had thought. Experience, in the form of what are variously known as sense impressions, sense data, sensations, etc., plays an important, perhaps even an all-determining, role. This insight was carried to its logical conclusion by a line of philosophers known as the British empiricists.

John Locke

The first of this group was John Locke (1632–1704), who made important contributions to both psychology and political philosophy.

Locke's Contributions to Psychology

A close friend of Newton, Locke, like Hobbes before him, looked on the mind as a mechanism instead of a supernatural entity. Locke compared the mind with a *tabula rasa*, a blank slate, that is written on by experience. Thus, according to Locke, the basic images with which we think come from sense impressions—that is, from external objects that, by causing some sort of motion to continue through the nerves to the brain, impress themselves on the mind. Note that these images are copies of the external objects; hence, this theory is a version of the copy theory that we have seen was held by many ancient philosophers, such as Empedocles, Democritus, and Plato.

Images or ideas, according to Locke, can be of simple or complex forms. The simple ones come directly from experience; the complex ones come from recombination of the simple images (e.g., the first person to imagine a unicorn did so by combining the image of a horn with the image of a horse). Locke formalized the distinction that others (e.g., Galileo, Newton) had made between primary and secondary qualities. Primary qualities according to Locke consist simply of matter—extended substance—in motion, whereas secondary qualities exist in the mind. For example, Locke maintained that the quality we experience as heat comes from the rapid motion of small particles in objects that we perceive to be hot. The rapid motion of the small particles is a primary quality (i.e., it exists in the external world); the experience of heat is a secondary quality (i.e., it is produced in the mind by the movement of the small particles).

Although Locke emphasized external sensation, he acknowledged that some sensation is internal, which he called "reflection." He also did not deny the existence of the soul, although he thought it was impossible to demonstrate such an entity.

Locke's Contributions to Political Philosophy

Locke developed a political philosophy that conceived of primitive humans making a contract with a ruler who would govern and protect them. This was similar to the social contract Hobbes postulated, except that the ruler in Locke's contract was bound by constraints that recognized certain basic rights of the individual. Locke's political philosophy had strong effects on some of the governments in his time. For example, Locke's influence on Thomas Jefferson led to the checks and balances between the branches of government specified in the U.S. constitution.

George Berkeley

After Locke, George Berkeley (1685–1753) and David Hume (1711–1776) are the two most famous British empiricists. Berkeley contributed to psychology in questioning the distinction between primary and secondary qualities and in providing a theory of space perception.

Primary and Secondary Qualities

For Berkeley, Locke's distinction between primary and secondary qualities was arbitrary. Specifically, Berkeley did not see any basis for regarding extension and motion as primary qualities as opposed to other qualities. He regarded all qualities to be in the mind. This implies that for anything to exist, it must be observed. The question immediately arises: Why do things seem to exist even when they are not being observed? Berkeley's answer is that God observes them.

Space Perception

Berkeley provided the first detailed theory of space perception. He disagreed with Descartes, who believed that space perception is due to an innate geometry. Instead, Berkeley argued that space perception is learned through the associations that occur between various muscle movements and corresponding sense impressions as we move about in our environment. The view that learning occurs through the associations between sense impressions or between ideas was to characterize British philosophy, and hence came to be known as British associationism. There was an inkling of associationism in Locke, although he saw it mainly in a negative sense—chance associations interfere with reasoning. Berkeley, however, formalized the doctrine of associationism by explicitly positing associations as the mechanism of learning.

David Hume

David Hume accepted Berkeley's reasoning regarding the logical invalidity of distinguishing between primary and secondary qualities, but took the argument one step further.

Absence of Object Permanence and Self

Hume did not believe that we have any basis for concluding that God exists. Therefore, we cannot conclude that objects have permanence. Things that have an external existence and which impress themselves on our sense organs might exist, as Locke proposed, but it might just as easily be the case that there are no external causes of our images and ideas. Even the self has no permanent existence, but is merely a loose collection of percepts, which include sense impressions, thoughts, images, and so on. To Hume, Descartes' "I think therefore I am" contains a logical fallacy known as "begging the question," that is, assuming beforehand what one is attempting to prove. According to Hume, all that Descartes actually showed was that thinking exists, not that there is an "I" that does the thinking.

We shall see later in this book that Buddhists make a similar argument when they advocate dispensing with an "I"—an ego, soul, or self. Like Hume, they argue that thinking occurs without these.

Cause-and-Effect is Merely Correlation

Hume also challenged the notion of cause and effect. For any two events A and B, where B consistently follows A, we have no empirical or logical basis for concluding that A causes B. We never actually see causation. All we can really conclude is that there exist sequences of events, some of which are repetitive.

GERMAN IDEALISM

Hume had taken empiricism to its logical conclusion, which seemed to deny the most essential aspects of what was previously thought to characterize humans. There was a strong reaction to British empiricism, especially as expressed by Hume, and this came primarily from a line of philosophers known as the German idealists. Four representatives of German idealism are Immanuel Kant (1724–1804), Georg Hegel (1770–1831), Arthur Schopenhauer (1788–1860), and Friedrich Nietzsche (1844–1900). Leibniz is often considered to be a precursor or an early representative of this group.

Like many philosophical terms, the word *idealism* is somewhat vague or imprecise. It generally refers to the view that reality is dependent to a large extent, if not exclusively, on thought. In this sense, at least one of the British empiricists, Berkeley, has been called an idealist. However, in contrast to the British empiricists, the German idealists stressed the innateness of our most fundamental concepts of reality (e.g., the concepts of space and time).

Immanuel Kant

Immanuel Kant, who credited Hume with having woken him from his "dogmatic slumbers," wrote a work entitled *The Critique of Pure Reason* (1781), which was designed largely as an answer to Hume. Strongly influenced by the French philosopher and social reformer Jean Jacques Rousseau (1712–1778), who is perhaps most noted for his concept of the "noble savage" (that humans are good in the natural state but corrupted by civilization), Kant wanted his philosophy in some way to help improve the human condition. He attempted to rigorously clarify our innermost percepts about reality and morality. Two of the most important concepts in Kant's philosophy are the-thing-in-itself and the categorical imperative.

Things-in-Themselves

According to Kant, Hume notwithstanding, external reality exists but we can never know it directly. Within this external reality are "things-in-themselves," or "things as they really are objectively," which Kant called *noumena*; however, our percepts or concepts of noumena, which Kant called *phenomena*, exist only in a realm of appearances. We perceive things-in-themselves to have certain qualities, such as spatiality (i.e., they exist in space and have spatial extent), temporality (i.e., they exist in time), and causal connectedness (they operate on each other to produce certain effects, including operating on our senses to give rise to innate percepts, such as those of space, time, and causality). These percepts are totally subjective. In addition to percepts relating to things-in-themselves, we have percepts that arise within ourselves through thinking. One of the most basic of these is that of a Supreme Being or God.

The Categorical Imperative

Another of our most basic percepts, according to Kant, is the ethical concept of the categorical imperative, which provides a way of distinguishing ethical from unethical behavior. Everyone, according to Kant, has an innate sense of morality, but for those who are not trained to think deeply it is usually vague or unclear. As with our innate sense of reality, the job of the philosopher is to make our sense of morality clear—at least for those who can follow the technical reasoning required.

There are two forms of the categorical imperative, a strong form and a weak form. The strong form, which is called "contradiction in conception," tells us that we should not will an act if it would be impossible for everyone to will it. This would rule out, for example, lying, because if everyone lied, there would be no distinction between lying and truth telling (hence, it is logically impossible for everyone to lie). The weak form, which is called "contradiction in the will," tells us that we should not will an act if we would not will everyone to will it. This would rule out stealing. It is not logically impossible for everyone to be a thief; but, nevertheless, it obviously is not a desirable state of affairs for anyone.

Kant's Answer to Hume

Kant criticized the view that the concept of God or any other innate concept could be proved, such as Descartes had attempted to do. In fact, he saw what, to him, appeared to be a serious logical problem in attempting to prove anything about the nature of reality. Specifically, Kant maintained that when one attempts to make such a proof certain contradictions, which are called *antinomies*, arise. Perhaps the most famous of these were discovered in ancient times by the Greek philosopher Zeno of Elea (495?–435? BCE). An example of one of these antinomies is the paradox of the many, which basically is as follows: A finite continuous line or a finite continuous period of time must be infinitely divisible; but then it must consist of the sum of an infinite number of small segments and hence be infinite in magnitude. Hence, finite lines or finite periods of time cannot exist, although of course they do.

It should be pointed out that mathematicians today generally believe that calculus and the modern mathematical theory of limits have resolved Zeno's paradoxes. Kant, however, interpreted these paradoxes—or as he viewed them, "contradictions"—to mean that space and time, as we (innately) conceptualize them, belong to the realm of appearances rather than reality, which is unknowable. Hence, Kant agreed with Hume that our intuitive percepts such as time, space, and causality can never be formalized using pure reason; however, this, according to Kant, demonstrates a limitation of pure reason rather than a problem with those percepts which, properly understood, belong only to the realm of appearances and not to the underlying reality.

Georg Hegel

Georg Hegel saw what he took to be the solution to the problem Kant had identified with pure reason or logic. In Kant's view, anything we attempt to say about that reality (thesis) divides it and therefore must be false and generate its opposite (antithesis). The thesis and antithesis together lead to a synthesis, which is a new thesis that therefore produces its antithesis. Kant saw this process as circular and unproductive. Hegel, in contrast, saw the process as progressive, not circular. He agreed that the synthesis, being a statement about reality, must, like the thesis and anti-thesis that gave rise to it, be false. However, he maintained that, in gen-eral, it must be (if properly formulated) truer or more perfect than the pre-vious thesis. Thus, through the formula of thesis, antithesis, and synthesis, Hegel envisioned a progression toward greater truth, the end product of which is the highest level of knowledge or consciousness of reality. This process is known as *Hegelian logic* or *Hegel's dialectic*.

Plato had a strong influence on Hegel, who acknowledged him as the originator of what is known as Hegel's dialectic. According to Hegel, it was no accident that Plato used dialogues to convey his philosophy. These dialogues typically proceeded with one participant stating a posi-tion (thesis) that was contradicted by another participant (antithesis), which, out of the ensuing discussion, led to a new position (synthesis) that could not have occurred without the participation of the previous two positions. The synthesis that emerges out of one dialogue might then form the thesis that initiates a subsequent dialogue. This back-and-forth process occurs even when one dialogues with oneself to arrive at a more correct position than one previously held on some particular topic. Fur-ther, even what appears to be straight linear logic (e.g., a mathematical proof) necessarily involves a dialectical process, although here it is not as obvious as in the case of a Socratic dialogue. Even the most rigorous of proofs, however, requires an intuitive understanding of what a proof is (which, by its very nature, cannot be proved in a linear way).

According to Hegel, reality itself develops in a dialectical manner. This follows because, in Hegelian logic, the line between our statements about reality and reality itself tends to blur (because of the synthesis that occurs). Thus, to Hegel, as to Berkeley, the apparent distinction between the per-ceiver and what is perceived—that is, between subject and object—is false or illusory.

Arthur Schopenhauer

Arthur Schopenhauer retained Kant's thing-in-itself and, in addition, picked up on Kant's concept of will. To Kant, will is a thing-in-itself that corresponds not to a percept, but to the body. This is because the body is the instrument that carries out the will through behavior. One needs to have a strong will to behave according to the categorical imperative; hence, a good person, defined as one who acts with "moral worth," is one who wills in accordance with the motive of duty (or, roughly, does the right thing for the right reason). According to Kant, such a person must have a strong will.

Schopenhauer made will the centerpiece of his philosophy and conceptualized a universal will common to all humans. However, Schopenhauer turned Kant's philosophy on its head and saw will not as the source of good, but as an evil. Influenced strongly by Indian religions, specifically Hinduism and Buddhism, Schopenhauer saw will as something to be extinguished similar to the way these religions seek to extinguish desire through meditation, foregoing pleasures of the flesh, and striving to attain toward total selflessness. Curiously, Schopenhauer seems to have practiced the opposite of what he preached, leading one to question how seriously committed he was to his own philosophy.

Friedrich Nietzsche

Friedrich Nietzsche's philosophy is difficult to summarize because, instead of attempting to convince merely by logical argument, he typically wrote as though he wanted his readers to question their cherished beliefs and to think in ways that involve the emotions as well as reason. His writings are filled with aphorisms and allegories.

Stress on Will

Nietzsche followed Schopenhauer in making the will the centerpiece of his philosophy, but considered the will in a positive or optimistic way against an extremely pessimistic background. He was an atheist who did not believe in free will, who saw life as filled with suffering (he was ill throughout most of his own life), and who (in what he called "the endless return")" believed that we are doomed to continually repeat our lives down to the last detail over and over again throughout eternity. He believed this last point was supported by scientific evidence, although it is not clear why on the basis of the science of his day. If he had lived after the formulation and support for the theory of the big bang—that is, the view that the universe, after having exploded into existence, is rapidly expanding and may someday contract and repeat the cycle—he likely would have taken this as further support for his theory of the endless return.

Nietzsche saw the will, specifically the will-to-power, as a way of turning this pessimistic view around—at least in a manner of speaking. According to Nietzsche there are, or there will be, certain individuals who would have extremely strong wills; it is unclear whether Nietzsche thought he was one, or even whether he thought they existed in his day or would be a future evolution of the human race. Nietzsche called this type of individual an *Übermench*, that is, an *overman* or a *superman*. Such individuals will not have super powers, but they would have superior wills-to-power. The power they will glory in, however, would not be the power to rule the world (as the Nazis, in misinterpreting Nietzsche's philosophy, thought). Rather, the special power they will have would be the ability to relish the suffering inflicted on them by the world. Such people will find supreme joy in every moment of their lives, no matter how terrible, to the extent that they will want that moment to last forever. These people will definitely not subscribe to a religion, such as Christianity, that teaches that they are sinful and should meekly suffer the misfortunes of the present life in the hope of a reward in an afterlife.

Opposition to Institutionalized Religion

The abstractions and hypocrisies of organized religion greatly disturbed Nietzsche. He opposed Christianity because it seemed to him to be a religion of weakness, at least as professed by the churches of his day. Hinduism and Buddhism were better, in his view, although he was not fond of any modern religion. In 1883, Nietzsche published his most famous book, *Thus Spoke Zarathustra*, in which a character having the same name as the prophet of the ancient Persian religion—from which, it might be argued, stem the three preeminent modern monotheistic religions, Judaism, Christianity, and Islam—declares that God is dead. Apparently the cause of God's death, a theme repeated throughout Nietzsche's writings, was the rise of mechanistic science and the distortions that had occurred in organized religion since the time of Zarathustra.

Similarity to Kierkegaard

Near the end of Nietzsche's life, a friend told him about an earlier Danish philosopher, Søren Kierkegaard (1813–1855), whom Nietzsche had never read but whose philosophy was similar to his. Like Nietzsche, Kierkegaard opposed what he perceived as the stultifying abstractions and adulations that had taken over Christianity. Both tried to chip away at the inauthenticity in people and in religion—Nietzsche from the point of view of an atheist, Kierkegaard from that of a devout Christian. Like Nietzsche, Kierkegaard felt that an exertion of will was necessary to go beyond the hypocritical abstractions that had arisen around religion. In 1849, he published one of his most important works, *The Sickness unto Death*. Nietzsche and Kierkegaard had little or no immediate effect on psychology, but they did have a large delayed effect.

SUMMARY

Going against the earth-centered teaching of Aristotle and Ptolemy, Copernicus provided a heliocentric theory. Galileo, following Copernicus, argued vehemently that the earth revolves around the sun. While Galileo's ingenious examples of the experimental method influenced subsequent generations of scientists, Francis Bacon provided influential philosophical arguments supporting the development of science, or natural philosophy as it was called at that time.

Influenced by Galileo's writings, William Harvey took a strong mechanistic view toward the heart, basically thinking of it as functioning much like a pump within a system of wheels and cogs. The British philosopher Thomas Hobbes adopted a thorough-going materialistic position.

Two important trends culminated in the French philosopher René Descartes. One was a trend toward the complete distinctness, called dualism, between body and soul. The other was the view that unlike the soul, the body is a machine.

Newton's law of inertia, which Galileo had also suspected, contradicted Aristotle's teaching that the natural state of objects is rest. According to the law of inertia, an object at rest will tend to stay at rest and an object in motion will tend to stay in motion, and these tendencies will be in proportion to the mass of the objects. In Newton's formulation, any object tends to move toward the earth because of the mutual gravitational attraction between the object and the earth. Newton's theory of motion not only established physics as a precisely predictive science, but also provided a model that other sciences, including present-day psychology, have attempted in some measure to emulate.

The German philosopher-mathematician Gottfried Leibniz developed the concept of parallelism, which answers the criticism of Descartes' philosophy that the body and soul cannot interact as Descartes asserted if they are composed of completely different substances. Leibniz postulated that each monad is a separate substance, that the universe is composed entirely of monads, and that monads do not interact. Whether an individual becomes conscious of a particular object or event is a function of the number of monads reacting to it, which in turn is a function of the number or intensity of the sensations produced by that object or event.

The first of the British empiricists, John Locke, formalized the distinction that others (e.g., Galileo, Newton) had made between primary and secondary qualities. Primary qualities according to Locke consist simply of matter, extended substance, in motion; whereas secondary qualities exist in the soul. He postulated that the mind is a *tabula rasa*, a blank slate.

Two other British empiricists were George Berkeley and David Hume. Berkeley contributed to psychology in questioning the distinction between primary and secondary qualities and in providing a theory of spatial perception. Hume accepted Berkeley's reasoning regarding the logical invalidity of distinguishing between primary and secondary qualities, but took the argument one step further, denying the existence of a permanent self and arguing that causation is nothing other than correlation.

German idealism was largely a reaction to British empiricism. Immanuel Kant stressed the thing-in-itself and the categorical imperative. Georg

Hegel dispensed with Kant's things-in-themselves, but agreed that there exists a fundamental unknowable reality. Unlike Kant, however, Hegel thought that the underlying reality may be approximated through a dialectical process involving the repetition of the sequence thesis, antithesis, and synthesis. Arthur Schopenhauer retained Kant's thing-in-itself and, in addition, picked up on Kant's concept of will. Friedrich Nietzsche stressed the importance of will in overcoming the meaninglessness of the universe. A philosophy similar to his was developed independently by the Danish philosopher Søren Kierkegaard.

Discussion Questions

1. Discuss Aristotle's role—both positive and negative—in the development of science. (Note: this question pertains to material in both chapters 1 and 2.)

2. Relate the contributions of Galileo and William Harvey to the development of modern science.

3. Discuss why science developed in Europe rather than in another part of the world.

4. Relate the contributions of Thomas Hobbes and René Descartes to the development of modern science.

5. Discuss the specific contributions Descartes made to the development of psychology.

6. Discuss the versatility of natural philosophers in the 1600s in comparison with today.

7. Discuss the contributions Leibniz made to the development of psychology. Are there modern psychological concepts that are similar to Leibniz's monads?

8. Discuss Newton's contribution to psychology.

9. Explain the major differences between the British empiricists and the German idealists.

10. Zarathustra was mentioned twice in chapter 1 and once in chapter 2. Discuss and relate the contexts in which he was mentioned.

CHAPTER 3

The Beginnings of Psychology as a Separate Field of Study

D uring the early history of psychology neither the word *psychology* nor any of its cognates in other languages existed. It was not until the early 1500s (probably sometime between 1510 and 1517) that the term made its first recorded appearance in a treatise by Marko Marulić (1450–1524), a Croatian best known for his epic poem *Judita*. The title of the treatise, which has long been lost and is known only because of the inclusion of its title in a listing of Marulić's works by one of his contemporaries, was *Psichiologia de ratione animae humanae*, which is Latin for *Psychology: On the Nature of the Human Soul* (Krstić, 1964). The first existent work containing the word *psychology* is a treatise published in 1590 by the German philosopher Rudolf Göckel. The title of his treatise was ψυχολογία· *hoc est de hominis perfectione, anima, ortu*, with *psychology* written in Greek and the rest of the title in Latin. A translation of the title from the Greek and Latin is: *Psychology: On the Perfection of Humans by the Development of the Soul*. Use of the term *psychology* spread gradually at first and then at a continually increasing rate.

THE FIRST SCIENTIFICALLY ORIENTED PSYCHOLOGY BOOKS

In 1732 and 1734, respectively, the German philosopher-mathematician Christian von Wolff (1679–1754) published two volumes in Latin with psychology in their titles: *Empirical Psychology* and *Rational Psychology* (*Psychologia Empirica* and *Psychologia Rationalis*). Wolff was attempting to make psychology into an empirical science, thereby bringing it into line with the proliferating physical sciences. His stated purpose in the first volume was to describe the principles about, as he put it, "things that are in the soul"; the purpose of the second volume was to explain the reasons for these principles. Mainly the books are compendiums of much that was believed about the mind at that time. Some of the major topics included were the senses, imagination, memory, attention, perception, and the appetites. Wolff adopted a modified form of Leibniz's philosophy. He emphasized that the mind is active, as opposed to being a passive receiver, as the British empiricists tended to hold. Like Descartes and many other philosophers since, Wolff emphasized a two-way interaction between the soul (or mind) and the body.

FACULTY PSYCHOLOGY

Wolff had opened up an approach called faculty psychology, which was based on the idea that the mind is composed of abilities or propensities (called faculties) such as attention and memory that vary in their degrees of strength across individuals. In this connection Leibniz's influence is apparent, for the faculties resemble Leibniz's monads in being divisions of a person's mind. The Scot Thomas Reid (1710–1796) also developed a faculty psychology, which was taken up by compatriots such as Dugald Stewart (1753–1828) and Thomas Brown (1778–1820). The latter combined faculty psychology with associationism and adopted Berkeley's theory of space perception.

Following the publication of Wolff's and Reid's works on psychology, the term became increasingly used. In addition, the term *mind* increasingly substituted for *soul*. Gradually, psychology became recognized as a special field of study. Developments occurred, in fits and starts as it were, along several lines: (a) attempts to understand the machinery or mechanisms of the mind; (b) attempts to understand the physiological basis for the mind; and (c) application. With regard to (a), the experimental method did not immediately take hold. Psychology was still an area for philosophical speculation. However, the speculation began to take on a more scientific bent in that by degrees it began to resemble the mechanistic approach that was taking place in natural philosophy (i.e., what today we call science).

ASSOCIATIONISM

The associationism introduced by the British empiricists to explain how ideas get chained together was a popular approach to explaining the workings of the mind.

David Hartley

Somewhat ahead of his time, a physician named David Hartley (1705–1757) provided a theory of a physiological basis for associationism. According to his theory, when one has a sensation, vibrations occur in the white medullary substance of the nerves corresponding to that sensation. If two vibrations occur together, the occurrence of one alone may tend to start the nerves corresponding to the other sensation to start vibrating. This mutual vibration is what we experience as an association.

The French connection: Julien de La Mettrie and Étienne de Condillac

The French writer Voltaire (1694–1778) visited England from 1726 to 1728, in time to witness the elaborate funeral for Sir Isaac Newton (one of the few commoners in that time period to be knighted) in 1727 and the great outpouring of adulation toward this great scientific genius. Voltaire could not fail to notice the widespread interest in science and philosophy that pervaded Britain. Greatly impressed, he took the enthusiasm for empiricism and associationism back to France. Among those on whom his writings had an impact was the French philosopher Julien de La Mettrie (1709–1751), who was also influenced by the mechanical side of Descartes' dualism. Voltaire influenced La Mettrie to think of thinking as mechanical. Regarding the brain to have "thought muscles," La Mettrie saw no need to postulate a soul as Descartes had done. Étienne de Condillac (1715–1780) went further and converted Locke's associationism into a deterministic system based entirely on external sensations. Whereas Locke had maintained that there were two sources of knowledge, namely external and internal stimulation (or "reflection"), de Condillac proposed that external sensations (or sense impressions or sense percepts) could account for all experience, that is, it was unnecessary to postulate internal sensations as distinct from external sensations.

Jeremy Bentham

Jeremy Bentham (1748–1832) was a British philosopher who also used associationism to explain the events (ideas, thoughts, etc.) that occur in the mind. He was also noted for systematically developing the "greatest happiness" principle, which is the essence of the ethical philosophy known as utilitarianism. According to this philosophy, the ethical person will act in such a way as to bring about the greatest happiness for the greatest number of people. Happiness according to Bentham is a direct function of pleasure and an inverse function of pain. A good government will, according to Bentham, act in such a way as to bring about the greatest happiness for the greatest number of its citizens.

James Mill and John Stuart Mill

The British philosopher James Mill (1773–1836) was strongly influenced by Bentham and, like him, carried on the trend started by the British empiricists. According to Mill, sensations or ideas are associated as they are received in the brain. Complex ideas are mosaics of simple ideas that are associated. In addition to following Bentham regarding associationism, Mill was also a believer in utilitarianism. His more famous son, the philosopher John Stuart Mill (1806–1873), accepted his father's utilitarian philosophy—the greatest good for the greatest number—but rejected his strict associationism. In place of what some considered mental mechanics, he preferred mental chemistry. He regarded the mind not to be a passive receptor but an active participant in its functioning. He also tended to reject the hedonistic (i.e., equating happiness with pleasure) aspect of Bentham's ethics.

Johann Herbart

The German philosopher Johann Herbart (1776–1841) was strongly influenced by the British mechanistic approach and ideas stemming from German idealism. Kant had asserted that psychology can never be an experimental or a mathematical science. Herbart agreed with the former assertion but not the latter, and attempted to develop a mathematical theory of psychology similar to Newtonian physics. His view of the way in which ideas came to be associated was more dynamic than that of the British empiricists. According to Herbart, ideas can both repel and attract each other. Ideas come into consciousness on the basis of their strength, and the strength of competing ideas tends to keep them out of consciousness.

Herbart was influenced by Leibniz's concept of the apperceptive mass. This is the view that ideas (monads) that are too weak by themselves to have an effect will have an effect if they occur in large enough numbers (thereby enlisting a large enough number of monads to enlist the dominant monad or soul). Their algebraic sum may put these ideas over the threshold of consciousness. This concept formed the rationale for Herbart to stress the educational importance of adequate preparation for the learning of new material. We more readily learn things that we are prepared for by exposure to similar things, just as we more readily detect a stimulus in a modality we have been prepared to detect it in. For his contributions to education, Herbart is known as the father of scientific pedagogy.

THE BEGINNINGS OF MODERN PSYCHIATRY

During the later half of the eighteenth century, physicians began to take a strong interest in psychological problems, leading to two noteworthy developments. One development involved the treatment of mental patients. Until near the end of the eighteenth century, across Europe people with mental illness had been put in asylums to remove them from society. Then, physicians in several European countries almost simultaneously began to view people with mental disorders as suffering from an illness that should be amenable to treatment by medical specialists (Shorter, 1997). The illness was given the name *mental alienation*, and accordingly medical doctors treating it were called *alienists*. (Although the German physician Johann Christian Reil [1759–1813] coined the term *psychiatry* [*Psychiatrie*] in 1802, the term *psychiatrist* did not replace *alienist* until near the beginning of the twentieth century.) Treatments frequently involved inducing patients to engage in various regimens to enhance sensory and social stimulation.

The other development leading to modern psychiatry was that physicians began treating patients having various disorders that were considered to be of neurological origin. People suffering from these complaints could function in society and would have rejected any implication that they were mentally alienated (i.e., mentally ill). Thus they were treated by ordinary physicians or by specialists in neurology, rather than by alienists. Later medical doctors with a specialty in psychiatry treated both the mentally ill and people with less severe neurological or psychological disorders.

Philippe Pinel

The French physician Philippe Pinel (1745–1826), considered the founder of psychiatry, is noted for humanizing the treatment of individuals suffering from mental disorders. Like Hippocrates and Galen over a millennium before him, he considered mental disorders to be due to natural causes. When appointed director of a mental institution in Paris (the

Bicêtre) in 1793, one of his first acts was to remove the chains from the inmates. He is also noted for developing an influential classification scheme for types of mental disorders.

Franz Mesmer

The French physician Franz Mesmer (1733–1815) developed a curious method of psychological treatment. He found that he could induce a trance in some people by having them drink a solution containing magnetized iron filings or simply passing a magnet over them. Mesmer claimed that this procedure, which he called *animal magnetism* but which came to be better known as *mesmerism*, had curative powers. Charged by the French government to investigate this process, as a result of complaints by French physicians, was a royal commission whose membership included Benjamin Franklin, the American scientist-statesman, who was ambassador to France at the time. The general conclusion was that neither magnets nor any special powers of the mesmerist were necessary. The procedure had its effect simply by working on the imagination of individuals who were susceptible to it. The commission established this by showing that members could obtain the effect simply by making people believe that Mesmer's techniques were being used on them. As a result, mesmerism fell into disrepute.

Nevertheless, given more respectability by being renamed hypnosis and studied experimentally, the technique eventually had a profound effect on the development of psychiatry and psychology, as will be seen in the next chapter.

NEUROLOGICAL ADVANCES

The late eighteenth and early nineteenth centuries saw rapid developments in neurology. These developments had major effects on the burgeoning sciences of psychiatry and psychology.

Pierre Cabanis

The French physician Pierre Cabanis (1757–1808) had the job of examining the corpses of guillotined individuals during the French Revolution. From observing the contortions of decapitated victims, he concluded that the muscles are under the control of the brain. He also drew conclusions about brain organization from accidental slips of the guillotine.

Franz Gall

The Viennese physician Franz Gall (1758–1828), in dissection studies of animals and humans, distinguished gray and white matter in the brain and spinal cord. He found that the white matter consisted of fibers that connect the gray areas, and discovered that the white fibers, which are on the outside of the spinal cord, cross the gray areas at the base of the brain. Unfortunately, he also went on to propose that mental traits or faculties can be predicted by the size of certain bumps and depressions on the head supposedly corresponding to the size of specific brain regions under the skull. Gall called this approach *craniology*, but it became better known as *phrenology*. Johann Spurzheim (1776–1832), a follower of Gall, coined this name from the Greek *phren* for the perceiving part of the soul (see chapter 1). Spurzheim popularized phrenology among the general public.

Rolando, Bell, and Magendie

Luigi Rolando (1770–1831) performed crude electrical stimulation experiments on the exposed brains of monkeys and was able to draw certain conclusions about the involvement of the brain in motor activity. Largely on the basis of anatomical studies, Charles Bell (1774–1842) suggested that the dorsal roots of the spinal cord are sensory in function while the anterior roots are motor. François Magendie (1783–1855) confirmed this through experiments demonstrating that paralysis results in dogs when the dorsal roots are cut and lack of sensation when the anterior roots are cut. The fact that sensory and motor nerve fibers group exclusively in the dorsal and anterior roots of the spinal cord, respectively, is called the Bell-Magendie law. Sometimes called the father of experimental physiology, Magendie made numerous other contributions to physiology and medicine, including the introduction of morphine and other compounds into medical practice.

Pierre Flourens

The French physiologist Pierre Flourens (1794–1867), in opposition to phrenology, argued that the nervous system functions as a unified whole. He refined and made sophisticated use of the ablation technique of studying the nervous system, whereby specific tissue in an animal is destroyed to discover the involvement of that particular tissue in a specific function. Using this technique on a variety of species, Flourens made a number of important discoveries. For example, he discovered that the cerebral lobes are involved in voluntary activity, the central part of the medulla oblongata in breathing, the cerebellum in muscular coordination, and the semicircular canals of the inner ear in balance. His discovery that large portions of the cerebral cortex could be destroyed without having any apparent permanent effect, provided that the animal did not die, led him to conclude that the cerebral cortex serves a general or holistic function.

James Braid

Neurological progress was also made when it was concluded that mesmerism was not due to any simple or straightforward neurological process. The British surgeon James Braid (1795–1860) investigated mesmerism and concluded that it was a real phenomenon. He initially advanced a physiological theory that it is a sleep-like state caused by a tiring of muscles of the upper eyelids. However, he later found that the state could be induced without straining the eyelid muscles. Furthermore, not everyone appears to be subject to mesmerism, so Baird rejected his physiological theory and attributed the state to the mental concentration of the recipient. He replaced the term *mesmerism* with *neuro-hypnotism* (from *hypno-* which is Greek for *sleep*), which was later shortened to *hypnotism*.

Johannes Müller

Johannes Müller (1801–1858) addressed the question of why we perceive different qualities in different senses. Why, for example, don't we (generally) see sounds, hear smells, or taste colors? He proposed the theory of specific nerve energies, which states that specific nerves energize or produce specific sensations (e.g., vision vs. touch) regardless of how those nerves are stimulated. In other words, qualitatively different sensations are a reflection of our nerves (or where those nerves connect in the brain) rather than the external environment. Thus, pressing a finger on the eye is experienced as a dark disc because the pressure stimulates nerves specific to a visual experience.

Müller argued against the copy theory—such as we have seen proposed by theorists from Empedocles to Locke—that is, the theory that the senses convey copies of external objects to an inner entity (i.e., the soul or mind) that analyzes and responds to those copies as one would to a picture or other representation of an object. However, Müller accepted the concept of a sensorium—basically, a place in the nervous system that senses or experiences states of the nerves that connect to it. Thus, like many of his contemporaries and others who followed him, Müller regarded the brain to contain processes or states that were representations of the external world. He believed that the fact that he did not postulate a nonmaterial entity, such as a soul, enabled him to avoid the philosophical difficulties involved in the copy theory (e.g., the problem of who or what looks at the internal representation, and the subsequent question of whether that entity also has internal representations of the internal representations, and so on in a never-ending, or infinite, regress). However, critics pointed out that he had not contended with the question of who or what looks at the images on the sensorium.

Hermann Lotze

The physician-philosopher Rudolph Hermann Lotze (1817–1881) criticized Müller's theory of specific nerve energies on the grounds that: there are no detectable differences between the nerves involved in different senses (e.g., the optic nerves look anatomically exactly like the auditory nerves); there are few experiments appearing that support the theory; and those experiments that do appear to support it involve abnormal or pathological forms of stimulation and produce abnormal sensations.

Although Lotze accepted the view that mechanistic analyses are necessary in science, he believed that all phenomena are the manifestations of an underlying unified spirituality (which could be called God). He accepted Kant's distinction between phenomena (things that we perceive) and noumena (the way things really are; i.e., things in themselves). Following Liebniz and Kant, Lotze believed that the mind is innately disposed to experience the universe in certain ways.

Lotze is perhaps best noted, at least in the history of psychology, for his solution to the problem of space perception. Given that space does not really exist as we perceive it, how is it that our experience of space is so strong and, apparently, so accurate? His answer was that the spatial locations of things are encoded by the patterns of stimulation that they produce with respect to their locations. Lotze extended his theory to other types of sensations. For example, visual experiences are different from auditory ones because the sensations are encoded differently. As to why the different modalities appear to be separate, Lotze answered that the sense organs filter out certain types of encoding; for example, the auditory code tends to be filtered out by the eye and the visual code tends to be filtered out by the ear. In addition, Lotze emphasized that learning plays a role in differentiating stimuli presented by different senses; for example, to a certain extent we learn to see, not hear, stimuli impinging on the retina.

Because he attempted to extend the views of the earlier German idealists to the increasingly mechanistic thinking of the dawning scientific era, Lotze is often viewed as a transitional thinker.

Hermann von Helmholtz

Hermann von Helmholtz (1821–1894) measured the speed of the transmission of a nervous impulse from the sense receptor to the brain through studies of reaction time. A student of Johannes Müller, he also refined his mentor's theory of specific nerve energies by formulating the theory of specific nerve fiber energies, particularly in relation to color vision. Helmholtz supported an earlier theory by Thomas Young that stated—correctly, as it turned out—that the eye contains different primary color receptors (i.e., specific receptors for red, green, and violet). The theory of specific nerve fiber energies postulates that different nerve fibers lead from each of these receptors to the brain, which enables us to see different colors.

Similarly, Helmholtz developed a theory of hearing that, again correctly, stated that there are different receptors for different pitches in the cochlea. Helmholtz also produced a theory of unconscious inference for space perception that was an extension of a popular theory going back to Berkeley (see Chapter 2) of how we come to perceive objects in our environment in general. We see a piece of iron for the first time and consciously learn by contacting it that it is hard. Later, when we see a piece of iron we unconsciously infer that it is hard. In basic agreement with Berkeley, Helmholtz maintained that space perception is no different (Schwartz, 2006, p. 126). A baby spends much time, according to the theory, learning how to manipulate objects (including him or herself) in space. Later, the baby maneuvers expertly in space largely because of unconscious inferences resulting from the earlier experience with objects in space.

THE ASTRONOMY CONNECTION

In the eighteenth and nineteenth centuries, a need arose for more accurate astronomical data to test Newton's theory of the physical universe and to aid in navigation as European countries expanded their exploration and trade. The British astronomer James Bradley (1693–1762) introduced a method for determining the position of a given star at a given time that involved listening to the ticks of a clock while observing the star through a telescope as it crossed a wire in the eyepiece of the telescope. As this method spread, however, it became obvious that astronomers using it showed variability in their measurements: the same astronomer observing the same star under the same weather conditions on different occasions when the star should be in the same position obtained different results; and even highly skilled astronomers consistently obtained average results that differed from each other. A major discovery was that the errors that an individual makes could be represented by the probability distribution that we now call the normal curve.

At about the same time, nation states became interested in collecting data (e.g., number of crimes of various types, number of births of each gender, number of marriages, and number of deaths at various ages per year) about their populations, and it was found that the normal distribution was not confined to errors of astronomers. It was also prevalent in these social data in particular localities. This finding, and the consistency of the means over the years of various categories of data, began to intrigue individuals known as *statists*, who were concerned with data collected by and pertaining to states. Hence the term *statistics* to refer to such data, and eventually the term *statistician* to refer to individuals who analyzed such data.

The errors people make in observing the physical universe began to intrigue psychologists. These errors suggested, in accordance with philosophers such as Kant, that people see the universe differently from the way it actually is. These errors therefore appeared to open a window to the human soul or mind as it relates to the physical universe. In addition, psychological researchers (who were not always psychologists by training) began gradually to adopt and refine the statistical methodology that was originally designed to deal with errors in astronomical observations (Stigler, 1986).

PSYCHOPHYSICS

Although experimentation had become well established in the more basic sciences by the beginning of the nineteenth century, it was conspicuous mainly by its absence in psychology. Around the middle of the century this began to change. Research began in an area that came to be known as psychophysics because its purpose was to relate psychology to physics— specifically, to show how measured physical properties such as weight, brightness, and loudness correspond to the sensation of those properties.

Ernst Weber

Ernst Weber (1795–1878), a German professor of anatomy, performed experiments on human judgments of the differences between weights. In fact, he has the distinction of publishing, in 1830, the first psychological law. Weber's law, as it is now known, states that the just-noticeable difference between two stimuli is a constant fraction of the ratio of the magnitudes of the two stimuli. This can be expressed mathematically as follows:

$$\frac{S_2 - S_1}{S_1} = c.$$

where c is a constant. In other words, the greater the stimulus (e.g., weight 1) the larger the change in that stimulus (e.g., the difference between weight 2 and weight 1) must be in order to detect a difference between the stimuli. Although Weber's pioneering work was on human judgments of the difference between weights, he extended his law to other sensory inputs.

Gustav Fechner

Gustav Fechner (1801–1887), a professor of physics at the University of Leipzig, appears to have coined the term *psychophysics*, which designates the study of the correspondence between physics (specifically, physical stimulation) and psychology (specifically, sensation). Fechner is most noted for formulating a mathematical relationship that turned out to be a generalization of Weber's law (although this was not Fechner's original purpose). Fechner's generalization states that the magnitude of a sensation is proportional to the logarithm of its stimulus. A simplified mathematical derivation of Weber's law from Fechner's generalization will help clarify why Fechner's generalization is important. In mathematical terms, Fechner's generalization states:

$$S = C \log R,$$

where S is a sensation, R (for the German *Reiz*) is a stimulus, and C is a constant. Now consider two sensations, S_1 and S_2 that are exactly one just noticeable difference (jnd) apart. Then we may continue the derivation as follows:

$$S_2 - S_1 = C(\log R_2 - \log R_1).$$

One of the rules of logarithms is that $\log a - \log b = \log a/b$. Therefore,

$$S_2 - S_1 = C \log (R_2 /R_1).$$

We are assuming that all jnds are equal; therefore, $S_2 - S_1$ is a constant, and thus $C \log R_2/R_1$ is a constant, and therefore $(R_2 - R_1)/R_1$ is a constant, which is Weber's law.

What is remarkable about Fechner's generalization is that Weber's law itself says nothing directly about sensations. What Fechner's generalization—which is now referred to as the Weber-Fechner law—does is to relate units of the environment (stimuli) to units of the mind (sensations). Fechner would likely have preferred the English word *soul* to *mind* (a word corresponding directly to *mind*, it will be recalled, does not exist in German) as he was mystical in orientation and his ultimate goal was to discover how the material and spiritual worlds are related.

Fechner published his psychophysical work in a book entitled *Elemente der Psychophysik* (1860), which launched psychophysics as a scientific field of study. The Weber-Fechner law occupied only a small portion of that book. By far the largest portion was devoted to the experimental methodology, including statistical design and analysis, that Fechner used to collect and analyze his data, which consisted of the judgments of the differences between weights. For example, he described how he carefully counterbalanced the order in which the weights were presented, and he estimated differences in the judgments between different weights by using the theory of errors (essentially, the normal distribution) that had been originally developed in astronomy. Fechner proposed that his methodology be used to study the effects of a plethora of factors on sensitivity, for example, time interval between trials, order of weights, fatigue, lack of food, lack of sleep. Although the experimental control he described was far in advance of his day, there were several features of his research that would strike the modern methodologist as questionable: (a) he used just one experimental subject—himself, (b) although the weights to be compared were in identical containers, he did not use a blind procedure (i.e., he knew which weight was in which container), and (c) he did not use a randomization procedure.

Fechner also studied aesthetics, which is of historic interest largely because his studies in this area constituted the first use of public opinion polls.

Frans Donders

Impressed by the fact that different astronomers differed consistently in their estimates of the times that a star crossed a wire in the eyepiece of a telescope, Frans Donders (1818–1889) reasoned that different individuals have different reaction times to particular events. This prompted him to embark on a study of reaction time to study psychological processes. First he obtained an individual's reaction time to particular stimuli, for example, the individual might be required to press a switch when an electric light turned on. Then the individual was required to discriminate between two different colored lights by pressing a button when one was presented but not when the other was presented, or by pressing one button when one of the stimuli was presented and another button when the other was presented. Donders used the difference between the discrimination reaction time and the simple reaction time to infer the time taken by higher mental processes to make the discrimination. Of particular interest, note Donders' incorporation of the fledgling electronic technology in his research method. This use of technology was a practice that would become increasingly prevalent as psychology matured as a science. Although many psychologists rejected Donders' subtraction method, it eventually was highly influential in later research in cognitive psychology.

DARWIN'S THEORY OF EVOLUTION

As remarkable as Fechner's book on psychophysics was, it pales in comparison to a book published a year earlier entitled the *Origin of Species*

(1859). Its author, Charles Darwin (1809–1882), was inspired by the many exotic species he had observed on some Pacific islands several decades earlier (1831–1836) as a naturalist on a British ship engaged in a surveying expedition (see Gould, 1977, pp. 28–33). His observations led him to conclude that animals had evolved differently on the different islands. A book by Thomas Malthus (1766–1834), describing what would be a competition for food on the British Isles as the availability of resources decreased in the face of an ever-increasing population, convinced Darwin of an underlying struggle for survival throughout nature. Over three decades he amassed evidence showing countless species throughout the world, including humans, as the product of a gradual process of evolution from a common ancestor. In addition, Darwin proposed a mechanism for evolution: natural selection. Organisms are similar to, but also differ from, their parents. Those organisms that are most likely to survive are most likely to pass on their characteristics to their offspring. However, there is a competition for food and, with higher multicellular organisms, for mates. Individuals whose differences give them advantages over other members of their species in these competitions are thus more likely to produce offspring. Over time this process has produced the different species throughout the world, including humans.

Darwin's theory of natural selection was not original; as we have seen, the ancient Greek thinker Empedocles, for example, had conceived the idea. However, it was Darwin's massive data and eloquent arguments that eventually overwhelmed scientific opinion. Data collected over the subsequent century-and-a-half have largely served to buttress and expand the theory. Today Darwin's theory of evolution, with some modifications, is the basic organizing theory for all the life sciences.

Darwin's theory of evolution is actually two theories rolled into one: (1) the theory that species evolved, and (2) the theory that the mechanism of evolution consists of random variation of inherited characteristics combined with the weeding out processes of natural and sexual selection. The French naturalist Jean-Baptiste Lamarck (1744–1829) published a theory of evolution in a book entitled *Philosophie zoologique* in 1809 (the year of Darwin's birth). The main difference between Lamarck's and Darwin's theories is that the former proposed that the mechanism of evolution involved the inheritance of characteristics acquired by the parents prior to the birth of the individual, whereas the latter proposed random variation of inherited characteristics as the main mechanism. (Notably, Darwin did allow for some inheritance of acquired characteristics in his theory, but this was not the major mechanism he proposed.) Lamarckianism continued as an alternative or supplement to Darwinianism until the early twentieth century when data and theory in genetics strongly indicated that parents cannot transmit acquired characteristics to their offspring and identified random mutation with Darwin's mechanism of random variation. Until that time, Lamarckianism had a certain appeal because it implied a biological striving toward perfection, as opposed to the random progression that Darwin's theory implied. In fact, for political reasons Lamarckianism was the state-supported theory of biological evolution in the Soviet Union until the 1960s. The Soviet hierarchy thought that its suggestion of sudden purposeful rather than gradual random-based change in species was more in keeping with the revolutionary change in societies that Marx proposed.

IMPACT OF DARWIN'S THEORY

Whereas Lamarck's theory had not attracted much attention during his lifetime, Darwin's *Origin of Species* had an immediate impact on science and on society as a whole. Nowhere was its influence felt more strongly than in psychology. If humans evolved from animals through natural processes, then there was no need to postulate a supernatural soul. The mind still existed, most felt, but as a purely natural part of the person. An empirically based science of the mind now seemed not only possible but also inevitable.

Emphasis on Heredity

The tendency for individuals to differ from, as well as be similar to, their parents, is crucial to Darwin's theory. Thus, his theory inspired a number of theories and studies based on the concept of heredity.

Alexander Bain

A close friend and colleague of John Stuart Mill, Alexander Bain (1818–1903) combined associationism with physiology and with evolutionary theory. Thus, not just associations, according to Bain, but also inherited factors such as differential sensitivity to stimuli are important in an individual's psychological makeup. Interestingly, Bain anticipated what was later to be called the law of effect: some movements bring pleasure or reduction of pain while others bring pain; animals and humans will tend to repeat the former and not to repeat the latter. In 1876 Bain founded the first psychological journal, *Mind*.

Herbert Spencer

While Bain emphasized the mind's dependence on physiology, specifically the nervous system, a contemporary British philosopher, Herbert Spencer (1820-1904), emphasized the mind's dependence on the environment in a two-volume work entitled *Principles of Psychology*. In this book, which went through four editions between 1855 and 1887, Spencer proposed that psychology is properly a subdivision of biology. This was a radical view at that time because of the strong distinctions that people made between humans and animals, between the mind and the environment, and between the mind and the body. In keeping with his position that psychology is a specialized part of biology, Spencer advocated an evolutionary approach to psychology before Darwin had published his theory of evolution, and well before in subsequent writings he suggested applying his theory to intelligence and emotion. At first Spencer took a Lamarckian approach to evolution, but adopted natural selection as the main mechanism of evolution after Darwin's *Origin of Species* appeared in 1859. In fact, it was Spencer who coined the expression "survival of the fittest" to describe Darwin's natural selection process.

Interestingly, Spencer formulated the view that an individual's movements in a particular situation would be increased in probability in that situation if those movements were followed by favorable effects, similar to the way that Darwin's theory proposes that favorable characteristics of organisms come about through natural selection of those characteristics by the environment. Thus, like Bain or perhaps from Bain's influence, Spencer formulated an early version of the law of effect (see Leslie, 2006).

In addition to psychology, Spencer applied evolutionary theory to society, thus helping to promulgate a position called "Social Darwinism" that was used with little logical basis to justify an extreme form of capitalism in the late 19th century and beyond.

Francis Galton

Francis Galton (1822–1911), an explorer and anthropologist, was strongly influenced by the writings of two individuals to turn his attention to the study of heredity. One of these individuals was Charles Darwin, who happened to be his cousin. The other was the Belgian astronomer turned social scientist, Adolphe Quetelet (1776–1874), who had applied statistical methods developed from astronomy to data collected by European states on their citizens. From his analyses, Quetelet had developed the concept of the "average man" (*l'homme moyenne*) as an abstraction from which actual men vary in their characteristics. Of course, the concept also applied to women, and to other groups of people as well. As a result of Quetelet's work, it became fashionable to speak of how the average Frenchman and average Englishman, for example, differed in various characteristics.

Following Quetelet in noting the law-like tendency for various characteristics to be normally distributed, Galton turned his attention on the tendency for various physical and mental characteristics to run in families—notwithstanding the large variability in those characteristics both within and between families. In 1869, he published a book entitled *Hereditary Genius: An Inquiry into its Laws and Consequences*. Lacking formal mathematical training, Galton studied the mathematical laws of variation in an empirical manner. He invented a device, which he called a quincunx, in which small balls of shot dropped into the top of the device and deflected in a random or haphazard manner by a series of pins formed an approximation to the normal distribution in compartments at the bottom of the apparatus. He then extended his statistical study to peas, noting that, unlike the results suggested by his quincunx, the variability in the weights of peas did not increase over successive generations. Extending his study to the inheritance of height in humans, he discovered the tendency for successive generations of a population to revert or regress to the mean of that population, which is what keeps variability from increasing over generations. In his endeavors to study the relationship between parents and the characteristics of their offspring, Galton provided the foundation for the statistical technique of correlation. Karl Pearson (1857–1936) and other mathematicians took Galton's basic correlation concept and developed it further in a rigorous mathematical manner.

Galton was extremely inventive and devised a number of instruments for measuring characteristics and abilities in large groups of people. For example, he designed one of the first large questionnaire studies in his investigation of the clarity and strength of mental images. He also made use of physical instruments for measuring characteristics such as strength of push, pull, and punch, and force of breath. In addition, he appears to have been the first to devise a word-association test. Using a simple apparatus he presented words to himself and noted his responses to a list of words. He found that presentation of an unforeseen word would produce an associated word in about 5/6 of a second. He also observed that most of his responses were taken from his childhood experiences.

In 1901, along with Pearson and another scientist, W. F. R. Weldon, Galton founded the journal *Biometrika*, which is devoted to the mathematical study of biological and psychological processes.

Animal Studies

Animal studies were important to demonstrate the continuity that exists across species with regard to their mental functioning. Darwin himself had pointed the way with his publication of a book entitled *The Expression of Emotions in Man and Animals* (1872).

George Romanes

George John Romanes (1848–1894), a British biologist, is credited with writing the first book on comparative psychology, *Animal Intelligence* (1881). A staunch Darwinian—he was Darwin's research associate from 1874 until Darwin's death in 1882—he used anecdotal evidence (i.e., casual and unsubstantiated observations rather than rigorously controlled studies) to try to demonstrate the evolution of intelligence across species. In addition, it was well known by this time in biology that developing embryos undergo stages that resemble the embryonic stages that species from which they evolved undergo—or, in other words, that ontogeny recapitulates phylogeny, as the saying goes. For example, early in its development, a human embryo has gill pouches due to its fish ancestry. (This, in fact, is one of the lines of evidence supporting evolutionary theory.) Romanes argued that from infancy through to maturity, humans proceed through stages of intellectual development that recapitulate the intelligences of organisms from which they evolved.

Lloyd Morgan

Conwy Lloyd Morgan (1852–1936), an English zoologist, pioneered rigorous observation of animal behavior, particularly in the natural environment. He was critical of theories based primarily on anecdotal evidence, and of theories that postulated higher mental processes in animals. He is most remembered today for a rule or canon that bears his name. There are a number of different formulations of Morgan's Canon, but basically it states that in attempting to explain any instance of animal behavior one should not postulate a higher mental function than is necessary. For example, one presumably should not postulate the use of reasoning by an animal to solve a problem that the animal conceivably could have solved through an associative process. As to how one could tell which mental processes are higher or lower than others, Morgan advocated the use of introspection (Wozniak, 1993)—a method that was becoming increasingly popular and systematized in psychology, as described in the next chapter.

Morgan's Canon is often regarded as a special case of a rule called Occam's razor, named after the scholastic philosopher William of Occam (c.1285–c.1349), who formulated it. He used it to "cut off" (as with a razor) excess speculation, such as appealing to abstract entities (e.g., an ideal circle) to account for specific instances (e.g., an actual circle). There are several versions of Occam's razor, but essentially it states that given a choice between postulating fewer and more kinds of entities to explain a phenomenon, one should postulate fewer. In scientific theorizing, Occam's razor is often equated with the rule of parsimony, which in essence states that one should be parsimonious (or stingy) in the number or complexity of concepts one uses to explain a phenomenon. It should be noted that Morgan did not equate his canon with the rule of parsimony (as he did not regard explanations involving lower mental processes to necessarily be simpler than those involving higher mental processes).

SUMMARY

Attempting to make psychology into an empirical science, the German philosopher-mathematician Christian von Wolff published the first two scientifically oriented books with psychology in their titles. Wolff had opened up an approach called faculty psychology, which was based on the idea that the mind is composed of faculties—abilities or propensities such as attention and memory that vary in their degrees of strength across individuals. Gradually, psychology became recognized as a special field of study.

David Hartley provided a theory of a physiological basis for associationism. According to his theory, when one has a sensation, vibrations occur in the white medullary substance of the nerves corresponding to that sensation. Jeremy Bentham also used associationism to explain the events (ideas, thoughts, etc.) that occur in the mind. James Mill was strongly influenced by Bentham, and like him carried on the trend started by the British empiricists. In place of what some considered mental mechanics, his son John Stuart Mill preferred mental chemistry.

The German educational philosopher Johann Herbart attempted a compromise between the British mechanistic approach and the more idealistic German approach. He proposed a mathematical psychological theory that ideas come into consciousness on the basis of their strength and the strength of competing ideas tending to keep them out of consciousness.

The French physician Philippe Pinel humanized the treatment of individuals suffering from mental disorders. The Viennese physician Franz Gall distinguished gray and white matter in the brain and spinal cord. Johannes Müller developed the theory of specific nerve energies, which states that qualitatively different sensations (e.g., vision vs. touch) energize different nerves.

Ernst Weber provided evidence that the ratio of two stimulus intensities that differ by a just-noticeable amount is a constant. Gustav Fechner generalized Weber's law to the statement that the magnitude of a sensation is proportional to the logarithm of its stimulus. Through his methods, Fechner launched psychophysics as a scientific field of study.

Charles Darwin provided massive evidence that species evolved and that the mechanism of evolution consists of random variation of inherited characteristics combined with the weeding out processes of natural and sexual selection. Nowhere was his theory's influence more strongly felt than in psychology. If humans evolved from animals through natural processes, then there was no scientific need to postulate a supernatural soul. Darwin's theory inspired a number of theories and studies based on the concept of heredity.

Studies of the mind had considered it as a general or universal property. Francis Galton was interested in individual differences in human characteristics and abilities, especially those pertaining to the mind. He focused on developing instruments for measuring characteristics and abilities in large groups of people. In his endeavors to study the relationship between parents and characteristics of their offspring, and to study the relationship between physical and mental traits, he provided the mathematical foundation for the technique of correlation.

Frans Donders used reaction time to study higher mental processes. He used the difference between the discrimination reaction time and the simple reaction time to infer the time taken by the higher mental processes to make the discrimination.

Hermann von Helmholtz measured the speed of the transmission of a nervous impulse through studies of reaction time. He also formulated a theory of color vision and a theory of space perception.

After Darwin's *Origin of Species* appeared, animal studies became important to demonstrate the continuity that exists across species with regard to their mental functioning. George Romanes is credited with writing the first book on comparative psychology. Lloyd Morgan, an English zoologist, pioneered rigorous observation of animal behavior.

Discussion Questions

1. Discuss why psychology developed so gradually as a separate field of study.

2. Discuss the differences between faculty psychology and associationism.

3. Discuss advances in neurology in the late 1700s and early 1800s.

4. Discuss why Fechner's modification of Weber's law had such a strong impact on psychology.

5. Discuss the early impact of Darwin's theory of evolution on psychology.

6. Describe how experimentation began to replace speculation in psychology.

7. Describe the contributions of astronomy to psychology.

8. Discuss how Leibniz influenced Christian von Wolff and Johann Herbart.

9. Discuss Kant's likely influence on early psychophysicists.

10. Discuss the development of the copy theory from the ancient Greeks to Johannes Müller.

CHAPTER 4

The Rise of Competing Schools of Psychology

A major milestone in the history of the experimental method in psychology occurred when Wilhelm Wundt (1832–1920), who had studied with Müller and with Helmholtz, founded what is regarded to be the first psychological laboratory in the latter part of the nineteenth century (the specific date of 1879 is often given) at the University of Leipzig. Whether or not it was the first depends on how one defines *laboratory*; however, there is no doubt that it was a highly influential laboratory that was widely emulated around the world. Its founding marked not only the beginning of experimental psychology, but also of competing schools of psychology.

VOLUNTARISM AND STRUCTURALISM

Wundt was strongly influenced by Fechner and by the mental chemistry of John Stuart Mill. His primary interest was the analysis of consciousness into its elements (i.e., sensations) and the study of how these elements synthesize into the more complex contents of the mind such as images, ideas, and feelings. In other sciences, specialists are trained to observe the phenomena of that science. Wundt believed that this should also apply to psychology, but there was one problem. The phenomena of other sciences are public, that is, they can be observed directly by anyone. Psychology, however, is different in that mental phenomena are private. They can only be observed through introspection (i.e., looking inward). There-

73

fore, Wundt developed a highly systematic introspective methodology using trained subjects, who were analogous to trained lab assistants in a science such as physics, chemistry, or biology that studies publicly observable phenomena.

Not all of Wundt's experiments involved introspection. He followed Donders, for example, in using reaction time to infer mental processes. Of particular note is his adaptation of Galton's association experiment to study the amount of time taken for a stimulus word to elicit an association versus the amount of time needed simply respond to the word. One observation, for example, was that an American took longer to produce an association to a German word than a native German did.

Wundt attracted a large number of students, many of whom went on to establish their own psychology laboratories in universities throughout Europe and North America. In the United States it was standard to advise aspiring psychologists to study with Wundt in Germany. If this was not possible, the budding psychologist was told to study at least with someone who had studied with Wundt. In this way psychology as an experimental science began to be propagated.

Wundt called his approach *voluntarism* because he thought that mental (i.e., conscious) phenomena are primarily acts of will or voluntary. For example, one generally can voluntarily select what one will attend to, or, to use Wundt's terminology, apperceive. Often confused with Wundt's approach is an approach called *structuralism*. This term is used to describe Edward Titchener's approach, which was based on Wundt's but differed in some significant ways from it. Titchener (1867–1927) was an Englishman who had studied with Wundt, translated the third and fourth editions of his *Physiological Psychology* into English, and immigrated to the United States where he obtained a position at Cornell University in 1892. Whereas Wundt had used other methods in addition to introspection, Titchener focused exclusively on introspection. He was in this sense narrower than Wundt; however, Titchener believed the analysis of physiological processes, which parallel mental processes, may sometimes provide useful information about mental processes.

The goal of psychology for Titchener, as for Wundt, was to analyze the contents of consciousness into their elements and determine how these elements combine to form conscious experience, or, in other words, how they are synthesized into mental compounds. The elements of consciousness, according to Titchener, are sensations, images, and feelings. Titchener did not, however, emphasize the importance of acts of will to conscious experience as Wundt had done. Because Wundt and Titchener were interested in studying the elements of the mind, their approaches are sometimes called elementarianism.

REACTIONS TO WUNDT'S AND TITCHENER'S APPROACHES

European Opponents

There were opponents to Wundt's and Titchener's approaches in Europe and America. These opponents gave rise to competing schools. We focus first on the European opponents, who for the most part were Austrian.

Franz Brentano

Although Wundt is generally credited with founding scientific psychology, the perhaps even greater influence of the Austrian psychologist-philosopher Franz Brentano (1838–1917) is just beginning to be appreciated (Polkinghorne, 2003). Prior to Brentano, philosophers generally agreed that mental or subjective phenomena are distinct from objective physical events. However, no one had formulated a clear difference between mental and physical events other than the debatable distinction of Descartes and others that mental and physical events are made of different types of substances and occur in different types of space. Brentano attempted to remedy this deficiency by stating a clear difference involving a concept that he borrowed from the scholastic philosopher Thomas Aquinas. Brentano called this concept *intentional inexistence*, although it has more recently simply been called *intentionality*. To say that something is intentional philosophically (not to be confused with the ordinary English meaning of *intentional*, i.e., on purpose) means that it is *about* or *of* something other than itself. Brentano argued that mental phenomena could be distinguished from other phenomena in that they are always intentional. My thought of lightning, for example, is about lightning, a physical event. Lightning, however, is not about anything (other than itself); it is simply lightning. Some philosophers have quibbled about this distinction by arguing that pains and itches, being conscious, are clearly psychological but are not of or about anything other than themselves. Brentano argued, however, that even these examples are about something else. A pain or itch in my foot, for example, is something about my foot.

This "of-ness" or "about-ness" of mental phenomena is, according to Brentano, an active, not passive, quality. That is, mental phenomena are actively directed toward whatever it is that they are of or about. My feeling of hunger, for example, is actively directed toward food. Brentano thus believed that mental acts, not the contents of the mind (as Wundt maintained), comprise the main subject matter of psychology. According to the school of thought Brentano founded, psychology should study not perceptions but the act of perceiving, not images but the act of imaging, not feelings but the act of feeling, not judgments but the act of judging, not memory but the act of remembering, and so on. Hence, Brentano's approach is called *act psychology*.

The difference between Wundt's and Brentano's approaches is important enough that it will be useful to illustrate it with a concrete example. Suppose that while walking in the woods I see something that at first I think is a snake, but on closer inspection turns out to be a stick. Wundt would be interested in the specific stimulus elements—the fact that it was long, black, shiny, rough in texture, and so forth—that that led me to perceive the object as a snake and the stimulus elements that led me later to perceive it as a stick. Brentano, however, would point out that I was not directly conscious of putting these elements together to form a particular perception. What I actually experienced was a mental act, namely a perception of a snake, followed by another mental act, namely a perception of a stick. I may later analyze these perceptions into elements, but what I was initially consciousness of were the perceptions, not the elements, of which they were composed.

By way of preview, we shall note that Brentano was particularly influential in the later development of two areas of study: the study of perception and the study of conscious experience. Perceptions are a clear form of intentionality (as the above example of falsely perceiving a snake and correctly perceiving a stick illustrates), and Brentano strongly influenced the approach to the study of perception developed by a school of thought called Gestalt psychology. Conscious experience consists of intentional phenomena that can themselves be objects of intentionality, and Brentano strongly influenced the study of these phenomena in a field that came to be called, appropriately enough, phenomenology. We detail the development of these approaches later.

We may sum up Brentano's contribution by saying that he provided a new way to look at mental phenomena and their relation to physical objects and events. Although his best-known book was entitled *Psychology from an Empirical Standpoint*, he was not an experimentalist and did not have a laboratory. Nevertheless, he influenced many students, a number of whom became extremely well known.

Ernst Mach

Ernst Mach (1838–1916) was an eminent Austrian physicist who worked on measuring the speed of sound, and in whose recognition the ratio of an object's velocity relative to the speed of sound is named. Mach's interests ranged from physics to psychology, which he believed was fundamental to all the other sciences because psychology in Mach's time was

largely the study of how we come to know the world about us. Thus Mach focused his interest on sensation and perception.

Although Mach believed that sensations are the fundamental elements of perception, he also thought that Wundt's focus on the individual sensations that produce images was misplaced. Mach pointed out that geometrical shapes, for example, are more than the sum of the lines (i.e., the elementary sensations) that make them up. Still, he did not abandon the idea that all perceptions are made up of elementary sensations; instead, he believed that in addition to the obvious sensations involved in a perception there is one that serves to bind together the elements into the perception. Thus, when we see a triangle as a triangle (rather than a collection of three lines) this is because of another elementary sensation—perhaps caused by the feedback from the movement of our eye muscles—that somehow binds the other sensations together to make them appear as a unitary whole.

Mach is noted for a philosophical position called *positivism*, which maintains that all proper scientific concepts must be based on sense impressions or sense data. He was not the originator of this position—that distinction belongs to the French philosopher Auguste Comte (1798–1857). Mach, however, was a strong and consistent advocate who applied it to all his scientific endeavors. He believed that physics should be based on the science of psychology—hence, his interest in studying the psychology of sense data and applying it to physics. For example, contrary to most physicists up to and including his time, he took the view that absolute rest is not a valid physical concept because it cannot be defined in terms of our senses, and hence that motion must be regarded as a relative concept. He related this relativism to psychology by noting, for example, the feeling that a bridge one is standing on is moving in the opposite direction of a river flowing below it after staring down at the river for a while.

Mach's writings on the relativity of motion had a profound influence on Albert Einstein (1879–1955) in the development of his theory of relativity. Given Mach's atomistic approach to psychology, it is perhaps noteworthy that he disputed atomic theory in physics in part because atoms cannot be sensed directly (although he had other reasons as well; Laudan, 1981, pp. 202–225).

A strong believer in evolution, Mach maintained that science is part of the evolutionary process. This is because science is an outgrowth of human intelligence, which evolved because it promoted the survival of our species. The ultimate effect of science, according to Mach, is to promote our survival by enhancing our control over the environment. Mach came close to holding an evolutionary criterion of truth—that is, ideas that people ultimately accept as true are, in the long run, those that best promote our survival as a species.

Carl Stumpf

Carl Stumpf (1848–1936), an eminent student of Brentano, attempted to reconcile Wundt's content psychology with Brentano's act psychology. According to Stumpf, the mind consists of both contents (which he termed phenomena) and acts (which he termed psychic functions). He agreed with Brentano that the contents or events of the mind are never experienced in isolation.

Alexius Meinong

Another eminent student of Brentano was Alexius Meinong (1853–1920). This philosopher is best known for the way he tackled an issue that Brentano's philosophy seemed to leave unresolved, namely, how is it that objects of mental acts appear to be differentiated on the basis of whether or not they are real? To put the problem another way, if an intention is a relation between a mental act and an object, how is it possible for a non-existent object to enter into a relation with a mental act? For example, my idea of a horse has as its object at least one real horse, whereas my idea of a unicorn appears to have no real existing object—so what is it exactly that is in relation with my unicorn idea that makes it intentional? Brentano's solution to this problem was to say that real objects are less subject to the will and can be interacted with more effectively than unreal objects. For example, I can easily make my imaginary horse do back flips, but I can't ride on it.

Meinong's solution to the problem of philosophically distinguishing between real and unreal objects was essentially the opposite of Brentano's. He maintained that all objects are equally real, but that objects that we consider unreal exist in a world of abstractions. His position in this regard was similar to Plato's view that abstractions have a reality that transcends the reality of concrete objects.

Meinong also has the distinction of having founded the first psychological laboratory in Austria.

Christian von Ehrenfels

Christian von Ehrenfels (1859–1932) studied with Brentano and Meinong. He agreed with Mach that a perception of an object seems to involve something more than just the elementary sensations that make it up. He disagreed, however, that there was an additional element that bound the other elements together. Instead, he believed that a perception exists as a unified whole apart from the separate sensations of which it is composed. Thus, when I view a triangle, for example, I see not only the individual lines that make it up but also the whole triangle, not as a separate sensory element (as Mach believed), but as something that exists apart from and in some sense at a higher level than the individual sensations. Ehrenfels coined the term *Gestaltqualität* (*Gestalt quality*, where *Gestalt* is German for form, shape, or figure) to characterize a combining of sensations to form a unified whole. He also suggested a hierarchy of Gestalt qualities, so that a group of Gestalt qualities could form a higher Gestalt quality. Indeed, he suggested that sensations might themselves be Gestalt qualities composed of lower-level sensations.

Ehrenfels generalized his Gestalt concept to all sensory modalities. A talented musician, he was especially interested in applying it to music. There his theory seems more plausible than Mach's, for it is difficult to conceptualize a single sensation that would bind together separate notes into a melody, for example.

Other former students and followers of Brentano coined similar terms to describe what Ehrenfels referred to as Gestalt qualities, but Ehrenfels is credited with the most extensive early writing on the topic, and his term *Gestalt* tended to stick (as we shall see later).

Edmund Husserl

Edmund Husserl (1859–1938), who was a student of both Brentano and Stumpf, founded phenomenology as a systematic philosophy. The subject matter of phenomenology is immediate experience, that is, that which is immediately given to consciousness without any type of formal analysis. Thus, trained subjects such as Wundt used are not needed in phenomenological studies and would in fact, according to Husserl, distort rather than reveal the true nature of consciousness. His method was to describe specific percepts or data of consciousness in the absence of any preconceptions about or interpretations of them. Husserl accepted Brentano's idea that all mental acts involve intentionality, that is, they are always directed toward an object. He based his phenomenological approach on the assumption that mental acts could be themselves the object of other mental acts. Husserl's goal was to discover through his phenomenological method the structure of and the laws determining conscious experience.

Oswald Külpe

A different kind of challenge to the approaches of Wundt and Titchener occurred when Oswald Külpe (1862–1915), working at the University of Würzburg with colleagues and students, decided to use Wundt's introspective method on higher mental processes, even though Wundt recommended against this. Külpe and his associates asked trained introspectionists to report on their conscious experiences while solving various higher-level problems. The result was that significant parts of the process appeared not to be accessible to conscious observation. There seemed to be unconscious mental processes or mechanisms at work.

Some of the concepts the researchers developed from these experiments were conscious attitudes (e.g., doubt or uneasiness produced by the problem), determining tendencies (i.e., the unconscious mechanisms that did not seem accessible to introspection), level of consciousness, task set (Einstellung), and imageless thought. The researchers also found that training the subjects seemed to affect the number of introspective states that they identified.

Titchener criticized these studies on the grounds that the researchers committed what structuralists called the stimulus error—focusing on the stimulus producing the sensations to be studied, that is. the problem to be solved in this case, rather than the sensations resulting from it. Researchers in Titchener's lab did not obtain imageless thought.

A cardinal rule of science is that results must be replicable. Scientists, sooner or later, shun any approach that does not yield replicable results. Thus, the fact that different results were obtained with different amounts or types of introspective training and from different laboratories did not bode well for the fate of Wundtian and Titchenerian introspective techniques.

Opposition in America: Functionalism

In America an approach called functionalism held sway. This approach was strongly influenced by Darwin's theory of evolution, in the sense that the focus was on the function of psychological processes, not their structure, as was the case with Wundt's and Titchener's approaches. In other words, the focus of functionalism was on how mental processes such as consciousness led to survival and reproduction during the evolutionary history of humans and other species.

William James

In 1875, William James (1842–1910), who was both a philosopher and the most eminent American psychologist of his day, began conducting psychological research at Harvard University. Like Wundt and Titchener, James was interested in consciousness but, unlike them, he saw it as a continuous flowing stream (he coined the term *stream of consciousness*) rather than consisting of isolated elements or events. In this regard his view was similar to Brentano's, whom he greatly respected. Like Brentano, James believed that consciousness is perceived as continuous in time, and that it cannot meaningfully be analyzed into discrete elements as Wundt tried to do. Although one may try to identify what appear to be elements in the stream, these so-called elements were not actually immediately present in consciousness. One had to mentally produce them after the fact. In effect, they were artifacts.

As a philosopher, James is noted for his writings on pragmatism, which is the view that the truth of a belief is a function of the usefulness or practical or pragmatic value (or "cash value," as James sometimes colloquially put it) of that belief. James obtained this philosophy from a friend who at been a fellow student at Harvard, the American philosopher Charles Peirce (1839–1914).* However, to Peirce's chagrin, James' version of pragmatism allowed for contradictory personal views, such as opposing religious claims, to be considered as true. According to James, a given religious belief, for example, is true for a particular person to the extent that it serves a useful function in that person's life.

Although James' pragmatism stressed the utility of religion, it also emphasized the utility of intellectual activity. In this latter respect, his view was similar to Mach's, whom he greatly admired. Like Mach, James argued that the high level of intellectual functioning in humans is due to instincts implanted in them through the process of evolution. Thus, far from having fewer instincts than other animals, James argued that they have more. However, instincts to James were much more flexible than the rigid unvarying behavior patterns they are commonly thought of as being today.

James' pragmatism, in essence, was the philosophy behind the school of psychology called functionalism, which, as mentioned, was the view that psychology should study not the structure of the mind but the function of mental processes. Thus three major schools of psychology had emerged in Europe and America: structuralism (a term that increasingly came to be applied to Wundt's as well as Titchener's approach), act psychology, and functionalism.

G. Stanley Hall

G. Stanley Hall (1844–1924) was the first American to have studied with Wundt, and is generally credited with founding, at Johns Hopkins University in 1883, the first Wundtian laboratory in America. However, Hall became an eminent functionalist. He had studied with William James prior to studying with Wundt, which no doubt predisposed him to functionalism. In 1887, Hall founded the first psychological journal in America, the *American Journal of Psychology*. He focused on child development psychology, and proposed a theory corresponding to the biological theory that ontogeny recapitulates phylogeny. He believed that child

---

*Peirce, whose forte was logic, also made methodological contributions to psychology. In collaboration with Joseph Jastrow (1863–1944), a graduate student at Johns Hopkins University when Peirce was a lecturer in the psychology department there, he improved on Fechner's methodology for judging weights by incorporating randomization of trials and using an assistant to ensure that the subject was blind with respect to which container held the heavier weight and which the lighter weight.

development (e.g., the development of the grasping reflex in infants) recapitulates stages that our primate ancestors went through (e.g., the development of climbing). In 1892, Hall became the first president of the American Psychological Association.

James Baldwin

Another important functionalist of this period was James Mark Baldwin (1861–1934), who worked in the area of child psychology and theorized on how children perceive the world. Both Hall and Baldwin were therefore founders of developmental psychology. Baldwin is also noted for having established the first psychological laboratory in Canada at the University of Toronto, and for having brought evolutionary psychology to Canada (Murray, 1988). He later taught at Princeton and Johns Hopkins.

APPLICATIONS

During the late nineteenth and early twentieth centuries three applications of psychology were the treatment of mental patients, the development of mental testing, and the founding of clinical psychology. An interesting aspect of these applications is the fact that the individuals involved in their development were strongly influenced by academic psychology.

Mental Patients

Emil Kraepelin

Emil Kraepelin (1856–1926) continued in the tradition of Philippe Pinel and other early psychiatrists working with people with mental illnesses. After receiving an M.D. from the University of Würzburg and studying with Wundt, Kraepelin became Director of the Psychiatric Clinic in Munich. In 1883, on the basis of his observations in this position, Kraepelin published a classification system for mental illnesses which, with only slight modification, is still used. He distinguished three types of serious mental disorders, which he labeled dementia praecox (because he believed it to be a premature deterioration of the nervous system), manic-depressive psychosis, and paranoia. He was the most influential psychiatrist of his day.

Eugen Bleuler

Eugen Bleuler (1857–1939) was a Swiss psychiatrist who was director of the Burghölzli Mental Hospital in Zürich. He is noted today for (among other things) renaming dementia praecox, which he did not believe was due to a physical deterioration. He gave it the name schizophrenia because he believed that it was due to contradictory (i.e., split), disharmonious, or conflicting tendencies in the mind (recall that *phren* comes from the Greek word for the perceiving part of the soul).

Mental Testing

Psychologists developed mental tests because of the practical question of how to enhance the efficiency of education.

Alfred Binet and Théodore Simon

In 1905, Alfred Binet (1856–1911), who had studied with Freud's mentor, Charcot, and his student, Théodore Simon (1873–1961), were assigned by the Ministerial Commission for the Study of the Retarded in the French school system to develop a means to separate normal from abnormal children in a scientifically precise manner. Binet and Simon developed a variety of tests for measuring the average age at which children are able to solve the various tasks in the tests. Thus, Binet and Simon were able to identify children whose mental functioning was well below their age levels. These were the first intelligence tests.

Hermann Ebbinghaus

Binet and Simon borrowed heavily from the work of others, but especially from that of German psychologist Hermann Ebbinghaus (1850–1909), who had done prior work in developing tests for school children. The school board of Breslau had commissioned Ebbinghaus, among others, to construct a test to measure the buildup of mental fatigue in school children over the duration of a 5-hour school day.

James McKeen Cattell

James McKeen Cattell (1860–1944), an American functionalist at Columbia University, had studied with Hall at Johns Hopkins, Wundt at Leipzig, and Galton at Cambridge. From both Wundt and Galton he acquired techniques for studying reaction time and discrimination, and Galton helped stimulate his interests in individual differences. Using instruments derived largely from Wundt and Galton, he devised a number of *mental tests* (a termed he coined) for studying individual differences. In keeping with the functionalists' interests in application, Cattell envisioned a future in which psychological tests would enable employers to match employees with the jobs they were best suited for, help physicians diagnose treatable abnormalities, and facilitate selective breeding directed toward improving the human race. The dangers of eugenics were not as clear then as they are today.

Clinical Psychology

Lightner Witmer (1867–1956), a psychologist who had studied under Cattell and then (like many Americans) went to Leipzig to earn his Ph.D. under Wundt, established the first psychological clinic at the University of Pennsylvania in 1896. Borrowing the term *clinic* from medicine, Witmer wrote of the need for the field that he christened *clinical psychology*, which he clearly distinguished from medicine. Witmer stressed that basic research and application in psychology, as in other sciences, go hand-in-hand. Witmer's clinic dealt mainly with children who had severe problems learning in school. However, although other psychologists did not respond immediately to his call, eventually they did and the field of clinical psychology gradually grew to include the treatment of all forms of psychological distress. Offshoots, such as counseling psychology, also developed.

STUDIES OF MEMORY

Although Ebbinghaus' applied work on testing is of historical importance, he is best known for his prior experimental research on memorization and remembering. Impressed with Fechner's quantitative results on the psychophysics of judging weights, he wanted to apply a similar quantitative method to the study of memory. He reasoned that when we memorize a tract of verbal material such as a poem, what we are doing is associating words together, and he wanted to study this associative process. He reasoned that the process of forming associations occurred too fleetingly for introspection to be of any use in capturing it, and so a different method would have to found. He also reasoned that he could not use actual poems or other meaningful material because there would already be strong associations between the words in even unfamiliar material. Therefore, he devised a method of forming random combinations of letters into pronounceable syllables and putting them randomly into lists to be memorized. Some of these syllables would be meaningless, and some would by chance be real words; however, when put together randomly in lists, they would essentially form nonsense; hence, he called them *nonsense syllables*.

Following Fechner's example of using only himself as the experimental subject, Ebbinghaus recorded the number of repetitions required to memorize a list and the number of correct responses and errors as he learned such lists. Among his discoveries were the shape of the retention curve (showing that the rate of forgetting drops more and more slowly as time following learning increases) and the existence of associations between items far removed from each other as well as adjacent items. Ebbinghaus is also noted for his development of the savings method, which is a measure of the effect of learning a previous list on a subsequent list of the same nonsense syllables in a systematically altered order (called a *derived list*). In 1885, Ebbinghaus published *On Memory*. The book received a cool reception from functionalists who did not see it as furthering their objective of discovering how mental associations function to promote survival in an evolutionary context. It was also not well received by structuralists in general because it did not involve introspective methods, although Titchener praised it highly.

Like Fechner, Ebbinghaus played an important role in importing statistical methods from astronomy to psychology. Noting that the measurements of natural processes, such as the position of a star, tend to following a normal curve, Ebbinghaus reasoned that if his measurements of the time he took to learned lists of a given size tended to follow a normal distribution, this would indicate that he had in fact tapped into a natural process. Thus he developed a method for comparing his measurements with a normal curve. Interestingly, when he found that his measurements were not normally distributed, he aggregated them, which, in effect, mathematically forced them into a normal distribution (due to what is known as the Central Limit Theorem). Although Ebbinghaus' rationale for aggregating his data is questionable, the fact that he did so is in accordance with accepted modern statistical methods. The next step Ebbinghaus took, however, was remarkably in keeping with modern statistical methods. Having established a way of putting his measurements into a normal distribution, he used that distribution to test whether a given result—for example, less time to learn lists when he used his savings method—was real or due to random fluctuations in his data. Although he gave no firm rule for (in modern statistical language) rejecting the null hypothesis, he seems to have considered a result with a chance probability less than 0.25 to be worthy of note and one with a chance probability less than 0.00003 to be certain proof. Thus, Ebbinghaus appears to have been the first to apply formal statistical hypothesis testing (or something remarkably close to it) in psychology (Stigler, 1986, pp. 254–261).

Another German researcher, Georg Müller (1850–1934), and his student Alfons Pilzecker (1865–1949) expanded on Ebbinghaus' memory work. They developed a method in which items are paired and the experimental task is to recall each member of a pair when the other member is presented. This makes the associations more explicit than they are in Ebbinghaus' method. Ebbinghaus' method is called serial learning and Müller's and Pilzecker's is called paired-associates learning.

THE STUDY OF REFLEXES

The history of the concept of reflexes goes back to Descartes (see Chapter 2), but it came into their own in the mid-to-late nineteenth century. While experimental psychology was making progress in the area of associative learning, neurological advances were also occurring. Helmholtz had used reflexes to measure the speed of transmission of impulses in the nerves. The Russian Ivan Sechenov (1829–1905) demonstrated the involvement of the brain in reflexes. He is generally credited with being the founder of Russian physiology. In 1863, Sechenov published *Reflexes of the Brain*. Charles Sherrington (1857–1952) was a British neurophysiologist who also did early research on reflex activity. He introduced the concept of reciprocal inhibition, in which inhibitory nerves relax one muscle when an antagonistic muscle is activated. He postulated that the reciprocal processes of excitation and inhibition operate throughout the nervous system, including the brain, and introduced the concept of integrative action in regard to the nervous system. In 1906, he published *The Integrative Action of the Nervous System*.

Ivan P. Pavlov

Work on reflexes led naturally to the conditioned reflex. Ivan P. Pavlov (1849–1936), a Russian physiologist who was a follower of Sechenov (although he had not been his student), did important work on digestion that won him the Nobel Prize. While researching the food-salivation reflex in dogs, Pavlov serendipitously observed that the stimuli preparatory to presenting food came to elicit salivation. This observation led him to a new line of research, the investigation of the conditional reflex. He called the reflex conditional because it was conditional on a prior pairing process, as opposed to an unconditional reflex (e.g., food in the mouth eliciting salivation), which did not depend on a prior pairing. Due to a mistranslation, the Russian word for *conditional* was rendered in English as *conditioned*, which has remained the operative term because it is a handy verb as well as an adjective with which to describe the procedure and its result. Pavlov went on to make a number of important discoveries about the conditioning process, such as extinction of the conditioned reflex, generalization, and discrimination. He attempted to work out a neurological theory of conditioning. Pavlov published his first conditioning studies in 1906.

Vladimir Bekhterev

Pavlov's compatriot, Vladimir Bekhterev (1857–1927), also contributed greatly to the study of reflexes. Bekhterev was also a follower of Sechenov, and had worked with Wundt at Leipzig, Du Bois-Reymond (the leading neurophysiologist in the mid-nineteenth century) at Berlin, and Charcot (an eminent French psychiatrist who was Binet's mentor and who also influenced Freud) at Paris. He thus was well attuned to psychological as well as neurological issues. While Pavlov worked primarily with the salivary reflex, Bekhterev developed a procedure for studying conditioned leg and finger reflexes. In the procedure he developed, an arbitrary stimulus occurs followed by a mild shock through electrodes attached to a leg or finger. Over several trials, the leg or finger jerks upon the presentation of the arbitrary stimulus, whereas it did not do so before. This fits the model of Pavlov's conditional reflex; however, Bekhterev (perhaps because he was attuned to psychological issues) used the term *association reflex*. In 1907, Bekhterev published a book entitled *Objective Psychology* in which he opposed the use of introspection as a fundamental psychological method. He disbelieved in the mind as an independent entity and hypothesized that, rather than taking place in a special mental realm, thinking is subvocal speech—that is, inaudible movements of the vocal cords as though making speech sounds, but with no overt speech occurring.

Bekhterev coined the word *reflexology* to describe the work that investigators such as Sechenov, Pavlov, and himself did, and these three individuals are considered preeminent among the Russian reflexologists.

PSYCHOANALYSIS

In the early twentieth century, another approach burst on the scene. Sigmund Freud (1856–1939), an Austrian medical doctor who started out doing traditional medical research, became interested in hysteria through collaborating with an older colleague, Joseph Breuer (1842–1925), in the treatment of one of Breuer's patients. Hysteria consists of various physical impairments without any clear physical cause. For example, Breuer's patient had, among other disorders, impaired vision and a paralysis of both right extremities although there was no evident physical basis for these disorders. Under hypnosis the patient revealed certain incidents in her life that appeared to be related to the development of the hysterical symptoms. To do more work on hypnosis, Freud went to Paris in 1885 to study with Jean Martin Charcot (1825–1893), the eminent French psychiatrist. Charcot had done much work with hypnosis and at first believed that susceptibility to hypnosis is one manifestation of hysteria. Later, as a result of debate and discussion with colleagues, he came to believe that hypnosis is similar to normal waking behavior and can be produced in nearly everyone.

Freud was particularly impressed with Charcot's suggestion that hysteria has a sexual basis. Upon Freud's return to Vienna to resume his collaboration with Breuer, he and Breuer abandoned the use of hypnosis because not all patients could be hypnotized and the removal of symptoms that it afforded tended not to be permanent. In lieu of hypnosis, Freud and Breuer had the patient free associate in a relaxed state. This is the therapy that came to be called *psychoanalysis*—literally, the analysis of the mind. In 1895, Breuer and Freud published a book entitled *Studies in Hysteria*.

Perhaps the most significant moment in Freud's thought occurred when he moved from the view that neurotic individuals' symptoms were the result of sexual molestation by relatives and family friends to the view that these events were mere fantasies stemming from unconscious wishes. As Freud increasingly emphasized what he saw as the sexual motivation underlying the symptoms, Breuer broke with him. Continuing on his own, based on the psychoanalyses of his patients, Freud went on to develop a general theory of the mind that viewed the sex drive, the libido, as the chief motivating factor. According to Freud this motivation is kept largely unconscious by processes of inner censorship called repression and suppression. It can, however, slip past the censor in various disguises that manifest themselves in dreams, slips of the tongue, art, literature, choice of profession, and various aspects of the normal personality, as well as (in extreme cases) neurotic symptoms such as hysteria, phobias, obsessions, and compulsions. According to Freud psychoanalysis is the treatment of choice not only to alleviate debilitating symptoms, but even for apparently normal persons—for repressive forces of society acting on us from infancy have made us all somewhat neurotic. These forces continue to operate internally through a kind of warfare (or tug of war) that goes on among the three parts of the mind: the id, the ego, and the superego. The id is unconscious and is the seat of the libido; the superego represents the repressive and suppressive forces instilled in us by society. The superego, too, is largely unconscious. The ego, which is partly conscious, functions to mediate between and reconcile the opposing forces of the id and superego. Freud put forth a theory of personality development in which these three entities play the major role in psychosexual stages that the child undergoes. In conducting psychoanalysis Freud particularly exhorted his patients to dredge up repressed material from their childhood in order to bring childhood traumatic events into consciousness where they can be dealt with and resolved by the ego. In 1900, Freud published *Interpretation of Dreams*.

Freud's theory of conflict between the various parts of the mind is similar, in some ways, to Plato's conflict between the parts of the soul. Thus, the base appetites are similar to the vegetative soul and the ego is similar to the thinking, rational, or conscious part of the soul. However, the analogy breaks down when we move to the emotional part of the soul, which bears little or no resemblance to the superego. The emotional part of the soul may take offense at injustice and passionately seek justice, but it is passionate about many other things as well. This is not to say, however, that Plato did not influence Freud.

Another, more contemporary, influence on Freud was Brentano. As a student at the University of Vienna, Freud had enthusiastically taken several philosophy courses from Brentano and may have been strongly influenced by Brentano's emphasis on intentionality, that is, the directedness of the mind toward objects in the world or the motivated nature of thought. Brentano believed that intentionality was the essence of consciousness, however, and thus would not have accepted Freud's view of the unconscious.

Although Freud's views were initially ridiculed and staunchly rejected by mainstream psychiatrists, such as Kraepelin, psychoanalysis eventually came to dominate most of psychiatry and clinical psychology until the 1950s. With the rise of modern pharmaceutical methods for controlling mental disorders, along with the advent of modern brain imaging techniques, most of psychiatry gradually returned to its biological roots (Paris, 2005). Other theories and methods have also tended to replace psychoanalysis in clinical psychology, as we shall see in the second part of this book.

FURTHER DEVELOPMENTS IN FUNCTIONALISM

While Wundt's elementarianism, Brentano's act psychology, and Freud's psychoanalysis were flourishing in Europe, functionalism thrived in North America. The main opposition to functionalism was Titchener's interpretation of Wundt's approach, called, as already mentioned, structuralism.

John Dewey

At the University of Chicago, John Dewey (1859–1952), who had studied with Hall at Johns Hopkins University, espoused functionalism, based on the psychology of William James. According to Dewey, to break psychological processes into elements, as the structuralists tried to do, reduces them to meaninglessness. It makes about as much sense, Dewey asserted, as trying to separate the stimulus and response in a reflex arc. This is a futile endeavor because one implies the other. According to functionalism, psychological processes, for example, perception, emotion, volition, and thought, should be understood in terms of how they enable an organism to adapt to its environment.

As a rough analogy to help clarify the difference between structuralism and functionalism, think of the difference between anatomy and physiology in zoology. Structuralism purports to look at the structure of the mind similar to the way in which anatomists look at the structure of the body; functionalists look at the function of the mental processes similar to the way in which physiologists look at the functions of the parts of the body. The analogy is only rough, however, because while anatomy and physiology are complementary, structuralism and functionalism are incompatible—at least from the point of view of the functionalists, who felt that mental phenomena cannot be meaningfully broken into elements. The structuralists, in contrast, believed that studying function before the elements are known is premature. Structuralists also tended to look down on the application of psychology to practical matters. In contrast, functionalists as a whole relished it. Adaptation to the environment was the essence of functionalism, and adaptation and application are closely related. The applied side of functionalism probably accounts for its dominance in America, for the country had a large practical streak stemming from its frontier days when survival depended on practicality. It is not surprising, then, that Dewey applied his theory to education. Dewey viewed learning as a prime example of an adaptive process. He therefore did not see education as an activity in which the student passively takes in information from the teacher. On the contrary, Dewey is noted for advocating that one learns by doing.

James Angell and Harvey Carr

Two other Chicago functionalists of note were James Angell (1869–1949) and his successor, Harvey Carr (1873–1954). Angell was an eminent functionalist, although he is perhaps most notable for the large number of doctoral students that he graduated. He strongly advocated the study of the functions of consciousness. Carr continued in the tradition of Dewey and Angell. He dealt with the mind-body problem in a manner similar to that in which Dewey dealt with the reflex arc: looked at separately they are meaningless abstractions because one implies the other. He attacked the charge that functionalism is teleological—that is, that behavior is caused by pulls from the future rather than pushes from the past—by distinguishing between proximate and consequent causes. For example, a proximate cause for eating would be things like an animal's gastrointestinal condition and the sight and smell of food leading to eating. The consequent cause, which gives the behavior its function, is accounted for by evolution.

Edward Thorndike

Functionalism was amenable to animal studies because, following the theory of evolution, it assumes a continuity between animals and humans. Structuralism did not deny the continuity, but could not take advantage of it because animals cannot tell us about their consciousness. Indeed, the direction of generalization went in the opposite direction for structuralists, in that experiments on humans were used to infer conscious processes in animals.

Functionalism viewed animal studies not only as a way to obtain basic knowledge, but also as a source of discovering general principles that can be applied to practical concerns, such as education. Edward Thorndike (1874–1949) was an animal researcher who studied with James at Harvard and Cattell at Columbia. While at Harvard, Thorndike did research on chickens. Illustrative of the importance functionalists placed on animal research is the fact that Thorndike's advisor, William James, gave him the loan of his basement to house the animals because there was no space for them at Harvard (Menand, 2001, p. 321). After transferring to Columbia to pursue his doctorate, Thorndike pioneered the study of a kind of animal learning that was different from that studied by Pavlov and Bekhterev. The type of learning Thorndike studied is the type that is often characterized as intelligent. Darwin's research associate, Romanes, and other early investigators of animal behavior had written about animals supposedly figuring out how to perform intelligent feats, such as opening door latches. Thorndike decided to put these observations to experimental test, and, on the basis of his findings, argued that a simple principle of association could account for these manifestations of animal intelligence.

In many of Thorndike's controlled experiments, animals learned simple responses to escape from a situation and obtain a reward. For example, a cat might learn to escape from a box, called a *puzzle box*, by pulling a cord that operated a latch, whereupon the cat obtained food placed outside the box. Thorndike plotted the amount of time the cat took to pull the cord on each trial. In this manner, he was able to show that the shapes of the learning curves across a wide variety of species are similar, indicating that the learning process is the same across species. On the basis of his research and on the basis of work on the nervous system, Thorndike developed a connectionist type of theory. According to Thorndike's theory, if a specific response occurs in a specific situation and is followed by an event called a satisfier, a connection between that situation or stimulus and the response will be established (or, as he put it, "stamped in"). The result of this connection is that the response will tend to occur the next time that the animal is in that situation. Thorndike formulated this observation in a principle he called the *law of effect*. It is only natural that Thorndike, who as a graduate student had begun his animal research with the support and encouragement of his mentor, William James, emphasized the importance of the effects—or *function*—of behavior. Thorndike's emphasis on the effects in a given situation of behavior on its tendency to reoccur in that situation was a logical extension of James' functional approach to psychology. In 1911, Thorndike described his research in a book entitled *Animal Intelligence*.

Thorndike extended his studies to humans. As an example, the situation might be the task of drawing a line a given length while blindfolded; the response would in that case be drawing the line, and the satisfier would be the word *right*. Thorndike also investigated the effects of punishment (with humans the word *wrong*) and concluded that while reward strengthens stimulus-response connections, punishment does not weaken them. Punishment, according to Thorndike, simply causes an individual to do something else that may be rewarded (which led him to modify the law of effect, which had originally referred to the stamping out as well as stamping in of stimulus-response connections). Under the influence of Cattell, Thorndike also worked on extending his methods and findings to the development of psychological tests.

Robert Yerkes

Another functionalist animal psychologist of note during the early 1900s was Robert M. Yerkes (1876–1956). In 1908, Yerkes, in collaboration with John D. Dodson, published a paper on a curvilinear relationship (since termed the Yerkes-Dodson law) between arousal or stress and learning. The study showed that mice learned a black-white discrimination more rapidly to avoid receiving a shock when the intensity of the shock was at an intermediate level rather than at its highest or lowest levels. In another paper, which received little attention at the time but later turned out to be quite important, Yerkes, in collaboration with Sergius Morgulis, provided the first description in English of Pavlov's research on the conditioned reflex. Yerkes is also known for his work with chimpanzees and gorillas, and for founding and directing the Yale Laboratories of Primate Biology (which today is the Yerkes National Primate Research Center of Emory University).

SUMMARY

Wilhelm Wundt founded the first psychological laboratory in the latter part of the nineteenth century at the University of Leipzig. He developed a highly systematic introspective methodology—later called structuralism because its objective was to study the structure of the mind—which involved training individuals to observe carefully images and the other contents of their minds while being presented with various stimuli and tasks.

There were opponents to Wundt's structural approach in Europe and America. Franz Brentano's act psychology maintained that mental acts, not the contents of the mind, are the proper subject matter of psychology. Brentano and his followers, with their emphasis on the intentional (i.e., the about-ness or directedness) and active nature of mental phenomena, prepared the groundwork for Gestalt psychology, as later initiated by Christian von Ehrenfels, and phenomenology, as later developed by Edmund Husserl. The former is the study of perceptions (broadly conceived) as unified wholes and the later is the study of conscious experiences.

There was also opposition to Wundt's approach in America where an approach called functionalism held sway. This approach was strongly influenced by Darwin's theory of evolution, in the sense that the focus was not on the structure of psychological processes but on their functions. William James was the earliest exponent of functionalism.

Stanley Hall was another eminent American functionalist. Hall had studied with James prior to studying with Wundt, which no doubt predisposed him to functionalism. In 1887, Hall founded the first psychological journal in America, the *American Journal of Psychology*. He focused on child development psychology and proposed a theory corresponding to the biological theory that ontogeny recapitulates phylogeny.

Edward Titchener, a student of Wundt, was the chief structuralist in America. The goal of psychology for Titchener, as for Wundt, was to analyze the contents of consciousness into their elements and determine how these elements combine to form conscious experience, or, in other words, how they are synthesized into mental compounds. The elements of consciousness, according to Titchener, are sensations, images, and feelings.

A serious blow was dealt to introspection by the phenomenon of imageless thought. That is, in working on complex problems there seemed to be unconscious mental processes or mechanisms at work that could not be discerned through introspection.

During the late nineteenth and early twentieth centuries applications of psychology included the treatment of mental patients (Emil Kraepelin), mental testing (Alfred Binet and Théodore Simon), and the founding of clinical psychology (Lightner Witmer).

Impressed with Fechner's quantitative results, Herrmann Ebbinghaus applied a similar quantitative method to the study of memory. Using himself as subject, he learned lists of nonsense syllables, demonstrated transfer and interference phenomena, and produced orderly forgetting curves over time. Through his memory research, he developed new techniques for studying learning and recall.

Ivan Sechenov demonstrated the involvement of the brain in reflexes, and theorized that thinking is a form of reflex activity. His followers, Ivan P. Pavlov and Vladimir Bekhterev, pioneered the study of conditioning. While Pavlov worked primarily with the salivary reflex, Bekhterev developed a procedure for studying conditioned leg and finger reflexes.

He sought to develop an objective psychology and theorized that thinking is subvocal speech.

Sigmund Freud collaborated with Joseph Breuer to treat hysteria in one of Breuer's patients. Breuer and Freud parted company, however, as Freud began to emphasize sexual motivation as a key factor in cases of hysteria. According to Freud this motivation is kept largely unconscious by processes of inner censorship called repression and suppression. Freud believed that unconscious sexual motivation manifests itself in normal behavior also.

At the University of Chicago, John Dewey espoused functionalism, based on the psychology of William James. Dewey viewed learning as a prime example of an adaptive process, and incorporated this insight in his theory of education. James Cattell, an American functionalist at Columbia University, basing his work on Galton, used techniques for studying reaction time, discrimination, and individual differences. Using instruments derived largely from Wundt and Galton, he devised a number of mental tests, a termed he coined, for studying individual differences.

Edward Thorndike pioneered the study of animal learning, but not the kind of learning studied by Pavlov or Bekhterev. The type of learning Thorndike studied is the type that is often characterized as intelligent. The animals in his experiments learned to make simple responses that were followed by a "satisfier" in a specific situation. On the basis of his research Thorndike formulated the law of effect.

Discussion Questions

1. Discuss the major schools of psychology and how they differed at the time of Wundt.

2. Critically discuss the advantages and disadvantages of functionalism relative to structuralism.

3. It has been said that functionalism more than structuralism fit the American character that emphasized practical know-how around the turn of the nineteenth to the twentieth century. Discuss whether you agree with this assessment.

4. How did the work of Pavlov and Bekhterev follow from that of Sechenov? Discuss the similarities and differences between the work of Pavlov and that of Bekhterev.

5. Explain how Thorndike's formulation of the law of effect can be seen as a natural outgrowth of the functionalism of William James.

6. Compare and contrast the functionalism of Hall, Dewey, Cattell, and Thorndike.

7. Discuss the relationship between functionalism, pragmatism, and Darwin's theory of evolution.

8. Discuss the likely effect of the British empiricists on Ebbinghaus, Pavlov, Bekhterev, and Thorndike.

9. Speculate on how the study of animal behavior might have developed under the structuralists if there had been no functionalists.

10. Discuss how Brentano's act psychology gave rise to phenomenology and the beginnings of Gestalt psychology.

CHAPTER 5

The Behavioral Revolution

O ne of Angell's most industrious graduate students was John B. Watson (1878–1958). While at the University of Chicago, Watson focused on research with animals and was impressed with how much he could learn about them without knowing anything about their consciousness, or even whether they had such a thing (Buckley, 1989).

BEHAVIORISM: AN OUTGROWTH OF FUNCTIONALISM

After leaving Chicago with his doctorate for a position at Johns Hopkins, Watson began increasingly to believe that the functionalists had not gone far enough in their criticisms of structuralism. He saw a problem not just with introspection, but also with the concept of the mind itself. Watson believed that psychology should be like other sciences in its methods of observation, as well as in other ways. He proposed that psychology should be the science of behavior, and thus founded the school of psychology he called behaviorism. Believing that the contents and processes of the mind, such as ideas and associations, needed to be replaced by a behavioral unit of analysis, Watson at first suggested habit as the unit.

The concept of habits had long been important in associationism and in functionalism, both of which stressed the formation of fixed and repetitive ways of thinking and behaving called habits. These were considered to be much like instincts, except that they were acquired through repetitive experiences—repeated associations of stimuli in the environment or ideas—rather than through heredity. Recall that it was James' student, Thorndike, who, with his mentor's encouragement (and loan of his basement), studied the formation of habits in chicks. Yet to James, as to other functionalists, habits were important theoretically because of their mental aspect, especially in their lack of dependence on consciousness. Moreover, habits referred not just to overt behavior—one could have habitual ways of thinking or of feeling, such as a habitual attitude of cheerfulness. To Watson, however, habits were simply fixed observable behavior patterns whose relation to consciousness or other unobservables was of no interest.

In 1913, Watson published an article entitled, "Psychology as the Behaviorist Views It," which was the opening salvo in what some have called the behavioral revolution.

A Unit of Behavior: The Conditioned Reflex

Members of the American Psychological Association were so impressed with Watson that in 1914 they elected him president of the organization at the youthful age of 36. After being introduced to Pavlov's research by his friend Robert Yerkes, and becoming familiar with the works of Pavlov and Bekhterev in translation, Watson saw the conditioned reflex as the behavior unit he sought, as opposed to the vague or poorly defined concept of habit. Conditioned reflexes in Watson's view were overtly observable habits.

Watson confirmed the fertility of the concept of conditioned reflex by conditioning motor responses in adult humans, using Bekhterev's procedures—motor responses being more manageable than salivation. Through his research and theoretical work, he then attempted to use the conditioned reflex to explain everything that had previously been considered a mental process. For example, in Watson's behavioral theory, speech is not a product of the mind but is conditioned vocal reflexes. Thinking does not occur in the mind, but in imperceptible activity of the vocal cords, and hence is subvocal speech—a concept that was originally proposed by Bekhterev (although Watson may not have been aware of this).

Applications

In 1917, when the U.S. entered World War I, American psychologists were quick to join the war effort with the application they knew best: testing techniques. The psychologists designed these tests to assign military personnel to positions for which they were best suited (although it is not clear how useful the tests actually were or how much credence the army gave to them). Watson was at the forefront of this effort, along with Cattell, Thorndike, Yerkes, and others. Lewis Terman (1877–1956), who in 1916 had developed the Stanford-Binet Intelligence Test (a revision of Binet's test), was also involved. The field of psychology gained some prestige from the work on testing that psychologists did for the U.S. Army during World War I.

Clinical psychology also began to make small strides during the war, for psychotherapists treated cases of what was then called *shell shock* (now known as post-traumatic stress disorder) and the problems of so-called "nervous soldiers" (Reisman, 1966). While behaviorism was advancing in most of psychology, the psychoanalytic approach was gradually starting to take hold in clinical psychology, where it eventually became predominant, as it was also doing at a more rapid pace in psychiatry, especially in North America. Later, some behaviorists began to give behavioral interpretations of psychoanalytic concepts, as will be seen in the next chapter.

Dualism

Back at Hopkins after the war, Watson received an inquiry from the eminent British philosopher Bertrand Russell (1872–1970). Russell was intrigued with behaviorism because he saw it as a potential way out of the problem of dualism, which had plagued philosophy at least since the time of Descartes. However, Russell had two serious reservations about behaviorism: he could not accept (1) Watson's restriction of thinking to subvocal speech; and (2) Watson's denial of the reality of images. It may be that Watson had few images and thought mainly in words. In any case, Watson, in response to the renowned philosopher, made two concessions. He admitted that thinking includes more than subvocal speech, that indeed, people think not just with their vocal cords, but with their entire bodies. In addition, Watson conceded that images exist and are a phenomenon that behaviorism will have to deal with as it matures, but that they have a purely physiological explanation. Russell, through his writings about behaviorism, helped to introduce it into Britain.

Extension to Emotions

Seeking the widest possible generality, Watson extended conditioning theory to emotions. In one of the best known experiments in the annals of psychology, he and his graduate student, Rosalie Rayner (1899–1935), conditioned a 9-month-old child to show fear (i.e., cry) at the sight of a white rat by pairing a loud noise with the rat. In a follow-up to the Watson and Rayner (1920) study, Mary Cover Jones (1924) demonstrated the unconditioning of a fear response in a child.

Despite Watson's towering reputation in psychology, he was forced to resign due to a sex scandal involving him and Rayner, whom he later married after divorcing his wife. Unable to obtain another university position, Watson went into marketing. He devoted as much energy and creativity to this profession as he had to research, and is directly responsible for some of the most powerful advertising techniques still in use. For example, he invented the concept of changing the styles of products in order to stimulate a felt need for the new product before the old one is worn out. He also developed the technique of pairing a product with a respected or desired person, as opposed to making a case for the actual merits of the product as advertisers had done prior to Watson. In other words, consistent with his behavioral approach, he applied straightforward conditioning and other behavioral strategies to advertising.

Opposition to Proliferation of Instincts

Although preoccupied with his marketing job, Watson maintained some contact with academic psychology for a while. A consistent advocate of the view that humans are born with only a few instincts, he became involved in a controversy with William McDougall (1871–1938) over instincts. McDougall was a follower of William James, who had held that instincts were an important component of human psychology. (James, in fact, had postulated that far from having fewer instincts than other animals, humans have many more.) Over a number of decades, beginning with the 1912 publication of his book *The Study of Behavior*, McDougall had developed a theory of instincts to account for human social behavior. According to McDougall, there are three components to an instinct: a cognitive or stimulus component, an affective or emotional component, and a conative or purposeful striving component. The middle component is relatively unmodifiable, although the other two can be modified through learning.

A serious problem with McDougall's system was that the number of instincts to explain behavior seemed to proliferate endlessly. Explaining any given behavior was easy—in fact, too easy. If the behavior seemed difficult to explain, all one has to do, following McDougall, is postulate a new instinct. Because this procedure can explain everything, in the end it explains nothing. McDougall saw the danger and warned against it. He maintained that, for example, an instinct for gregariousness was acceptable, but not one for religiosity because animals do not show anything like it. However, he apparently could not avert the danger. Once he opened Pandora's box of instincts, he apparently could not shut it, and the proliferation of instincts continued. Under strong attack by Watson and others, such as the psychologist Knight Dunlap (1875–1949), McDougall's system fell and the word *instinct* was essentially banned from respectable psychological discourse for decades. (With the rise of evolutionary psychology, the idea that humans have many instincts is becoming acceptable again to some psychologists. See chapter 6.)

LOGICAL POSITIVISM

A movement in philosophy that disposed psychologists toward an acceptance of behaviorism was logical positivism. This school of philosophy was founded in Vienna in the 1920s (hence, it is also known as the Vienna school). Drawing inspiration from the writings of Ernst Mach (they initially called themselves the Ernst Mach Association), the group's founding members included Moritz Schlick (1882–1936), Rudolf Carnap (1891–1970), and Kurt Gödel (1906–1978). The primary objective of this school of thought was to rid philosophy of problems that had generated interminable discussion over the centuries and that seemed to be irresolvable. The reason the solutions to these problems had eluded some of the greatest thinkers in history, the group maintained, is not because these problems are difficult but because they are meaningless.

Logical positivism held that there are only two kinds of meaningful utterances: logical and empirical. The former follow by logical deduction from definitions and assumptions. The latter are based on sense experience or sense data, that is, their meanings are their verification conditions in terms of the kinds of sense data that would be required to verify them. An example of a logical utterance would be the statement, "Socrates is mortal," given the assumptions that Socrates is a man and that all men are mortal. An example of an empirical utterance would be the statement that some swans are black. Verification of this proposition would requiring viewing swans and noting if any black sense data occur (i.e., whether we observe any that are black). In one version of logical positivism, consensual validation is required to verify the sense data satisfying the verification conditions. Thus, according to this version of logical positivism, two or more observers must see a black swan under appropriately controlled scientific conditions to confirm the proposition that some swans are black.

A statement that logical positivists would find suspect is the statement that the fundamental substance of the universe is mental. According to logical positivism, the philosopher's task, when confronted with such a proposition, is not to decide whether or not it is true, but rather to determine whether it is meaningful. The statement is considered meaningful only if it is clear what sense data would be required to verify it. For example, does it mean that I can kick a tree hard (as the renowned critic Samuel Johnson [1709–1784] allegedly did in a facetious refutation of Berkeley) without hurting my foot? Hence, an important tenet of logical positivism is that observers must agree on what would constitute a valid test of the meaningfulness of a proposition.

Because Watson's behaviorism rejected mind as an ill-defined concept, we can see why the arguments of the logical positivists gave support to behaviorism. It is well to understand, however, that the logical positivists did not necessarily directly influence the positivistic views of behaviorism. There was already plenty of influence on behaviorism in this regard through the influence of Ernst Mach on William James and other functionalists who, as we have seen, were the forerunners of behaviorism.

Logical positivism eventually suffered a sharp decline in the number of its adherents, and today there are very few, if any, logical positivists in philosophy. One criticism against logical positivism is that it is self-refuting or self-contradictory, in that it cannot itself be verified by sense experience.

OPERATIONISM

Another philosophical movement that fits well with behaviorism—and indeed that overlapped with logical positivism—is operationism. This approach was developed most extensively by the physicist Percy Bridgman (1882–1961) on the basis of Einstein's special theory of relativity. As with the logical positivists, a major influence on Einstein, as mentioned earlier, was the writings of the positivist Ernst Mach. Einstein made a revolutionary revision to Newton's theory. Newton had assumed the existence of absolute space and absolute time. In revising the theory in what Einstein called the special and general theories of relativity, Einstein assumed that the speed of light is constant for all observers regardless of their velocities relative to each other. The special theory, published in 1905, dealt only with constant velocities and not with acceleration or gravitation. In the general theory, the final version of which was published in 1915, Einstein equated acceleration with gravity, and proposed that objects moving under the influence of gravity are simply following the curvature of space into the time dimension.

In a book called *The Logic of Modern Physics* (1927), Bridgman argued that Newton's theory required Einstein's revision because Newton and the physicists who followed him had not properly defined space and time. He believed that if physicists had taken more care to define space and time in terms of the operations they used to measure them, Einstein's revision would not have been necessary. He coined the term *operational definition*. This had a strong effect on many psychologists, who advocated for the operational definition of all psychological concepts in terms of measurable behavior. Like logical positivism, operationism supported Watson's assertion that the proper subject matter of psychology is behavior.

To operationally define mentalistic concepts—that is, concepts about the mind and its supposed elements, processes, and functions—means to define them in terms of the behavior one must measure in order to make empirical statements regarding those concepts. For example, the operational definition of the sensation of red in an introspection experiment is the subject's verbal report of having a sensation of red. Verbal reports are vocal behavior. Hence, if psychologists using introspective methods defined their terms properly, according to operationists, they would realize that they are actually studying behavior. Following this line of argument, the behaviorists argued that not only is behavior the proper subject matter of psychology, it is the only possible subject matter of psychology.

It is noteworthy that although Bridgman was very supportive of the special theory of relativity, he was much less supportive of the general theory due to the difficulty of casting the curvatures of space and time in operational terms. Eventually, both logical positivism and operationism fell because of the difficulty, or at least extreme awkwardness, of defining all scientific concepts (even relatively simple ones, such as temperature) in terms of sense data or operationally. The influences of logical positivism and operationism, however, are still prevalent in psychology.

GESTALT PSYCHOLOGY: AN EARLY OPPONENT OF BEHAVIORISM

As behaviorism was gaining strength in America, Gestalt psychology was coming to occupy a predominant place in Germany under the leadership of its founder, Max Wertheimer (1880–1943). Behaviorism is analytic and focuses on the observable; specifically, it divides its subject matter into observable units of stimuli and responses. In contrast, Gestalt psychology is holistic and focuses on unobservable mental processes. Gestalt psychology arose largely in reaction to Wundtian and Titchenerian elementarianism. However, as these approaches lost adherents and faded into history, Gestalt psychology focused its critique on behaviorism. Rather than viewing psychological phenomena as composed of stimuli and responses, Gestalt psychology sees the mind as organizing external stimuli into perceptual wholes that are qualitatively different from the aggregate of their constituent elements.

Despite their differences, behaviorism and Gestalt psychology have one thing in common: they both were influenced by Ernst Mach. Accordingly, both emphasized the importance of empirically testing their theories in terms of observable phenomena. Mach's views also influenced Gestalt theory. Recall from chapter 4 that he had emphasized that perceptions of geometrical forms are not simply combinations of the sensations the elements of those forms produce, but rather that the elements

are combined into a whole by some other factor. For Mach this other factor was another element. Similarly, for Christian von Ehrenfels perceptions consisted of organized wholes separate from, but dependent on, the elements of which they were composed.

Although Max Wertheimer has been credited with founding Gestalt psychology, he modestly gave the credit to Ehrenfels, who, as we have seen, coined the term *Gestaltqualitäten* (form-qualities). Ehrenfels assumed that elementary sensations occur prior to the form or Gestalt, whereas, according to Wertheimer the opposite is true: we sense or perceive the form before the individual sensations.

Behaviorism came under strong attack by Gestalt psychologists, who considered the conditioned reflex to be an artificial unit that can tell us nothing about the organizing properties of the mind. As a simple example, consider that three lines are not a triangle—they have to be arranged in a certain way. In addition, one still strongly perceives a triangle even if part of it is obstructed, showing to the Gestalt psychologist that the mind is structured to perceive triangles and other standard geometrical forms. The mind, in other words, is a field not unlike a gravitational field in physics as described by Einstein (cf. Michael Wertheimer, 1965), except that instead of organizing bodies such as planets into an organized whole such as a solar system, the mind organizes its components into a Gestalt— an organized mental whole that is different from the aggregate of its parts. In 1921, the Gestalt journal *Psychologische Forschung* was first published, and in 1923, Wertheimer published *Laws of Organization*.

In a study with chimpanzees, the Gestalt psychologist Wolfgang Köhler (1887–1967) offered an impressive demonstration of what appeared to be the mind's organizing properties. He showed that some of the animals could solve certain novel problems (e.g., putting two sticks together to reach a banana) in a way that suggested sudden insight into the solution. Köhler argued that this was due to a sudden reorganization in the mind that permitted the solution to occur. In addition to supporting Gestalt theory, these studies also challenged the behaviorist assumption that all learning occurs in a trial-and-error manner. In 1927, Köhler published *The Mentality of Apes*. These studies came under severe criticism because it is difficult to define what is meant by sudden, and also because there is difficulty repeating these experiments with the same results.

A colleague of Wertheimer and Köhler, Kurt Koffka (1886–1941), introduced Gestalt psychology into the United States as an immigrant from Germany. Koffka did much to systematize Gestalt theory and extend it to developmental psychology. In 1924, he published *The Growth of Mind*.

Another German immigrant to the U.S., Kurt Lewin (1890–1947), extended Gestalt theory to social psychology. Lewin developed a field theory consisting on the one hand of mental events such as needs, tensions, and impulsions, and on the other of environmental variables consisting of incentives and barriers to those incentives. The organism moves through this field, which exists within a psychological space. Lewin developed and tested his theory with laboratory rats and with people. He expanded his theory to groups, and in this respect is one of the founders of social psychology. In 1935, he published *A Dynamic Theory of Personality*.

THE PREDOMINANCE OF BEHAVIORISM

With the rise of behaviorism, structuralism ceased to be a viable approach because its results could not be reliably replicated. Functionalism also disappeared, as it had no clear methodology for studying the mind. Gestalt psychology's influence as a school of thought or theoretical approach steadily diminished until it was virtually nonexistent by the 1950s. Its demise may have been mainly due to theories propounded by its exponents concerning electrical fields on the surface of the brain, which were disproved or unsupported. Gestalt psychology's methods, findings, and insights, however, had a positive effect on behaviorism (Sokal, 1984), and on other contemporary approaches to be discussed in subsequent chapters—humanistic psychology (Decarvalho, 1991), cognitive psychology (e.g., see Palmer, 1990), and possibly at least one version of psychodynamic psychology (namely, Adler's; see Ansbacher & Ansbacher, 1967).

Having eclipsed structuralism, functionalism, and Gestalt psychology, behaviorism held sway for some time with psychodynamic psychology as its only serious competitor. The demise of the other approaches is often attributed to behaviorism, but operationism may have been the key factor. First, through the doctrine of operationism, psychologists became acutely aware of the importance of defining their concepts in terms that can be tested through observation if psychology is to emulate other sciences. Second, the doctrine seemed to suggest that although the mind cannot be studied directly, it could be studied indirectly. An image or a perceptual illusion, to mention two examples, can be operationalized as verbal reports. Thus, operationism provided a way to study the mind. Psychodynamic psychology remained fairly immune to operationism, possibly because its therapeutic applications were supported by the impression that they seemed to be working. Thus, psychodynamic psychology, in particular Freudian psychoanalysis, was left to share the field of scientific psychology with behaviorism.

SUMMARY

John B. Watson argued that psychology should be like other sciences in its methods of observation, as well as in other ways. He proposed that psychology should be the science of behavior, and thus founded the school of psychology he called behaviorism. When he learned of the work of Pavlov and Bekhterev, Watson made the conditioned reflex the unit of behavior.

Seeking the widest possible generality, Watson wanted to extend conditioning theory to emotions. Before this goal could be fully achieved, however, Watson's appointment at Johns Hopkins was terminated. Forced out of academia due to an illicit affair, he went into marketing.

William McDougall developed a theory of instincts to account for human social behavior. McDougall's system was vulnerable to at least two serious criticisms. Under strong attack by Watson and others, such as the psychologist Knight Dunlap, McDougall's system fell and the word *instinct* was essentially banned from respectable psychological discourse.

Two philosophical movements helped promote behaviorism: logical positivism and operationism. The former requires terms to be defined by sense data, often in a way that can be consensually validated; the latter requires terms to be defined by the operations used to measure them.

Max Wertheimer founded Gestalt psychology. Initially directed primarily against elementarianism, this school of thought is opposed to all forms of analysis into arbitrary or artificial units or elements.

With the rise of behaviorism, structuralism ceased to be a viable approach. Gestalt psychology also was no longer a force, although many of its methods, findings, and theoretical insights have been absorbed into contemporary approaches. Functionalism also was no more, although its legacy continues with the emphasis in psychology on evolution. Only psychoanalysis continued as a strong competitor to behaviorism.

Discussion Questions

1. Discuss the similarities between behaviorism and functionalism. Given these similarities, is it reasonable to argue that behaviorism is a natural outgrowth of functionalism? Why or why not?

2. Discuss how and why Watson incorporated the concepts and findings of Pavlov and Bekhterev into behaviorism.

3. Discuss how Watson extended behaviorism to include both thinking and emotions. Is it possible that he borrowed heavily from Bekhterev in making this extension? What indications are there of this? (Hint: see the section on Bekhterev in the previous chapter.)

4. Discuss the similarities among behaviorism, logical positivism, and operationism.

5. Discuss how and why behaviorism replaced structuralism, functionalism, and Gestalt psychology. Discuss whether any aspects of these ways of thinking are still present in some form in contemporary psychology.

6. Did behaviorism replace psychoanalysis? Why or why not?

7. Soon after the behavioral revolution, a common saying was that psychology first lost its soul, then it lost its mind. Discuss whether the subject matter of psychology changed after each of these changes, whether only its methods changed, or whether only its underlying philosophy changed.

8. What philosophical problem prompted Bertrand Russell to contact John B. Watson? Discuss whether Watson's approach provides a satisfactory solution to that problem.

9. Discuss the potential problem with using instincts to explain behavior, as McDougall attempted to do, and whether Watson's approach completely avoided this pitfall.

10. Discuss the similarities and differences among Watsonian behaviorism and Gestalt psychology.

CHAPTER 6

The Aftermath of the Behavioral Revolution

*I*n the immediate aftermath of the behavioral revolution, two forces dominated psychology: behaviorism and psychoanalysis. The former was mainly an American phenomenon, and had little influence in Europe; the latter was of European origin, but had considerable influence in North America as well. With the increasing political and military power of the Nazis in Germany and the concomitant persecution of European Jews prior to and during World War II, many European psychologists sought refuge in North America. They brought with them psychological orientations of European origin.

Beginning around the middle of the twentieth century, several important developments occurred. First, the offshoots of psychoanalysis became stronger. Second, a movement called third force, or humanistic, psychology arose in opposition to the domination of psychology by the dual forces of psychoanalysis and behaviorism. Third, sometime around the 1970s, an approach called cognitive psychology gained considerable strength in opposition to behaviorism's exclusion of the mind from psychology. This is sometimes called the cognitive revolution. In addition, throughout these developments, interest continued in the study of the adaptive and neurological bases of behavior or the mind. The former is now generally called evolutionary psychology, and the latter neuropsychology or (somewhat more broadly) neuroscience.

Thus by the 1970s, six identifiable strands in psychology were evident: (1) behavioral psychology; (2) cognitive psychology; (3) psychodynamic psychology—which is the collective term for psychoanalysis and its offshoots; (4) humanistic psychology; (5) evolutionary psychology; and (6) neuroscience. Hillner defines "system of psychology" as follows:

> At an informal level, a system is any conceptual approach to psychology. A system entails the specific set of beliefs that underlie a given psychologist's brand of psychology. At a more formal level, a system is a set of philosophical assumptions relative to what constitutes (1) the proper object of study of psychology and (2) the acceptable methodology of psychology. As such, a psychological system is a specific philosophical approach to organismic (human) experience, behavior, or both. (Hillner, 1984, p. 2)

According to this definition, the first four strands are systems of psychology. They are collections of closely related theories that have similar underlying philosophies and attempt to provide an integrated view of psychology. The last two relate psychology to subdisciplines in biology, namely, evolutionary biology and neurology. They provide data and theory that inform the first four.

The remainder of this chapter provides an overview of the history of the above approaches following the behavioral revolution.

BEHAVIORAL PSYCHOLOGY

After the behavioral revolution, behaviorism focused on three areas: learning, memory, and behavioral applications.

In the area of learning, there were four main theorists: Guthrie, Tolman, Hull, and Skinner. Their research was primarily with laboratory animals in simple learning situations.

Edwin Guthrie

Edwin Guthrie (1886–1959) adopted an extremely simple principle of association. According to this theory, a response is associated with a particular stimulus if the stimulus changes immediately after the response occurs. For example, an animal in Thorndike's puzzle box learns to pull the latch when in the box not because escape from the box and food occurred following the latch pull, but because the stimulus changed. In Guthrie's research a camera photographed the cat at the instant it pulled on a cord that operated the latch. The pictures supported Guthrie's theory in that the pictures showed identical positioning of the cat on every trial at the instant of release. Guthrie was ingenious in the way in which he used this counterintuitive theory to explain complex learning.

Edward Tolman

Edward Tolman (1886–1959), although a behaviorist, believed that it was necessary to introduce cognitive variables into his theory in order to give a complete account of behavior. All behavior, according to Tolman, is a function of environmental variables mediated by intervening variables. These intervening variables include cognitions, such as mental "maps" that a rat may use in navigating a maze. Although he freely used mentalistic or cognitive terms, he was a strict operationist—that is, he believed and practiced the philosophy that all terms in a theory must be operationally defined. In 1932, Tolman detailed his cognitive behavioral approach in a book entitled *Purposive Behavior in Animals and Men*.

Clark Hull

Clark Hull (1884–1952) attempted to produce a system of behavior modeled on Newton's system of physics. As with Watson, Hull's system was based on the conditioned reflex as the fundamental unit of behavior. However, he believed that conditioned reflexes occur as a result of reinforcement or reward following the response. Thus, Hull did not distinguish between animals learning to salivate to a conditioned stimulus and learning to run to the goal box in a maze. Just as Newton had created postulates about the physical universe from which physical phenomena can be derived, Hull created postulates about behavior. Based mainly on studies with rats, Hull's postulates dealt with the ways in which variables such as habit strength, drive (or motivation), incentive, stimulus intensity, stimulus generalization, etc. interact mathematically (e.g., habit strength and drive were said to multiply together) to produce a given response. Each term was given a precise operational definition (e.g., the hunger drive was defined in terms of number of hours of food deprivation, habit strength in terms of the number of reinforced, i.e., rewarded, trials). In 1943, Hull published *Principles of Behavior*, which contained the first complete version of his theory.

Burrhus Frederick Skinner

B. F. Skinner (1904–1990) was strongly influenced by Francis Bacon and Ernst Mach. As already discussed, both of these individuals had stressed science as the study of observable events as a function of other observable events. Thus, while other learning theorists developed hypotheses about unobservable events and tested those hypotheses experimentally, Skinner avoided making hypotheses about unobservable events and devising predictions from them. Instead, he studiously followed the advice of Francis Bacon to collect data systematically and organize the facts in a way that seems most suited to them. He developed a device with a lever that the experimental organism—a white rat in his early studies—could press to obtain reinforcement. Hull, who adapted the device to his research, named it the Skinner box, although Skinner himself never called it that.

Skinner focused on obtaining findings that were so reliable that they could be demonstrated in individual organisms without requiring inferential statistics.

One of the most important distinctions he made was between what he called respondent conditioning, which is Pavlovian conditioning, and operant conditioning in which a response (e.g., lever press) is strengthened because it is followed by reinforcement. Skinner was, however, not the first to make this distinction; it was made independently by the Polish psychologist Jerzy Konorski (1903–1973). However, Skinner was the first to develop a highly systematic theory of psychology based largely on the principle of operant conditioning.

Of the four leading learning theorists, Skinner was the closest to Watson's position, especially as Watson explained it to Bertrand Russell. Skinner acknowledged the existence of images but did not postulate a specific locus for thinking. Skinner called this position radical behaviorism, distinguishing it from what he called methodological behaviorism, which assumes that images and thinking are not behavior. Although scrupulously following the positivism of Mach in precisely defining the terms he used in his system, Skinner argued that there is no need for operationally defining mentalistic terms in general because he doubted that most are useful in a science of behavior.

In 1938, Skinner published his book *The Behavior of Organisms*, which was the first formulation of his system. The operant conditioning device that he described in that book bore a striking resemblance to Thorndike's puzzle box, and the principle of reinforcement that Skinner formulated was essentially Thorndike's law of effect. Yet for some reason Skinner neglected to cite Thorndike's work—an oversight for which he apologized profusely in a 1939 letter. The following quotation from that letter provides an interesting insight into Thorndike's influence on Skinner's early work:

> . . . In searching my soul to learn why the acknowledgments were never made I get only this far: (1) I have never seen an advertised and promoted "system" under your name and, (2) I seem to have identified your point of view with the modern psychological view taken as a whole. It has always been obvious that I was merely carrying on your puzzle box experiments, but it never occurred to me to remind my readers of that fact. I don't know why I mention this, because I can't imagine that it bothers you in the least. [Thorndike graciously replied: "I am better satisfied to have been of service to workers like yourself than if I had founded a 'school.'" (Hearst, 1999, p. 445; Jonçich, 1968, p. 506)]

In 1953 and 1957, respectively, Skinner published his books *Science and Human Behavior* and *Verbal Behavior*. In the former he extended his theory to all areas of human behavior and in the latter he extended it specifically to human language. While the theories of Guthrie, Tolman, and Hull did not survive, Skinner's continues to thrive with a large number of adherents.

Memory Research: Benton J. Underwood

In addition to animal research, behaviorists carried out memory research in the style of Ebbinghaus—with the exception that they used group designs (Ebbinghaus, it will be recalled, had used a single subject, namely, himself) and modern inferential statistical methods. A notable example is the work of Benton J. Underwood (1915–1994). Toward the end of his research career, Underwood began to compare the recall of meaningful material with that of nonsense syllables (which in Underwood's research were, unlike Ebbinghaus', never real words). This research may not have sparked what has been called the cognitive revolution, but it fits in with the trend toward cognitivism that began to develop.

Applications

Behaviorism also gave rise to practical applications. Mary Cover Jones (1896–1987) had suggested how conditioning principles could be applied to the treatment of maladaptive fears, and Joseph Wolpe (1915–1997), a South African psychiatrist, developed a behavioral procedure called systematic desensitization that proved successful in treating phobias and other debilitating anxieties. Skinner extended his approach to education in the form of devices called teaching machines. In addition, some followers of Skinner's approach developed an approach called behavior modification or applied behavior analysis. This approach has proved effective in the treatment of autism and other developmental problems. The term behavior therapy is often used to refer collectively to therapies such as those developed by Wolpe and by applied behavior analysts.

COGNITIVISM

As we have seen, individuals in many different specialties outside of psychology have been involved in the development of psychology. This is particularly true with regard to the development of cognitivism, which is therefore often referred to as *cognitive science* rather than the more narrow term *cognitive psychology*. Since the focus of this text is on psychology, however, it should be understood that even when we refer to cognitivists in other fields, our interest in this book is directed toward their impact on the field of psychology.

Lev Vygotsky

With the advent of Pavlovianism in Russia and behaviorism in North America, interest in the mind decreased. Then in Russia, the conditioned reflex began to take a back seat to more cognitive concerns. The Soviet psychologist Lev Vygotsky (1896–1934) stressed the importance of the individual's active interaction with society in the development of language and higher mental or cognitive functioning. According to Vygotsky an individual creates meaning through social interaction. Vygotsky's views are fundamental to the rise of social constructivism, which is the view that meaning and truth are in the individual rather than in the environment. Alexander Luria (1902–1977), a Soviet psychologist who worked closely with Vygotsky, continued the development of a social constructivist theory, integrating it with Pavlovian theory and with cognitive theories of the West. Luria adopted a materialistic position, however, as had Vygotsky.

Jean Piaget

The Swiss psychologist Jean Piaget (1896–1980) had been a student of Théodore Simon, who had worked with Binet on the development of intelligence tests. Put in charge of administering Binet's reading tests to Parisian children, Piaget was impressed with the role age plays in children's ability to solve certain cognitive problems. This sparked Piaget's interest in the field of child psychology. He found that children go through specific developmental stages. For example, at an early stage a child may have no concept that the amount of liquid is conserved or remains the same when a liquid is poured from one container to another with a different shape. Thus, a child who is shown a liquid in a short, fat container that is then poured into a tall, thin container, or vice versa, will, when asked, indicate that there is more liquid in the tall, thin container than in the short, fat one, even though both held exactly the same amount. Piaget became famous for his studies of the cognitive and ethical development of children.

Alan Turing

The advent of the computer was especially important for the development of cognitive psychology because it provided a potential model for the mind. A large measure of credit for this goes to the British mathematician Alan Turing (1912–1954) who, prior to the advent of the computer, conceptualized a universal problem-solving machine and analyzed its logical properties. As Turing conceptualized it, this hypothetical machine

could, on the basis of binary coded instructions, be converted into any given type of problem-solving machine. What Turing had conceptualized is the modern day computer, which gave rise to the view that the human brain might also be a universal problem-solving machine. In this view the mind corresponds to the general set of instructions that converts the machine into any type of problem-solving machine. Turing's conceptualizations opened the door for the development of cognitive psychology as the study of the mind as an information processing system. The appeal of this approach is that it seems to escape the yoke of behaviorism while at the same time avoiding the philosophical problem of dualism. A computer program is just as physical as the hardware that it runs on, but at the same time quite different from that hardware. In 1936 Turing published an article that introduced his conceptual machine.

Herbert A. Simon and Allen Newell

An American economist who also worked in computer science and psychology, Herbert A. Simon (1916–2001) was among the first to recognize and act on a direct analogy between the computer and the mind. This insight led him to team up with the computer specialist Allen Newell (1927–1992) to devise computer algorithms that attempted to model human mental processes. Strongly influenced by work in the areas of feedback mechanisms or cybernetics (e.g., Norbert Wiener, 1948), information theory (e.g., Claude Shannon, 1938), and the burgeoning computer technology (e.g., Alan Turing, 1950, John von Neuman, 1958), Simon and Newell conceptualized the mind as a symbol-manipulating or information-processing system (Simon, 1991). Together Newell and Simon began to create computer programs that attempted to simulate human logical reasoning and problem solving (e.g., Newell & Simon, 1956, 1963). This marked the beginning of the field of artificial intelligence (AI).

George Miller

In 1956, the psychologist George A. Miller (1920–), formerly a self-proclaimed behaviorist, published a paper entitled, "The Magic Number 7 Plus or Minus 2: Some Limits on Our Capacity for Processing Information" in which he showed that the number of well-learned units (called *chunks*) that one can readily recall shortly after a single exposure appears to be about seven. This paper is sometimes considered to be the "first shot" in the cognitive revolution. In any case, it contributed to the cognitive revolution by indicating a remarkable—as the word *magic* in the title suggests—quantitative uniformity among humans in information storage to and retrieval from short-term memory. Miller is also noted for his work on rule-following as a higher type of conceptual activity. In 1960, he published *Plans and the Structure of Behavior*.

Noam Chomsky

The American linguist Noam Chomsky (1928–) developed a theory to account for why humans possess the competency for language. According to Chomsky, humans are linguistically competent because in the deep structure of their minds they absorb the rules of grammar in a particular language by listening to speech in that language. The central idea of the theory is that there is a universal grammar that is merely refined or specified by hearing local speech. In 1957, Chomsky published *Syntactic Structures*, in which he described his theory of a universal grammar—a grammar that, according to the theory, underlies all the grammars of the world, and thus makes it possible for any human to learn any human language. Chomsky is also noted for a scathing critique of Skinner's book *Verbal Behavior*. Although it had little impact on Skinner and his closest followers, it appears to have been profoundly effective in causing many behavioral psychologists to become cognitive psychologists, and thus helped to spark the cognitive revolution.

Ulric Neisser

In 1967, a book entitled *Cognitive Psychology* appeared which gave the new field of cognitive psychology its name. The author of that book, Ulric Neisser (1928–), argued that concepts from computer science, such as information, representation, memory, storage, and retrieval, are especially appropriate for psychology. He also argued, and has continued to argue, that the human mind is far more complex than any current computer and that, accordingly, cognitive psychologists should use computer concepts only as a stepping stone to concepts that more accurately reflect cognitive processes in real people as opposed to computer models or simulations.

Albert Ellis and Aaron Beck

Starting from premises similar to those of cognitive psychologists, although not directly influenced by them, Albert Ellis (1913–) and Aaron Beck (1921–) pioneered a type of psychotherapy called cognitive therapy as an alternative to psychoanalysis, which they saw as ineffective. Cognitive therapists work on changing cognitions in order to change behavior. Like behaviorists, cognitive therapists focus on changing behavior rather than on the individual's childhood or dreams. Whereas the fundamental assumption of behavior therapy is that maladaptive behaviors have been conditioned, the basic assumption of cognitive therapy is that they are due to irrational or maladaptive thinking. Despite this difference, most cognitive therapists have adopted some behavioral techniques, and vice versa. Hence, the two approaches have tended to blend into one general approach called cognitive-behavioral therapy.

PSYCHODYNAMICS

The term *psychodynamics* comes from psycho + dynamics, where the latter root means force. Psychodynamics thus focuses on forces operating deep within the mind. Hence, another name for psychodynamics is depth psychology.

Sigmund Freud

Psychoanalysis dominated clinical psychology and psychiatry at the same time that behaviorism was at its apex in experimental psychology. In fact, there were attempts by behaviorists, most notably by John Dollard (1900–1980) and Neal Miller (1909–2002), to show that behavioral theory is compatible with Freudian psychoanalysis. Somewhat ironically, however, a number of nonbehaviorists who were attracted to Freud's theory, including some of his initial followers, began to have problems with it.

Alfred Adler

Alfred Adler (1870–1937) started out as one of Freud's closest followers, but later withdrew his allegiance as a result of a disagreement over the primacy of sexual motivation. Adler believed that the basic motivation is for power and superiority, and that individuals compensate for failures to achieve these. He developed a type of psychodynamics called individual psychology.

Carl Jung

Another close follower who withdrew from the psychoanalytic movement was Carl Jung (1875–1961), a Swiss psychiatrist. As a young medical doctor, Jung had done research under Eugen Bleuler at the Burghölzli Mental Hospital in Zürich. There, upon learning of Wundt's association experiments and Freud's use of the free-association method in psychoanalysis, he conducted research on word associations with schizophrenic patients. One of his findings was that certain words, which seemed to cluster around particular themes, took longer for the patients to respond to than did other words. From this research, Jung formed the concept of a complex—essentially a set of repressed thought patterns.

Jung believed that he had obtained data supportive of Freud's concept of the unconscious and sought a meeting with the older man. Freud was extremely impressed with Jung and eventually began to groom him as his successor. However, Freud was intolerant of any attempts by his followers to modify his theories. Thus, when Jung broadened the concept of libido to include all life processes, not just sexual energy, a break between the two men occurred. Jung went on to develop a theory of the collective unconscious, which is supposedly a repository of hidden meanings shared by all humanity. Jung also developed a theory of personality traits. He called his psychodynamic approach analytical psychology.

Neo-Freudians

Many in the next generation of psychoanalysts adopted some, but not all, of Freud's teachings. Some of these neo-Freudians were strongly influenced by existential and phenomenological philosophies stemming from Brentano, and in this regard they helped provide a bridge from psychodynamics to humanistic psychology (see the next section).

HUMANISTIC PSYCHOLOGY

Humanistic psychology was originally called third force psychology because it was a reaction to the two dominant forces, behaviorism and psychoanalysis. When cognitive psychology emerged during the cognitive revolution, humanistic psychologists considered it to have the same problems as they found with behaviorism. The main issue of contention was that behaviorism, cognitivism, and psychoanalysis, in their abstractions about the individual, had eliminated what humanistic psychologists considered most essential about the individual, namely, the fact that each person exists as a real entity and not as an abstract collection of behaviors or drives.

Early Humanistic Psychologists

Gordon Allport

Gordon Allport (1897–1967) opposed the trends toward abstraction in behavioral psychology and psychoanalysis. He believed that the strong psychological concern for general laws, which he called the nomothetic approach, was overemphasized, and there should be more focus on understanding the individual, the idiographic approach. In 1937, Allport published his views in a book entitled *Personality*, which provided a strong impetus for the movement toward humanistic psychology.

Carl Rogers

Two individuals who led the movement to humanistic psychology were Carl Rogers (1902–1987) and Abraham Maslow (1908–1970). Rogers developed person-centered therapy, which is a form of therapy in which the objective is to facilitate the course of therapy rather than to direct it. The emphasis is on allowing the client rather than the therapist to determine the outcome. In this approach the client is viewed as a person rather than an embodiment of a set of psychological principles, which is seen as inimical to viewing the client as a person. In 1951, Rogers published *Client-Centered Therapy*.

Abraham Maslow

Maslow emphasized that once their basic needs are met, people have a tendency toward self-actualization, or, in other words, to fulfill their true potential, which is unique to each individual. In 1954, Maslow published *Motivation and Personality*, and in 1968, he published *Toward a Psychology of Being*.

Branches of Humanistic Psychology

Humanistic psychology in its most general sense incorporates four approaches: (1) humanistic psychology in a specific sense, as described above; (2) phenomenology, (3) existential psychology, and (4) transpersonal psychology.

Phenomenology

Originated by Brentano's student, Husserl, phenomenology was developed further by his student, Martin Heidegger (1889–1976). Phenomenology holds that it is incorrect to focus exclusively on the objective or the subjective; the observation of any phenomenon requires both. For every phenomenon there must be a subject who observes the phenomenon, that is, one cannot view these two aspects of a phenomenon independently. A phenomenological approach focuses on how individuals respond subjectively to events in their lives; for example, during extreme sorrow or boredom, time may seem to move slowly, whereas during extreme joy it seems to move rapidly. Space also is experienced subjectively. A loved one far away may seem closer than a stranger in the same room. In 1927, Heidegger published his most influential work, *Being and Time*. While

Heidegger's brilliance as a philosopher is widely acknowledged, his reputation as a person is tarnished by his active support of the Nazi Party and his deception regarding his involvement with the Nazis following World War II.

Existential Psychology

Existentialism focuses on the reaction of an individual to the fact of his or her existence. I am engaging in existential thinking, for example, when I experience awe and wonder that I exist now at this particular place at this particular instant, as opposed to not existing or being nothing (which we might suppose or imagine, if we can, would be the existential situation of an inanimate object). While phenomenology stresses the importance of that which is immediately presented to consciousness, existentialism emphasizes the importance of existing in a world that may or may not be meaningless. In either case, will and free choice are of paramount importance in determining one's fulfilment and meaning in the world.

Nietzsche and Kierkegaard, although little recognized in their times, were extremely influential in the development of existentialism in the twentieth century. The writings of these philosophers influenced Heidegger, who was an existentialist as well as a phenomenologist. His most fundamental existentialist concept is that of *Dasein*, which translates into English as *being-there*, that is, being or existing in the world. Another contributor to existentialism was the novelist and philosopher Jean-Paul Sartre (1905–1980). In 1943, Sartre published his best-known philosophical work, *Being and Nothingness*.

In Europe, a number of psychiatrists and psychotherapists practicing various forms of therapy began to incorporate phenomenological and existential outlooks into their therapies. Two of the most notable of these were Ludwig Binswanger (1881–1966) and Medard Boss (1903–1990). Rollo May (1909–1994) is most responsible for introducing existential therapy into North America. In 1958, May, in collaboration with two colleagues, edited a book entitled *Existence: A New Dimension in Psychiatry and Psychology*.

Existential psychotherapists are acutely aware that each individual they treat is first and foremost not a collection of abstractions, that each lives in a universe of subjectivity much like their own subjective universes. Although by definition no one except the client can enter the client's subjective universe, existential psychotherapists try to understand deeply— through knowledge of their own subjective universes—what it is like to be the client, that is, they empathize with the client. Existential psychotherapy thus focuses on helping individuals to develop or restore meaning to their lives. They do this by emphasizing that their clients are free to make choices that determine the course of their day-to-day lives. Existential psychotherapy is thus highly compatible with humanistic psychology in the specific sense, which also stresses the importance of empathy and treating the client like a subjectively experiencing autonomous person. One difference is that humanistic psychologists tend to believe that people are inherently good, whereas existentialists believe that to be good or not is a choice people make.

Transpersonal Psychology

In addition to being a leader in the founding of humanistic psychology, Abraham Maslow was also instrumental in founding transpersonal psychology, which focuses on the spiritual aspect of the person. He saw transpersonal psychology as an extension of humanistic psychology. Transpersonal psychology, however, is sometimes called the fourth force.

EVOLUTIONARY PSYCHOLOGY

As we have seen, there has historically been a close connection between all schools or approaches to psychology and evolutionary theory. This connection eventually evolved to the point that a field called evolutionary psychology has appeared. This section considers the major contributors to this field.

Karl von Frisch, Konrad Lorenz, and Niko Tinbergen

Although behaviorism replaced functionalism during the behavioral revolution, there was renewed interest in the concept of instincts in the mid-twentieth century. This was due largely to the work of three European biologists: the Austrian zoologists Karl von Frisch (1887–1982) and Konrad Lorenz (1903–1989), and the Dutch zoologist Niko Tinbergen (1907–1988).

Von Frisch is most famous for showing that honeybee scouts returning to their hive communicate to other honeybees in the hive the distance and direction of food through very specific types of movements on a wall of the hive: a so-called circular dance and a waggle dance. These dances are highly similar across honeybee groups and no type of learning process can account for them. They must therefore be innate; that is, the tendency for honeybees to engage in specific dances to communicate the location of honey to their fellow bees must have evolved through natural selection.

Lorenz is most famous for his studies on imprinting, which specifically is the tendency for a young duck or goose to follow the first moving object that it sees after hatching. Imprinting can be described as an innate tendency to learn a specific type of behavior. Lorenz extended his theories regarding instincts to humans in a way that sparked controversy. In 1963, he published a book entitled *On Aggression*, in which he argued that humans are instinctively aggressive and warlike. This evoked strong criticism because of its apparent implication that aggression and war cannot be reduced or eliminated through learning. Lorenz argued for eugenics, or planned breeding of humans, to solve cultural and social problems supposedly stemming from our genetic makeup. Since Lorenz's death, his reputation as a person has been tarnished by increasing evidence that he actively supported the Nazis during World War II, going so far as to offer to help them in their efforts to achieve "racial purity" through the science of genetics.

Tinbergen is famous for his studies of what he called innate releasing stimuli or innate releasers. A male stickleback fish, for example, will attack another male stickleback that comes too close to his territory. Experiments show that it is not the other fish per se, but the red coloring of its body that elicits the attack response. Again, this behavior cannot have been learned and so must be innate.

Von Frisch, Lorenz, and Tinbergen developed the field of ethology, the study of animal behavior as a subdivision of zoology, which had a strong impact on the study of animal behavior in psychology. In 1973, as a result of their contributions, these three individuals jointly received the Nobel Prize in Physiology or Medicine.

William Hamilton

William Hamilton (1936–2000) proposed a modification of evolutionary theory that had a strong effect on evolutionary theorizing by psychologists. Prior to Hamilton, biologists had assumed that the evolutionary principle of survival of the fittest occurs at the level of the individual as individuals compete for resources and for mates. However, this assumption does not explain instances in which individuals show altruistic behavior or act unselfishly. In Hamilton's theory, which is called the theory of inclusive fitness, competition occurs at the genetic level rather than at the level of the individual. That is, according to this theory an individual's genes cause that individual to behave in ways that facilitate making and distributing genes that are close replicas of themselves. In metaphorical language, the theory says that an organism is a gene's way of making more genes like itself.

To use another metaphor, what appears to be altruism or unselfishness at the level of the individual is actually selfishness at the genetic level (Dawkins, 1976). Parents typically have more genes in common with their offspring than any other organism, and therefore according to the theory of inclusive fitness we would expect to see parents making the most efforts to help their offspring even at significant costs to themselves. The theory also predicts that individuals will show altruism, but to a lesser degree, to individuals that are more distantly related to them. The theory even predicts that individuals will show altruism to individuals who may simply have a chance of being related to them. Of course, the decision to be altruistic in a specific instance requires complex computations that take factors in addition to relatedness into account, such as the amount of risk involved and the extent to which the recipient of the altruistic act is likely to be able to reproduce.

E. O. Wilson

Hamilton's theory of inclusive fitness had a strong impact on the biologist E. O. Wilson (1929–), who immediately saw the relevance of the theory to his special area of expertise, insect behavior. He believed that the theory could account for all social behavior, and on that basis founded a field called sociobiology—the contribution of genetics to animal social behavior, including that of humans. Although he is a biologist, Wilson had a much greater effect on psychologists than on other biologists.

To take one example of an application of sociobiology to human behavior, followers of this approach typically (1) assume that men are genetically predisposed to greater promiscuity than women, and (2) explain this as due to the fact that men can physically impregnate a much greater number of women than the number of men women can be impregnated by. More specifically, the cost of producing offspring is lower for men (who only invest sperm) than it is for women, who invest more biologically speaking. Supposedly, then, men are genetically disposed to impregnate as many women as possible (hence to be more promiscuous), whereas women are predisposed to be extremely selective in whom they allow their eggs to be fertilized by. Some sociobiologists extend this explanation to account for the fact that men commit the vast majority of rapes.

This view has been strongly criticized on the basis that it is sexist (which is actually a political rather than scientific judgment) and not supported by scientific evidence (Coyne, 2003). In particular, there is considerable evidence that sexual selection, as conceptualized by Darwin—whereby individuals tend to select mates on the basis of the quality of their genetic material (as indicated by their physical characteristics)—is considerably complicated by other factors. For example, the theory has a great deal of difficulty accounting for the growing evidence that homosexuality, both male and female, is widespread throughout the animal kingdom, including among our closest primate relatives (Roughgarden, 2004). It appears that sex serves a strong social function in addition to its reproductive function.

Stephen Pinker

Another person impressed by the theory of inclusive fitness is the psychologist Stephen Pinker (1954–). He believes that since the behavioral revolution the importance of genetics to behavior has been greatly underemphasized. In support of Chomsky, Pinker emphasizes that our capacity to learn language is genetically programmed. In 1994, Pinker published *The Language Instinct*.

John Tooby and Leda Cosmides

In an edited book entitled *The Adapted Mind*, published in 1992, John Tooby (1952–), an anthropologist, and Leda Cosmides (1957–), a psychologist, co-authored a chapter entitled "The Psychological Foundations of Culture." This chapter was instrumental in launching evolutionary psychology as a perspective within psychology. There are critics who maintain that evolutionary psychology is merely sociobiology under a new name. However, it appears that evolutionary psychology is broader than sociobiology in that it is not restricted to social behavior, and at the same time narrower in that its focus is on human cognition. Evolutionary psychologists tend to view the mind as consisting of an integrated set of modules designed by evolution to solve specific problems, for example, a language-learning module designed to enable humans to learn languages. As evolutionary psychologists point out, if we consider each module to represent an instinct, this position harks back to William James' view that humans have many instincts.

However, there is no reason that evolutionary psychology should necessarily be restricted to the cognitive approach. As the evolutionary psychologist David Buss has pointed out, "Because all behavior depends on complex psychological mechanisms and all psychological mechanisms at some basic level of description are the result of evolution by selection, then all psychological theories are implicitly evolutionary psychological theories" (Buss, 1995, p. 2).

Thus, each of the four systems to which the rest of this book is devoted consists of a set of psychological theories which, if correct, must be consistent with evolution. Therefore, although evolutionary psychology may inform the four systems, it is not itself a system of psychology as that term is used in this book.

NEUROSCIENCE

Interest in the role of the nervous system in behavior, especially the higher cognitive functions, continued unabated throughout the behavioral revolution and beyond. During most of the twentieth century, psychologists who focused on the nervous system were called physiological psychologists. Behavioral neuroscientists, cognitive neuroscientists, or simply neuroscientists are more modern terms for these individuals. In addition, they may be in disciplines other than psychology, such as zoology with a specialization in neurology.

Historically there have been two views about the role of the cerebrum, the two large lobes that form the top part of the brain and that, in humans, overhang the midbrain and brain stem. One view is that of *specificity*, that is, that different areas of the cerebrum are involved in different mental functions. The other view, called *equipotentiality*, is that all parts of the cerebrum are equally capable of serving any function.

Specificity

The cerebrum is believed to be involved in higher mental functions. Phrenology held that different areas of the cerebrum correspond to different personality traits. Paul Broca (1824–1880), a French surgeon, and Carl Wernicke (1848–1905), a German neurologist and psychiatrist, made discoveries that seemed partially to support phrenology in the sense of showing that some specific brain areas serve different functions. Broca treated a patient who had a particular type of aphasia. Although this patient could understand speech, he could not articulate words. Upon the death of the patient, an autopsy revealed damage to a specific area of the cerebral cortex—the outer layer of the cerebrum where the cell bodies of the neurons are located—that today is called Broca's area. Similarly, Wernicke found an area in the cortex that seemed to cause a different type of aphasia. Individuals with damage to what is now called Wernicke's area can articulate words, but they have extreme difficulty coming up with the correct word. Thus, specific areas of the brain are involved in specific faculties of speech, suggesting that other mental faculties might also depend on specific brain functions.

Equipotentiality

A physiological psychologist named Shepherd Franz (1874–1933), using the ablation technique, shifted the emphasis toward a more holistic view of the cerebral cortex. He noted that functions lost through the destruction of some neural tissue can be recovered, to some extent, through training and reeducation. He concluded that the cerebrum has a high degree of generality. A former student of John B. Watson, Karl Lashley (1890–1959), following up on work done by Franz, discovered that large portions of the cerebral cortex appear to have general rather than specific function.

Conducting experiments with rats, Lashley found that ablation of parts of the cerebral cortex does not have any specific effects, but may decrease learning ability. He also found that when a particular function is destroyed, other regions may take over that function.

Lashley's protégé, Donald Hebb (1904–1985), proposed a method by which events or ideas can be associated or connected in the nervous system. The method involves neural circuits in the brain growing together as a result of being activated at approximately the same time. Hebb's theory (which was not new—other associationistic philosophers and psychologists, including William James, had proposed a similar neural mechanism) is consistent with a generalized view of the cerebral cortex, since it does not specify different types of connections for different functions. Like the individual neurons in the brain, the connections are all of one type and can serve any function. In 1949, Hebb outlined his theory in a book entitled *The Organization of Behavior: A Neuropsychological Theory.* His theory is recognized in the field of artificial intelligence (AI) as describing one way in which intelligence may be programmed in computers.

Combined Specificity and Equipotentiality

In addition to its generalized functions, the cerebral cortex has specialized functions. This fact was underscored in mid-twentieth century by the neurologists Wilder Penfield (1891–1976) and Roger Sperry (1913–1994). Penfield is famous for, among other contributions, mapping regions of the brain involved in motor and sensory functions. Sperry received the Nobel Prize in medicine in 1981 for research demonstrating that the two sides of the cerebral hemispheres have different functions and even, at least when surgically separated, different consciousnesses.

Research beginning around the middle of the twentieth century also clarified functions of brain regions below the cerebral hemispheres. In the midbrain and brainstem there are regions that are involved in sensation, cognition, short- and long-term memory, emotion, motivation, pleasure, and pain.

Neuroscientists have also found that specific learning experiences may affect specific brain regions. For example, in what is known as "the cabbie study," it was found that the posterior hippocampus (a region involved in navigation in animals) in London taxi drivers is larger than in individuals who do not have extensive navigational experience, and it grows as a function of length of time in the job (Maguire, Gadian, Johnsrude, Good, et al., 2000). Other brain regions do not appear to be similarly affected.

Thus, both evolutionary psychology and neuroscience are currently moving toward a modular view, which is reminiscent of the faculty psychology of the eighteenth and nineteenth centuries. Neuroscience is often associated more with cognitivism than with the other four systems. This may be because in the computer model typically adopted by cognitive theorists, the nervous system is the hardware on which the software called the mind runs, and there is a growing appreciation by cognitivists that knowledge of the hardware may be important in understanding the workings of the software. However, there is no logical reason for neurology to be any more or less important for cognitivism than for any of the other systems. Like evolutionary theory, neuroscience informs the four systems discussed in this book, but is not itself a system of psychology.

SUMMARY

By the last quarter of the twentieth century, six clearly identifiable strands in psychology were evident: (1) behavioral psychology; (2) cognitive psychology; (3) psychodynamic psychology; (4) humanistic psychology; (5) evolutionary psychology; and (6) neuroscience. The first four approaches are systems of psychology in that they are collections of closely related theories that attempt to provide an integrated view of psychology.

After the behavioral revolution, behaviorism focused on three areas: learning, memory, and behavioral applications. The major learning theorists were Edwin Guthrie, Edward Tolman, Clark Hull, and B. F. Skinner. All behavior, according to Tolman, is a function of environmental variables mediated by intervening variables. Hull attempted to produce a system of behavior modeled on Newton's system of physics. While the other learning theorists developed and tested hypotheses, Skinner avoided making formal hypotheses and devising predictions from them. Instead he adopted an approach based on the inductive philosophy of Francis Bacon.

Behavioristic memory researchers, such as Benton J. Underwood, continued Ebbinghaus' research program. With regard to application, Skinner extended his approach to education in the form of devices called teaching machines. In addition, some followers of Skinner's approach developed an approach called behavior modification or applied behavior analysis. The term behavior therapy is often used to refer collectively to therapies such as those developed by Wolpe and by applied behavior analysts.

Cognitive psychology continued trends stemming from the work of Lev Vygotsky and Jean Piaget, with an information-processing model based on advances in computer science. Vygotsky stressed the importance of the active interaction of the individual with society and of the development of language in higher mental or cognitive functioning. Piaget, a development theorist, studied the stages in the cognitive and ethical development of children.

Cognitive psychology brought the mind back into psychology after its banishment by the behaviorists. In most contemporary cognitive approaches, the mind is viewed as an information-processing system—the software of the brain. Two individuals who were extremely influential in the development of cognitive psychology were George Miller and Noam Chomsky. Miller studied the effects on memory of chunking information and rule-following as a higher type of conceptual activity. Chomsky developed a theory to account for why humans possess the competency for language. Much cognitive research attempts to determine algorithms by which people process information. Applications are mainly in the areas of cognitive behavior modification, which consists primarily of behavior modification or behavior therapy procedures that incorporate either mediating behavior or information-processing concepts.

Psychodynamic approaches focus largely on unconscious motivations. These approaches stem mainly from the work of Sigmund Freud. Psychoanalysis dominated clinical psychology and psychiatry at the same time that behaviorism was at its apex in experimental psychology. However, a number of psychoanalysts broke with Freud to form their own theories of unconscious motivation. In general these approaches downplayed sexual motivation and stressed other types of motivation. For example, Alfred Adler stressed the drive for power within a social context, and Carl Jung stressed the integration of the personality based on his theory of personality traits.

Humanistic psychology was originally called third force psychology because it was a reaction to the two dominant forces, behaviorism and psychoanalysis. When cognitive psychology emerged during the cognitive revolution, humanistic psychologists considered it to have the same problems as they found with behaviorism. Two individuals who led the movement to humanistic psychology were Carl Rogers and Abraham Maslow. Rogers emphasized taking a nondirective approach to therapy; Maslow emphasized the drive for self-actualization, that is, realizing one's full potential.

Two philosophical movements that strongly influenced humanistic psychology are phenomenology (based on the philosophy of Edmund Husserl) and existentialism (based on the philosophies of Søren Kierkegaard and Friedrich Nietzsche). Phenomenology stresses the importance of that which is immediately presented to consciousness; existentialism emphasizes the fundamental fact of one's existence and the importance of will and choice in determining one's fulfilment and meaning in a world that either is (according to some existentialists) or merely appears to be (according to others) deterministic and meaningless. Existential psychotherapy, which focuses on helping individuals to develop or restore meaning in their lives, is closely allied with humanistic psychotherapy.

Transpersonal psychology is sometimes called the fourth force; however, since the spiritual side of a person is a part of that person's phenomenology and provides meaning to a person's life, it makes sense to consider transpersonal psychology a branch of humanistic psychology. Thus, broadly conceived, there are four branches to humanistic psychology: humanistic psychology proper, phenomenology, existential psychology, and transpersonal psychology.

Evolutionary psychology focuses on how past evolutionary processes account for current behavior and the mind. Neuroscience has received impetus from advances in technology for studying the nervous system. In both evolutionary psychology and neuroscience there has been movement away from general processes (e.g., the evolution of general learning processes in evolutionary psychology and general neural processes that mediate many functions in neuroscience). Both evolutionary psychology and neuroscience are compatible with and inform the four broad systems.

Discussion Questions

1. Discuss the similarities and differences between the four major behaviorist learning psychologists (Guthrie, Tolman, Hull, and Skinner).

2. Of the four major behavioristic learning theories, which one survives today? Discuss possible reasons for this.

3. Discuss how Ebbinghaus' research gave rise to behavioristic studies of memory. Given that Ebbinghaus was strongly influenced by Fechner and Wundt, does this seem strange? Why or why not?

4. Discuss the reasons for the cognitive revolution. What was Alan Turing's role in its occurrence?

5. Discuss what gave rise to humanistic psychology. What were the roles of Husserl, Kierkegaard, and Nietzsche in the development of humanistic psychology?

6. Discuss whether evolutionary psychology is an outgrowth of functionalism.

7. Discuss how Freud's, Adler's, and Jung's views differed, and how they were similar.

8. Discuss whether behaviorism is compatible with any of the views of the soul in the first two chapters of this book.

9. Discuss how evolutionary theory can inform each of the four systems, and whether it is more or less important for any of the systems.

10. Discuss how neuroscience can inform each of the four systems, and whether it is more or less important for any of the systems.

CHAPTER 7

The Four Systems Up Close: Internal Differences

*T*his chapter takes a closer look at the four systems of the previous chapter—behavioral psychology, cognitive psychology, psychodynamic psychology, and humanistic psychology—with emphasis on the differences within these systems and the historical bases for those differences.

BEHAVIORAL APPROACH

For over 2,500 years, psychology had been the study of the mind. In the first part of the twentieth century, this changed. The change came about under the leadership of John B. Watson. In the first paragraph of his famous 1913 article ("Psychology as the Behaviorist Views It") that sparked the behavioral revolution, Watson redefined the goal of psychology as follows:

> Psychology as the behaviorist views it is a purely objective experimental branch of natural science. Its theoretical goal is the prediction and control of behavior. Introspection forms no essential part of its methods, nor is the scientific value of its data dependent upon the readiness with which they lend themselves to interpretation in terms of consciousness. The behaviorist, in his efforts to get a unitary scheme of animal response, recognizes no dividing line between man and brute. The behavior of man, with all of its refinement and complexity, forms only a part of the behaviorist's total scheme of investigation. (Watson, 1913, p. 158)

129

This article, which is sometimes called the "behaviorist manifesto," consisted largely in an attack on the introspective method, primarily on the basis that it is unreliable (i.e., findings using it cannot be reliably replicated). Six years later, he followed this article with a book entitled *Psychology from the Standpoint of a Behaviorist*, which went through three editions and numerous printings. In that book he attempted to provide the knowledge base of a science of behavior without resorting to any mention of introspection. As he stated in the preface,

> The present volume does some violence to the traditional classification of psychological topics and their conventional treatment. For example, the reader will find no discussion of consciousness and no reference to such terms as sensations, perception, attention, will, image and the like. These terms are in good repute, but I have found that I can get along without them both in carrying out investigations and in presenting psychology as a system to my students. I frankly do not know what they mean, nor do I believe that any one else can use them consistently. (Watson, 1919, p. 1)

Although Watson ruled out introspection as a scientific method, he accepted self-observation as a means to obtain information about one's own behavior. He also accepted an individual's verbal report of his or her self-observation as a means of obtaining information about that person's behavior (e.g., Watson, 1920).

An indication of the speed of behaviorism's takeover of psychology is contained in the following from a letter by Wundt's most famous student, E. B. Titchener, written to Robert Yerkes in 1914:

> [T]here is now a flurry in favour of behaviourism, but that is largely because the thing is so far all positive, and no criticism worth mentioning has appeared. No doubt the point of view will permanently appeal to certain temperaments (as it has happened in the past; it is no more new than pragmatism was!). But the present hullabaloo will quiet down after a few critical papers have made their appearance; and then we shall get our perspective again. I do not belittle behaviourism by hoping that it may soon be set in its right place! but I get a trifle tired of unhistorical enthusiasms. (Quoted in Larson & Sullivan, 1965, p. 342)

Titchener was right about the "present hullabaloo" eventually quieting down, but when it did behaviorism had replaced the introspective approach as the experimental method of psychology. As discussed in chapter 5, three related movements in other fields helped in the spread of behaviorism: positivism in physics and logical positivism and operationism in philosophy.

After Watson's early departure from academia, behaviorism fragmented into a number of camps. These appear to represent practically all the logically possible variations of behaviorism. They may be classified as belonging to one or the other of two broad types: methodological and radical.

Methodological Behaviorism

Methodological behaviorists accept behaviorism as the method of psychology. Mental phenomena such as the phenomenological experience of consciousness may exist, but cannot be studied by psychologists. Such phenomena must either be ignored or left to other disciplines or fields, such as philosophy or religion. We may distinguish two types of methodological behaviorism: empty-organism and intervening-variable.

Empty Organism Behaviorism

Empty-organism or EO behaviorism is the view that psychology should deal only with units of the environment called stimuli (plural of stimulus) and units of behavior called responses, and should not postulate anything intervening between these two. The noted early behavioral theorist E. R. Guthrie (1886–1959), who worked primarily on learning in cats, expressed this view (along with a colleague) as follows:

> We do not at all deny that the cat undoubtedly has experience analogous to ours. But it appears to us highly desirable to find an adequate description of the cat's behavior without recourse to such conscious experience. . . . [T]he unobservable and unverifiable supposititious mental life of the cat is of no use in a theory of learning. That should be confined to observable antecedents and observable results. . . . If we lean too heavily on conscious ideas in explaining behavior we may find ourselves predicting what the cat will think, but not what we can observe it to do. (Guthrie & Horton, 1946, p. 7)

This type of behaviorism is called an "empty-organism" approach because it seems to take the stance that one should assume that there is nothing inside the organism under study. This is the type of behaviorism, also known as strict behaviorism, that many people think of when they come across the word *behaviorism*, and it is also the type that is frequently attacked in numerous textbooks, as well as in many popular books.

EO behaviorism is the type of behaviorism that is frequently said to be dead. Clearly it is dead, in that there are few, if any, EO behaviorists left and they produced no major writings in defense of their viewpoint. Therefore, this type of behaviorism will receive no further consideration in this book.

Intervening-Variable Behaviorism

Under the category of intervening-variable or IV behaviorism are included many psychologists who might not label themselves as behaviorists. Many psychologists who attempt to study "mental" processes such as thinking, and who perhaps label themselves as "cognitive psychologists," are actually IV behaviorists. That is, they implicitly or explicitly consider behavioral data to be the only type of acceptable psycho-logical data. They believe that behavioral data may be used to make constructs and theories about variables that are purely hypothetical, but that may be useful in predicting behavior. IV behaviorists generally subscribe to the scientific philosophy that holds that only that which can be directly observed by more than one person (i.e., only that which is objective) can be dealt with scientifically, that is, to logical positivism (or some variant of it). However, they have no problem postulating unobservable nonbehavioral processes to account for behavior, provided that these unobservables are operationally defined in terms of things (e.g., objects, events, behavior) that can be directly observed by more than one person. In fact, they see the goal of psychology as being to develop a theory of behavior that incorporates such processes.

The following statement by Edward Tolman (1886–1959) provides one of the earliest examples of the approach of methodological behaviorism:

> A theory, as I shall conceive it, is a set of "intervening variables." These to-be-inserted intervening variables are "constructs," which we . . . evolve as a useful way of breaking down into more manageable form the original complete [empirical] function. . . . And I have conceived a set of . . . functions to connect these intervening variables severally to the independent variables [objects and events in the external environment], on the one hand, and a function . . . to combine them together and connect them to the final dependent variable (behavior), on the other. (Tolman, 1938, p. 9)

Tolman's theory, or set of intervening variables, involved a construct termed a "cognitive map"—a hypothesized internal map that an animal or human uses to get around in its environment. Tolman studied the cognitive map primarily through experiments with rats in mazes. His purpose in studying the function relating behavior (e.g., errors and correct responses in a maze) to the environment was to formulate and test hypotheses about the cognitive map. Behavior was of interest to Tolman, not in its own right, but only insofar as it provided information about the cognitive map and other cognitive processes. Of course a cognitive map could not be directly observed, and so the concept had to be operationally defined. An operational definition of the existence of a rat's cognitive map of a specific maze, for example, would be the observation that the rat reliably takes the most direct route to the goal box of the maze regardless of where the rat starts out in the maze.

There is no commitment on the part of the IV methodological behaviorist that an intervening variable actually exists apart from the operations (i.e., procedures) used to define it. Thus, in the preceding example, Tolman was not committed to the view that some sort of real map actually exists inside the rat. The rationale for using intervening variables is that they are scientifically useful, not that they really exist. Hence, they are sometimes described as "convenient fictions."

In the first chapter of his classic work, *Purposive Behavior in Animals and Men*, Tolman explained his rationale for intervening variables as follows:

> Finally . . . it must . . . be emphasized that purposes and cognitions which are thus immediately, immanently, in behavior are wholly objective as to definition. They are defined by characters and the relationships which we observe out there in the behavior. We, the observers, watch the behavior of the rat, the cat, or the man, and note its character as a getting to such and such by means of such and such a selected pattern of commerce-with. It is we . . . who note these perfectly objective characters as immanent in the behavior and have happened to choose the terms *purpose* and *cognition* as generic names for such characters. (Tolman, 1932, pp. 12–13)

In the concluding chapter of that book he reiterated his rationale in more detail:

> Our system has been presented. It conceives mental processes as functional variables intervening between stimuli, initiating physiological states, and the general heredity and past training of the organism, on the one hand, and final resulting responses, on the other. These intervening variables it defines as behavior-determinants. And these behavior-determinants it subdivides further into (1) immanent purposive and cognitive determinants, (2) capacities and (3) behavior-adjustments. All three of these types of determinant are to be discovered, in the last analysis, by behavior experiments. They have to be inferred "back" from behavior. They are precipitated out from the empirical correlations which can be observed between specific stimuli and initiating physiological states, on the one hand, and specific resultant acts, on the other. They are to behavior as electrons, waves, or whatever it may be, are to the happenings in inorganic matter. There is nothing private or "mentalistic" about them. They are pragmatically conceived, objective variables the concepts of which can be altered and changed as proves most useful. They are not the dictates of any incontrovertible moments of immediacy. (Tolman, 1932, p. 414)

Tolman is respected not only as a leading early behaviorist, but also as an early cognitive psychologist. This illustrates the close connection between methodological behaviorism and cognitive psychology.

Other noted early IV behaviorists include Clark Hull (1884–1952) and Donald Hebb (1904–1985). Hull developed a set of intervening variables that were more behavioral and physiological sounding (e.g., his theory contained constructs such as need, drive, and habit strength) and more quantitative than Tolman's. Hull developed intervening variables that sounded more behavioral (e.g., habit strength) or physiological (e.g., need or drive reduction) than Tolman's intervening variables did. Hebb developed intervening variables that referred to the nervous system (e.g., the cell assembly, which is a group of neurons or nerve cells that cycle neural activity among themselves and thus keep the activity going indefinitely). Hebb is considered an early pioneer of neuroscience, which illustrates the close connection between methodological behaviorism and neuroscience.

Radical Behaviorism

There is some confusion about radical behaviorism due to the word *radical*, which can connote either extremism (as in EO behaviorism) or consistency with fundamental principles (the word *radical* deriving from the Latin for *root*). It is the latter meaning that applies to radical behaviorism. Essentially, radical behaviorists maintain that not only is behaviorism the only valid method of psychology, but that all psychological phenomena are behavior and as such can be studied with the methods of behaviorism. Radical behaviorists do not accept logical positivism—at least not the version that states that scientists must confine themselves to events that are publicly observable (i.e., can be consensually validated; see chapter 5). They believe that everyone engages in behavior that, although unobservable by anyone else, is observable to the person engaging in it.

There are at least four versions of radical behaviorism: Skinnerian behaviorism (e.g., Skinner, 1953, 1957, 1974), interbehaviorism (e.g., Kantor, 1942, 1970), psychological behaviorism (e.g. Staats, 1994, 1996), and teleological behaviorism (e.g., Rachlin, 1992, 2000). We now look briefly at each of these.

Skinnerian Behaviorism

Radical behaviorism's most famous advocate was B. F. Skinner (1904–1990), who coined the terms radical behaviorism and methodological behaviorism (Skinner, 1945). Skinner was quite clear that private events exist and must be considered in a science of behavior. In the two most comprehensive books describing his behavioral philosophy, *Science and Human Behavior* (1953) and *Verbal Behavior* (1957), Skinner used the example of a toothache to illustrate how he conceptualized the differences and similarities between public and private events in a science of behavior:

> When we say that behavior is a function of the environment, the term "environment" presumably means any event in the universe capable of affecting the organism. But part of the universe is enclosed within the organism's own skin. Some independent variables may, therefore, be related to behavior in a unique way. The individual's response to an inflamed tooth, for example, is unlike the response which anyone else can make to that particular tooth, since no one else can establish the same kind of contact with it. Events which take place during emotional excitement or in states of deprivation are often uniquely accessible for the same reason; in this sense our joys, sorrows, loves, and hates are peculiarly

our own. With respect to each individual, in other words, a small part of the universe is *private*. (Skinner, 1953, p. 257; italics in original)

The response *My tooth aches* is controlled by a state of affairs with which no one but the speaker can establish a certain kind of connection. A small but important part of the universe is enclosed within the skin of each individual and, so far as we know, is uniquely accessible to him. It does not follow that this private world is made of any different stuff—that it is in any way unlike the world outside the skin or inside another's skin. Responses to private stimuli do not appear to differ from responses to public events (Skinner, 1957, p. 130)

In reply to a commentary on the position he took early in his career with regard to radical and methodological behaviorism, Skinner stated:

Methodological behaviorists also talked about private events that serve as stimuli and also about private (covert) behavior. The part of methodological behaviorism I rejected was the argument that science must confine itself to events accessible to at least two observers (the position of logical positivism) and that behaviorism was therefore destined to ignore private events. (Skinner, 1988c, p. 217)

In addition to developing a radical behaviorist philosophy, Skinner and his followers applied that philosophy to develop an extensive program of experimental research. Skinner's behavioral philosophy and research led him to systematize an elaborate set of functions or theory describing the relationship of behavior to the environment. Moreover, Skinner and his followers attempted to extrapolate these functional relations to complex human behavior (e.g., Skinner, 1957, 1953).

It is important to note that in reinterpreting certain processes behaviorally, Skinner was not (as is often thought) denying those processes. For example, consider the following reinterpretation by Skinner of the Freudian concept of sublimation (which, according to Freud, is the process by which sexual motivation is changed into socially more acceptable motives such as artistic ones):

To say that artistic and musical activities "express sexual impulses" may mean that characteristic behavior in this field *resembles* sexual behavior in topography. The sculptor modeling a human figure is behaving to some extent as he would behave toward a human body; certain temporal aspects of musical behavior resemble the temporal pattern of sexual behavior. This is simply induction [i.e., generalization] from one stimulus to another or from one response to another on the basis of similarity. (Skinner, 1953, pp. 152–153; italics in original)

Most of Skinner's research was with animals—especially rats and pigeons. The chief difference that Skinner saw between animals and humans is that the latter have *verbal behavior* (a term he coined to emphasize that language can be studied from a behavioral point of view without recourse to the mentalistic terms—i.e., words referring to the mind and related concepts—of cognitive psychology or methodological behaviorism). Indeed, in his book entitled *Verbal Behavior* (1957), Skinner extensively and systematically argued that language behavior follows the same laws as other behavior. The linguist Noam Chomsky (1959) wrote a critical review of *Verbal Behavior* that became almost as famous as the book (and which, as mentioned in chapter 5, helped to spark the cognitive revolution). Skinner started to read the review, but put it aside when it appeared to him that Chomsky had missed the point of the book. In Skinner's words, "I could not see how a review beginning that way could be of any value, and I stopped reading" (Skinner, 1983, p. 152). Thus, Skinner never wrote a reply to Chomsky's review, which seems to have led most cognitive psychologists and others interested in language to believe that Chomsky's arguments are unanswerable. However, authors typically do not respond publicly to reviews, whether favorable or unfavorable.

A decade later, one of Skinner's former students, Kenneth MacCorquodale (1970), wrote an answer to the review, but little attention has been paid to his article. Most radical behaviorists agree that Chomsky misunderstood Skinner's book, whereas cognitive psychologists tend to disregard the book. This is unfortunate because there is much in the book that could be seen to be interpretable as cognitive processing, such as Skinner's discussion of the grammatical ordering and grouping of responses, which he hypothesized is done by means of verbal responses (or verbal operants) that he called *autoclitics* (Skinner, 1957, p. 332). In Skinner's theory, autoclitics—or what we might call *grammar responses*—add structure or meaning to more primordial verbal responses. For example, a thirsty person might tend to request water by saying, "me, water." However, this response is more likely to be more quickly reinforced if the responses "please," "give," and "some" are added in the appropriate positions, so that the complete response becomes, "please give me some water."

Although he published no comparisons of his theory with Chomsky's, Skinner acknowledged in one of his notebooks a correspondence between the two theories:

> An account in the Sunday *Times* suggests to me that Chomsky's deep structure is what I have been calling primordial verbal behavior—before autoclitics are added. At least that is true of the examples given in the article. (Skinner, 1980, p. 131)

The adding of autoclitics that Skinner referred to could be interpreted as cognitive processing. It is interesting that through his theoretical analysis of verbal behavior, Skinner independently arrived at a position similar in some respects to that of Chomsky (1957, 1963) regarding the processing of verbal behavior. This observation provides a foretaste of the numerous points of rapprochement between the approaches that we shall see throughout this book.

There is also similarity between what cognitive psychologists call *schemata* (or *schemas*) and Skinner called *rule-governed* behavior. According to Skinner, rules are stimuli that specify contingencies of reinforcement, where a contingency of reinforcement is a relationship between some behavior and a reinforcer for that behavior (Skinner, 1969). Thus, if in playing tennis I execute my backhand swing in a particular way because in the past executing my backhand swing in that manner had been reinforced by the trajectory of the ball over the net, my backhand swing is under the control of a specific contingency of reinforcement. Skinner would have said that my backhand swing has been *contingency-shaped*. If instead, however, my backhand swing was under the control, not directly of a contingency, but of a rule that I said to myself—perhaps one that I had read in a tennis book or one that a tennis instructor had given to me—then Skinner would have said that my backhand swing was rule-governed. The rules that govern behavior may be either emitted by oneself (as in self-control) or by someone else. If oneself emits them, they may be public or private. It is the latter that most closely resemble schemas as hypothesized by cognitivists. Despite the similarity between schemas and privately emitted rules, however, it is important to note that cognitive psychologists typically view schemas as being unconscious static structures rather than behavior.

It should be noted, however, that cognitive psychologists do not make a strong distinction between behaviors that radical behaviorists consider contingency shaped and those that Skinner called rule governed. Both types of behavior are assumed to follow what are called *scripts*. For example, the distinction between an actor following a script and speaking extemporaneously, or between a musician following a score and improvising, might be considered to be the distinction between different types of *mental scripts* for the cognitive psychologist. To the radical behaviorist the distinction is between the presence and absence of a specific type of stimulus called a *rule*. (Schemata and scripts are discussed further on page 146.)

Interbehaviorism

J. R. Kantor (1888–1984) developed his interbehavioral psychology prior to Skinner's development of his approach. Kantor seems to have had some influence on Skinner, but Kantor rejected certain aspects of Skinner's approach. One point of contention was the heavy emphasis that Skinner placed on operant behavior—that is, behavior that is strengthened by its consequences—as the most fundamental behavioral process and the rate of emitting an operant response as the fundamental datum of psychology. Another was Skinner's downplaying or apparent dismissal of many of the traditional psychological topics (e.g., perception, the participation of physiological processes in behavior), even when interpreted in behavioral terms. Modeling his approach on field theory in physics (e.g., gravitational fields, electromagnetic fields), Kantor conceived of an interbehavioral field that consists of the organism and the stimulus objects in its environment reciprocally relating to each other according to psychological laws, the discovery of which is the purpose of psychology. However, Kantor did not develop his system as extensively or to the same degree of detail as Skinner did his system.

Unlike Skinner, Kantor was not an experimental psychologist. Under the *nom de plume* "Observer," Kantor wrote articles and a regular feature based on interbehaviorism for the *Psychological Record*, a journal that he founded. Many of these writings were reprinted in a collection of readings (Observer, 1984). Although Kantor considered Skinner's views on private events to be a step in the right direction, he did not believe they went far enough in disavowing dualism. Referring to Skinner as "a behaviorist" rather than directly by name in the following quotation, apparently to give more generality to his argument, Kantor wrote:

> An interesting attitude is assumed by a behaviorist not completely emancipated from a dualistic background and who uses the term "private" in its popular connotation when he asserts that the individual's response to an inflamed tooth, for example, is unlike the response which anyone else can make to that particular tooth (Skinner, 1953, p. 257). What the behaviorist overlooks is that the same statement can be made of any stimulus object, say, the catching of a frisbee, even by the same individual at a second trial. What is the case here is simply the specificity of the factors in a particular field. If the inflamed tooth is in John Jones' mouth it is *he* who is interacting with his tooth, but the inflamed tooth is a public object specifically and professionally interacted with by Dr. John Doe, dentist.
>
> The behaviorist enlightens the reader when he says, "with respect to each individual, in other words, a small part of the universe is private" (Skinner, 1953, p. 257). The behaviorist does not realize that in a world where every event is "private," that is unique, there is no problem of privacy. Everything is public in the sense of being directly or inferentially available for observation. There is no problem to be solved if one is concerned with fields, so that there are several components of an event to supply information. Mysteries of privacy owe their source only to unacknowledged vestiges of transcendental thinking. (Observer, 1984, p. 230; italics in original)

In other words, no stimulus object or event can in principle be seen simultaneously from the same physical perspective by more than one observer, and therefore every object and event is private; however, every stimulus object or event can in principle be seen from *some* perspective by more than one observer, and therefore every stimulus object and event is public. Thus, according to Kantor, there is no scientific or logical basis for distinguishing between public and private events. It is unclear, however, whether Kantor took into consideration that it is much easier for observers to exchange perspectives on events ordinarily considered public, for example, a star seen through a particular telescope by two observers taking turns looking through the telescope, than events ordinarily considered private, for example, an inflammation in a tooth felt as pain by John Jones but not by Dr. John Doe, dentist.

Kantor eschewed intervening variables of all sorts, describing them with such pejorative terms as *ghosts* and *spirits* to indicate his view that they reflect the failure of psychology to abandon dualism. At the same time, he considered Skinner's systematic approach (which Kantor called *operantism*) to be too limited. For example, he wrote:

> One of the strongest bits of evidence of the disparity between operant processes and psychological behavioristics is the limited foundation upon which operantism was erected. That foundation is the conditioning of Pavlov. The superstructure implied that all behavior, including thinking, speaking, feeling, and all other complex activities, is simply conditioned action based on the sovereign principle of rewards. It is well to note that the fault of operantism lies precisely in the arbitrary expansion of an excellent behavioral procedure into a psychological system.
>
> Great merit accrues to Pavlovian conditioning. It showed the way to the modification of behavior by observable means instead of metaphysical processes. However, the inflation of the conditioning process into an explanatory principle to account for the most complicated interactions of persons in human situations constitutes a violent travesty of scientific thinking. The conclusion is inevitable. Insofar as operantism is the investigation of primarily animal behavior, it constitutes a definite department of behavioristic psychology, but in no sense the whole of it. (Observer, 1984, pp. 107–108)

Psychological Behaviorism

Like J. R. Kantor, Arthur Staats (1924–) regards Skinner's system as too narrow to account for the full complexity of human behavior. Staats (1994, 1996) has developed an approach called psychological behaviorism (PB) which disavows, among other things, (a) the emphasis that Skinner placed on rate of responding as the basic datum of psychology, (b) Skinner's emphasis on operant conditioning as opposed to Pavlovian conditioning, (c) Skinner's emphasis on studying behavior in the stable state as opposed to studying learning, and (d) Skinner's denial of emotions as potential causes of other behavior. Although Staats clearly rejects Skinner's radical behaviorism, he is a radical behaviorist in his acceptance of the reality of private events and his position on intervening variables. However, Staats considers Skinner's view on private events to have been too imprecise or vague to be of any scientific value. Regarding private events, Staats wrote:

> PB takes the position that there are internal behavioral events that have stimulus properties and thus can help determine the individual's behavior. PB considers this circumstance to represent a special problem for psychology, that is, that very generally events important in immediately determining human behavior lie within the individual, out of sight. The trick is to study those events as systematically as possible, not to refuse to consider those events or to do so only vaguely [as Staats believes that Skinner did]. It is systematic development that enables the internal event to be considered as a determinant of behavior. It is that development that provides a basis for doing something about such internal events in a way that has useful scientific outcomes. Without systematic development a concept such as the private event is not a useful "cause" in a behavior analysis. It is a concept that can be used to suggest that some question has been answered without actually doing so. (Staats, 1996, p. 367)

Staats' psychological behaviorism considers emotions to be Pavlovian conditioned responses that can indeed cause other behavior to occur. Moreover, Staats does not shun traditional psychological data, including data derived from tests of intelligence, attitudes, and personality. In Staats' psychological behaviorism, these concepts are not thought of as mentalistic or in mental terms (i.e., terms referring to the mind). Instead, they denote clusters of hierarchically organized behavior, called basic behavioral repertoires (BBRs), that enable or facilitate the learning of similar behavior (i.e., the adding of new behavior to a cluster). Measures such as intelligence, attitude, and personality tests tap into specific BBRs, which is why they can be fairly predictive of behavior. Thus, Staats does not consider concepts such as intelligence, attitudes, and personality to be intervening variables as methodological behaviorists do:

> When personality is considered an intervening variable, as it is in cognitive social learning theory (Bandura, 1978; Rotter, 1954), what personality *is* is not specified. The concept of the BBR, however, is not an intervening variable. PB makes, and calls for, empirical definition of the contents of the BBRs, how the contents are learned, and how they have their effects on behavior. It is because PB provides such analytic definition that its concepts of personality, such as intelligence, and the emotional-motivational repertoire, are not intervening variables. They are concepts that specify causes (the environment), the personality events, and the behaviors that are affected. Many of the BBRs involved in personality have not been identified yet. The theory thus calls for much additional theory, method, and empirical development. But the task is generally that of identifying actual repertoires, not inferred processes out

of reach of observational specification. (Staats, 1996, pp. 367–368; italics in original)

Staats believes that all of psychology can potentially be integrated under psychological behaviorism, and has devoted himself to this cause.

Teleological Behaviorism

Howard Rachlin (1935–) calls his approach teleological behaviorism because it places the emphasis on Aristotle's final cause rather than efficient cause (see chapter 1), as other forms of behaviorism (and most other psychological approaches) do. Consistent with his emphasis on goals in the distant future, Rachlin maintains that a number of psychological issues can be most effectively dealt with by appropriate adjustment of the time scale over which we examine behavior. This leads him to conclude, somewhat like Kantor, that there is no valid scientific distinction between public and private events. For example, Rachlin maintains that what Skinner called private events appear to be accessible to only one person, not because of technological limitations as Skinner maintained, but because these events by their very nature take a longer time to observe. Thus, I am more familiar with my private events than you are because I have a longer exposure to my behavior than you have. The longer another person has been exposed to my behavior, the more knowledge that person would have about my so-called private behavior. In the extreme case, someone who has had as much exposure to my behavior as I have had would know as much about my behavior as I do. None of my behavior would be private for that hypothetical person. Thus, while denying that there are any truly private events, Rachlin accepts the reality of what Skinner called private events.

In Rachlin's teleological behaviorism, the time period over which individuals can integrate their behavior is arbitrarily flexible. This allows for the ability of people to engage in self-control and to respond for long-delayed reinforcers or avoid distant aversive events. Skinner's radical behaviorism also deals with these issues but requires more explanatory steps.

For further distinctions between the various types of behaviorism, see Zuriff (1985.)

COGNITIVE APPROACH

Cognitive psychology is a direct descendant of the tradition, going back to the ancient Greeks and earlier (as we have seen in the previous chapters), that there exists a distinct entity, process, or collection of processes, called the soul or mind, that can be speculated about and possibly studied in some way. Following the French philosopher René Descartes (1596–

1650), many who speculated about the soul or mind (an English word whose only counterpart in French, German, and many other languages is the word for soul) tended to subscribe to a philosophical position called *dualism*. As we saw in previous chapters, this philosophy holds that there are two kinds of *stuff* in the universe: (1) material stuff, or matter; and (2) nonmaterial mental stuff, or mind. (Dualism is summed up flippantly by the interchange: "What is mind? No matter. What is matter? Never mind!"). There were some philosophers who thought that just as physical science studies matter, there should be an analogous empirical science that studies the mind. There were others such as the German philosopher Immanuel Kant (1724–1804) who doubted that such a science was possible, but eventually a science of mind did emerge.

Psychology as the Study of the Mind

Early psychologists proposed to study mind—which they equated with consciousness—in a manner analogous to that in which physical scientists study matter. Physicists and chemists study matter by observing it under controlled conditions, that is, conducting experiments on it, to determine its components or constituents and the manner in which they interact. Wilhelm Wundt, who in the latter quarter of the nineteenth century (1879 is the date usually given) established the first experimental psychology laboratory, outlined the goals of scientific psychology as follows:

> Now it is one of the first tasks of each science, that deals with the investigation of empirical facts, to discover the elements of the phenomena. Its second task is to find out the laws according to which these elements enter into combinations. The whole task of psychology can therefore be summed up in these two problems: (1) What are the elements of consciousness? (2) What combinations do these elements undergo and what laws govern these combinations? (Wundt, 1912, pp. 43–44)

Wundt's primary (but not exclusive) method of investigation was introspection—looking inward to draw conclusions about the mind and other psychological issues. Now, introspection was not new; philosophers had been introspecting for thousands of years prior to Wundt. What was new, however, was a radical break with the kind of imprecise introspection that philosophers had been doing. Psychology was to follow the example of physics and the other natural sciences that in previous centuries had broken off from philosophy to accept the "book of nature" as the primary source of knowledge about the world rather than the writings of the ancient philosophers. Thus, psychology was to become an experimental science, and a rigorous form of experimental introspection was to become its primary methodology. In keeping with the precision demanded in science, introspection as Wundt conceived, developed, and employed it was a highly systematic procedure. In fact, he was accused of being opposed to introspection because of the tight strictures he placed on his version of it. The following is an example of how he tried to distinguish his scientific introspective method from ordinary introspection:

> Our psychical experiences are, primarily, indeterminate magnitudes; they are incapable of exact treatment until they have been referred to determinate units of measurement, which in turn may be brought into constant causal relations with other given magnitudes. But we have, in the experimental modification of consciousness by external stimuli, a means to this very end—to the discovery of the units of measurement and the relations required. Modification from without enables us to subject our mental processes to arbitrarily determined conditions, over which we have complete control, and which we may keep constant or vary as we will. Hence the objection urged against experimental psychology, that it seeks to do away with introspection, which is the *sine qua non* of any psychology, is based upon a misunderstanding. The only form of introspection which experimental psychology seeks to banish from the science is that professing self-observation which thinks it can arrive directly, without further assistance, at an exact characterisation of mental facts, and which is therefore inevitably exposed to the grossest self-deception. The aim of the experimental procedure is to substitute for this subjective method, whose sole resource is an inaccurate inner perception, a true and reliable introspection, and to this end it brings consciousness under accurately adjustable objective conditions. For the rest, here as elsewhere, we must estimate the value of the method, in the last resort, by its results. It is certain that the subjective method has no success to boast of; for there is hardly a single question of fact upon which its representatives do not hold radically divergent opinions. Whether and how far the experimental method is in better case, the reader will be able to decide for himself at the conclusion of this work. He must, however, in all justice remember that the application of experiment to mental problems is still only a few decades old. (Wundt, 1910, p. 7)

It might seem that the introspective approach would rule out animal studies, but interestingly this was not the case. Wundt and his followers believed in Darwinian evolution and the continuity of species, and saw as a goal of psychology the elucidation of the animal mind as well as the human mind. What was going on in animal minds, however, had to be inferred from what was known about human minds. Wundt expressed this as follows:

> We have no other means of estimating the mental processes of animals than in the light of those of our own consciousness. We must employ these in such a way as to gain the best and surest knowledge possible of the animal mind. (Wundt, 1896, p. 345)

To Wundt, experiments with humans are needed to provide information about animal minds because we cannot observe their mental life directly. The following quote provides an interesting glimpse of Wundt's view of animal studies and associationism:

> Indeed the importance of association for the animal consciousness recalls what we have already said of its value for the human mind. When we began our consideration of the mental life of animals, we condemned the tendency of animal psychology to translate every manifestation of "intelligence" into an intellectual operation. The same reproach could be made against certain more or less popular views of our own mentality. The old metaphysical prejudice that man "always thinks" has not yet entirely disappeared. I myself am inclined to hold that man really thinks very little and very seldom. Many an action which looks like a manifestation of intelligence most surely originates in association. (Wundt, 1896, p. 363)

Wundt's hopes for the development of an objective, scientific method of introspection were not realized. As data came in from different laboratories attempting to use Wundt's method, it became apparent that many results obtained by different laboratories were inconsistent, and there appeared to be no way to resolve these inconsistencies. Such a state of affairs is intolerable in science because scientific progress depends on results by one investigator being repeatable by other investigators in the same field.

Although in one sense behaviorism was clearly a radical departure from the introspective approach, in another it was a natural offshoot of it. Behaviorism continued the interest in associations and provided a powerful experimental methodology for studying them.

Back to the Mind: The Cognitive Revolution

The cognitive revolution did not begin all at once. There was no *cognitive manifesto* in the mode of Watson's so-called *behaviorist manifesto*. Rather, starting sometime in the 1960s or 70s (depending on one's perspective), a critical mass of psychologists began expressing dissatisfaction with many of the restrictions of behaviorism (e.g., that all psychological concepts must be formulated in terms of stimuli and responses, that all psychological theories must be related in some form to conditioning, and that principles of animal learning are fundamental to understanding human behavior) a renewed interest in studying the mind. Psychology, which since the behavioral revolution of Watson had been defined simply as the science of behavior, now increasingly became defined as the science of the mind *and* behavior (or sometimes just the science of the mind). From Ulric Neisser's (1967) book title psychologists interested in studying the mind took on the name *cognitive psychologists* (from the Latin *cognito*, meaning *knowledge*), and their approach is called *cognitive psychology*.

Dissatisfaction with the perceived limitations of behaviorism rendered the situation ripe for another drastic change. Some have suggested that the change from behaviorism to cognitivism as the dominant force in psychology constituted the kind of scientific revolution that Thomas Kuhn wrote about in his classic work, *The Structure of Scientific Revolutions*. Kuhn (1962) argued that scientists in any given field are problem solvers working within a set of basic assumptions called a *paradigm*. For example, the paradigm in Europe prior to the 1600s concerning the earth's relation to the rest of the universe described the sun and other heavenly bodies revolving around the earth. Normally, science proceeds at an even pace as scientists continue solving problems within the prevailing paradigm. With the accumulation of data and observations (e.g., Galileo's telescopic observations of moons revolving around Jupiter), further problem solving within that paradigm becomes extremely difficult due to anomalies between the paradigm and scientific data or observations. At the same time, a competing paradigm (e.g., the earth goes around the sun rather than the sun around the earth) emerges that offers, at least to the majority of (generally younger) scientists, a more satisfactory way to deal with phenomena and solve problems. This process results in a scientific revolution called a paradigm shift—a change from the old to the new paradigm.

We have already seen how the change from the introspective approach to behaviorism could be considered to be a paradigm shift. Many have argued that the change from behavioral to cognitive psychology by the majority of psychologists was a second paradigm shift in psychology. Still others have argued that neither the shift from introspection to behaviorism nor the shift from behaviorism to cognitivism satisfies the criteria for paradigm shift or scientific revolution in Kuhn's usage of those terms. The reason, they argue, is that none of these approaches were well-developed scientific theories or paradigms like those involved in the paradigm shifts in physics.

It should be noted that the shift from behaviorism to cognitivism did not entail a return to the introspective method of early scientific psychology. Following the lead of early behaviorists (e.g., Bulbrook, 1932; Duncker, 1926; Watson, 1920; Woodworth, 1938, pp. 785–786), cognitive psychologists generally consider the use of verbal report to describe thought processes to be an acceptable research tactic. Herbert Simon and his associates, for example, developed a method called protocol analysis, which involved individuals thinking aloud as they solved various intellectual problems. Simon and his associates recorded these verbalized thoughts and used them to develop computer programs that simulate human thought patterns (Ericsson & Simon, 1984, 1993; Newell & Simon, 1972).

The Informational or Computational Model

Several important things happened to help bring about the cognitive revolution. One was dissatisfaction with behaviorism's focus on correlating stimuli with responses with seeming disregard for what goes on between the stimulus and the response. Much evidence seemed to suggest that there are important processes that mediate between stimuli and responses, and that these mediating processes seem to be similar to what people often refer to as mental activity. Another thing that happened to bring about this resurgence of the mind in psychology was the rise of information-processing theory and computer technology, which provided a model—a paradigm competing with the behavioral one—for the mind. To understand this model, note that a computer consists of (1) hardware (i.e., electronic components put together in a certain manner) and (2) software (i.e., a computer program directing the hardware to carry out certain functions). The software, or computer program, is coded (i.e., written) from an algorithm, which is a precise, step-by-step procedure for carrying out some function. The model on which cognitive psychology is based, then, is this: the brain corresponds to the hardware of a computer (it is sometimes therefore called *wetware*, because like the rest of the body the brain is mostly water), whereas the mind is the program that runs on that hardware (or wetware). Cognitive psychologists see their goal as being to discover—or construct in a step-by-step fashion—the program, or its algorithm, that the brain runs (e.g., Simon, 1981). The function of a computer can be seen as that of carrying out computations or information processing; thus, another way to look at the mind is as a computational device (a *number cruncher*) or as an information processor.

Cognitive psychologists consider the mind to be furnished with what they call schemas or schemata, the plural of schema, and scripts. A dictionary definition of *schema* is a diagram or plan, but cognitive psychologists use the term to refer to a program in the mind that tells us how to interpret a given situation. Thus it is an attitude, an assumption, a belief, or an expectation. Scripts are the roles or rules for acting in given situations or context. To illustrate what has been called "the restaurant script," consider the following set of statements:

1. Sally was hungry, so she went into a restaurant.
2. She ordered a delicious meal consisting of roast chicken, potatoes, and salad.
3. She left the restaurant feeling satisfied.

If after reading the above you were asked the question, "What did Sally eat in the restaurant?" you academic almost certainly would reply, "roast chicken, potatoes, and salad." But nowhere is this actually stated. Instead, cognitive psychologists would maintain, the restaurant script placed in your mind by your culture provides it.

The computer model, computational model, or information-processing model of mind (depending on which term one prefers) gives cognitive psychologists an answer to the behaviorist argument that science cannot study an immaterial object. Cognitive psychologists point out that a computer program, or an algorithm, is an abstraction rather than a material object, yet it can clearly be studied. In addition, the cognitive psychologist would point out that behavior patterns, as opposed to individual behaviors, are also abstractions.

The Dynamical Interactions Approach

Although the computational approach to cognition is currently dominant within cognitive psychology, there is a growing number of psychologists, philosophers, and other scientists who reject this model in favor of studying cognition as brain processes in continuous dynamical interactions (i.e., interactions that have a cumulative effect on subsequent interactions, as described by a particular mathematical approach known as dynamical systems theory) with the environment (e.g., Beer, 1995; Brookes, 1991; Haselager, de Groot, & van Rappard, 2003; Keijzer, 2001; Varela, Thompson, & Rosch, 1991).

Cognitive Science: An Interdisciplinary Approach

As mentioned earlier, whether the mind is an algorithm in the computational approach or the way in which the brain interacts dynamically with the environment, there are many specialists other than psychologists who contribute to its study. Computer scientists, philosophers, linguists, neurologists, psychiatrists, and others have entered the enterprise, and indeed have been part of the cognitive revolution. Thus, when we refer to cognitivists, we are not necessarily referring to individuals within psychology; however, whether or not these individuals received formal training as psychologists, it is their impact on psychology with which we are concerned. This applies to individuals outside of psychology who have contributed to the other approaches as well. For example, as we have seen and will see throughout this text, psychiatrists have contributed greatly to psychology in general and specifically to each of the four broad systems with which we are concerned.

PSYCHODYNAMIC APPROACH

Although the psychodynamic approach was once extremely popular within psychology, most academic psychologists have abandoned it as a part of mainstream psychology. Nevertheless, it has enriched psychology tremendously with its concepts, many of which are still current.

Sigmund Freud (1856–1939) is known as the founder of psychoanalysis, which was the original psychodynamic approach. Like cognitive psychologists, Freud's goal was to understand the mind, although his approach was quite different. A neurologist by training and a materialist by conviction, Freud regarded the mind to be physically the brain (or at least a part of the brain). Because in his studies and theorizing he did not actually observe the brain, he developed a special language to talk about the mind. His observations were of his patients as they described their psychological problems to him in the course of undergoing the treatment that he developed.

Freud revised his theory many times. The following describes the final version he held, unless otherwise indicated. In reading it, however, it is important to keep in mind that Freud died in 1939. Much of what he said we now know to be either partially or completely wrong. However, much of what he said, which the majority of psychiatrists and psychologists of his day rejected, is—at least in some version—widely accepted today. This especially includes the views that much of our thinking and behavior is influenced by factors that are largely unconscious, and, to a lesser extent, the views that much of our behavior seems designed to resolve conflicts within ourselves and that personality development depends to a large extent on childhood experiences and involves moving from immature to mature states (Westen, 1998).

Parts of the Mind

Fundamental to Freud's theory is the assumption that the mind is divided into two realms: *consciousness* and the *unconscious*. Within consciousness there is a part called the *subconscious* or the *preconscious*, which is not to be confused with the unconscious. The subconscious consists of material (i.e., thoughts) that is not conscious, strictly speaking, but that usually can be brought into consciousness rather easily. The unconscious consists of material that normally almost never becomes conscious without being distorted beyond recognition. Practically the only way to get at this material is through psychoanalysis. According to Freud, the unconscious is a much more important determiner of behavior than consciousness is. In other words, most of what we say and do is more strongly influenced by the unconscious than by consciousness, regardless of what we feel to be the reasons for our behavior. To illustrate the importance of the unconscious, Freud likened the mind to an iceberg where the visible tip is consciousness and the much more massive and powerful submerged part is the unconscious.

As mentioned earlier, in addition to dividing the mind into conscious and unconscious parts, Freud also divided the mind into three entities that were rather like separate personalities: the *id*, the *ego*, and the *superego*.

(The terms Freud actually used in German, the language in which he wrote, translate more directly into English as the *It*, the *I*, and the *Over-I*, respectively.) The id consists of the instincts, of which there are two types: (1) a general desire for expansion of the self by union with other persons or things, and (2) a desire to annihilate the self. The former is a generalized sex drive, called *libido*; the latter is the death wish, called *thanatos*. Libido usually predominates, often by helping to redirect thanatos from aggression toward the self to aggression toward others. However, thanatos always achieves its objective in the end.

The id presses for immediate gratification of its instincts. This can be dangerous, however, in that it may provoke punishment either from the physical environment or from other people. For example, a child who puts steaming hot food into his or her mouth will be burned; a child who steals a cookie from the cookie jar may be spanked. The ego comes into being to prevent the id from getting the individual into trouble through impulsive actions. The id resides entirely in the unconscious; the ego, being the rational part of the mind, is largely conscious.

Besides protecting the individual from punishment from the outside world, the ego also protects the individual from punishment from the superego. The superego is a part of the mind which identifies with the punishing parent, and thus in a sense is society's representative within the self. As such, it can punish the individual with guilt feelings for transgressions against society. Moreover, the superego, which is largely unconscious and hence not rational, does not distinguish between the desire to perform some forbidden action and the actual performance of that action; both are equally deserving of punishment. Even if the individual merely thinks about committing some transgression, the superego punishes the individual just as though he or she had actually committed the transgression. Thus, to protect the individual from the wrath of the superego, that part of the ego which is not conscious must prevent prohibited thoughts which arise in the unconscious from reaching consciousness. The ego does this by, in a sense, posting a censor at the "gate of consciousness." The function of the censor is to keep prohibited thoughts out of consciousness. Prohibited thoughts can slip by the censor, however, by assuming various sorts of disguises, especially at times when the censor is "off guard"—as when a person is sleeping. Much of the content of dreams, art, and literature is disguised sexual material, which is therefore said to symbolize sex. For example, a man who dreams he is fighting with another male may be expressing an unconscious wish to engage in homosexual relations—a thought that would be severely punished by his superego if it were expressed in an undisguised form. Prohibited thoughts also sometimes get past the censor as various kinds of everyday accidents and slips of the tongue, which are therefore often called *Freudian slips*. For example, the physician who accidentally said to his patient, "Don't forget to take your bill [instead of pill]," was possibly revealing his strong interest in money as opposed to his patient's health. An example from Freud's book, *The Psychopathology of Everyday Life*, that introduced what are now called Freudian slips, is as follows:

> A similar mechanism is shown in the mistake of another patient whose memory deserted her in the midst of a long-forgotten childish reminiscence. Her memory failed to inform her on what part of the body the prying and lustful hand of another had touched her. Soon thereafter she visited one of her friends, with whom she discussed summer homes. Asked where her cottage in M. was located, she answered, "Near the mountain loin" instead of "mountain lane." (Freud, 1901/1914, p. 83)

The Defense Mechanisms

The dynamics manifested by the ego in avoiding punishment from the superego are termed *defense mechanisms*. Freud distinguished the following defense mechanisms:

- *Repression.* This is the action of the censor in excluding unacceptable unconscious impulses from consciousness.
- *Projection.* This is attributing one's own thoughts and feelings to other people. For example, a person who feels that other people are hostile toward him or her may be projecting his or her own feelings of hostility onto others. Thus the ego can maintain, "It is not me who is hostile, it is other people," thereby avoiding punishment from the superego for being hostile instead of kind and loving.
- *Reaction formation.* Reaction formation is engaging in behavior that is the opposite of what one really desires to do in order to keep the forbidden desire out of consciousness. The classic illustration of this is the line in Shakespeare's play Hamlet: "Methinks the lady doth protest too much." This was in reference to Hamlet's mother's extreme expression of grief over the death of Hamlet's father, whereas her true feeling was the opposite. It is characteristic of reaction formation that the behavior it produces occurs in an extreme form.
- *Displacement.* This is the shifting of an instinctual urge from its original object of gratification to an object that is in some way similar to the original object. Although the second object does not provide as much gratification as the original object, it also does not provoke punishment from the superego. For example, a man may form a relationship with a woman who resembles his mother, or a woman with a man who resembles her father, because of a displaced sexual desire for the parent of the opposite sex. When an instinctual urge is displaced toward some activity that is highly valued socially, the term sublimation is often used. Thus, a person who displaces his or her sexual urges toward an artistic or professional activity is said to have sublimated these urges.

- *Rationalization.* This is the substitution of socially acceptable reasons for the real reasons for a behavior when the real reasons would be punishable by the superego. For example, a person may become a medical doctor because it is a lucrative profession but, not being able to acknowledge this in consciousness, believe that the reason is the more socially acceptable desire to serve humanity.

Stages of Development

According to Freud, the libido goes through five stages in the psycho-sexual development of the individual. For various reasons, however, a portion of the libido can become fixated at any of the first three stages; that is, not all of the libido may progress through all of these stages despite normal physical growth. This can result in psychological problems for the individual during adulthood. These problems can be treated by psycho-analysis, in which the fixated portion of the libido is made to resume its arrested progress toward the fifth stage. The stages are as follows.

- *Oral stage.* During this stage, which occupies the first year of life, the libido is focused in the region of the mouth and directed toward such activities as feeding, sucking, chewing, and biting.
- *Anal stage.* During this stage, which occupies the second and third years, the libido is focused in the region of the anus and directed toward the act of defecation.
- *Phallic stage.* During this stage, which occurs during the third to fifth years, the libido is focused in the sex organs. At this stage, the individual (whether male or female) develops an attraction toward the mother and sees the father as a rival. This is the *Oedipus complex*: the desire to kill the father and have sex with the mother. If the male child resolves the Oedipus complex satisfactorily, he identifies with the father (and the rules of the father become internalized in the form of the superego). The female child, if development proceeds normally, does not identify with the father. Instead, recognizing that she lacks a penis, the female child becomes attracted to the father as a love object because of what Freud termed penis envy. She envies all males, but particularly the father, for their penises. Freud initially called this attraction to the father as a love object the *Electra complex,* but later changed its name to the *female Oedipus complex.* Analogously to the male Oedipus complex, to successfully resolve the Electra or female Oedipus complex, the child must renounce her sexual attraction toward her father, identify with her mother, and find another man to replace her father as a sex object. It should be noted that the originator of the concept of the Electra complex was not Freud, but his follower, Carl Jung (see Kilmartin & Dervin, 1997), and that Freud had trouble deciding whether he liked the concept or not.
- *Latency period.* During this stage, which occurs from about five-and-one-half years of age to puberty, the libido is turned away from the erogenous zones (i.e., the mouth, the anus, and the genitals), previous sexual feel-

ings are repressed, and sexual urges lie dormant. This is also a period of *latent homosexuality* (i.e., boys want to associate only with boys, and girls only with girls).

- *Genital stage.* During this stage, which begins at puberty and lasts throughout the remainder of the individual's life, the libido is again focused in the sex organs. This is the stage of normal heterosexual relationships.

Two Leading Dissidents: Adler and Jung

In 1899, Freud published *The Interpretation of Dreams*, which began to attract adherents to psychoanalysis. In 1901, he published *The Psychopathology of Everyday Life*, which further enhanced his reputation as a theorist—although it took some time for his theories to gain respect in the larger psychiatric profession.

Although Freud and his adherents considered psychoanalysis to be a science, under his leadership it took on some of the characteristics of an ideological movement. An inner circle of psychoanalysts coalesced around him, and the punishment for disagreeing with him was expulsion from this inner circle. Two of the most influential members of the inner circle were Alfred Adler (1870–1937), who was about 15 years Freud's junior, and Carl Jung (1875–1961), who was about 20 years younger than Freud. Adler, who had been invited to join the inner circle in 1902, was one of the earliest members. Jung, prior to his first meeting with Freud in 1907, had done research on associations and had published a book that was positive toward Freud's theory. Freud was so impressed with Jung that he began to groom him as his successor. In 1910, he chose Jung to be president of the International Association of Psychoanalysis. In that same year, as a consolation to Adler, Freud chose him to be president of the Vienna Psychoanalytic Society. However, Adler, soon finding himself in conflict with some aspects of Freud's theory such as the sexual basis of the Oedipus complex (Adler thought it had more to do with a struggle for power over the father), resigned this office and left the Vienna Society to form his own organization. Shortly thereafter, Jung also provoked Freud's displeasure by publishing a book that broadened the concept of the libido. In 1913, fearful that psychoanalysis was in danger of being eroded by dissidents such as Adler and Jung, Freud established a secret committee, composed of his loyal disciples. The main purpose of this committee apparently was to let Jung know that he was no longer welcome in the psychoanalytic movement. As if this were not strange enough for someone who considered himself a scientist, Freud presented each member with an intaglio as a symbol of the elite group to which they belonged, which the members had mounted into rings (Grosskurth, 1991, 1998). A little less than a year later, Jung resigned from the presidency of the International Association for Psychoanalysis and severed all ties with Freud and the psychoanalytic movement.

Regarding his break with Freud, Jung later wrote:

> When I was working on my book about the libido and approaching the end of the chapter "The Sacrifice," I knew in advance that its publication would cost me my friendship with Freud. For I planned to set down in it my own conception of incest, the decisive transformation of the concept of libido, and various other ideas in which I differed from Freud. To me incest signified a personal complication only in the rarest cases. Usually incest has a highly religious aspect, for which reason the incest theme plays a decisive part in almost all cosmogonies and in numerous myths. But Freud clung to the literal interpretation of it and could not grasp the spiritual significance of incest as a symbol. I knew that he would never be able to accept any of my ideas on this subject.
>
> I spoke with my wife about this, and told her of my fears. She attempted to reassure me, for she thought that Freud would magnanimously raise no objections, although he might not accept my views. I myself was convinced that he could not do so. For two months I was unable to touch my pen, so tormented was I by the conflict. Should I keep my thoughts to myself, or should I risk the loss of so important a friendship? At last I resolved to go ahead with the writing—and it did indeed cost me Freud's friendship. (Jung, 1961, p. 167)

Both Adler and Jung went on to formulate influential psychodynamic theories that, although strongly influenced by Freud's theory of psychoanalysis, differed markedly from it. Adler, who coined the term *inferiority complex*, saw the major motivating force to be, not sex, but that of overcoming feelings of inferiority through the attainment of some master goal in life. He especially stressed the role of the individual in his or her society or community. In Adler's psychology, *Gemeinschaftsgefühl* (variously translated from the German as social interest or community feeling) is the cornerstone of the individual's psychological well-being or mental health. Adler's approach to psychology is called individual psychology, and the main Adlerian journal is called (appropriately enough) the *Journal of Individual Psychology*.

Jung, who originated the use of the term *complex* to refer to subsidiary aspects of the personality, also disagreed with Freud about the importance of sexual motivation and stressed the integration of the personality as the primary directing force in personality development. He postulated the collective unconscious, which supposedly consists of representations of universal human experiences, as being important in the goal of personality integration. Jung's approach to psychology is called *analytical psychology*, and the major Jungian journal is called the *Journal of Analytical Psychology*.

Freud and Jung's impacts on psychology have been much greater than that of Adler. The following chapters, therefore, will mainly focus on the Freudian and Jungian variations of the psychodynamic approach.

The Neo-Freudians

Born too late to be members of the inner circle, a new generation of leading psychoanalysts arose who were heavily influenced by Freud's theories. Like Adler and Jung, they accepted certain parts of Freud's theories, but rejected or modified other parts.

Some of the most prominent of these neo-Freudians were:

- Karen Horney (1885–1952). Horney (pronounced "horn-eye")" disagreed with Freud's emphasis on sex. She regarded the sexual urge to be a manifestation of the need to be loved. The most basic need, according to Horney, is the need for safety. Horney also disagreed with much of Freud's theorizing about women. In particular, she rejected the idea that penis envy is a biologically determined reaction of little girls. Horney agreed that penis envy occurs; however, she saw it as being due to the cultural advantages that little girls saw accorded to males. Horney disagreed with the Freud's view of the exclusively sexual nature of the libido. She thought it should also include the desire for other satisfactions and safety needs. In addition, she emphasized how the child is treated and cultural factors—as opposed to Freud's psychosexual stages—in the development of the personality.
- Harry Stack Sullivan (1892–1949). Sullivan postulated two basic motives: satisfaction and security. He placed a great deal of emphasis on the child-parent and adult-adult relationships, and conceptualized relationships between people (real or imaginary) as occurring within a Lewinian-type field (i.e., a field within a psychological space).
- Erich Fromm (1900–1980). Fromm rejected Freud's emphasis on adaptation to society as being a criterion for mental health. Fromm maintained that ideals such as truth, justice, and freedom are basic human strivings rather than merely rationalizations of baser motives. He argued that society imposes "filters" on individuals that suppress their ability to think critically, which leads to "socially patterned defects." A goal of psychoanalysis, according to Fromm, is to alleviate these defects. In 1941, Fromm published Escape from Freedom, in which he made a strong distinction between freedom from and freedom to. Society has freed us from a number of undesirable things, but to exercise our freedom to express ourselves creatively requires courage because society tends to repress free expression.
- Erik Erikson (1902–1994). Although also considered to be a neo-Freudian, Erikson developed ideas that were significantly different from Freud's basic theories. One of his most influential notions is that of the importance of

developing a sense of identity—that is, a sense of "who one is"—in the development of the personality. Erikson coined the term *identity crisis* to refer to the lack of a sense of identity.
* R. D. Laing (1927–1989). Laing, a Scottish psychiatrist, was strongly influenced by his reading of Husserl, Heidegger, and other philosophers whose thinking stemmed from Brentano. Although Freud was of the view that psychoanalysis could not be effective with psychotic disorders such as schizophrenia, Laing's early work involved attempting to understand the phenomenology of and treatment of persons with schizophrenia. Also in disagreement with Freud and most psychoanalysts, Laing maintained that psychoanalysis could never be a natural science because the nature of its subject matter is totally unlike that of the natural sciences. That is, unlike stones, stars, trees, and other objects studied by the natural sciences, people have subjective experiences (i.e., intentionality), which, according to Laing, cannot be dealt with adequately in the mechanistic manner that characterizes the natural sciences. Laing did believe that psychoanalysis is a useful tool, and he accepted many of Freud's concepts, such as the unconscious, the defense mechanisms, and regression. A highly original thinker, however, he reconceptualized, and in some cases relabeled, these concepts in accordance with his own approach. In many respects both Fromm and Laing anticipated and contributed to developments in humanistic psychology.

It should be recognized that all psychodynamic theorists today are neo-Freudians, in that they accept heavily modified versions of Freud's theory. For example, most psychoanalysts today do not believe in Freud's dual instinct theory in which sex and aggression are the only primary motives, with other motives being derived from them. As Westen (1998, p. 334) observes, "most contemporary psychodynamic psychologists hold that humans have a number of motives, many of them rooted in biology but nearly all elaborated upon by culture and experience." Still, as Westen also points out, this does not necessitate an outright rejection of Freud: "To reject psychodynamic thinking because Freud's instinct theory or his view of women is dated is like rejecting modern physics because Newton did not understand relativity" (Westen, 1998, p. 334).

HUMANISTIC APPROACH

Humanistic psychology arose largely as a reaction to psychoanalysis and behaviorism, and for this reason was originally called third-force psychology. This was before the emergence of cognitive psychology; otherwise, it likely would have been called fourth force psychology, since many humanistic psychologists are as opposed to the cognitive approach as they are to the other two.

Humanistic Psychology Contrasted with Philosophical Humanism

Although it is related in some sense to the philosophical movement known as *humanism*, and is also referred to as humanism, humanistic psychology should not be confused with philosophical humanism. Philosophical humanism, which dates back at least to the beginning of the period known as the Renaissance (around 1350, when the writings of the ancient Greeks began to be rediscovered by Western Europeans and profoundly affect their thinking; see chapter 2), emphasized the importance of humanity's relation to nature rather than its relation to supposed supernatural forces. Accordingly, these early humanists stressed reliance on human reason rather than subservience to religious authority as the means of achieving understanding of nature and solving human problems. Whereas by opposing the scholastics these early humanists were influential in the rise of modern science (Dijksterhuis, 1961, pp. 223–240), humanistic psychologists have serious reservations about the application of modern scientific methods to human behavior. One reason for this can be traced at least as far back as Brentano (see chapter 4); namely, the objects effectively studied with modern scientific methods do not show intentionality, whereas humans do. Nevertheless, humanistic psychology and philosophical humanism do have one feature in common, which is a strong emphasis on the primacy of experience as the guide to human conduct and action as opposed to blind adherence to arbitrary abstractions and authority figures.

Although just about all that philosophical and psychological humanism share is a name, the name is important in understanding the emergence of humanistic psychology. Early humanism gave rise to what is today commonly called *secular humanism*. This is the viewpoint adopted by the American Humanist Association, whose magazine *The Humanist* takes a strongly atheistic or nontheistic stance. An eloquent expression of the rationale behind secular humanism was given by Kurtz (1983), who stated:

> Any account of nature should pass the tests of scientific evidence; in our judgment, the dogmas and myths of traditional religions do not do so. . . . We find insufficient evidence for belief in the existence of a supernatural being; it is either meaningless or irrelevant to the question of the survival and fulfillment of the human race. As nontheists, we begin with human not God, nature not deity. (p. 41)

This is a philosophy with which many behaviorists agree. In fact, the radical behaviorist B. F. Skinner wrote in the third volume of his autobiography: "I had been a contributing member of the American Humanist Association for many years, and I was an honorary member of the Rationalist Press in Britain, which published the *New Humanist*, a journal more militantly anticlerical and anti-big-state than the American *Humanist*" (Skinner, 1983, p. 343). Skinner was named "Humanist of the Year" in 1972 by the American Humanist Association.

Deciding on a Name for the New Movement

Humanistic psychologists tend to be inclusive rather than exclusive. Secular humanists and other nontheistic individuals, as well as theists, can be humanistic psychologists. Humanistic psychologists tend to believe that the problem with other approaches is not that they are wrong, but that they are too restrictive. They believe that the other approaches, in their abstract theoretical characterizations of humans, exclude much that is essentially human. Rather than being contentious or argumentative toward other approaches, humanistic psychologists tend to encourage other approaches to broaden their perspectives. It is therefore characteristic of humanistic psychology that the most contentious issue within the movement was probably the selection of a name that would not be too restrictive.

The first formal meetings that led to the launching of humanistic psychology were held in Detroit in 1957 and 1958 (Greening, 1985). Many names were considered: orthopsychology, ontopsychology, axiopsychology, metapsychology, self-psychology, autonomous psychology, self-directive psychology, and person psychology. Abraham Maslow's son-in-law suggested the name *Journal of Humanistic Psychology* for the official journal of the organization in a letter in 1959. Maslow liked the name, as evidently did most other third-force psychologists, for they voted to adopt it. The American Association for Humanistic Psychology came into existence in 1961, and the first issue of the *Journal of Humanistic Psychology* appeared in the spring of that year. In 1970, the name of the organization was changed to the Association for Humanistic Psychology to reflect its international focus.

Not all members of the new movement were happy with the name *humanistic* because of its association with philosophical humanism. These psychologists believed that the name *humanism* implied a de-emphasis of the spiritual or transpersonal side of the person, which they thought was important. Regarding this, Clark Moustakas (1985) wrote:

> As members of the Organizing Committee, both Dorothy Lee and I opposed the "humanistic" identification because of what we regarded as confusing and limiting associations with humanism. We preferred "self-psychology" or "holistic psychology," while Abe Maslow, perhaps because of closer ties with secular humanism, or perhaps because he

sensed that the distinction between humanistic and transpersonal was essential, opted for "humanistic." It is likely that Tom Sutich was influenced by Cohen's letter. Joe Adams, the other member of the Organizing Committee, apparently accepted "humanistic," for through majority vote the word was adopted. (p. 5)

Nevertheless, the term *humanism* continues to be troublesome. For example, Eugene Taylor (1999) wrote:

Although it is true that the Greeks are often referred to as humanist philosophers because their subject matter was person-centered and humanism was a theme of the Renaissance scholars, the modern meaning of the term *humanist* refers, in the public's mind, to the American Humanist Association, started by Madelene Murray O'Hare and the atheists who became politically active and were responsible for spearheading the movement that removed prayer from the schools. At the height of the humanistic movement in psychology, for instance, led by Rogers, Maslow, and May, the American Humanist Association elected arch opponent B. F. Skinner as Humanist of the Year. Maslow himself was a member of both groups. (p. 15)

Transpersonal Psychology

Led by Maslow, a group of humanistic-oriented psychologists founded transpersonal psychology, which is sometimes regarded as a fourth psychology (or fourth force). Transpersonal psychology is considered in more detail in chapter 13, which deals with spirituality. The ties and similarities of transpersonal psychologists with humanistic psychologists are so strong that, for the purpose of this book, they are treated as variations of the same approach.

Existentialism

Although humanistic psychology is not closely related to philosophical humanism, it is closely related to the philosophy known as *existentialism*, which was strongly influenced by the philosophy of Friedrich Nietzsche (1844–1900). Nietzsche believed that although we are at the mercy of an uncaring, meaningless universe, it is still possible to live with courage and dignity. Since scientists of his day thought that the universe would continue forever, Nietzsche believed that the universe must repeat states that it has already been in. Moreover, it must do this an infinite number of times. From this premise, Nietzsche drew the inference that each of us must have lived the exact same life we are living now an infinite number of times and are destined to live it again an infinite number of times. From this he concluded that any notion of progress is illusory, and that life is essentially meaningless. In addition, there can be no God—or if there is, God must also be destined to continual repetition. Despite all this meaninglessness, there is a way to rise above it. Only an individual of superior intellectual integrity—whom Nietzsche called an *overman* (also translated from the word Nietzsche used in his native German, *Übermensch*, as *superman*)—would be able to do this, however.

Although some existentialists have adopted Nietzsche's rather gloomy outlook, there are others who are more positive. In fact, many existentialists were more influenced by the optimistic aspects of his philosophy—especially the notion that we have free will and can in some sense use it to achieve dignity regardless of the apparent indifference of the universe. Humans can create their own meaning, whether or not there is meaning in the universe, according to this view. Although there are differences between different existentialist philosophers, according to Sartre (1948), "What they have in common is simply the fact that they believe that existence comes before essence—or, if you will, that we must begin with the subjective" (p. 26).

According to *A Dictionary of Philosophy* (Flew, 1979):

> In the existentialist view the problem of being must take precedence over that of knowledge in philosophical investigations. Being cannot be made a subject of objective enquiry; it is revealed to the individual by reflection on his own unique concrete existence in time and space. . . . Each self-aware individual understands his own existence in terms of his experience of himself and of his situation. The self of which he is aware is a thinking being which has beliefs, hopes, fears, desires, the need to find a purpose, and a will that can determine his actions. (p. 115)

Humanistic Psychotherapy

Humanistic psychologists conducting therapy emphasize the client's subjectivity (feelings) and his or her freedom to choose. Some humanistic psychotherapists practice a type of therapy called *existential psychotherapy*, although not all existential psychotherapists would necessarily call themselves humanistic psychotherapists. Existential psychotherapists tend to focus on the feelings of meaninglessness clients often experience.

Relation to the Other Psychological Approaches

Humanistic psychology is a reaction to the other approaches, on the grounds that the other approaches, while not necessarily wrong as far as they go, have neglected certain issues that have been central to psychology throughout its history. Other approaches have focused on problems such as understanding perception, attention, learning, memory, thinking, and the behavior of nonhuman animals. In general, humanistic psychologists have not taken issue with specific theories about these phenomena, nor have they proposed their own theories about these phenomena. Moreover, unlike therapists of other persuasions, humanistic psychotherapists do not draw on a systematic theory of mind or behavior. There are no humanistic theories of perception, attention, learning, memory, nonhuman behavior, and so forth, as there are in other psychological approaches.

The issues that humanistic psychologists believe have been inappropriately neglected by other psychological approaches are whether our consciousness is more than a passive bystander in our lives, whether we are completely the product of our genes and history, whether cause-effect laws like those in the physical sciences govern our behavior, what the place is of morals and spirituality within psychological science, what form of therapy psychologists should provide, and how we can best generate psychological knowledge. Part II of this book examines the stance humanistic psychology has taken with respect to these issues and the positions and reactions of the other approaches to that stance. In many instances we will see the other approaches moving closer to the humanistic position while retaining their own respective individualities. In the process we will obtain a comprehensive overview of the differences and the similarities among these four approaches or systems of psychology.

Positive Psychology and Humanistic Psychology

Recently, an approach that has much in common with humanistic psychology has emerged. This new approach is called positive psychology (Aspinwall & Staudinger, 2003; Seligman, 2002; Seligman & Csikszentmihalyi, 2000; Snyder & Lopez, 2002/2005). Its goal is to counteract what its adherents see as excessive negativity in other psychological approaches. As opposed to focusing on human weaknesses or failings such as proneness to aggression, self-centeredness, passivity, and psychological distress, positive psychology emphasizes qualities such as courage, love, hope, optimism, wisdom, self-directedness, the tendency to self-actualize, altruism, and creativity. Positive psychology, as stated by Sheldon & King (2001) in a special issue of the *American Psychologist* devoted to positive psychology, "is nothing more than the scientific study of ordinary human strengths and virtues" (p. 216).

The founder of positive psychology, Martin Seligman (2002), acknowledges a debt to humanistic psychology. However, he and his followers maintain that positive psychology is distinctly different from humanistic psychology, as well as from any other form of psychology. The main difference between positive psychology and humanistic psychology, according to Seligman, is that the latter has built no strong research tradition. In short Seligman asserts that humanistic psychology is unscientific. In addition, Seligman maintains that humanistic psychology has tended to generate a cult of narcissism by emphasizing the importance of the self (e.g., self-determination, self-actualization). For example, Seligman and Csikszentmihalyi asserted:

> Unfortunately, humanistic psychology did not attract much of a cumulative empirical base, and it spawned myriad therapeutic self-help movements. In some of its incarnations, it . . . encouraged a self-centeredness that played down concerns for collective well being. . . . [O]ne legacy of the humanism of the 1960s is prominently displayed in any large bookstore: The "psychology" section contains at least 10 shelves on crystal healing, aromatherapy, and reaching the inner child for every shelf of books that tries to uphold some scholarly standard. (Seligman and Csikszentmihalyi, 2000, p. 7)

Humanistic psychologists have responded vociferously to these charges. For example, Taylor (2001) wrote:

> After 1969 . . . the content and methods of humanistic psychology were appropriated by the psychotherapeutic counterculture, causing the humanistic movement in academic psychology to recede. This was because it fractionated into at least three separate streams—transpersonal interest in altered states of consciousness, experiential bodywork and group dynamics, and radical political psychology. From there, the original humanistic psychologists went through a series of transformations, from group leaders and individual therapists to biofeedback researchers, ethnobotanists, transpersonal psychologists, yoga and meditation teachers, martial arts experts, shamanic counselors, and now mind-body practitioners of alternative therapies who focus on consciousness and healing. Seligman mistakes this group for the original personality theorists who led the humanistic movement for more than a quarter of a century in the academy and were concerned first and foremost with generating a "rigorous" research tradition—variously called personality, personology, and a science of the person (Allport, 1968; Rogers, 1964). (Taylor, 2001, p. 23)

In addition, some humanistic psychologists challenged the scientific practices of positive psychology (Held, 2004; Smith, 2003). Positive psychologists frequently assert or imply that individuals who are optimistic—even unrealistically so—cope more effectively, are less prone to depression, and may even live longer than pessimistic individuals (e.g., Seligman, 2002, pp. 129, 200). Humanistic psychologists counter that the evidence for these claims is weak, and, moreover, that there is also evidence that there may be some benefits to negativity. Defensive pessimism, for example, may be a more effective coping strategy than optimism—at least for individuals who suffer from excessive anxiety (Norem, 2001; Norem & Chang, 2002). That is, some individuals appear to cope better by anticipating and preparing for worst-case scenarios, as opposed to trusting that nothing bad will happen. Sometimes bad things do happen, and the person who has anticipated them may be in a better position to cope. Moreover, positive psychologists maintain using mature, accurate judgment is a human strength; recommending that individuals be even slightly unrealistically optimistic would seem to contradict the emphasis on strengths.

More recently there has been a detectable softening of some advocates of positive psychology toward humanistic psychology and toward considering the full range—negative to positive—of psychological phenomena (e.g., Linley, Joseph, Harrington, & Wood, 2006). At present it appears that positive psychology may be best classified as either (1) a close relative of humanistic psychology, or (2) a general movement to accentuate the positive within all four systems. We will therefore not consider it as a separate system in this book.

SUMMARY

Since Watson, behavioral psychology has had as its objective the prediction and control of behavior. There has been disagreement among behaviorists over how to deal with covert or private behavior. Methodological behaviorists accept behaviorism as the method of psychology. Mental phenomena such as the phenomenological experience of consciousness may exist, but cannot be studied by psychologists. There are two types of methodological behaviorists: Empty-organism or EO behaviorism holds that psychology should deal only with units of the environment called stimuli and units of behavior called responses, and should not postulate anything intervening between these two. Intervening-variable or IV behaviorists postulate conceptual variables that mediate between the environment and behavior. These intervening variables are assumed to be something other than behavior. Radical behaviorism maintains that not only is behaviorism the only valid method of psychology, but that all psychological phenomena (overt or covert) are behavior and as such can be studied with the methods of behaviorism. To radical behaviorists, private events (i.e., private stimuli and responses) are no different in principle from other behavior.

There are at least four versions of radical behaviorism: Skinnerian behaviorism, interbehaviorism, psychological behaviorism, and teleological behaviorism. Skinnerian behaviorism takes the operant (i.e., reinforced) response as the fundamental unit of analysis; interbehaviorism holds that behavior cannot be considered as distinct from the stimulus field in which it occurs; psychological behaviorism accepts all psychological measures as valid measures of behavior; teleological behaviorism accepts long range goals as valid determinants of behavior.

Although it arose as a reaction to behaviorism, cognitive psychology stems from a deep philosophical tradition. Early psychologists proposed to study mind in a manner analogous to that in which physical scientists study matter. Around the 1960s, increasing numbers of psychologists began to express a renewed interest in the study of the mind, which had been eclipsed by the rise of behaviorism. Many have argued that the change from behavioral to cognitive psychology by the majority of psychologists was a second paradigm shift in psychology. Still others have argued that neither the shift from introspection to behaviorism nor the shift from behaviorism to cognitivism satisfies the criteria for paradigm shift or scientific revolution in Kuhn's usage of those terms. The computer model, computational model, or information-processing model of mind (depending on which term one prefers) gives cognitive psychologists an answer to the argument that science cannot study the mind because it is immaterial. The answer cognitive psychologists generally give is that the mind is no more immaterial than a computer program is, and science clearly can study a computer program.

Freud's goal also was to understand the mind. Fundamental to Freud's theory is the assumption that the mind is divided into two realms: *consciousness* and the *unconscious*. According to Freud, the unconscious is a much more important determiner of behavior than consciousness is. In addition to dividing the mind into conscious and unconscious parts, Freud divided the mind into three entities that were rather like separate personalities: the *id*, the *ego*, and the *superego*. Freud distinguished a number of defense mechanisms, designed to protect one from seeing undesirable social tendencies in oneself. According to Freud, the libido—or sexual energy—goes through several stages in the psychosexual development of the individual. The successful completion of each stage is critical for normal development. The later followers of Freud, called neo-Freudians, continued with his methods but introduced modifications to his theories. Most psychodynamic psychologists today put less emphasis on sexual motivation than Freud did and more emphasis on social factors.

Both Adler and Jung, who were originally leading disciples of Freud, departed drastically from his theories and went on to formulate influential psychodynamic theories of their own. Adler's approach to psychology is called individual psychology. Jung's approach to psychology is called analytical psychology.

Humanistic psychology arose largely as a reaction to psychoanalysis and behaviorism, and for this reason was originally called third-force psychology. Rather than being contentious or argumentative with other approaches, humanistic psychologists tend to encourage other approaches to broaden their perspectives. Basically, humanistic psychologists believe that other approaches have neglected certain fundamental issues involving consciousness, feelings including our feeling of freedom, and meaning—issues that are also emphasized by phenomenologists, existentialists, and transpersonal psychologists.

Discussion Questions

1. State five assertions that Watson made in his so-called "behaviorist manifesto," and discuss how (or whether) each of these claims represented a fundamental break with traditional psychological approaches.

2. Discuss how positivism in physics and logical positivism and operationism in philosophy aided in the spread of behaviorism.

3. Relate logical positivism to the concept of private events in each of two broad types of behaviorism: methodological and radical.

4. Discuss the similarities and differences between Wundt's approach to studying the mind and that of modern cognitive psychology.

5. Discuss the similarities between methodological behaviorism and cognitive psychology.

6. Explain what a paradigm is, and discuss whether the change from behaviorism to cognitivism in psychology can be considered to be a paradigm shift.

7. Discuss how the ideas of Adler, Jung, and at least two neo-Freudians differed from those of Freud. Do you see a commonality in these differences?

8. Why do you think it was so difficult to find a name for humanistic psychology? Is the name humanistic psychology ideal? Why or why not? What in your opinion would be a better name, and why?

9. How is humanistic psychology related to other approaches to psychology?

10. Discuss whether positive psychology is best classified as a form of humanistic psychology, a general movement toward accentuating the positive in all four psychological systems, or a system in its own right.

A Contemporary Look

Although there are differences among and within systems, there are also striking similarities. This is because underneath, as a result of their common history, they share assumptions that bind them together and distinguish them. The chapters in Part II examine these similarities and differences, and show that in some respects the systems appear to be converging.

The four approaches will be examined with respect to issues that have been fundamental to psychology throughout its history. The issues are: (a) the importance of consciousness and how best to study it; (b) the extent to which we can understand the whole individual by analyzing him or her and into what kinds of units or elements; (c) the role the future plays in influencing present behavior; (d) whether we are merely the product of our genes and environments or something more; (e) the role of morals or values in the science of psychology; (f) how psychology should approach or study spirituality; (g) how clients should be treated both therapeutically and as individuals; and (h) how psychological research should be conducted so as best to advance psychological knowledge.

In each chapter the four systems will be covered in the following order: humanistic approach, psychodynamic approach, cognitive approach, and behavioral approach. This is the reverse of the order used in chapters 6 and 7. There the order reflected that humanistic psychology was a reaction to psychodynamics and behaviorism, and cognitive psychology was a reaction to behaviorism. The reason for this reversal in Part II is to allow psychodynamics and behaviorism to respond to humanistic psychology, and behaviorism to respond to cognitivism.

CHAPTER 8

Consciousness

A s discussed in chapter 4, one need only look at the three major leaders of psychology in the latter part of the nineteenth century to realize how central the problem of consciousness was to psychology at its birth as a science. Each of these leaders proposed a different plan of attack on the problem of consciousness. Wundt attempted to analyze it into its elements; Brentano focused on intentionality or the act of making conscious representations; and William James directed his attention to the flow or stream of consciousness. Yet despite the efforts of these giants, the problem of consciousness remains as elusive as ever. Perhaps there is something about the word *consciousness* itself that is problematic.

As with many everyday words, there is more than one meaning of consciousness. In fact, one can identify at least two meanings of the word. One meaning is that of being responsive to complex stimuli. Someone who has been knocked *unconscious* shows no differential responding at all to complex stimuli that are presented to him or her. The other meaning, which is the one used in the text, is that of self-awareness—especially, the subjective feeling or experience of being aware. Consciousness in this sense was originally an important topic in psychology, but it suffered a decline in the interest showed to it early in the twentieth century. This decline has been attributed to the rise of behaviorism in psychology, and to positivism in physics and logical positivism in philosophy. More recently, however, there has been an upsurge in interest in consciousness.

To understand the problem with a concept such as consciousness, it helps to take a deeper look at the principle of operationism. This principle, which was first formulated by the physicist P. W. Bridgman (1928), as discussed in chapter 5, was based on the approach taken by Einstein in constructing his special theory of relativity. Prior to Einstein, two findings that troubled physicists concerned the propagation of light. One was

167

that light waves travel through interstellar space even though no material medium for its propagation could be detected in interstellar space. The other was that no difference could be detected in the speed with which light moves past an observer whether the observer is moving toward or away from the light source, even though ingenious experiments with very precise measurements were conducted to detect such a difference. The general feeling was that if such a difference exists, it should have been detected. In order to account for these facts, most physicists accepted the idea that space is filled with an intangible substance called the *ether*. The ether was supposed to be the medium for the propagation of light waves in the same sense that water is the medium for the propagation of water waves and air the medium for the propagation of sound waves. Most physicists also accepted the idea that on the whole the ether is at rest in what was regarded to be absolute space. However, there could be local disturbances in the ether, just as there can be local disturbances in water or air. Physicists proposed a number of theories concerning how local disturbances in the ether could make it appear that light moves at the same speed regardless of whether one is moving in the same or the opposite direction in which light is moving. For example, one theory proposed that the earth pushes some of the ether along with it so that light moving in the same direction as the earth is speeded up and light moving in the opposite direction is slowed down, so that light moves by at approximately the same speed regardless of its direction. There were a number of problems with these theories, however. For example, one problem was that if the earth pushes the ether, the ether in turn should be slowing the earth down; yet all available evidence indicated that the earth continues moving at the same speed in its orbit.

Einstein discarded the concept of the ether in his special theory of relativity. He simply assumed that light can move through space with no medium being necessary for its propagation, and that its speed is always constant regardless of one's direction of movement relative to the light source. Discarding the concept of the ether, Einstein found that he had to discard two other concepts of physics that depended on it, namely, those of absolute space and absolute time. He then found that, in order to develop his theory, he had to define the concepts of *space* and *time* more precisely than had been done previously.

The principle of operationism is essentially the following rule that Bridgman abstracted from Einstein's general approach in constructing his special theory of relativity: *all concepts in science must be defined in terms of the operations used to measure them.* Such definitions are called *operational definitions.* According to Bridgman, physics was in trouble prior to Einstein because physicists had failed to provide satisfactory operational definitions for some of their major concepts. The ether, absolute space, absolute time, and absolute motion have no operational definitions because there is no way to measure them. The success of Einstein's theory lay in his having eliminated concepts that could not be operationally defined and providing more precise operational definitions for the concepts of space and time.

Psychologists who were influenced by Bridgman thus questioned whether it is possible to give a satisfactory operational definition of consciousness. In general, the answer many gave was that it is not possible and that therefore consciousness, like certain concepts in physics, is not a valid scientific concept.

HUMANISTIC APPROACH

Humanistic psychologists are generally unconcerned about the problem of operationally defining consciousness; instead, they tend to adopt a *phenomenological* approach (Tageson, 1982). By this it is meant that they emphasize the importance of understanding consciousness as an immediately given experience that needs no definition. In their view, the other approaches have severely neglected the study of consciousness and the importance of consciousness to human behavior. Humanistic psychologists generally use the term consciousness in the sense of "self-awareness." According to humanistic psychologists, consciousness (in this sense) is uniquely human. It is acquired though social experience, because in order to have self-awareness we need to be aware of how others view us. Although acquired through interaction with others, it is a totally private experience. Moreover, rather than the negative function hypothesized by Freud, humanistic psychologists believe that consciousness has a positive function: "Consciousness, instead of being the watchman over a dangerous and unpredictable lot of impulses, of which few can be permitted to see the light of day, becomes the comfortable inhabitant of a society of impulses and feelings and thoughts, which are discovered to be very satisfactorily self-governing when not fearfully guarded" (Rogers, 1961, p. 119).

Levels of Consciousness

Although humanistic psychologists generally have deep reservations about giving theoretical status or credence to an unconscious, they recognize that there are different levels of consciousness. For example, Nuttin (1953, pp. 205–210) identified three levels:

- *Psychophysiological level.* At this level one is aware of one's bodily states, for example, aches, pains, feelings, desires, and sensations.

- *Psychosocial level.* At this level one is conscious of oneself as a separate entity apart from other objects and people in one's immediate environment. One is also conscious that other people are conscious, although one cannot experience their consciousnesses. It is at this level that one may experience a sense of loneliness at being separate from other people, even though they may be physically close.
- *Transpersonal level.* At this level one somehow transcends (or "goes beyond") the level of being separate from other people and objects in one's immediate environment, and even beyond one's immediate environment. At this level one may have the feeling of moving backward and forward in time, as when one recalls past experiences or anticipates future events; or one may have the feeling of being closely in touch with someone else's consciousness, as when one experiences a sense of empathy toward another person. These transpersonal experiences can range from the quite ordinary to the extremely profound—as when one has an "out-of-body" experience or experiences a sense of "oneness with the universe." (These more profound or unusual experiences of consciousness will be discussed in chapter 13.)

Similarly, Ken Wilber (1985) sees at least five levels of consciousness, each of which involves a distinction between self and nonself. At the lowest level one distinguishes one's desirable self (called the *persona*) from undesirable aspects of oneself (called, using terminology adopted from Jung, the *shadow*). At the next level, these two selves are united and one distinguishes that self (called the *ego*) from one's body. At the third level, called the *centauric level* (after the mythical animal that was part human and part horse) one's body and mind unite, but are seen as distinct from one's surroundings including other people (called the *environment*). At this level rationality has developed. At the fourth level one recognizes that one is inseparable from his or her environment. At this level, one begins to have transpersonal experiences. Finally, at the highest level, called *unity consciousness*, one sees oneself as one with the universe. At each level there is a corresponding form of psychotherapy that is appropriate. For example, Freudian psychoanalysis is appropriate for moving from the first to the second level. This type of therapy is not appropriate for moving to the higher levels, however; rather, humanistic, existential, and transpersonal forms of psychotherapy are appropriate therapy.

Carl Rogers spoke of a "field of experience" which contains "all that is going on within the envelope of the organism at any given moment which is potentially available to awareness" (Rogers, 1959, p. 197). This field of experience includes events, perceptions, and sensations of which a person may not be aware, but could be if he or she focused on them. This field of awareness has psychological limitations (i.e., what we are willing to be aware of) and biological limitations (i.e., what we are capable of being aware of). One of the goals of therapy might be to help a person become more aware of certain things contained in their field of experience. Consciousness is also important in Rogers' approach with regard to what he called *interpersonal knowing* or *phenomenological knowing*. This is obtained through the therapeutic practice of "empathetic understanding" which is "to sense the client's private world as if it were your own, but without ever losing the 'as if' quality" (Rogers, 1961, p. 284). The therapist demonstrates and tests his or her empathetic understanding of the client through tentative confronting (e.g., "You're upset this morning"). This helps the client become more aware of the things in his or her field of experience.

Maslow (1971) emphasized the importance of consciousness with regard to the *peak experience*, which is supposed to be a heightened state of consciousness. Peak experiences are especially joyous and exciting moments, lasting from a few minutes to a few hours. They are often inspired by intense feelings of love, exposure to great art or music, or experiencing the overwhelming beauty of nature. The most powerful peak experiences have been portrayed by poets as moments of ecstasy, and by the religious as deep mystical experiences.

Toward the end of his life, Maslow began to emphasize another type of experience which he called the *plateau experience*. He stated that as he got older the number of peak experiences he had became fewer, and were replaced by another type of experience which he described as follows:

> A sort of precipitation occurred of what might be called the sedimentation or the fallout from illuminations, insights, and other life experiences that were very important—tragic experiences included. The result has been a kind of unitive consciousness which has certain advantages and certain disadvantages over the peak experiences. I can define this unitive consciousness very simply for me as the simultaneous perception of the sacred and the ordinary, or the miraculous and the rather constant and easy-without-effort sort of thing.
>
> I now perceive under the aspect of eternity and become mythic, poetic, and symbolic about ordinary things. This is the Zen experience, you know. There is nothing special, but one lives in a world of miracles all the time. There is a paradox because it is miraculous and yet it doesn't produce an autonomic burst. (Maslow, in Krippner, 1972, pp. 112–113)

Maslow was differentiating between two qualitatively different types of subjective experiences: the peak experience, which is associated with a high degree of activation of the nervous system, and the more subtle plateau experience, which is not associated with a high degree of neural activation (autonomic bursts). In his reference to Zen, Maslow was relating the latter experience with the peaceful, calming effect of Zen Buddhist meditation.

Existential Psychotherapists

As mentioned in chapter 6, humanistic psychology, broadly conceived, includes elements of existentialism and phenomenology. Hence, there is an overlap between existential psychotherapy and humanistic psychotherapy. Existential psychotherapists stress ontology (the study of existence or being) over phenomenology (the study of the experience of consciousness), although the two are intimately related. According to existential psychotherapists, the first thing that is important about human beings is that they exist for a finite time in a finite space. The roots of psychological problems can often be traced to this fact, since the finitude of existence—the fact that we exist for only a finite period and then cease to exist—can give rise to anxiety, although it can also lead to psychological growth. Given that we exist, phenomenology pertains to our perceptions of our existence in relation to the world, that is, our being in the world. As Norcross (1987) stated: "The existential approach deals with clients' immediate, unique perceptions from within their frames of references" (p. 50).

Altered States of Consciousness

Stressing the importance of understanding consciousness, humanistic psychologists are naturally interested in *altered states of consciousness* (ASCs) as they tend to believe that this knowledge could aid in our understanding of all conscious states. Tart (1969) defined an ASC as follows:

> An altered state of consciousness for a given individual is one in which he (or she) clearly feels a *qualitative shift* in his (or her) pattern of mental functioning, that is, he (or she) feels not just a quantitative shift (more or less alert, more or less visual imagery, sharper or duller, etc.) but also that some quality or qualities of his (or her) mental *processes* are different. Mental functions operate that do not operate at all ordinarily, perceptual qualities appear that have no normal counterpart. (pp. 1–2; italics in original)

Baruss (2003) suggests that ASCs may give us alternative perspectives on reality.

ASCs may be induced by: (1) normal biological processes (e.g., sleep, orgasm); (2) extreme physiological states (e.g., high fever, dehydration, food deprivation, sensory deprivation); (3) drugs (especially hallucinogenic ones such as LSD); and (4) cultural stimuli (e.g., hypnosis, meditation, religious, and other rituals). Humanistic psychologists find meditative and ritual ASCs to be particularly interesting because of their spiritual or religious associations. The two types of states can be distinguished on the basis that meditative ASCs are brought about by a detachment from the environment while ritual ASCs depend on external sensory stimulation (e.g., music, clapping, chanting, rhythmically shouting religious formulas). There is an interesting difference between Western and non-Western attitudes toward ritual ASCs. In the West, individuals who engage in them are often regarded as being abnormal and even bordering on mental illness. Just the opposite is the case in most non-Western cultures. Tart (1972) pointed out that in non-Western societies people "believe that almost every normal adult has the ability to go into a [religious] trance state [and] the adult who cannot do it is a psychological cripple" (p. 3). The normality of the ritual ASC for most cultures is indicated in a study by Bourguignon (1973) and her co-workers who found that "of a sample of 488 societies, in all parts of the world, for which we have analyzed the relevant ethnographic literature, 437, or 90% are reported to have one or more institutionalized, culturally patterned forms of [religious] altered states of consciousness" (pp. 9–11).

An interesting finding concerning ritual ASCs is that apparently they can be experienced independent of any particular belief system or commitment to any particular religious dogma. Goodman (1986) noted that particular postures, as well as auditory stimulation, are involved in ritual ASCs. Recognizing that posture can affect a number of metabolic functions, including oxygen consumption, carbon dioxide elimination, heart rate, blood flow, intestinal mobility, EEG (brain waves), and various endocrine gland secretions, she hypothesized that the ASCs may be induced purely by physiological processes apart from any initial religious significance. To test this hypothesis, she requested subjects to assume postures used in various cultures when inducing ASCs. The postures came from East Indian, Native Australian, and Native American cultures. For example, in the "singing shaman" posture from the Northwest coast of the U.S., the feet are straight forward, the knees are loose, the head is slightly tilted toward the back, and the hands are held loosely in a fist and joined above the heart. One posture was even taken from a stone-age painting found in Lascaux Cave. When the participants assumed the postures, Goodman provided rhythmic auditory stimulation (which she called *auditory driving*) by shaking a gourd rattle. In some cases, the participants hummed as well.

Despite the fact that none of the participants had any prior knowledge of the religious significance of the postures, most of them experienced ASCs similar to those experienced by practitioners of the various religions represented. Some of the experiences reported included seeing colors (blue, yellow, and orange were common), seeing spinning objects (e.g., a church steeple), feeling that one is spinning, slowly rotating, or floating freely at will, feeling warm and dry sensations in the head, perceiving everything to be bright or perfectly still, feeling strong stimulation in the head as though everything were streaming into it, having a feeling of "piercing a veil and gaining understanding," seeing costumed dancers, feeling that one is dancing, feeling afraid but not knowing of what, feeling being looked at by repulsive eyes and being afraid, feeling that one is sitting in a large bottle, feeling one's body growing very large or very small, and feeling energy whelming up in the body and flowing outward. Many of the experiences were reported as being beautiful.

The posture depicted on the stone-age cave painting produced surprising results because they seemed at variance with the restful appearance of the pose. Four of the more elaborate descriptions of the effects of this posture were as follows:

- I felt a wave coming from the extremities and getting dammed up in my chest. I struggled desperately, I knew it had to pass on to my head, through my neck. Then there was this frightful pressure in my head, and I could not feel the rest of my body, only my head. A second rattle sound appeared, which turned into circular motion. Suddenly I saw the energy spiraling out from the top of my head.

- There was a tremendous wave of heat that moved from my feet to my head. When it arrived there, my head turned into a mountain peak. That peak kept growing higher and higher, giving me the feeling that I was the highest mountain peak in the world.

- The entire world stretched out before me, infinitely far and limitless, and I could see it all. Not only the earth was without boundaries, but also the sky, the entire cosmos, as it opened up above me. Then I could feel the heat no longer, and from the tip of the mountain, I fell into this infinity. A soft wind carried me through the eternal expanse. There was no distance, neither toward the horizon nor into the depth. I could allow the wind to waft me where I pleased, and it was exceedingly beautiful.

- I received power from my tense left arm. There was a feeling of effort, but not torture, milky white, and everything was concentrated in my abdomen. There was excitement, but also a letting go, and suddenly I knew that these were precisely the same emotions as when I gave birth. All of a sudden the pressure in my abdomen was gone and I went up and up to a mountain top. It was fabulous, because giving birth was such an experience for me that I thought I should have a hundred children, just to be able to go through that over and over again, and now, in this way, I was able to experience the birth of a child once more. (Goodman, 1986, pp. 104–105)

To control for the possibility that the ASCs obtained in the study were simply the result of suggestion, the participants were asked to assume a control posture (resembling the conventional ballroom dance position). Despite the fact that the participants were not told that this was not a posture used in a religious ritual, no one achieved a trance using it. It would seem that various cultures have, probably over many centuries of trying out different postures, hit upon just those postures that are most effective in producing ASCs.

PSYCHODYNAMIC APPROACH

As mentioned previously, consciousness is accorded less prominence than the unconscious in psychodynamic theories. It would be incorrect, however, to say that consciousness has no importance in these theories. The opposite is true, as indicated by the following consideration of two major psychodynamic theories.

Role of Consciousness in Psychoanalysis

Consciousness is the seat of the ego, and the ego is important in protecting the individual from punishing consequences in the external environment and in resolving conflicts between the id and the superego. Accordingly, consciousness plays an important role in the treatment of neurotic disorders. Consider, for example, the role of consciousness in the treatment of a difficulty stemming from an unresolved Oedipus complex. According to Freud, every little boy has an unconscious urge (stemming from the id) to kill his father and have sex with his mother. The superego, however, does not permit this wish to surface in consciousness. If the father has been extremely punitive to the child, the superego—being the internalization of the father's discipline—will be extremely strong relative to the id. To prevent the prohibited urge from being carried out, the superego may produce various sorts of neurotic, or maladaptive, symptoms. For example, the superego may produce a hysterical paralysis of the dominant arm (i.e., a paralysis with no known physiological basis). It is as though the individual reasons, "I cannot kill my father if my dominant arm is paralyzed." This reasoning occurs in the unconscious, which is not as rational as consciousness is, and therefore does not distinguish between the urge to do something and the actual commission of the act. Therefore, the only way to cure the neurosis is for the urge to be brought into consciousness where the ego can deal with it in a rational manner. Psychoanalysis is the technique Freud developed for bringing repressed material into consciousness so that conflicts between the id and superego can be resolved by the ego in a way that enables the individual to adapt functionally to society. Having the client free-associate in the presence of the therapist, who provides a nonpunitive audience, can help bring such material into consciousness. The therapist also helps the client interpret the material he or she brings to consciousness, including material from dreams, which are considered especially important in revealing the conflicts occurring in the client's unconscious. When this material is made fully conscious, so the theory goes, the ego will resolve the conflicts in such a way that the individual will not need his or her neurotic defenses, and will be cured. As a by-product, the individual will gain a greater understanding of the factors determining his or her behavior. This is called *insight*. When insight occurs, it can be like Maslow's "peak experience," that is, a heightened state of consciousness. Thus, although the emphasis in psychoanalysis is on the unconscious, it is fair to say that the goal of psychoanalysis is to enhance consciousness by making what was unconscious about oneself conscious.

The Role of Consciousness in Jungian Psychology

As in Freudian psychology, the unconscious is the focus of Jungian psychology. However, in Jungian psychology the unconscious is not the seat of repressed desires. Instead it is the basis of the individual's potential for growth, in the sense of obtaining balance among all the sides of the individual's personality. When the individual becomes too weighted on one particular side of the personality, the unconscious sends messages in the form of symbols that show up in dreams. Hence, dreams are not, as in Freudian theory, the unconscious' way of trying to hide something from us. On the contrary, in Jungian theory dreams are the unconscious' way of trying to tell us something. In Jungian therapy the interpretation of the client's dreams is important in helping the client to change in a positive way. Thus, both Freudian and Jungian therapy focus on enhancing self-knowledge or consciousness of oneself.

COGNITIVE APPROACH

In general, cognitivists have tended to assume that any adequate simulation of mind will also simulate whatever subjective states are correlated with the mind—including consciousness. Recently, interest by cognitivists in understanding and explaining consciousness has grown. For example, Howard Gardner observed: "For centuries humanists have cherished consciousness as their domain. . . . For most of the last century, behavioral scientists eschewed that territory. But in recent years, cognitivists and neuroscientists have begun at least an assault on the fortress" (Gardner, 2001).

Philosophical Considerations

Philosophers have provided a number of basic concepts in the cognitive scientific approach to consciousness. Foremost among these is the concept of *qualia* (plural of *quale*). A quale is something one is directly conscious of, such as an experience of seeing the color red, having a toothache, hearing a note of music. A closely related term is *raw feel*, which is basically an unanalyzed feeling or sensation. For example, when I glance at my brown coffee mug I have a sensation of brownness. Another closely related concept is *something it is like*. For example, there is something it is like to have your experience of red. My experience of red may be quite different from yours; in fact, logically speaking, my experience of red could be like your experience of green and vice versa. Nevertheless, we may assume that my experience of red is something like your experience of red. More generally, we may say there is something it is like to be you, or to be me, or to be any human. We may also assume that there is something it is like to be a dog, or a cat, or a bat—although it is difficult for us to imagine what it would in fact be like to be a bat due to its quite different sensory apparatus, locomotion method, etc. (Nagel, 1974). There are also entities for which there is nothing it is like. There is, for example, nothing it is like to be a car. Hypothetically, there could be people who appear totally normal in every respect but whom it is nothing to be like. Some philosophers use the term *zombie* to describe these hypothetical individuals, and a certain amount of philosophical literature is devoted to answering the question of whether zombies are genuinely possible.

Cognitivists tend to shy away from that question because there seems to be no answer to it experimentally. However, there are some related questions that some cognitivists believe may be eventually answerable with the development of appropriate experimental techniques and a valid theoretical model. One of these questions concerns whether it is possible to devise a computer algorithm that produces qualia; that is, could a computer be made to be conscious, in which case (unlike the case with something like a car) there would be something it is like to be that computer. Another question concerns whether it is possible to discover what it is that produces qualia, or consciousness, in humans (and other animals, assuming that they also have qualia). Much of this effort has focused on discovering neural correlates of consciousness. Thus, the cognitive approach to consciousness has focused on discovering what produces it naturally and how, or whether, it can be produced artificially.

Artificial Intelligence

A branch of computer science spearheads the search for a means of developing artificial intelligence (AI) in the form of a computer program that duplicates or simulates human intelligence or mentality. This field of computer science is related to cognitive psychology in that both fields search for an algorithm that, when programmed into a computer, will simulate thinking. The field of cognitive psychology searches for the algorithm that is used by the human brain, whereas the field of AI searches for any algorithm that simulates thinking, whether it is the one the human brain uses or not. For an analogy illustrating the differences between the two fields, consider a biologist attempting to determine how birds fly versus the Wright brothers attempting to develop a flying machine regardless of whether it resembles a bird or not. Although airplanes and birds fly in very different ways, both use similar physical principles in flying. By analogy, the attempt to build an intelligent machine may not produce a machine that thinks exactly like a human, but may give us some insight into how humans do think. One of the most intriguing questions about such a machine, were it to be developed, is whether it would be conscious. It is doubtful, however, that there would be any empirical way to answer this question.

The AI Approach

Many experts in AI have adopted an *operational definition* of *intelligent* machine that might be a suitable operational definition of *conscious machine*. This definition is known as the *Turing test*, named after Alan Turing (1950), the pioneering computer scientist who first proposed it. (Turing called it the *imitation game*, because it involves programming a computer to imitate a human.) The Turing test consists of having a person in one room converse by typed communication with either another person or a machine in another room, where the person in the first room cannot see into the second room. If the person in the first room cannot tell whether he or she is conversing with a human or a machine, then the machine is deemed to be intelligent.

Criticisms of the Strong AI Approach to Consciousness

If the specification of certain atmospheric conditions is put into a weather-predicting computer program, and the program predicts rain, one does not expect the computer to output real rain. The situation is a bit different with regard to AI. Many cognitivists believe that a program that simulates human intelligence would in fact be conscious. They believe that consciousness, unlike weather, is in essence a computational process. The view that a program that simulates a mind will produce subjective conscious states is called *strong AI*, to differentiate it from the view that such a program would no more be conscious than that a program that simulates weather patterns produces real weather.

Chinese Room Argument. The philosopher John Searle (who coined the term strong AI) devised a famous critique of the Turing test as a means of demonstrating understanding and consciousness by a computer (Searle, 1980, 1992). The argument is as follows. Suppose you put a person who has no knowledge of Chinese into a room with a comprehensive book of rules for responding with appropriate strings of Chinese characters to every conceivable statement or question that can be written in Chinese characters. (Of course this rulebook would have to be absolutely enormous, so it would be impractical actually to do this, but since it would be finite, it would in principle be possible to do it.) The task of the person in the room would be simply to look at Chinese characters written on pieces of paper passed into the room through a slot in the door, look in the rulebook for a set of Chinese characters that would constitute an appropriate response, copy this set onto a slip of paper, and pass this piece of paper back through the slot in the door. The effect of this procedure would be that (except for the extreme slowness of the replies, which is not considered important to the argument) a Chinese-speaking person on the other side of the door passing statements and questions written in Chinese characters into the room would be unable to tell that the person in the room doesn't understand Chinese. Yet the person in the room would in fact have no understanding of—hence, no consciousness of—the content of the conversation, or even necessarily that he or she is carrying on a conversation at all. Similarly, Searle argues, a computer that passes the Turing test would simply be acting according to a set of rules of which it has no understanding, and thus have no consciousness at all.

Searle's Chinese Room Argument continues to have a profound effect on cognitive science decades after he first published it, even though most cognitivists disagree with it. In an edited book devoted entirely to the argument, Preston (2002) wrote, "there is (still) little agreement about how the argument goes wrong, or about what should be the exact response on behalf of computational science and strong AI" (p. 47).

Searle's definitional problem.   Searle (1992) has also made a more general argument against the brain as a computer and the mind as a program that runs on that computer. There are several aspects to his argument, but the central point is that a computer and its program must, by definition, have a user. Who is the user of the computer and computer program that is said to be the brain and mind, respectively? If it is said the person who possesses that particular brain and mind is the user, then we have to imagine that the person is somehow distinct from his/her brain and mind. That is, according to Searle, computers and their programs are not objects with the same logical status as stones, trees, stars, and brains. These can exist in the absence of people. Instead, computers and their programs are logically more like chairs, bathtubs, diving boards, and pets. The names of these objects imply their functions, and these functions are meaningless in the absence of anyone to carry them out.

To make the point another way, note that computers are frequently said to "process information." Now, what is information? It is meaningful statements or data coded into the computer as patterns of electricity. (For example, the information on a computer screen is simply patterns of electricity produced by corresponding patterns of electricity inside the computer.) But without someone to interpret those patterns of electricity, they would remain just that—patterns of electricity. A user is required to extract meaning from the patterns of electricity and, hence, turn them into information. Thus, without a user, what we would call a computer is not an information processor, but simply a box with certain patterns of electricity in it, and hence not a computer.

Where does all this leave consciousness? According to Searle, consciousness exists, but not as a computer program in the brain. Rather, it is a subjective experience produced by the brain as a biological organ. A computer program might be able to simulate brain functions, even those that give rise to the experience of consciousness—but it would not actually be conscious, any more than a computer simulation of weather patterns would produce real hurricanes or snowstorms.

Consciousness and quanta. A number of theorists have argued that consciousness cannot be explained by ordinary mechanistic principles, such as those by which a modern computer operates. For example, the mathematical physicist Roger Penrose (1989, 1994, 2002) has argued that consciousness cannot be generated by any computer operating according to the laws of physics as we understand them today. According to Penrose, the brain must be operating according to the laws of quantum physics—that is, the laws of subatomic particles. He bases his argument on a famous proof by the mathematician Gödel, independently discovered by Turing, demonstrating that any mathematical system at least as complex as simple arithmetic contains truths that cannot be proved. Yet, presumably, we humans can intuit these truths; therefore, we must be using some principle outside the realm of computation to accomplish this. That is, these intuitions supposedly involve an inferential leap from premises that could not be used to calculate the conclusion in an algorithmic procedure. Hence, Penrose agrees with Searle that the human brain cannot be a mere computer, as we understand that term today (e.g., see Penrose, 2002). He also agrees that consciousness is a biological process. He differs from Searle and the vast majority of other cognitivists in that he thinks that the biology of the brain must somehow reach into the quanta level in order for the phenomenon of consciousness to emerge.

As Casti (2000, p. 161) pointed out, Turing anticipated Penrose's arguments regarding the noncomputability of consciousness—and similar ones made earlier by the philosopher John Lucas (1961)—and rejected them. For arguments, pro and con, see Hodgson (1991, pp. 154–156.)

Neural Networks

So far, we have considered the familiar type of computer in which one inserts a program that is, essentially, a set of rules. There is, however, another type of computer that is relevant to the above arguments against the idea of mind, intelligence, or consciousness being a computer algorithm. This type of computer consists of several kinds of elements that are connected together. There are inputs, which are connected to intermediate elements, which are connected to other intermediate elements in a layered fashion, with the last layer of intermediate elements being connected to output elements. Inputting information into the input elements causes current to travel through the intermediate elements, depending on how they are connected to each other, until finally the last layer of intermediate elements transfers the current to the output elements. The input and output can be a keyboard and a computer screen, just as in a standard computer. Unlike a standard computer, however, what determines the output for a given pattern of input are the strengths of the connections, called the connection weights, between the intermediate elements. Note the similarity of this type of computer with the kinds of connections that seem to exist in the nervous system, in which sensory organs are attached to neurons (nerve cells), which are attached to other nerve cells, which are attached to still other nerve cells, through an extremely complex chain of connections leading through the brain and eventually to the muscles and glands. Because of its similarity to the nervous system, this type of computer is called a *neural net* or *network*.

In addition to the way in which their components are organized, neural networks are quite different from standard computers and quite similar to the nervous system in another way. They are programmed in a quite different way from that in which a standard computer is programmed, yet similar to how the nervous system presumably is programmed. Essentially, one programs them by altering the weightings of the connections (the connection weights) between the intermediate elements. There are two general methods for doing this: (1) if two elements are activated at the same time, increment the weight of the connection between them; (2) provide feedback to the system that causes it to adjust its connection weights according to how close it is to a desired output with respect to some specific input. In other words, unlike ordinary computers, neural nets learn—and the way to program them is to teach them. For example, a neural net might be given the problem of attaching the correct names to pictures of particular faces shown in various orientations. The teaching process would consist of providing feedback for responses to many orientations of different faces. Typically, after many trials the neural net would with above-chance accuracy attach the correct name to faces it has practiced on shown in completely new orientations. Interestingly, since the programming is indirect, the only way to find out how the connection weights have changed is by having the neural net print out the states of all its components—an advantage that one does not have with an actual nervous system.

The view that neural nets can explain the properties of mind, including consciousness, is called connectionism. Neural nets have a number of attractive features as a plausible model of the mind or the way the brain works. For example, they are biologically plausible because the connections at least superficially resemble the way that neurons connect; they appear to be good candidates for modeling animal and human learning because they learn gradually when being trained and show gradual degradation of learning when damaged or when feedback no longer occurs; and they generally show high computational speeds for pattern recognition tasks. However, there are criticisms of neural nets. Many cognitivists find this approach too behavioristic for their tastes, since neural nets learn by association. According to these cognitivists, the mind is primarily a symbol processor and any approach that ignores or downplays this aspect must be wrong. In addition, there is nothing in a neural net that seems to correspond to thinking, as we understand it. The failing of either standard computers or neural networks to model the mind adequately has led some to propose that the correct model might be one that combines these two types of computation (e.g., Marcus, 2001).

Interestingly, the lack of obvious symbols in neural networks allows them to escape Searle's criticisms of standard computer models of mind. He stated:

> Among their other merits, at least some connectionist models show how a system might convert a meaningful input into a meaningful output without any rules, principles, inferences, or other sorts of meaningful phenomena in between. This is not to say that existing connectionist models are correct—perhaps they are all wrong. But it is to say that they are not all obviously false or incoherent in the way that the traditional cognitivist models that violate the connection principle are. (Searle, 1992, pp. 246–247)

Neural nets do not, however, answer the criticism of those who subscribe to a quantum mechanics interpretation of mind. Penrose, for example, argues—somewhat ironically—that standard computer programming can model precisely any neural net (in fact, that is how neural nets are studied). The only difference is that the speed of an actual neural net would be much faster, because neural nets engage in simultaneous processing across their elements (i.e., parallel distributed processing) whereas a standard computer proceeds in a step-by-step fashion. Logically, however, there is no difference; Gödel has established that consistent mathematical or logical systems of the complexity of arithmetic or greater hold truths that no neural net can fathom but, presumably, any normal human with the proper training and motivation can.

The Homunculus and the Cartesian Theater

There is an explanation of consciousness that goes back at least as far as Descartes. Recall that for Descartes the soul or mind, through contact with the pineal gland deep within the brain, receives input from the senses and controls bodily movements. For Descartes, the soul (or mind) is the seat of consciousness and the pineal gland is the seat of the soul. Today this theory still exists, but in a modified form. It is no longer scientifically acceptable to say that it is the soul that receives input from the environment and controls behavior. Rather, these functions are now considered to occur in some part of the brain, although exactly what part is unknown. Further, in this revised version of Descartes' theory, characteristics belonging to a conscious person, that is, consciousness, are ascribed to this unknown part of the brain.

Much as it was for Descartes, it is as though there is a little person inside the brain who views the external world on a screen and controls the actions of the body like the operator of a vehicle. Skinner (1963, p. 191) in his critique of mentalism referred to this hypothetical inner person as the *homunculus* (literally, little man); and the philosopher Gilbert Ryle (1949/1990), in his similar critique of the concept of mind, referred to this inner person as the *ghost in the machine*, and the hypothetical space in which this inner person supposedly views images or representations from the world as the *Cartesian theater*. Both Skinner and Ryle argued that using an inner person as an explanatory concept explains nothing until you explain the inner person, which is difficult to do unless you postulate an inner person inside the inner person, and so on in an infinite regress that ends up explaining nothing. The implication is that it is pointless and even counterproductive to postulate an inner person (or a soul, or mind) to begin with.

There are many cognitive theories that oppose the Cartesian view of consciousness. Here we focus on two of these.

Dennett's Explanation of Consciousness

Following Gilbert Ryle, whose work strongly influenced him, the philosopher Daniel Dennett (1991) attacked the idea of the homunculus in explaining consciousness. The homunculus idea implies that any event that impinges on consciousness does so at a particular point in time, that is, that it makes sense to ask at what point in time you became aware of a specific event. However, it appears that awareness of an event does not take place at a single point in time. One way to demonstrate this experimentally is as follows. If a person in a dark room views two lights, fairly close together, flashed on and off consecutively, it will appear to him/her that a single light has moved continuously from the location of the first light to that of the second. (This effect, called the *phi phenomenon*, is familiar to everyone who has observed signs made of electric lights that appear to move, and is also responsible for the appearance of motion on movie and TV screens.) However, if the first light is red and the second green, the perceived single, continuously moving light will appear to change from red to green midway between the red and green lights—even on the subject's first exposure to this situation. Dennett takes the fact that it is possible for the subject to be aware of the light changing to green before being aware of the green light itself as evidence that consciousness is not a unitary experience.

To experience a related, although less dramatic, effect, simply touch the tip of your nose with the index finger of either hand. Note that you do not feel the touch on your nose before you feel the touch on your finger. Instead, the two sensations appear to occur simultaneously. Yet because nerve impulses from the nose travel a shorter route to the brain than nerve impulses from the fingertip, the former reach the brain sooner than the latter. Somehow the brain treats two events that occur sequentially as simultaneous. Similar to the way that the light is seen as changing from red to green before green is actually seen, the touches are felt to be simultaneous even though impulses from the nose reach the brain before the impulses from the finger do.

A simple way to understand these effects is by the *Pandemonium* analogy. This analogy is based on the mythical Pandemonium, which was a place inhabited by numerous shouting demons. In the analogy, the system—that is, the computer program that is the mind—is composed of shouting demons, and what gets shouted the loudest is what has the most effect on the system. According to Dennett these demons are not homunculi in the sense he and others have criticized. Each only has one function that does not have to be explained by another demon inside of it. Each homunculus performs a simpler function than the one it and its colleagues are being invoked to explain. Some demons might have the function of detecting a specific color, and others that of detecting motion. What gets shouted the loudest is determined by the number of demons shouting it and the weights of those demons. For example, if a red light turns on somewhere in a person's environment, some of the color-detecting demons in that person's brain may begin shouting, "red!" Other demons may be shouting the names of other colors, but many more will likely be yelling, "red." Thus, the loudest shouting will be, "red," and so the person will think, and perhaps also say, "red."

Now let's apply this to the problem of being conscious of the red light changing to green midway between the positions of the red and green lights. When the red light goes on, a number of red-detecting demons begin shouting, "red!" and then when the green light goes on, a number of green-detecting demons begin shouting, "green!" In addition, when the green light goes on, a number of motion-detecting demons begin shouting, "moving light!" and a number of change-detecting demons begin shouting, "change to green!" Moreover, other demons—those in charge of assigning times to events—begin shouting times to assign to the four events (a, b, c, and d) being shouted by the preceding demons. The time-assigning demons are weighted such that they assign a time for the color change that is intermediate to the times assigned to seeing the red and green lights in their actual position. The totality of the shouting demons constitutes the awareness or consciousness of the events in the sequence.

Dennett calls his theory a multiple-drafts model. The analogy is with a writer who is constantly revising a manuscript, or a painter who keeps making changes to a canvas. At no one point in time can we say precisely what the writer has written or what the painter has painted. Similarly, at no one point in time does it make sense to ask exactly what a person is conscious of at that point in time. Stimuli act upon sense organs and the resulting information is transmitted to the brain; however, at no time does the information from the sense organs end up at a central location to be viewed by a homunculus in a Cartesian theater. To quote Dennett:

> These spatially and temporally distributed content-fixations in the brain are precisely locatable in space and time, but their onsets do not mark the onset of consciousness of their content. It is always an open question whether any particular content thus discriminated will eventually appear as an element in conscious experience, and it is a confusion . . . to ask when it becomes conscious. These distributed content-discriminations yield, over the course of time, something rather like a narrative stream or sequence, which can be thought of as subject to continuous editing by many processes distributed around in the brain, and continuing indefinitely into the future. This stream of contents is only rather like a narrative because of its multiplicity; at any point in time there are multiple "drafts" of narrative fragments at various stages of editing in various places in the brain. (Dennett, 1991, p. 113)

Dennett's account has been criticized (e.g., Searle, 1992) as explaining away consciousness, rather than explaining it. In other words, his account seems to leave no room for the actual subjective experience of consciousness as a unitary experience.

O'Regan and Noë's Sensorimotor Theory

Focusing on visual consciousness, the psychologist-philosopher team of J. Kevin O'Regan and Alva Noë (2001) proposed a theory of consciousness that is similar to Dennett's. O'Regan and Noë present their theory as an alternative to the representational theory of visual consciousness, which holds that the mind represents the environment by making pictures of it. The function of these pictures, according to the representational theory, is to allow us to interact effectively with the environment. Thus, according to the theory, when we see a scene a representation of that scene is contained in memory long enough to allow us to interact effectively with the objects in the scene. O'Regan and Noë marshal their attack first by arguing that the representational theory is a version of the homunculus theory because, if there are representations in the mind, in order to serve their supposed function they must be viewed. Whatever it is that views them must be, by definition, a homunculus. In addition, they describe phenomena that tend to show that the representational theory cannot be correct.

One phenomenon that O'Regan and Noë emphasize as particularly supportive of their position is called change blindness, which refers to a person not noticing a change in a scene that he or she is viewing. Normally if a person is viewing a scene (e.g., a picture on a computer screen) and a drastic change occurs, such as a car disappearing or changing colors, the person will immediately be conscious of this. According to the representational theory, this is because the person compares the scene with the representation of it in his or her mind and notes the discrepancy. According to O'Regan and Noë, however, the phenomenon of change blindness indicates that this explanation is incorrect. Change blindness can be demonstrated in a normal person by introducing the change—the car disappearing, or appearing, or changing colors—at the instant that some transient event, such as a light flash or an eye-movement, called a saccade, occurs. Changes in the scene may occur repeatedly and, as long as a transient event occurs at the same time, the person generally will be totally unaware of them. Even more dramatically, an unknowing subject talking to a stranger who is suddenly replaced by another person while the subject is momentarily distracted may be completely unaware that he or she is now talking to a different person (Simons & Levin, 1998).

O'Regan and Noë maintain that if the representational theory is correct, change blindness should not occur because the mental representation of the scene should not be affected by the transient event that causes change blindness. Their theory, which they believe accounts for change blindness and other phenomena that the representational theory does not account for, is that vision (and, by inference, other senses) should not be viewed as passive reception of stimuli. Vision, or seeing, is a behavior. It is not just sensory; it is motor as well, which is why O'Regan and Noë call their theory of visual consciousness a sensorimotor theory. We explore our environment with vision similar to the way in which we explore it with touch, although we tend not to think of vision that way. There are a number of reasons that we do not typically think of vision as an exploratory behavior like touch. One reason might be that we cannot see our eyes move. More importantly, when we view a scene it seems to us that we are seeing the whole scene all at once. However, as the phenomenon of change blindness shows, this is not the case. The reason that it seems to us that we are viewing the whole scene at once, according to O'Regan and Noë, is that we know that at any instant we can view any part of the scene that we want. We do not need a mental representation; we do not need an internal picture, or memory, of the scene. O'Regan and Noë use the

expression "world as outside memory" to indicate this; in other words, to have an internal representation would be unnecessary—and evolution tends not to develop unnecessary functions. According to O'Regan and Noë, as we explore our environment visually we typically notice changes in our environment not because we compare what we are seeing with a picture in our minds, but because a change in the environment attracts our attention to it. However, if a transient distracts us at the time of a change, or masks the change, then we are unaware—and typically remain unaware—of the change until, usually much to our surprise, someone points it out to us.

Another example of evidence supporting O'Regan and Noë's sensorimotor theory is that subjects who are asked to locate various items in a scene show little or no improvement as the task is repeated with the same scene but different items. If the individual were making a mental representation of the scene, one would expect the representation to become stronger with prolonged exposure to the scene, and hence that finding successive items would become easier. O'Regan and Noë's sensorimotor theory, however, correctly (it appears) predicts that individuals will explore and attend to only as much of the scene as necessary to perform each specific location task requested of them. Interestingly, if individuals are asked to memorize the scene before the locating task, however, they do better than if they do not memorize the scene beforehand. Apparently people can form images that are like what internal representations are thought to be, but this takes effort and does not happen automatically. Perhaps the fact that we can form mental images, in addition to the fact that we use the "world as memory," gives us the strong sense that we have internal representations of the world even though, at least according to O'Regan and Noë, this is not the case.

It has been argued that the phenomenon of change blindness does not disprove the existence of mental representations, as maintained by O'Regan and Noë. The representations may be there, but the individual may simply not attend to them or may not compare the before-change and after-change representations that would enable him or her to detect the change (e.g., Simons & Ambinder, 2005). However, this objection leads us to the homunculus problem once again; that is, who is it who is looking at the representations and attending or failing to attend to them, or comparing or failing to compare them?

But what does all this have to do with consciousness? What it has to do with consciousness is that O'Regan and Noë equate consciousness with the sensorimotor interaction with the environment. O'Regan and Noë believe that their theory solves some of the thorny philosophical problems about consciousness mentioned earlier. For example, the reason, according to O'Regan and Noë, that sensations from different sensory modalities appear qualitatively different to us is that they represent qualitatively different ways of interacting with the environment. The reason certain sensations from different sensory modalities are experienced as unitary (the binding problem) is because they occur together. That is, it is our tendency to associate things that occur together that binds them together.

One point critics of the theory make is that it does not seem to account for our being conscious of our dreams, or the fact that people who are totally (or almost totally) paralyzed appear to be just as conscious as individuals who are awake and in possession of all their faculties. O'Regan and Noë answer these points by asserting that knowledge of the sensorimotor contingencies—that is, that certain behavior will result in certain kinds of sensations—is sufficient for consciousness.

Like Dennett, O'Regan and Noë have been criticized for explaining away consciousness rather than actually explaining it. Interestingly, some have criticized Dennett's multiple-drafts theory and O'Regan and Noë's sensorimotor theory as being behavioristic. They have been considered to be behavioristic because they have denied the existence of mental representations and because they have focused on input–output (sense data–behavior) relations as defining criteria for consciousness. These theorists have denied both charges. With regard to the charge of explaining away consciousness, they have stated that what they have described is what consciousness is. If the critics can't see this, they say, it is simply because the critics are bound to traditional views of consciousness that impede the solution of the problem. With regard to the charge of being behavioristic, they reply that their theories are about more than simply sensation–behavior (stimulus–response). Internal events and states are important in their theories. In denying the charge of behaviorism, Dennett and O'Regan and Noë may be thinking of EO rather than radical behaviorism, which does take private events into account.

BEHAVIORAL APPROACH

Most behaviorists attempt to follow a rigorous operational approach. Accordingly, the concepts used by behaviorists, such as the concepts discussed in chapter 7, have strict operational definitions. Consider, for example, the term *positive reinforcer*. The operation one uses to determine whether a stimulus is a positive reinforcer is simply to present it following a response and note whether the response increases in frequency. If the frequency of the response does increase, the stimulus is a positive reinforcer; if the frequency does not increase, the stimulus is not a positive reinforcer.

Behavioristic Ways of Dealing with Consciousness

There are two general ways in which behaviorism can deal with the concept of consciousness: (1) decree that there is no satisfactory way in which the concept can be operationally defined, and that therefore it is not a valid subject for scientific study; or (2) attempt to define the term operationally. The first approach is the one methodological behaviorists typically adopt. Methodological behaviorists have been strongly influenced by logical positivism, and accordingly maintain that all scientific terms must denote publicly observable events. (Recall that logical positivists maintained that in order for a statement to be meaningful, the terms in it must be defined on the basis of sense impressions that could be had by more than one person.) The experience of consciousness is private—a person cannot experience someone else's consciousness. Therefore, a methodological behaviorist would probably say that consciousness cannot be studied scientifically.

Behavioral Definitions of Consciousness

Radical behaviorists do not accept the view that there are private events that cannot be dealt with scientifically. The world within the skin is just as real to them as the world outside the skin—it is simply less accessible. One can observe one's own private events such as one's own covert verbal behavior and images. The fact that others cannot does not make these events any less real, or any less worthy of scientific study. They are behaviors in the same sense that publicly observable behaviors are, and should be treated as such.

Although radical behaviorists thus do not accept logical positivism (or at least the version that requires consensual validation), they do accept the operationist principle that scientific concepts must be defined in terms of the operations used to observe them. How, then, might a radical behaviorist operationally define *consciousness*? Prior to answering this, we must consider how a radical behaviorist would operationally define *operational definition*. The operational definition of *operational definition* generally used by radical behaviorists is as follows. To operationally define any word (e.g., *consciousness*") used in common speech, first regard the word as a response that is emitted under certain stimulus conditions and then identify those stimulus conditions. In other words, the operational definition of a term is the stimulus conditions that control the emission of the term. For example, an operational definition of the word *chair* is the set of all stimulus objects in the presence of which a person is likely to emit the verbal response, "chair," when asked, "What is this?"

Let us now see how this definition is applied to the term *consciousness* from a radical-behaviorist point of view. The humanistic psychologist Joseph Nuttin's three levels of consciousness in this sense were summarized earlier. From a radical-behaviorist point of view, these three levels can be described as follows. The psychophysiological level is verbal responding to one's own physiological states. We do not do this very accurately because other people do not typically have direct access to our physiological states, and therefore cannot reinforce us for responding accurately to them (although they can provide approximately accurate reinforcement on the basis of indirect evidence). The psychosocial level is our verbal responding to our own behavior and the way in which it is being controlled by both the social and nonsocial aspects of the environment. The transpersonal level can be either, or both, of two things: (1) verbal behavior describing one's own responding to certain abstract verbal stimuli such as "the universe," "love," "history," "time"; (2) a change in one's verbal responding to one's own behavior due to a temporary change in the control exerted by the environment on behavior. Such a change can be produced by variables ranging from drugs to meditation, and is what is meant by an "altered state of consciousness."

Essentially, it can be seen that consciousness in the sense of self-awareness is, to a radical behaviorist, verbal responding under the control of one's own behavior. The subjective experience of consciousness is the private stimulation produced by our verbal responding to our own behavior. Looked at in this way, it can be seen why consciousness can appear to be a very profound thing: not only can one respond verbally to one's own behavior, one can respond verbally to one's verbal responding to one's own behavior, and so on—perhaps ad infinitum. (A crude analogy might be looking in a mirror at oneself looking in a mirror.)

It should be noted that this definition would rule out self-awareness by animals, because they do not have verbal behavior. A possible exception might be the great apes, which may be able to learn some rudimentary verbal behavior.

Consciousness as Self-Awareness

Thus, radical behaviorists would agree with humanists in identifying consciousness, at the human level, with self-awareness. Skinner put it this way:

> I believe that all nonhuman species are conscious in the sense [that] . . . [t]hey see, feel, hear, and so on, but they do not observe that they are doing so. . . . [A] verbal community asks the individual such questions

as, "What are you doing?," "Do you see that?," "What are you going to
do?," and so on, and thus supplies the contingencies for the self-descrip-
tive behavior that is at the heart of a different kind of awareness of consciousness. (Skinner, 1988d, p. 306)

It is interesting to note that despite his frequent references to consciousness in humans and other animals, such as previously noted, Skinner is commonly misinterpreted as denying the existence of consciousness. Just to take one of many possible examples in the literature, consider
the following from a popular book that purports to examine the minds
of monkeys:

> In the twentieth century, the descendants of the radical empiricists, the
> behaviorists, have taken a still more extreme stance (than the view that
> behavior is the product of associations between sensory inputs in a pas-
> sive mind), arguing in some cases that mental processes like thought and
> consciousness do not exist at all but have been mistakenly inferred from
> behavior (e.g., Skinner, 1957, 1974). (Cheney & Seyfarth, 1990, p. 7)

Consciousness According to Relational Frame Theory

Skinner's views have been elaborated in a theory developed by Steven
C. Hayes and his colleagues called relational frame theory (Hayes,
Barnes-Holmes, & Roche, 2001). According to this theory, through language individuals learn frames as operant responses and as discriminative stimuli. There are a vast number of frames in any human language. A
simple example of one of the countless frames in English is " _____ is
walking with _____." An individual learns from early childhood to
appropriately fill in the blanks of the appropriate frame or frames for each
situation (e.g., "*Tom* is talking to *Mary*," "*Mom* is talking to *Dad*," . . .). As
a result of learning many frames, an individual eventually appropriately
puts first person pronouns into appropriate frames (e.g., "*Dad* is talking
to *me*"). Consciousness or self-awareness to a large extent consists in
appropriately filling frames with first person pronouns, and responding
appropriately to frames that contain second person pronouns (e.g., *you*;
Barnes-Holmes, Hayes, & Dymond, 2001, pp. 130–131). (This suggests
that aphasia reduces a person's consciousness when it deprives him or
her of the ability to generate such frames. Unfortunately, there appears
to be no way at present to test this consequence of the theory.)

Unlike psychodynamic theorists, radical behaviorists do not reify consciousness—that is, they do not ascribe to it the status of a thing. It is not
a place where something happens. In this regard radical behaviorists are
like humanistic psychologists, who also treat consciousness as a process
rather than as a thing.

Behaviorism and the Unconscious

Recall that humanistic psychologists disagree with the strong emphasis placed on the unconscious by psychoanalysts. Radical behaviorists also disagree with psychoanalysts concerning the unconscious. In particular, radical behaviorists do not believe that there exists something called *the unconscious* that causes behavior. According to radical behaviorists, it is the environment acting on genetic variables that causes all behavior. Radical behaviorists do agree with the Freudians, however, that we are not conscious of the way in which much of our behavior is controlled. In fact, to start off with, the individual is totally unconscious of how his or her behavior is being controlled by the environment. The verbal community imposes consciousness (i.e., self-awareness) on us by, as indicated above, conditioning us to respond verbally to our own behavior and the variables controlling it (e.g., by reinforcing us for answering such questions as "What are you doing?" "Why did you do that?" "Where are you going?"). Radical behaviorists thus agree with both humanistic psychologists and psychoanalysts who point to the importance of socialization in producing consciousness. They agree with humanists and disagree with psychoanalysts concerning the reification of consciousness and the unconscious by psychoanalysts. However, they tend to agree with psychoanalysts in opposition to humanistic psychologists regarding the relative unimportance of consciousness; they believe along with psychoanalysts that much of our behavior (in fact, probably the greater proportion of it) is determined by variables of which we are not aware. However, they locate those variables in the environment rather than in a hypothetical entity called the unconscious.

Behaviorism and Artificial Intelligence

Artificial intelligence is usually thought to belong strictly to the province of cognitive psychology. From a behavioral point of view, however, there is no reason in principle why it would not be possible to construct a conscious machine.

Skinner on the Possibility of a Conscious Machine

According to Skinner, it might be possible to construct a conscious machine. Such a machine, however, may not experience consciousness in the same sense that we do. The reason is that (unless it was an exact duplicate of a human) it would be made out of different material than we are. Thus, in responding to its own behavior it would be producing and responding to stimuli that are quite different from the stimuli we produce and respond to when we are exhibiting self-awareness. To quote Skinner:

Theoretically, there is no limit to the extent to which a machine could respond to its own parts and activities. It may still be argued that this is not "real feeling," that no matter how sensitive a machine may be it is still not "conscious." But is this a matter of the behavior with which one responds to oneself or the self to which one responds? In human behavior the critical issue is not the feeling but what is felt, just as it is not the seeing but what is seen. A machine, no matter how sensitive, can feel only a machine. A machine is all a machine can possibly be conscious of.

This brings us to the one obvious and currently irreducible difference between men and machines. They are built differently. The ultimate difference is in componentry. To have human feelings a machine would have to have human things to feel. To be conscious or aware of itself as a man is conscious or aware of himself a machine would have to be what a man is aware or conscious of. It would have to be built like a man and would, of course, be a man. It would behave like a man and its behavior would include responding to itself in ways we call being conscious. Adam would not only be alive, he would be sentient, intelligent, and capable of becoming aware of himself as Adam. (Skinner, 1969, p. 294)

In other words, it follows from a radical behavioral point of view (at least Skinner's version), as it would from any mechanistic position, that an intelligent, conscious machine could exist. From any mechanistic point of view, there already is one—namely, humans—so why not more than one? The radical behavioral view differs from the cognitive view, however, in the nature of consciousness. From the behavioral point of view, consciousness is a person's responding to his or her own behavior. Hence, the experience of consciousness would be different for a machine, unless it were a close duplicate of a human, because the components of its body to which it was responding would be different from those of a human. From a cognitive point of view, in contrast, if the algorithm that produces consciousness for a machine is the same as that for a human, the subjective experience of consciousness should be the same for both. This may be an irresolvable issue, however, since it is unclear how it could be tested.

Behaviorism and the Turing Test

The Turing test for an intelligent machine is sometimes said to be behavioral because whether a machine is conscious depends solely on how the machine responds to verbal input. The machine passes the test simply by responding to verbal or other input in the same manner as a human would, so that an observer who does not see the machine cannot tell whether it is a machine or a human that is responding. Nothing that goes on inside the machine (whether, for example, it constructs the response according to an algorithm or simply looks it up in a table), including what it might be thinking if anything, is relevant to the Turing test. Nevertheless, the Turing test is not a good behavioral test from a radical behaviorist point of view. The Turing test consists primarily of a type of verbal responses that Skinner (1957) labeled intraverbals—that is, technically defined as verbal responses under the control of verbal stimuli to which they do not bear a point-to-point relationship. The test may also include some autoclitics: verbal responses that modify the listener's reaction to other verbal responses (e.g., "a," "and," and "are" that modify the listener's response to "table-chair-furniture" in "a chair and table are furniture")" are autoclitics. A person or machine whose repertoire of verbal behavior consists only of intraverbals and autoclitics would be extremely deficient verbally. Such a machine could conceivably pass a Turing test; but in the broader or natural environment in which most of us live, the gross deficiency in its behavior would be immediately obvious.

In order to pass a radical behaviorist version of the Turing test, an intelligent machine would need a sizeable number of other verbal operants. In Skinner's theory, verbal responses are classified according to the stimuli or states of deprivation that control them and the type of reinforcers that follow them. In addition to intraverbals and autoclitics, two extremely important categories of verbal responses are *mands*, which are verbal responses (e.g., "Can you tell me where the nearest washroom is?") that are reinforced with a characteristic consequence (e.g., directions to a nearby washroom resulting in bowel or bladder relief) and *tacts*, which are verbal responses (e.g., "It's raining") that are under the control of specific stimuli (e.g., rain) in which there is no point-to-point correspondence between the stimulus and the verbal response and the verbal response is reinforced by a generalized reinforcer (e.g., "Yes, you're right!").

In order to be a valid radical behavioral test of an intelligent machine, the Turing test would have to be modified to include mands and tacts. It is not easy to see how this could be done, as testing would have to be carried out in the natural environment—an environment containing houses, stores, drinking fountains, sunsets, people, and all the other features of the world that are lacking in Turing's sterile test room—using a machine that looked exactly like a human, so that only the behavior of the machine could potentially enable an observer to distinguish it from a human.

A Behavioristic Answer to Searle

The above is a version of an argument that Searle calls the robot reply. Recall that, according to Searle, the problem with the Turing test is illustrated by the fact that a person who understands no Chinese could in theory pass a Turing test of knowing Chinese by consulting a table of reasonable Chinese responses to statements and questions in Chinese. Searle maintains that the robot reply adds nothing new to the argument. According to him, the Chinese room could simply become the control room for operating a robot and then essentially the same argument would apply. All that one needs to change is the way in which the Chinese characters come into the Chinese room and the effect that the person's output of characters has. The input into the room would be from a TV camera attached to the robot; the output would be to motors operating the hands, arms, and legs of the robot. Although Searle, not being a behaviorist, mentions this, we could even have the robot operate according to behavioristic principles. Even so, according to Searle, all that the person in the Chinese room would understand would be how to manipulate symbols. In other words, he or she would still have no understanding of Chinese at all.

Interestingly, Searle (1980, p. 420) notes that the robot reply "tacitly concedes that cognition is not solely a matter of formal symbol manipulation" as many cognitivists maintain. Meaning, in other words, resides as much in the environment as in the individual, which happens to be what radical behaviorists maintain.

A radical behaviorist might also point out that the focus on "understanding" may be misdirected, because behaviorally the term *understanding* is not well operationalized—that is, it can have a number of different meanings. The critical question from a behavioral point of view is not whether the machine understands anything, but rather whether it functions adequately for some particular purpose. This suggests a modified version of the Turing test in which Searle's catalogue would be in effect a phrase book, similar to the phrase books travelers use to get around in a foreign country. Searle's argument, extended to this version of the Turing test, would state that the person using the phrase book would not understand Chinese even if the Turing test indicated otherwise (although it is hard to imagine carrying out the test in this way in the natural environment because the observer would see whether or not the speaker was using a phrase book; however, for our purposes here, we shall ignore this difficulty). From a behavioral point of view, a person who was able to use such a phrase book to communicate (with all classes of verbal operants represented) would be functioning effectively in Chinese. The difference between a native-speaking Chinese person and the speaker using the above-mentioned phrase book is that the phrase book is facilitating the verbal processing of the latter.

To use computer terminology, we could say that the speaker has offloaded much of the necessary processing onto the phrase book or catalogue, but this in no way detracts from the speaker's ability to communicate in Chinese which is comparable to that of a native speaker. Although it may seem to go against common sense, the philosopher Daniel Dennett appears to agree that offloading does not detract from understanding. In fact, he regards the offloading to facilitate our intellectual functioning to be characteristic of our species. He described it as:

> extruding our mind (that is our mental projects and activities) into the surrounding world, where a host of peripheral devices we construct can store, process, and re-represent our meanings, streamlining, enhancing, and protecting the processes of transformation that are our thinking. This widespread practice of offloading releases us from the limitations of our animal brains. (Dennett, 1996, pp. 134–135)

There are cognitive psychologists and philosophers who would disagree with Dennett on this point (e.g., Adams & Aizawa, 2001). One objection to Dennett's position is that there is no experience of consciousness associated with offloaded memory, as there appears to be with real memory. However, if we grant the validity of Dennett's position with regard to the concept of offloading, it appears that an argument can be made for a convergence of behavioral and cognitive positions against Searle's position denying the possibility of constructing a conscious machine. Both the behavioral and the cognitive positions (at least Dennett's cognitive position) maintain that there is nothing special about internal memory as opposed to external (offloaded) memory that would grant the status of understanding to the former but not to the latter.

SUMMARY

Humanistic psychologists are generally unconcerned about the problem of operationally defining consciousness, because consciousness is a subjective experience and they accept the primacy of the subjective. Some humanistic psychologists adopt a *phenomenological* approach. By this it is meant that they emphasize the importance of understanding the experience of consciousness. In their view, the other approaches have severely neglected the study of consciousness and the importance of consciousness to human behavior. Humanistic psychologists generally use the term consciousness in the sense of *self-awareness*. They would tend to agree with William James' view of consciousness as the self observing the self knowing or thinking. According to humanistic psychologists, consciousness is uniquely human. Moreover, rather than the negative function hypothesized by Freud, humanistic psychologists believe that consciousness has a positive function. Humanistic psychologists are particularly interested in what are termed altered states of consciousness.

Consciousness is given a back seat to the unconscious in psychodynamic theories. It would be incorrect, however, to say that consciousness has no importance in these theories. Indeed, the primary function of psychoanalysis and other psychodynamic approaches is to bring material into consciousness so it can be dealt with. Hence, the psychodynamic approach aims at expanding consciousness.

In general, cognitivists have tended to assume that any adequate simulation of mind will also simulate whatever subjective states are correlated with mind—including consciousness. Recently, interest by cognitivists in understanding and explaining consciousness has grown. Many experts in AI have adopted an *operational definition* of *intelligent machine* that might be a suitable operational definition of *conscious machine*. This definition is known as the Turing test, named after Alan Turing, the pioneering computer scientist who first proposed it. Quite likely a machine that passes the Turing test would have to be considered conscious, as well as intelligent.

There are, however, criticisms within cognitivism of various cognitive approaches to consciousness: Some cognitivists question the view that a program that simulates mental activity can produce subjective conscious states. The philosopher John Searle's Chinese Room Argument is a famous critique of the Turing test as a means of establishing understanding and consciousness. Searle argues that a computer that passes the Turing test would simply be acting according to a set of rules of which it has no understanding, and in fact no consciousness at all. More recently, Searle has argued that computers (and their programs) are not objects with the same logical status as stones, trees, stars, and brains. The philosopher Daniel Dennett argues that in order to understand consciousness, we must understand that consciousness is not a unitary experience. He has also proposed a multiple-drafts model in which the content of consciousness is just the content (meaning) of one's inner *draft* representation of what is happening in the world.

A methodological behaviorist would say that because the experience of consciousness is private it cannot be studied scientifically. Radical behaviorists, however, maintain that one can observe one's own private events such as one's own covert verbal behavior and images. A radical behaviorist might look at different levels of consciousness similarly to how a humanistic psychologist looks at them. The psychophysiological level is verbal responding to one's own physiological states. The transpersonal level can be either, or both, of two things: (1) verbal behavior describing one's own responding to certain abstract verbal stimuli such as the universe, love, history, time; (2) a change in one's verbal responding to one's own behavior due to a temporary change in the control exerted by the environment on behavior. Such a change can be produced by variables ranging from drugs to meditation, and is what is meant by an *altered state of consciousness*. Essentially, it can be seen that consciousness in the sense of self-awareness is, to a radical behaviorist, verbal responding under the control of one's own behavior. The subjective experience of consciousness is the private stimulation produced by our verbal responding to our own behavior.

One might also use the Turing test in a behavioral definition of consciousness. In order to pass a radical behaviorist version of the Turing test, an intelligent machine would need a sizeable number of other verbal operants. This might answer Searle's problem with the Turing test because consulting a table (e.g., of Chinese-English words) is only one type of verbal operant. Other types are needed in a behavioral definition of understanding.

Discussion Questions

1. Early psychologists had the goal of studying consciousness. What have we learned since then regarding the philosophical and technical problems involved in the study of consciousness?

2. Discuss what the difference is between different levels of consciousness and altered states of consciousness, or if there is a difference.

3. Compare and contrast the role of consciousness in Freudian and Jungian theories.

4. Discuss the problems involved in treating consciousness as the product of an information processing system (i.e., a computer). What might be a solution to these problems?

5. Describe and criticize the homunculus theory of consciousness.

6. Describe and criticize behavioral theories of consciousness.

7. Describe and criticize the Turing test of consciousness. Discuss whether there could be a more valid test and, if so, what it might be.

8. Discuss whether a radical behaviorist would be committed to the view that consciousness is different for speakers of American Sign Language, since their verbal behaviors are so different from those of speakers of spoken languages.

9. Discuss whether a machine could be conscious.

10. Discuss how consciousness might be studied from the perspective of each of the four systems.

CHAPTER 9

Divisions of the Whole Person

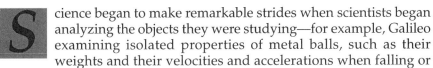cience began to make remarkable strides when scientists began analyzing the objects they were studying—for example, Galileo examining isolated properties of metal balls, such as their weights and their velocities and accelerations when falling or rolling down inclines (see chapter 2). In contrast to this approach is the holistic view that we must treat the objects of our study, especially humans, as integrated wholes. Adopting a holistic approach is not as simple as it might at first seem. There is a strong tendency to analyze any object of study into parts. We can group the ways in which psychologists and other scientists take a nonholistic approach into two categories: dualism and reductionism.

There are two types of dualism: (1) the mind-body distinction and (2) the self-other dichotomy.

- *The mind-body distinction.* According to a view first formalized by Descartes (see chapter 2), every human has both a body that is made of matter and a mind (or soul) that is composed of something that is not matter. The mind is not to be confused with the brain. It is connected to the body at a part of the brain called the pineal gland, and operates the body much as an engineer operates an engine. Or, if we think of the brain as a computer, the mind operates the brain much as a computer user operates a computer. The mind is the seat of reasoning, moral judgment, and the will.

- *The self-other dichotomy.* There is a strong tendency, especially in Western culture, to distinguish the self from others and from the rest of the universe (i.e., the rest of nature). Although the self-other distinction may seem so natural that it is difficult to understand how anyone could question it, there are grounds for questioning it, as will be seen.

Reductionism is the opposite of holism. It includes any approach that involves breaking or analyzing a subject matter into parts of which the subject matter is supposed to be composed. Two broad types of reductionism are: (1) strict reductionism (also called atomism or physicalism) and (2) the hierarchic systems approach.

- *Strict reductionism.* This is the belief that the phenomena in a science can be explained by using concepts and terminology that are assumed to be more fundamental. We may distinguish two types of strict reductionism: (a) within-science reductionism, and (b) across-sciences reductionism. An example of within-science reductionism in chemistry is explaining water as a combination of the elements hydrogen and oxygen. An example of across-science reductionism is using the laws of particle physics (e.g., physical laws concerning the parts of the atom) to explain chemical reactions. In psychology, an example of within-science reductionism might be explaining poor performance in school as a product of a lower-level psychological concept such as poor motivation. An example of across-science reductionism in psychology is attempting to explain behavior with concepts from neurology, such as explaining low motivation as due to a particular brain state.

- *Hierarchic systems approach.* This is the belief that nature is organized hierarchically, or into levels, and that the lower levels are not necessarily more fundamental than the higher levels. In fact, in a certain sense, the higher levels are more fundamental than the lower ones, since—according to this view—the lower levels are abstractions from the higher levels and thus can only be understood in the context of the higher levels. Hence, according to the hierarchic systems approach, explanation does not proceed only in the reductive direction (i.e., from lower to higher) as in strict reductionism. It also proceeds from higher to lower. There are within- and across-science explanations with this approach as there are with strict reductionism. An example of a within-psychology hierarchic systems explanation might be explaining poor performance in school as a product of dysfunctional family dynamics at home. An example of a between-sciences (psychology and sociology or anthropology) hierarchic systems explanation might be explaining low motivation to perform well in school as a product of a cultural bias.

To summarize, there are two types of nonholism: dualism and reductionism. There are two types of dualism: mind-body and self-other. There are two types of reductionism: strict and hierarchic systems. Finally, there are two types of strict reductionism: within-science and across-sciences.

There are a number of problems with each of the forms of nonholism. Regarding the mind-body distinction, there is no evidence of a separate, nonmaterial substance such as that of which the mind is supposed to be composed. In addition, even if such a substance existed, it is unclear how it could interact with a material substance such as the body. Clearly the details of Descartes' mind-body distinction (e.g., that the soul operates through the pineal gland) are no longer scientifically acceptable.

The problems with mind-body dualism impinge directly on the self-other distinction. For if there is no separate mind or soul substance, then it appears that the only thing distinguishing one person from another is either (a) the matter that makes up their respective bodies or (b) the organization of that matter. But both of these change over time. The cells in our bodies are continuously taking in new material and excreting old material, and are constantly dying and being replaced. Thus, very little of the physical material that existed in your body seven years ago is present now, and very little that is present now will be present seven years from now.

In his famous critique of the concept of a self as a distinct entity, the philosopher David Hume (see chapter 2) wrote:

> For my part, when I enter most intimately into what I call *myself*, I always stumble on some particular perception or other, of heat or cold, light or shade, love or hatred, pain or pleasure. I never can catch *myself* at any time without a perception, and never can observe any thing but the perception. (Hume, 1978, p. 252; italics in original)

In other words, Hume was denying that there is an entity that we can call a *self* as distinct from other aspects of the universe. The fragility of the self-other distinction can also be illustrated by the following thought experiment: Suppose that a new method of travel has been invented. You can be transported anywhere in the world at the speed of light. The method, called teleportation, involves a transmission apparatus that completely breaks down your body at its present location and reconstructs a duplicate from new matter at your desired destination. Although it seems farfetched, an apparatus that does this is theoretically possible (Zeilinger, 2003). If a teleportation apparatus were constructed and you were transported using it, the person stepping out at the new location would be indistinguishable from you, including having your exact personality and all your memories, and would undoubtedly be extremely pleased to have made the journey with such little time and effort. But, would it really be you?

Actually, it turns out that the person stepping out at the receiving end would not be exactly identical to the person that stepped into the transmitting end. There are laws governing subatomic particles that virtually prevent an exact duplicate of a complicated object from being generated. This is because in order to be an exact duplicate of a complicated object, all corresponding subatomic particles of the duplicate have to be in the same quantum states as the original. Because of the fragile nature of quantum states, this would be virtually impossible. According to the physicist Anton Zeilinger (2003, p. 41), "Even a tiny lump of matter would be disturbed merely by the thermal radiation from the walls of the apparatus." However, he goes on to point out, "Being in the same quantum state does not seem necessary for being the same person. We change our states all the time and remain the same people—at least as far as we can tell!" (Zeilinger, 2003, p. 41).

But do we really remain the same people if our quantum states are changing? The ancient Greek philosopher Heraclitus (540–circa 480 BCE) said that the same man cannot cross the same river twice, because (a) it is not the same river and (b) it is not the same man. In fact, he added, he cannot even do it once! But if I am not the same individual from one instant to the next, then either there are an infinite number of distinct "me's," each of which exists for only a split second (which, although logically possible, would seem to make life literally pointless) or all individuals are in essence me. To put the point in its most extreme form, the self-other distinction is, as a Buddhist would say, an illusion. (For further discussion of philosophical and rational problems regarding the self-other distinction, see Parfit, 1984; Perry, 1975; Rorty, 1976; Williams, 1973.)

The chief problem with strict reductionism is that in order to predict any complex phenomenon at a higher level, we must have almost perfect knowledge of what all the lower-level units are doing at each instant in time. In most cases this is impossible either from a practical standpoint or in principle (especially given the indeterminate principle in quantum physics, which will be discussed in chapter 11). Strict reductionism may perhaps be traced to the development of the atomic theory in physics. All matter is composed of atoms and all chemical reactions can be explained as interactions between atoms. Thus, the chemical reactions in the nervous system may be thought of as interactions between atoms. All activity in the nervous system can be thought of as due to chemical reactions, which are the result of interactions between atoms. All behavior is due to activity in the nervous system. Therefore, it follows that behavior can be thought of as due to chemical reactions in the nervous system, which are due to interactions between atoms. Therefore, all behavior can be thought of as due to—or, in other words, all behavior reduces to—interactions between atoms. Indeed atoms themselves are composed of smaller parts, namely subatomic particles, some of which are composed of still smaller entities called quarks. In a sense, then, everything is really composed of tiny particles much smaller than atoms. For an extreme strict reductionist, the idea that things like cars, trees, water, chairs, chalk, etc., exist is an illusion. Reality is simply a huge collection of small particles surrounded by large volumes of space. Less strict forms of reductionism stop short of attempting to reduce everything to elementary particles, although they may hold that this is possible in principle. Representative of these less extreme forms are the views that all biology can be reduced to DNA, or that all psychology can be reduced to neurology.

A problem that some have seen with strict reductionism is that a complete theory at each level must be formalized before any reduction is possible, and there must be bridge laws for connecting the two levels (Looren de Jong, 2002; Nagel, 1961, pp. 354, 433–435)—that is, there must be a theory for connecting the two theories.

A problem with the hierarchic systems approach is that there is no clear rule for deciding which level or levels to choose to analyze a phenomenon. The hierarchic systems approach agrees with strict reductionism that there are different levels on different scales of measurement (i.e., elementary particles exist and are on a smaller scale than forests). No level, however, is more fundamental than another: forests consisting of trees, animals, air, and so forth exist and are just as fundamental as subatomic particles. The former are on a relatively large scale, called a macroscale, whereas the latter is on a smaller, or microscale. To complicate matters, the levels may in fact interact. For example, successive mutations (changes in the DNA molecule) can cause a particular population of individuals to evolve into a new species. In order for a new species to form, however, one or more mechanisms at a level higher than the molecular level (e.g., geographical isolation) have to reproductively isolate a population from populations with which it might otherwise interbreed (Dieckmann, Doebeli, Metz, & Tautz, 2004).

The following statement by Paul Weiss nicely summarizes the hierarchic systems approach:

> Analysis focuses downward on ever smaller isolated samples of the Universe. In its descent, it encounters further compact packages of rather constantly recurring configurations—from organisms, down to organs, cells, organelles, molecules, atoms, and subatomic particles. Each downward step involves a further degree of dismemberment of the primary unitary image of the Universe; involves cumulative abstractions due to either the disregard or the deliberate mental severance of those relational ties that link the abstracted "units" into the cohesive total fabric of the Universe. The success of this analytic method has been immense. It must not be forgotten, however, that its gains have to be bought at the expense of corresponding losses of information about the mutual relations between the "units" severed in the analytic process. This information needs to be restored when one climbs back up the scale in the synthetic direction, trying to fit things again together into original context. . . . [B]ear in mind that in reality the "units" never have been, nor could have been, truly isolated in the sense of separation from the continuum of the Universe. The whole notion of "isolation" is an abstraction. (Weiss, 1971, p. 7)

Most succinctly, David McNeill stated this point of view as follows:

> "In systems of all kinds, not only is the structure of the whole independent in large measure of the parts, but understanding the interrelation of the parts requires knowing the state of the whole" (McNeill, 1971, p. 62).

In essence, both of these quotations point out that it is necessary to analyze phenomena in order to understand them, but by analyzing any phenomenon we are necessarily distorting it because nothing exists in isolation. The Universe is One.

HUMANISTIC APPROACH

Humanistic psychologists advocate a holistic approach to psychology—that is, they advocate treating the individual as a whole rather than as the product of interacting parts or processes. Thus, they are in fundamental agreement with the familiar Gestalt maxim that the whole is greater than or different from the sum of its parts. Accordingly, humanistic psychologists believe that breaking the individual into parts can never lead to a satisfactory understanding of the individual.

Rejection by Humanistic Psychologists of the Ways of Dividing the Person

- The mind-body distinction. Humanistic psychologists reject the mind-body distinction primarily because it divides the individual into parts, but also because it implies that the universe is composed of two fundamentally different kinds of substances.

- The self-other dichotomy. Humanistic psychologists believe that this is a dichotomy that we should strive to reduce, if not abolish entirely. One reason that humanistic psychologists are favorably impressed by Eastern religions is that these religions consider the self-other dichotomy to be an illusion and have developed techniques to attempt to free individuals from it.

- Reductionism. Humanistic psychologists believe that the emphasis of other psychological approaches on analysis is a major impediment to a deeper and more complete understanding of human psychological functioning. Specifically, they believe that analyzing a phenomenon into its components in some sense destroys the true nature of the phenomenon. For example, one cannot see subjective experience by looking into the brain; reductionism thus, in the view of humanistic psychologists, tends to minimize the importance of subjective experience. Of the four approaches, humanistic psychology finds animal research least relevant because it is generally reductive when applied to humans (Mehlman, 1967). In fact, animal research is typically of interest to humanistic psychologists only when it suggests that animals have unusual or paranormal powers, implying that humans also have or can access these capabilities (e.g., see the discussion of the "Hundredth Monkey Phenomenon" in chapter 13).

Existential psychotherapists put particular stress on holism in opposition to the analytic approaches of the natural sciences. For example, Norcross extolling individualism stated:

> Existentialism is individualism. Each individual is unique, whole, and irreplaceable and cannot be understood by arbitrary reductions or compartmentalizations of experience. . . . For many existentialists, the mind/body controversy is a pseudoproblem resulting from natural science's need to divide experience to suit itself. The unnatural division of people into subject and object creates a "thing" out of a phenomenologically experiencing being. (Norcross, 1987, p. 51)

The Necessity of Reductionism

Some form of reductionism seems to be essential to science as we currently know it. For example, chemistry analyzes compounds into the elements of which they are composed. It is true that the compound can be quite different from the elements of which it is composed. For example, water, being a liquid, is quite different from hydrogen and oxygen, which are both gases. Nevertheless, one cannot understand a compound scientifically until one knows what it is made of. In addition, further understanding is generally obtained by reducing the phenomena of one science to those of a more basic science. For example, a greater understanding of the chemistry of water is obtained when one learns the laws of physics that determine how atoms of hydrogen and oxygen combine to produce molecules of water.

Evidence Against Holism

Split-Brain Research

Although humanistic psychologists emphasize studying the individual as a unitary whole, there is reason to believe that even the phenomenon of consciousness—which humanistic psychologists consider fundamental—is not unitary. One type of evidence concerning this comes from what are known as *split-brain* experiments (Gazzaniga, Borgen, & Sperry, 1965; Sperry, 1961). These are experiments that have been carried out with people who have been subjected to an operation in which the corpus callosum (the major nerve tract connecting the two halves of the brain) has been severed to reduce the severity of epileptic seizures from which these people suffer. Although the behavior of these individuals is indistinguishable from the behavior of normal people under most conditions, special tests can reveal some surprising differences. The nervous system is so constructed that sensory input from the right half of the visual field and the right half of the body goes into the left half of the brain, and sensory input from the left half of the visual field and left half of the body goes into the right half of the brain. Moreover, movements of the right half of the body and (in most people) speech output originate in the left half of the brain, and movements of the left half of the body originate in the right half of the brain. Thus, for individuals whose brains have been split by severing the corpus callosum, it is possible to study the functioning of the two halves of the brain in relative isolation from each other. If such a person is shown one object in the left half of the visual field and a different object in the right half of the visual field, and is asked to point to an object matching the one shown, the individual will point to the object matching the one seen in the right visual field with the right hand and to the object matching the one seen in the left visual field with the left hand. In some cases, one hand may try to stop the other hand from pointing to the object matching the one in the corresponding visual field, or try to force it to point to the other matching object. In addition, if asked to name the object, the individual will name the one shown in the left half of the visual field (assuming that the person's speech area is in the left half of the brain, as is usually the case). These and many similar tests indicate that people whose brains are split behave as though they have two separate consciousnesses, in that one part of the individual is unable to describe what another part of the individual is doing or responding to.

Further split-brain research has indicated even stronger dissociations between the two hemispheres than the original work suggested (Gazzaniga, 2002). For example, each hemisphere possesses skills and behavioral tendencies that the other lacks. The left hemisphere is much better at searching for items in a scene because it uses highly systematic procedures. In fact, the left hemisphere on average performs better at this task than an individual with an intact brain, indicating that in the intact brain the right hemisphere inhibits systematic search strategies in the left brain. The left brain is also verbal whereas the right is not; thus the left hemisphere engages in verbal reasoning, even inventing reasons for things (e.g., for the choices of the right hemisphere) that it has no access to. The right hemisphere, for its part, is more skilled at detecting certain patterns (e.g., in certain types of illusions) than the left hemisphere is. From his recent split-brain research, Gazzaniga (2002, p. 31) concluded that both hemispheres can be considered conscious although "the left brain's consciousness far surpasses that of the right."

Dissociative States

Another line of evidence indicating that consciousness may not be a unitary phenomenon is the existence of dissociative states. These are any of a variety of states that function outside of the awareness of the state of consciousness that has primary or executive control of the body (Richards, 1990), or are a narrowing or fragmentation of awareness (Edge, 2001). There are various degrees of dissociation, ranging from performing routine tasks without being fully conscious that one is doing them (e.g., driving to work on automatic pilot), through acting as a *medium* or *channel*, in which one claims contact with entities (e.g., deceased spirits) that may to some extent take control of one's body, to *dissociative identity disorder* (*DID*; formerly called *multiple personality disorder* or *MPD*), in which the individual exhibits at different times different personalities, some of which may not be aware of some of the others. The personalities in DID often are radically different from each other in a number of ways, including dress, handwriting, speech patterns, interests, abilities, and even IQ scores. They may also assume different ages, nationalities, and even sexes.

Humanistic psychologists generally consider extreme cases of dissociation, such as DID, to indicate impaired development of the personality. They therefore tend to emphasize the desirability of synthesizing the different personalities into just one unified personality. Richards (1990), however, questioned the appropriateness of this approach and suggested that humanistic psychologists may have overemphasized the importance of developing a single personality in a single body. In other words, dissociation may not be as bad as has been thought, and may even have some beneficial aspects. Richards noted that the cases of DID that come for psychological treatment—that is, the clinical cases—may differ from non-clinical cases of DID. In addition, there are reports of DID in which the different personalities shared tasks, provided companionship and friendship for each other, and in general seemed to be instrumental in helping the individual function at a high level while manifesting no evident pathology (e.g., Kluft, 1986). Beahrs (1982) compared the individual to an orchestra: both consist of many parts. In this sense, we all have multiple personalities. Pathology occurs when the parts are not functioning harmoniously under the direction of a unifying conductor or executive function. Thus Beahrs emphasized strengthening the executive function as opposed to attempting to achieve a synthesis of the personalities into one unified personality.

Richards (1990) asserted that dissociative states appear to be positive not only in at least some nonclinical DID cases, but may also have been instrumental in the development of the world's great religions (assuming that prophets who heard and transmitted God's word were actually sensing another part of themselves of which they were not conscious). More recently, other humanistic psychologists (e.g., Edge, 2001, and Hunt, Dougan, Grant, & House, 2002) have argued that dissociative states can be used for personal growth and may contribute positively to psychotherapy.

Thus, even though dissociative states may appear to go against the principle of holism, humanistic psychologists seem to be giving more consideration to their possible constructive role in human development and functioning.

Sperry's Holistic Approach

It is noteworthy that the pioneer of split-brain research adopted a holistic approach. Roger Sperry (1980, 1995) argued that mental states are an "emergent property" of the nervous system, and thus depend on the nervous system for their existence; however, neural states are just as dependent on mental states as mental states are on neural states. Causation between neural and mental states, in other words, is bi-directional: neural states are just as much caused by mental states as the latter are by the former. Thus, there is an interaction between mental and neural states, so that it is impossible to understand mental states by simply studying neural states. To attempt to understand mental states by studying neural states would be as futile as a physicist trying to understand energy by only considering matter, although both matter and energy are (presumably) simply different aspects of the same underlying reality.

It should also be recognized that humanistic psychologists do not deny that there are parts to any whole. However, they maintain that the whole cannot be understood simply by studying its parts; rather the parts themselves cannot be understood apart from the whole (e.g., Slife, Hope, and Nebeker, 1999, p. 75). Perhaps an even better way to put it from a humanistic perspective is that although we may seem to identify *subpersonalities* within the personality of each individual, rather than being distinct entities, these subpersonalities are actually aspects of a dynamic whole (Frick, 1993).

PSYCHODYNAMIC APPROACH

The psychodynamic approach is nonholistic in most of the ways mentioned at the beginning of this chapter. It accepts the mind-body distinction in the sense that its goal is to study the mind as distinct from the body. However, it is nondualistic in that it assumes that the universe is composed only of matter as described by physicists. There is, according to the psychodynamic approach, no distinct mental substance separate from neural tissue.

Ways in Which the Psychodynamic Approach is Nonholistic

The psychodynamic approach accepts the self-other distinction as an essential aspect of healthy psychological functioning. According to Freud, the individual begins life as an undifferentiated ego that does not distinguish self from nonself:

> An infant at the breast does not as yet distinguish his ego from the external world as the source of the sensations flowing in upon him. He gradually learns to do so, in response to various promptings. He must be very strongly impressed by the fact that some sources of excitation, which he will later recognize as his own bodily organs, can provide him with sensations at any moment, whereas other sources evade him from time to time—among them what he desires most of all, his mother's breast—and only reappear as a result of his screaming for help. In this way there is for the first time set over against the ego an "object" in the form of something that exists "outside," and which is only forced to appear by some special action. A further incentive to a disengagement of the ego from the general mass of sensations—that is, to the recognition of an "outside," an external world—is provided by the frequent, manifold and unavoidable sensation of pain and unpleasure the removal and avoidance of which is enjoined by the pleasure principle, in the exercise of its unrestricted domination. . . . One comes to learn a procedure by which, through a deliberate direction of one's sensory activities and through suitable muscular action, one can differentiate between what is internal—what belongs to the ego—and what is external—what emanates from the outer world. In this way one makes the first step toward the introduction of the reality principle which is to dominate future development. This differentiation, of course, serves the practical purpose of enabling one to defend oneself against sensations of unpleasure which one actually feels or with which one is threatened. (Freud, 1961, pp. 66–68)

Thus, through development the individual moves from an undifferentiated unitary self to a self that is differentiated from the external environment. A Freudian might see humanistic psychology as an attempt to return to the earlier nondifferentiated self.

As its name implies, psychoanalysis is within-science reductionistic in that it studies the components of the mind and their interactions. In addition, it is also across-science reductionistic in that Freud believed that brain processes corresponding to the components of the mind would someday be discovered. These processes would not necessarily be localized in specific brain areas, but they would be clearly identifiable.

Holistic Tendencies in the Psychodynamic Approach

Other psychodynamic psychologies (e.g., those of Adler, Jung, Kohut) tend to be more holistic. For example, according to Cain, "Adler's psychology viewed living beings as connected wholes—biologically, philosophically, and psychologically. His view of the person was that of an indivisible unity. He rejected polarities, such as mind-body and conscious-unconscious, believing that all functions or subsystems of the person are in the service of the whole person" (Cain, 2002, p. 15)

In addition, there has been a movement in psychoanalysis away from interest in divisions of the mind, such as id, ego, and superego (Westen, 1998).

COGNITIVE APPROACH

The cognitive approach is nonholistic in at least some of the ways mentioned at the beginning of this chapter. It accepts, as we have seen, the mind-body distinction—with the mind being thought of as a computer program that runs on the brain.

Ways in Which the Cognitive Approach is Nonholistic

To determine whether it accepts the self-other distinction, we need to ask whether there is a *self* according to cognitivism, and if so what it is. If we think of the self as a little person inside the skull—that is, the homunculus mentioned in the previous chapter—then it appears that, from the viewpoint of cognitivism, the self doesn't exist and, hence, there is no self-other distinction. If we equate the self with the mind or some subprogram of that program, however, then the self exists as a pattern that is distinct and apart from the rest of nature or the universe. If this is the position of cognitivism, then it does accept the self-other distinction.

The self-other distinction also comes into play in cognitivism in the tendency of normal adults to attribute independent mental states to other individuals. Research has focused on issues such as when this tendency develops in normal children, the extent to which individuals with autism have it and how it can be further developed in them, and whether animals (especially those most closely related to humans) exhibit it. This ability or tendency to attribute mental states has been variously labeled *mental state attribution* (Cheney & Seyfarth, 1990), *metarepresentation* (Whiten & Byrne, 1991), *mind reading* (Krebs & Dawkins, 1984), *perspective-taking*

(Povinelli, Nelson, & Boysen, 1990), and *theory of mind* (Premack & Woodruff, 1978). Tests of it typically involve observing whether an experimental subject can correctly predict another individual's behavior in a situation in which the subject has information he or she is in a position to know that the other individual does not have. For example, in a study of children's development of a theory of mind, a child may be shown an object being hidden, and asked whether another child will know where the object is hidden when the first child knows that the second child did not see the object being hidden. Presumably, if the test child lacks a theory of mind, or an ability to attribute mental states (or a self-other distinction), he or she will predict that the other child will correctly identify the object's hiding place. Since the inability to attribute mental states is considered abnormal in humans older than a certain age, it would be interesting to determine where radical behaviorists stand with regard to this ability. For example, do they lack it, or do they have it but interpret it differently from the way that cognitivists do?

The cognitive approach is reductionistic because its ultimate goal is to understand the mind, which is regarded to be an information processing system—essentially, something like a computer program. Computer programs are usually based on algorithms that specify interacting components of computer code. Thus, cognitive psychology is within-science reductionistic in that its goal is to analyze mental phenomena into interacting modules of what code the mind is written in. Cognitivism is also across-sciences reductionistic to the extent that its goal is to reduce psychology to another science—namely, computer science. However, there is less interest among many cognitivists in reducing psychology to physiology or neurology. The reason is that cognitivists are interested in the mental program (i.e., the mind), not the particular hardware or wetware (i.e., the brain) on which it happens to be running. Since a given program can run on any computer with enough memory for it (or, more precisely the algorithm for any program can be coded to run on any computer with enough memory), most cognitive psychologists do not consider knowledge of the brain to be critical to understanding the mind. For example, the cognitive psychologist Herbert Simon stated: "I have discussed the organization of the mind without saying anything about the structure of the brain" (Simon, 1981, p. 97).

This approach to cognition is called *functionalism*, not to be confused with the functionalism of William James and John Dewey (see chapter 4). It is called that because it is concerned with how the mind functions, but not the physical medium (whether it is a computer or a brain) through which it functions.

However, there are cognitivists who consider knowledge of the brain to be very important or even essential. This is especially true of cognitivists specializing in the field of neuroscience. For example, Francis Crick, codiscoverer (in collaboration with James Watson) of the DNA molecule, who subsequently devoted his life to cognitive science, wrote:

> The brain does not make a distinction between hardware and software, as a computer does. Theories [of cognition] that have made this distinction are unfortunate. (Crick, 1994, p. 179)

Any reductionistic science must, by definition, explain its subject matter by using something that is simpler or more basic than that subject matter. In physics, for example, complex movements of inanimate objects (e.g., planets, projectiles) are explained by simple laws operating in a mechanistic manner. In cognitive science, computer principles are simpler than the complex thought processes they are trying to explain. For example, we mentioned the self above with regard to the self-other distinction. Cognitive psychologists tend to view the self in a reductionistic manner, in that they consider the self not be a module in the mental flowchart or algorithm, but rather the product of many other nonself modules being joined together in coherent, stable, interconnected ways.

Representations and the Problem of Reductionism

Reductions of cognitive science to computer science and to physiology are across-science reductions. Most reductive attempts within cognitivism are attempts at within-science reductions—that is, attempts to explain cognitive phenomena with fundamental cognitive concepts. According to the predominant form of within science cognitive reductionism, the mind is composed of modules, which consist of elements that process information in some way. The information that is processed is typically considered to be symbols, which are units of representation. That is, a symbol is a representation of something else; for example, the word *house* is a symbol for a particular house or the general idea or concept of house. Not all cognitivists are comfortable with the use of representations in cognitive explanations. In the previous chapter we saw that there are some problems with the notion of representation with regard to explaining consciousness. Similar criticisms apply with regard to the use of representation in a reductive manner in cognitivism.

Keijzer's Arguments

In a book called *Representation and Behavior*, Fred Keijzer (2001) has outlined practical and logical arguments against the use of representation as a reductive or explanatory concept. From a practical point of view he argues that the amount of memory required to represent the environment is so great that it is unlikely that the brain has evolved to accommodate it. From a logical point of view, he argues that the concept of representa-tion is not truly reductive even though cognitive psychology accepts reductionism in explaining the behavior of persons. In order for cogni-tivism to be reductive, Keijzer argues, its explanations should be at what he calls a *subpersonal* level, that is, at a level below that of the person.

In order to follow Keijzer's arguments, let us briefly take a look at how cognitivists use representations as explanations. There are three stages. In the first stage, the individual forms a representation of the environment. In the second stage, the individual processes the representation in some manner (most cognitive theories mainly differ in the algorithms that des-cribe how this processing occurs). In the third stage, the processed repre-sentations are translated into behavior.

All this seems very straightforward on the surface. Keijzer maintains, however, that closer analysis reveals that the concept of *representation* is not very well defined within cognitivism. Perhaps this is because repre-sentations seem so natural to us as humans that defining them precisely has not seemed necessary. Humans are distinguished from other species by the ease with which we engage in symbolic activity. If I draw a picture, for example, no normal person would have the slightest difficulty under-standing that the picture represents whatever it is that I drew (even though, given my poor artistic skills, it would probably not be a good likeness). In a sense, I can also draw pictures "in my head" (so to speak). Thus, I can draw a picture of a house; and, I can picture or imagine a house. In both cases it is clear that the picture is a representation of some-thing—either of a particular house or of the general concept of house. In this regard, there is no disagreement between a cognitivist and a radical behaviorist. Both a typical radical behaviorist and a typical cognitivist would probably agree that a private image of a house is no different in principle from an actual drawing or picture of a house, and that each could be a representation of an actual house. They would still not see eye-to-eye, however, because the cognitivist would not be particularly inter-ested in representation in this sense. The cognitivist would view repre-sentation in this sense only as a crude analogy of the type of representation he or she is interested in. The cognitivist is more interested in represen-tation in the sense of something taking place in the wetware (i.e., the brain) that is not necessarily at the conscious level (and that also occurs in the brains of nonhuman animals, which one would not think of as being symbolic in the ordinary sense of that word).

To understand how cognitivists use the concept of representation as opposed to the more commonsense way of viewing representations, con-sider the three stages in cognitive theory as described previously. In the first stage, when you see your house and respond to it (e.g., by walking toward it), you are not responding to your house per se. Rather, you are responding to a representation of your house in your mind. Keijzer points out that this explanation does not seem to serve any simplifying purpose (which a reductive explanation should do). It would be simpler, it seems, to say that you are responding to your actual house. Certainly there are changes in your brain that correspond to seeing your house; however, calling them representations does not seem to add to our knowledge of these changes (which is still very limited). Moreover, in the artificial intelligence endeavor, programming representations of the environment into robots has run into problems of memory storage. In fact, there is a thriving school of AI called *behavior-based robotics* that maintains that it is much more efficient to program robots to respond directly to the environment rather than to internal representations of the environment (Arkin, 1998; Brookes, 1991, 1999). Interestingly, this approach was used with good success to build the Martian-exploratory robots Spirit and Opportunity. Further, it can be argued that since evolution typically takes the most efficient route, it is questionable whether internal representations would have evolved to the extent required by many cognitive theories.

The second and third stages provide more serious difficulties for representation as a reductive (or primitive, to use a term more common in reductive theories) concept. To see these difficulties, consider how a computer processes a given symbol. Let us say, for example, that you type the word *house* into a computer. The word represents house just as in the above; to the computer, however, it is simply a pattern of electrons. The computer knows nothing about houses, let alone how a particular pattern of electricity corresponds to a house. At most, the pattern of electricity represents the sequence of letters *h-o-u-s-e* printed on the computer screen when given the appropriate command. But in what sense does it represent this? The pattern of electricity is simply translated into the letters. The computer, however, knows nothing about the translation of the pattern into the letters. Now suppose that the computer does some sort of processing on this word, and the end result of the processing is a certain pattern of electricity that corresponds to the sequence of letters *t-r-e-e*. Now a person can clearly see that the computer has gone through an algorithm that has translated the electrical pattern representing *house* into the electrical pattern representing *tree*. In a certain sense, a person might even say that for this computer program, the word *tree* represents the word *house*. The computer, however, knows nothing of representations; this is totally an interpretation of the human. To the computer, one pattern of electricity has simply been transformed into another. In other words, while a human can easily see that something is a representation of something else, there is no way currently known for a computer to know this.

In short, the concept of representation in cognitive theorizing remains, to use Keijzer's term, at the personal rather than at the subpersonal level, where he thinks it should be if it is to be a valid reductive or primitive concept. Keijzer calls this use of a higher-level term (e.g., symbol manipulation) in a lower level (e.g., brain processes) theoretical position *theoretical hitchhiking* because the term has been transported from a higher to a lower level without providing payment in the form of increased theoretical knowledge or understanding. It will be recalled that in the previous chapter we mentioned the problem of explaining the behavior of a person by attributing it to the behavior of a little person—a homunculus—inside of that person. Theoretical hitchhiking seems to be a version of this homunculus error, in that the property of a person (the ability to make and understand representations) is explained by reference to that very same property or ability.

Keijzer is far from being the only person to note the problem he calls theoretical hitchhiking. Steven Harnad, who calls it the "symbol-grounding problem," has expressed it succinctly as follows: "How can the semantic interpretation of a formal system be made *intrinsic* to the system, rather than just parasitic on the meanings in our heads?" (Harnad, 1990, p. 335; italics in original).

Bennett and Hacker (2003), writing about the problem in neuroscience, call it the *mereological fallacy*. They write, "It is the animal that perceives, not parts of its brain, and it is human beings who think and reason, not their brains" (p. 3). In philosophy, this problem is called "the problem of original intentionality"—that is, where does the meaning of a symbol, for example, originate?—where (as we have seen in our discussion of Brentano in chapter 4) intentionality is the property of being about something, the way a symbol is about the thing it represents.

Other Criticisms of Reductionism in Cognitivism

The view that the mind is a computational device that manipulates or processes representations has also received criticisms from some cognitivists as being hopelessly imprecise. The problem according to these cognitivists is that the concept of representation is not adequately operationally defined. For example, Cliff and Noble (1997, p. 1170) ask: "if evolution did produce a design that used internal representations, how would we recognize it?" In other words, what would a representation look like? If we looked for pictures or for words in a brain, we would not find them. It has been proposed that we could find representations by looking for processes or features that have isomorphism, that is, a one-to-one correspondence, with what it is they are supposed to represent (e.g., Kim, 1996, p. 89). It appears, however, that the concept of isomorphism is too inclusive to provide a useful theoretical definition of representation, because for any physical system one can always find isomorphism between the system and something that is causally connected to the system (Haselager et al., 2003; Putnam, 1998; Searle, 1992). For example, one can find isomorphism between movements of the shock absorbers in a car and bumps in the road, but saying that shock absorbers represent bumps in the road does not seem to add to our understanding of shock absorbers. More to the point, if representations reduce to such a simple physical correspondence, it is not clear how postulating them in the mind can help provide a deep understanding of how the mind, in all its complexity, works.

A Possible Solution: Dynamical Systems

One possible solution to the problem of operationally defining representation is to restrict the concept to situations in which the representation is "decoupled" in some way in time or space from the thing that it is represents, and the system uses the representation to respond to the thing being represented (Grush, 1997; Haselager et al., 2003, p. 20). This would, however, still leave the concept undefined for other situations for which cognitivists tend to use the concept, and it would seem not to solve Keijzer's theoretical hitchhiking problem. Another possible solution is to devise a cognitive theory that does not involve representations (although to at least some cognitivists this is tantamount to abandoning the cognitive approach altogether). For Keijzer, and a number of other cognitivists (e.g., Beer, 1995; Brookes, 1991; van Gelder, 1998; Varela et al., 1991), a dynamical interaction between the brain, the body, and the environment seems to fit the bill. Keijzer offers the broad outlines of an alternative theory, yet to be developed, that he calls *behavioral systems theory* (BST). He outlines the following two central commitments (a positive and a negative one) relating to the development of this theory, which is intended to apply to robots (or models) as well as to organisms:

a) The behavior of organisms (as well as of BST-based models) results from multiple, dynamical, reciprocal interactions between a neural system (or another control structure when it comes to the models), a sensory-musculoskeletal system (or just embodiment in the robotic case), and an interaction space (the environment incorporated in the behavioral regularities).

b) The postulation and use of subpersonal representations (interpreted as an internal structure isomorphic to the behaviorally relevant environment) to instruct behavior is rejected. (Keijzer, 2001, p. 226)

It remains to be seen whether the dominant view in cognitivism will continue to be that the mind is a computational system that manipulates representations or whether an alternative approach that does not involve representations will replace it.

BEHAVIORAL APPROACH

Both methodological and radical behaviorism are nonholistic in various respects; however, they differ somewhat in how they are nonholistic. Methodological behaviorists might be thought to be dualistic in their use of mentalistic terms (that is, language referring to the mind) in describing and theorizing about behavior. Terms like *cognition*, which suggests a mind that is cognizant of external stimuli, and *information processing*, which suggests a mind that treats stimuli as incoming information to be stored and manipulated, are popular among methodological behaviorists. It is true that methodological behaviorists maintain that these terms must be operationally defined in terms of overt behavior in order to be scientifically valid, and in this respect they clearly are not dualistic. Radical behaviorists, however, reject all mentalistic terms whether operationally defined or not. They maintain that the dualistic implications of such terms necessarily impede a scientific analysis of behavior. According to radical behaviorists, the greatest clarity and precision is achieved only when all psychological processes are addressed exclusively in behavioral terms (i.e., terms that refer clearly and directly to behavior). As mentioned earlier in this book, this does not rule out the treatment of private, covert, or internal events provided that such events are spoken of as stimuli and responses and are assumed to be no different in principle from public, overt, or external stimuli and responses.

Ways in Which the Behavioral Approach is Nonholistic

Both methodological and radical behaviorists accept the self-other dichotomy as valid. The view that this dichotomy is learned through interacting with the environment, and is functional to the individual, is consistent with both types of behaviorism.

Both methodological and radical behaviorists are clearly within-science reductionistic, in that they analyze their subject matter—behavior—into small units. The units of behaviorism are responses under the control of environmental events. Skinner was explicit about this. For example, he wrote:

> Various objections have been made to the use of rate of responding as a basic datum. For example, such a program may seem to bar us from dealing with many events which are unique occurrences in the life of the individual. A man does not decide upon a career, get married, make a million dollars, or get killed in an accident often enough to make a rate

of response meaningful. But these activities are not responses. They are not simple unitary events lending themselves to prediction as such. If we are to predict marriage, success, accidents, and so on, in anything more than statistical terms, we must deal with the smaller units of behavior which lead to and compose these unitary episodes. If the units appear in repeatable form, the present analysis may be applied. . . . In the field of behavior we arrange a situation in which frequencies are available as data, but we use the notion of probability in analyzing and formulating instances and or types of behavior which are not susceptible to this analysis. (Skinner, 1950, p. 199)

Skinner regarded rate of responding as the basic datum of psychology. Rate of responding is composed of individual, repetitive responses. In this quotation Skinner is saying that in order to understand complex human behavior such as deciding on a career, getting married, etc., we must understand the individual repetitive responses of which these activities are composed.

Role of Representations in Behavioral Theory

It is also important to note that radical behaviorism does not engage in what Keijzer has called *theoretical hitchhiking* with regard to the concept of representation (see above section on the cognitive approach). In radical behaviorism, representation is explained at the *subpersonal level* (again to use Keijzer's term). In other words, representation is derived, not primary. Indeed, from an evolutionary point of view, it is not clear how it could be primary. As the philosopher William Bechtel (2005) noted with regard to cognitive theories of animal behavior, "It seems peculiar to propose that symbol-processing components would have evolved in species that had yet to develop the capacity to manipulate symbols" (p. 321).

Thus, behaviorists see it as a theoretical necessity to account for how people come to manipulate symbols. For example, in his classic work *Verbal Behavior*, Skinner (1957) introduced the concept of the *tact*, which is a verbal response that is evoked in the presence of a specific object or property of an object because it has been reinforced (with what is called a generalized reinforcer—a conditioned reinforcer, such as praise, that has been paired with more than one primary reinforcer) in the presence of that object or property. The stimulus object or property of an object, the response, and the reinforcer constitute what Skinner calls a *three-term contingency*. The following quotation from *Verbal Behavior* illustrates how Skinner uses the lower (subpersonal) level concept of the tact to explain representations persons make:

The three-term contingency in this type of operant is exemplified when, in the presence of a doll, a child frequently achieves some sort of generalized reinforcement [i.e., a reinforcer such as praise] by saying *doll*; or when a teleost fish, or picture thereof, is the occasion upon which the student of zoology is reinforced when he says *teleost fish*. There is no suitable term for this type of operant. "Sign," "symbol," and more technical terms from logic and semantics commit us to specific schemes of reference and stress the verbal response itself rather than the controlling relationship. The invented term "tact" will be used here. (Skinner, 1957, p. 81)

Once a verbal response exists as a tact, it can enter into other types of verbal relations that would be called symbol manipulation.

While Skinner's is the best-known radical behaviorist theory of verbal behavior, it is not the only one. Steven Hayes and his colleagues have proposed an alternative based on relational frame theory, which was discussed in the previous chapter. Relational frames provide an alternative theoretical means for the manipulation of symbols.

Behavioral Approach and Physiology

Both methodological and radical behaviorism are also across-science reductionistic in the sense that both accept the view that, in principle, it should be possible to explain the laws of behavior in terms of physiology. (In fact, most behaviorists would probably agree that, since physiology can in principle be explained in terms of chemistry, and chemistry in terms of physics, it should be possible in principle to explain the laws of behavior in terms of physics.) However, methodological behaviorists seem to be more ready than radical behaviorists to use terms and concepts from physiology to explain behavioral processes. For example, Skinner argued that it makes little sense to talk about neurological correlates of behavior until we have clear functional relationships between behavior and the environment to correlate with neurological processes. According to Skinner, using physiological terms to explain behavior, given our present lack of understanding of physiology, has the same danger as that of using mentalistic terms: both impede a scientific analysis by giving a false sense of understanding.

A radical behaviorist view of across-science reductionism can perhaps best be summed up as follows: In principle, it is possible to explain all behavior on the basis of the science of physiology (i.e., the science of how the nervous system and other internal parts of the individual function and interact). However, behaviorists suggest that we cannot do this yet because too little is known about behavior as well as about physiology. Fortunately, it is possible to have an independent science of behavior that does not talk about physiological processes—for example, how the brain works—in order to formulate lawful relationships between the environment and behavior. This possibility follows from the reasonable assumptions that the relationship between the environment and physiological processes is lawful and that the relationship between physiological processes and behavior is lawful. Therefore, radical behaviorists are interested in developing psychology as the science that relates behavior to the environment, quite apart from any concern for the underlying physiological processes. However, Skinner always maintained that physiology and behavior are independent but complementary sciences. For example, referring to the fact that operant baselines are often used to study brain processes, he stated:

> The use of operant techniques in the brain science laboratory is the best demonstration I can offer of the contribution of an independent science of behavior in making the task of brain science clear. Valid facts about behavior are not invalidated by discoveries concerning the nervous system, nor are facts about the nervous system invalidated by facts about behavior. Both sets of facts are part of the same enterprise, and I have always looked forward to the time when neurology would fill in the temporal and spatial gaps which are inevitable in a behavioral analysis. (Skinner, 1988a)

That time may be approaching, as indicated by the 2005 special issue of the *Journal of the Experimental Analysis of Behavior* devoted to the relation of behavior and neuroscience.

SUMMARY

There are two types of nonholism: dualism and reductionism. There are two types of dualism: mind-body and self-other. There are two types of reductionism: strict and hierarchic systems. Finally, there are two types of strict reductionism: within-science and across-sciences.

Humanistic psychologists advocate a holistic approach to psychology—that is, they advocate treating the individual as a whole rather than as the product of interacting parts or processes. Accordingly, humanistic psychologists believe that breaking the individual into parts can never lead to a satisfactory understanding of the individual.

Humanistic psychologists reject the mind-body distinction not only because it divides the individual into parts, but also because it implies that the universe is composed of two fundamentally different kinds of substances. Although humanistic psychologists emphasize studying the individual as a unitary whole, there is reason to believe that even the phenomenon of consciousness—which humanistic psychologists consider fundamental—is not unitary.

The psychodynamic approach accepts the mind-body distinction in the sense that its goal is to study the mind as distinct from the body. The psychodynamic approach accepts the self-other distinction as an essential aspect of healthy psychological functioning.

The cognitive approach accepts the mind-body distinction—with the mind being thought of as a computer program that runs on the brain. The self-other distinction comes into play in cognitivism in the tendency of normal adults to attribute independent mental states to other individuals. This ability or tendency to attribute mental states has been variously labeled *mental state attribution, metarepresentation, mind reading, perspective-taking,* and *theory of mind.* The cognitive approach is reductionistic because it treats the mind as an information processing system, that is, a computer program. Computer programs are usually based on algorithms that specify interacting components of computer code. Thus cognitive psychology is within-science reductionistic in that its goal is to analyze mental phenomena into interacting modules. Cognitivism is also across-sciences reductionistic to the extent that its goal is to reduce psychology to another science—namely, computer science. However, there is little interest among many cognitivists in reducing psychology to physiology or neurology.

Terms like *cognition,* which suggests a mind that is cognizant of external stimuli, and *information processing,* which suggests a mind that treats stimuli as incoming information to be stored and manipulated, are popular among methodological behaviorists. Radical behaviorists, however, reject all mentalistic terms whether operationally defined or not. According to radical behaviorists, the greatest clarity and precision is achieved only when all psychological processes are discussed exclusively in behavioral terms. Both methodological and radical behaviorists accept the self-other dichotomy as valid. Both methodological and radical behaviorists are clearly within-science reductionistic, in that they analyze their subject matter, behavior, into small units (e.g., stimuli and responses).

Radical behaviorism does not engage in what Keijzer has called *theoretical hitchhiking* with regard to the concept of representation. In radical behaviorism, representation is explained at the subpersonal level. The stimulus object or property of an object, the response, and the reinforcer constitute what Skinner calls a *three-term contingency.* Skinner argued that it makes little sense to talk about neurological correlates of behavior until we have clear functional relationships between behavior and the environment to correlate with neurological processes. According to Skinner, using physiological terms to explain behavior, given our present lack of understanding of physiology, has the same danger as that of using mentalistic terms: both impede a scientific analysis by giving a false sense of understanding. A radical behaviorist view of across-science reductionism can perhaps best be summed up as follows: In principle, it is possible to explain all behavior on the basis of the science of physiology (i.e., the science of how the nervous system and other internal parts of the individual function and interact); however, it is possible to have an independent science of behavior that does not talk about physiological processes—for example, how the brain works—in order to formulate lawful relationships between the environment and behavior.

Discussion Questions

1. What are the two types of dualism discussed in the text? Is there a relationship between these, or are they simply two arbitrary ways of making a distinction or division? What do the two types of dualism divide?

2. Compare and contrast the two types of reductionism. Discuss whether one type is more valid.

3. Discuss whether it is possible for humanistic psychology to be completely holistic—that is, non-dualistic and non-reductionistic.

4. Discuss whether there are aspects of psychodynamic theories that are holistic. Are these aspects compatible with the humanistic approach?

5. Discuss whether there are aspects of the cognitive approach that are at least potentially holistic. Are these aspects compatible with the humanistic approach?

6. Discuss whether there are aspects of the behavioral approach that are holistic. Are these aspects compatible with the humanistic approach?

7. What are the problems with mental representations in psychology? Discuss possible solutions.

8. Discuss how a radical behaviorist would deal with the problem of representations. That is, is there anything in behavior theory that takes the place of representations in cognitive theory?

9. Discuss why we have such a strong sense of self according to each of the four systems.

10. Discuss whether self is an illusory concept, as some have suggested (e.g., Hume, Buddhists).

CHAPTER 10

Teleology: Can the Future Affect the Present?

ecall from chapter 2 that Aristotle postulated four different types of causes for each thing or event: (1) its material cause, (2) its formal cause, (3) its efficient cause, and (4) its final cause. These causes are typically illustrated by the way in which they are supposedly involved in the creation of, for example, a statue. The material cause of a statue is the block of marble with which the sculptor begins; the formal cause is the plan or blueprint of the finished form; the efficient cause is the force the sculptor applies to the chisel with the hammer to shape the block; and the final cause is the purpose or goal of the sculptor in creating the statue.

The fourth type of cause has sometimes been said to appeal to events in the future to account for events in the present (e.g., the future completed stature being the cause of the sculptor's behavior). Such explanations have also sometimes been labeled teleological. This is a familiar misunderstanding of teleology and Aristotle's fourth cause. The trouble may be in the word *cause*, which today is often taken to be synonymous with *efficient cause*. Instead of speaking of Aristotle's four causes, it is probably more accurate to call them his four "*be*causes." It is clear that Aristotle intended them to comprise the kinds of explanations that one might give in response to a *why* question (see Killeen, 2001, pp. 35–36). Thus, final (be)causes, according to Aristotle, are not efficient causes that work backward in time. Final causes are explanations in terms of purpose or intention, and purposes and intentions exist before their effects and therefore may be said to "efficient-cause" them in the normal way.

Nevertheless, teleological or final cause explanations are problematic when applied to natural phenomena, for they imply that nature has purpose or intentionality. Although it probably could not have been predicted at the time Aristotle was developing his philosophy, it was efficient cause that came to be the most productive of his causes in the development of science. In physics, for example, the gravitational attraction of the earth was found to be a more productive explanation of an apple's (or any object's) fall to the earth as opposed to the view that the apple was purposefully or intentionally moving toward its natural place. In the field of biological evolution, to take another example, it was Darwin's theory of natural selection of characteristics contributing to reproductive success, as opposed to organisms being purposely moving toward the goal of perfection, which resulted in a powerful science of biology.

However, there has been reaction against the exclusive dominance of efficient causes in science, especially human science. Some opponents of the exclusive focus on efficient causes, for example, postulate a goal or set of goals whose realization constitutes the highest end or purpose in human life. This end has been variously held to be happiness, contemplation, rationality, autonomy, attainment of certain forms of excellence, free and creative development of one's distinctively human powers, enlightenment, ego-loss, a higher state of consciousness, and union with God. Some theories maintain that if left to their own devices, humans move naturally toward this end; other theories hold that this tendency does not operate automatically, but must be brought into operation through special processes, for example, insight or understanding. In either case, it may be considered a final cause in Aristotle's terminology.

HUMANISTIC APPROACH

To humanistic psychologists, the emphasis of modern science, and especially that of the other approaches to psychology, on efficient causes to the exclusion of final causes has a dehumanizing effect because it seems to be equating humans with mere machines or other inanimate objects. Thus, they tend to show a strong partiality toward Aristotle's final causes. They generally believe that residing within everyone is an actualizing tendency through which we, unless impeded in some way beyond our control, move naturally toward fulfilling our unique potentials—that is, toward what, in some sense, we were meant to be. This is very similar to the way in which, according to Aristotle, a heavy object moves toward the center of the earth because that is its natural place or where it is meant to be.

Carl Rogers' Self-Actualizing Tendency

According to Carl Rogers, the self-actualizing tendency is the only motive that exists; all other motives are simply manifestations of it. He stated:

> It should be noted that this basic actualizing tendency is *the only motive* which is postulated in this theoretical system. . . . The self, for example, is an important construct in our theory, but the self does not "do" anything. It is only one expression of the general tendency of the organism to behave in those ways which maintain and enhance itself. (Rogers, 1959, p. 196)

Thus, an individual will do whatever is necessary for self-maintenance. However, the ultimate goal of each individual is self-actualization, which means to realize his or her full potential.

Abraham Maslow's Needs Hierarchy

Abraham Maslow (1970, pp. 35–46) provided what is probably the most systematically developed and best known theory regarding the actualizing tendency. He proposed that there are five categories of needs, which are organized in the following hierarchy, ranging from lowest to highest:

1. *Physiological*—the basic biological needs for food, water, pain reduction, and the biological aspects of sexual needs.
2. *Safety*—the needs to feel physically and psychologically safe and secure. They include the need for safety from physical danger and the need for economic security.
3. *Love*—the need to love others and to be loved by others, and the need to be an accepted member of a community of friends.
4. *Esteem*—the needs to achieve, to be competent, and to receive respect and appreciation from others.
5. *Self-actualization*—the need to fulfill our own unique potential. "A musician must make music, an artist must paint, a poet must write if he is to be ultimately happy. What a man *can* be, he *must* be" (Maslow, 1970, p. 46; italics in original).

According to Maslow, needs lower on the hierarchy must be satisfied before the higher needs can express themselves. He stated this as follows:

> Man's higher nature rests upon man's lower nature, needing it as a foundation and collapsing without this foundation. That is, for the mass of mankind, man's higher nature is inconceivable without a satisfied lower nature as a base. (Maslow, 1968, p. 173)

And again, "Growth is theoretically possible only because the 'higher' tastes are better than the 'lower' and because the 'lower' satisfaction becomes boring" (Maslow, 1971, p. 147).

An implication of this is that "the perfectly healthy, normal, fortunate man has no sex needs or hunger needs, or needs for safety, or for love, or for prestige, or self-esteem, except in stray moments of quickly passing threat" (Maslow, 1970, p. 57).

Maslow's needs hierarchy has been criticized as not allowing for the kinds of sacrifices that occur when people give up one good for another. For example, should we say that the starving person who shares a last piece of bread with another is not self-actualized? In other words, the needs hierarchy seems to promote a selfish, mechanistic view of humans. Regarding this, Daniels (1988) noted: "In Maslow's theory there are no equally valid, tragic alternatives. Choices, both within and among levels of the hierarchy, may be made simply by deciding which alternative promises greater 'subjective delight'" (Daniels, 1988, p. 23).

In other words, Maslow's humanistic philosophy seems to be lacking an ethical or moral aspect, which seems strange given the high place humanistic psychologists place on concern for others.

Levels of Motivation

Maslow described two levels of motivation and two levels of complaining or "grumbling" when motives are not fulfilled. The higher levels of each of these are called, respectively, *metamotivation* and *metagrumbles*. The closer the individual is to being self-actualized, the higher is the level of his or her grumbles. People who complain about the imperfections of the world instead of about their own lack of possessions, etc., have probably reached a high level of growth and are still striving for further growth. Maslow also distinguishes between (1) deficiency and being motivation, (2) deficiency and being cognition, (3) deficiency and being values, and (4) deficiency and being love. The term *deficiency* in each of these phrases refers to objects or people being seen in terms of remedying some deficit, whereas the term *being* in each of these phrases refers to objects or people being viewed as ends in themselves. For example, hunger is a *deficiency* motive, whereas curiosity is a *being* motive. Loving someone because you need that person is deficiency love; loving that person in the sense that you truly care about him or her is being love. Maslow argued that people who have more B-motivation, B-cognition, B-values, and B-love are closer to being self-actualized than those who have less. Because all of the lower needs are so seldom satisfied in our society, the highest need—that of self-actualization—is satisfied in only a few fortunate individuals.

The Self-Actualized Person

These people, called *self-actualizers*, can be recognized as being exceptional specimens of humanity. Maslow described them as follows:

> Such people become far more self-sufficient and self contained. The determinants which govern them are now primarily inner ones, rather than social or environmental. . . . They are the laws of their own inner nature, their potentialities and capacities, their talents, their latent resources, their creative impulses, their needs to know themselves and to become more and more integrated and unified, more and more aware of what they really are, of what they really want, of what their call or vocation or fate is to be. (Maslow, 1968, p. 35)

Rogers (1959) described the *fully functioning* (i.e., self-actualized) person as follows:

> "The fully functioning person" is synonymous with optimal psychological adjustment, optimal psychological maturity, complete congruence, complete openness to experience. . . . Since some of these terms sound somewhat static, as though such a person "had arrived," it should be pointed out that all the characteristics of such a person are process characteristics. The fully *functioning* person would be a person-in-process, a person continually changing. (p. 235)

Thus self-actualization includes continuing to be actualized. It is not an end or a final goal.

Maslow also emphasized the process aspect of self-actualization. He listed the following characteristics of self-actualizers:

- more efficient perception of reality and more comfortable relations with it;
- acceptance of self, others, nature;
- spontaneity, simplicity, naturalness;
- problem centering, as opposed to being ego-centered;
- the quality of detachment, the need for privacy;
- autonomy—independence of culture and environment;
- continued freshness of appreciation;
- mystic and peak experiences;
- *Gemeinschaftsgefühl* (feeling of kinship with others);
- deeper and more profound interpersonal relations;
- the democratic character structure;
- discrimination between means and ends, between good and evil;
- philosophical, unhostile sense of humor;

- self-actualizing creativeness;
- resistance to enculturation: the transcendence of any particular culture. (1970, pp. 153–172)

According to Maslow, self-actualization "is not an absence of problems but a moving from transitional or unreal problems to real problems" (1968, p. 115). In other words, once one becomes self-actualized, one can deal with the truly important problems of life as opposed to petty problems of everyday living.

According to Rogers, the fully functioning person has three characteristics: (1) Openness to experience, regardless of whether it is positive or negative. Rogers (1961) stated: "He is more open to his feelings of fear and discouragement and pain. He is also more open to his feelings of courage, and tenderness, and awe" (p. 188). (2) Living in the present—fully realizing each moment. This allows "the self and personality [to] *emerge* from experience, rather than experience being translated or twisted to fit preconceived self-structure" (pp. 188–189). (3) Trusting in one's inner urgings and intuitive judgments.

Humanistic psychologists believe that all sorts of good qualities emerge from people who are self-actualized. For example, most humanistic psychologists believe that people are basically altruistic and caring, and that it is only necessary to let them self-actualize for this basic characteristic to be manifested.

Huston Smith (1985) equates self-actualization with a *jivamukta*, which is the Indian term for a fully realized person, that is, a *jiva* (soul) that is *mukta* (liberated, enlightened) in this very life. Smith defines a jivamukta as follows:

> An enlightened being, I am proposing, is one who is in touch with his or her deepest unconscious, an unconscious which . . . deserves to be considered sacred (because being in contact with it enables one to be "holy" in the sense of being "whole"). Our century has acquainted us with regions of our minds that are hidden from us and the powerful ways they control our perceptions. My thesis is that underlying these proximate layers of our unconscious minds is a final substrate that opens mysteriously onto the world as it actually is. (p. 71)

Smith goes on to describe a jivamukta as follows:

> Basically, she lives in the unvarying presence of the numinous (a kind of spirit or creative energy). This does not mean that s-he is excited or "hyped"; his/her condition has nothing to do with adrenalin flow, or with manic states that call for depressive ones to balance the emotional account. It's more like what Kipling had in mind when he said of one of his characters, "He believed that all things were one big miracle, and when a man knows that much he knows something to go upon." The opposite of the sense of the sacred is not serenity or sobriety. It is drabness; taken-for-grantedness. Lack of interest. The humdrum and prosaic. (p. 73)

Generality of the Self-Actualizing Tendency

Some humanistic psychologists believe that the actualizing tendency is not only an important determinant of human behavior, but is present in all living things. Carl Rogers (1961) described it as "the urge which is evident in all organic and human life—to expand, extend, become autonomous, develop, mature—the tendency to express and activate all the capacities of the organism, to the extent that such activation enhances the organism or the self" (p. 35). Toward the end of his life he postulated that it may be present in everything:

> I hypothesize that there is a formative directional tendency in the universe, which can be traced and observed in stellar space, in crystals, in microorganisms, in more complex organic life, and in human beings. This is an evolutionary tendency toward greater order, greater complexity, greater interrelatedness. In humankind, this tendency exhibits itself as the individual moves from a single-cell origin to complex organic functioning, to knowing and sensing below the level of consciousness, to a conscious awareness of the organism and the external world, to a transcendent awareness of the harmony and unity of the cosmic system, including humankind. (Rogers, 1980, p. 133)

In the age-old controversy of whether good outweighs evil, Rogers came down squarely on the side of good. This is indicated in the following statement from Rogers (1969):

> I have little sympathy with the rather prevalent concept that man is basically irrational, and thus his impulses, if not controlled, would lead to destruction of others and self. Man's behavior is exquisitely rational, moving with subtle and ordered complexity toward the goals his organism is endeavoring to achieve. The tragedy for most of us is that our defenses keep us from being aware of this rationality, so that consciously we are moving in one direction, while organismically we are moving in another. (p. 29)

Not all humanistic psychologists agree with Rogers regarding the prevalence of good.

A Possible Dark Side?

In 1982, the existential psychotherapist Rollo May (see chapter 6) published an open letter to Rogers critical of his position minimizing the importance of evil in humans (May, 1982). Regarding May's view that, as Rogers paraphrased it, "the central tendency in human nature is a dual one, aiming both toward creative growth and destructive evil," Rogers (1982) stated, "I find in my experience no innate tendency toward destructiveness, toward evil" (p. 87). Maslow would have agreed with Rogers on this point, for he stated, "Human nature is not nearly as bad as it has been thought to be" (1968, p. 4). And again, "The fact is that people are good, if only their fundamental wishes (for affection and security) are satisfied. . . . Give people affection and security, and they will give affection and be secure in their feelings and behavior" (Maslow, in Lowry, 1973, p.18).

May (1989) pointed out that there are at least two kinds of humanism. One kind accepts Maslow's view of an actualizing tendency that moves us toward becoming more ethical, more spiritual, and closer to some ultimate goodness. The other kind, according to May, does not accept the idea of an actualizing tendency as innate. For this kind of humanism, a teleological cause is just as limiting as an efficient cause. As May put it:

> The other kind of humanism owes more to existential history, and is based on the belief that our own choices have much to do with whether or not we move higher, that we are set free in a universe and must take responsibility for our own future. This view holds that our lives are chiefly tests of character, that we can make a world of peace or its opposite, that life's anxiety, despair, hope, freedom, and love are not gained automatically but are gained through our choices and efforts. For me, this latter has more challenge. (May, 1989, p. 247)

Thus, according to May, self-actualization is the result of responsible choosing rather than an innate tendency. Note that May's theory is just as teleological as Maslow's is; only the source of the final cause is different.

Views of Existential Psychotherapists

Existential psychotherapists tend to speak of "potentiality" as opposed to self-actualization. According to existential psychotherapists, people have a potential which they may or may not realize, and there is no necessary motivation that impels them toward realizing that potential. Helping them to realize it is a major goal of existential psychotherapy. Norcross (1987) stated this as follows: "Existential psychotherapy aims at bringing people to the point of full authenticity-transcendence. The capacity to transcend the immediate situation is a unique characteristic of human existence" (p. 53).

Authenticity and transcendence are discussed in later chapters. It might be noted here that because they do not necessarily accept the notion that people move automatically toward self-actualization, existential psychotherapists often are not reluctant to incorporate psychoanalytic method and theory into their procedures. Existential psychotherapists who tend to use psychodynamic techniques are termed existential-analytic thera-pists, in contrast to existential-humanistic therapists (Norcross, 1987).

Arguments Against Self-Actualization Theories

A number of arguments have been raised against self-actualization theo-ries. These include a lack of an adequate operational definition of self-actualization, incompatibility of the self-actualization concept with mod-ern science, and the focus on self to the exclusion of broad social issues. Each criticism is discussed below.

Lack of Operational Definition

Geller (1984) has pointed out that in order for self-actualization theory to be correct, there must be an end with the following properties: (1) it must be objective; (2) it must apply to all humans, or at least all humans in "a particular type of society at a certain stage of socio-historical devel-opment" (p. 102); (3) realizing this end will enhance the quality of one's life to the greatest extent; and (4) this end has absolute priority over other ends, given certain moral constraints. Geller argues that there is no evi-dence that such an end exists, and that it may be impossible to provide evidence that it does exist—that is, it may be impossible to define the con-cept operationally in such a way that it can be tested scientifically. Cer-tainly, not all humans within a given society tend to pursue the same end, unless the various ends that they do strive for are given such a vague description as to be scientifically useless.

Arguments such as those advanced by Geller led Daniels (1988) to conclude that self-actualization should be considered to be a *myth* rather than a scientific proposition or theory. By myth, however, he does not mean that it should be considered to be false; rather, he means that it be considered to contain an important truth that can be used for the guidance of human conduct, just as many regard the stories in the Bible to be useful myths in helping people to recognize and act on funda-mental truths even though those Biblical stories cannot be demonstrated scientifically to be true (in the sense of having ever actually happened in the way that they are reported in the Bible). This is the pragmatic view of truth (i.e., that a proposition is true to the extent that believing it has useful or practical effects), which, as mentioned in chapter 4, stems from the philosophy of pragmatism put forth by the philosopher C. S. Pierce and famously elaborated by the psychologist-philosopher William James. In James' view, what is true for an individual is what works best for that individual in the long run. Thus, according to pragmatism, a particular myth is true for an individual if that individual finds that myth to be useful in providing meaning or fulfillment. Included in this pragmatic view is the stipulation that the myth does not result in harm to the individual.

Daniels (1988) pointed out that there are two potential pitfalls in the use of self-actualization as a myth: (1) the theory of self-actualization has often been interpreted as promoting the selfish view that the goal in life is to pursue self-gratification without regard for the needs and feelings of others; (2) the theory has often been regarded as promoting an elitist attitude in the sense that (so the objection goes) only very rare people—the elite—are capable of attaining it.

Science and Humanistic Teleology

Regardless of the merits or demerits of self-actualization as theory or myth, the teleological emphasis of humanistic psychologists seems to go against modern scientific theory and practice. Although once popular among scientists, teleology has gradually become less influential. For example, Aristotle postulated that objects fall because they have the goal of being near the center of the earth (i.e., being as close as possible to the center of the earth is the final cause of an object falling). Modern science rejects this teleological explanation. The reason is that a major function of science—and quite possibly its defining characteristic—is to enable us accurately to predict and (where possible) control future events. Even sciences that focus on the past such as paleontology and much of geology make predictions that confirm or disconfirm theories about the past. Scientific prediction must be done on the basis of states or events that have already occurred, since we have no direct access to what has not yet happened. Thus, modern science explains an object's fall to earth in terms of the gravitational field of the earth, the strength of which can be calculated at any point in space prior to the object's fall. In other words, as stated at the beginning of this chapter, modern science bases explanations on efficient causes rather than final or teleological causes.

Although biologists once saw living things as being governed by some overall purpose, they have abandoned this way of thinking because it has not been scientifically productive. According to modern biology, life has evolved into a wide variety of different forms because chance mutations (i.e., accidental changes in the genetic code) have occasionally given rise to forms that were more suited than others to survive in various environments. This process, operating over about 4.5 billion years, has produced some highly complex organisms—including humans. But modern biologists do not see any general purpose or overarching tendency in nature operating to produce more complex forms. They also do not regard humans to be higher than other species on some evolutionary scale; rather, they see humans as occupying one branch of an evolutionary tree that contains many branches.

Humanistic psychologists often use analogies like that of an acorn becoming an oak tree to illustrate the actualizing tendency. For example, Maslow wrote:

> Man demonstrates *in his own nature* a pressure toward fuller and fuller Being, more and more perfect actualization of his humanness in exactly the same naturalistic, scientific sense that an acorn may be said to be "pressing toward" being an oak tree, or that a tiger can be observed to "push toward" being tigerish, or a horse toward being equine. Man is ultimately *not* molded or shaped into humanness, or taught to be human. (Maslow, 1968, p. 160; emphasis in original)

Now it is true that it is standard biology to say that an acorn contains structures that have the biological function of producing an adult oak tree, and that many acorns will at least begin to fulfill this function by causing processes to take place that will tend, in favorable environments, to produce adult oaks. However, evolutionary biologists give an efficient-cause explanation for the potential of an acorn to develop into an oak tree. It is significant that Maslow gives no such efficient-cause explanation for the presence of the self-actualizing tendency in humans.

To an evolutionary biologist an acorn does not become an oak because that is its purpose or goal—that is, it does not become an oak because there is something in the future *pulling on it* to become an oak. It becomes an oak because *in the past* only acorns that became oaks produced new acorns, and because it, unlike some acorns, contains all the genetic material needed to make oaks. Although biologists may say that this material has the function of producing an adult oak tree, they use the word *function* here in a nonteleological sense. A biologist could just as well say that an oak tree has the function of producing acorns; or, in other words, that an oak is an acorn's way of producing more acorns. Most biologists, however, would caution against thinking that an acorn has a purpose or goal to produce more acorns, just as they would caution against thinking that becoming an oak is its purpose or goal.

Biologists have discovered a great deal about the way in which the genetic code enables organisms to reproduce themselves. This information does not support a teleological principle because an organism's genetic code exists prior to that organism reproducing itself. In fact, it is now possible to control in very precise ways what characteristics a new individual will have by manipulating the structure of its genetic code. Moreover, it is theoretically possible to grow a duplicate of a person from any of his or her cells that contain DNA (e.g., skin cells)—that is, to clone a person. This would seem to imply that if we accepted a teleological principle in biology, we would have to conclude that every cell in our bodies has the purpose or goal of becoming a duplicate of ourselves.

Moreover, the notion that the universe is evolving toward more order or complexity is not consistent with modern scientific thinking. In particular, it goes against the second law of thermodynamics in physics. Central to the second law of thermodynamics is the concept of *entropy*, which is the amount of energy in a closed system that is unavailable to do work. Essentially, the second law of thermodynamics states that in a closed system (a system into which no energy is being put, nor from which any energy is leaving), although the amount of energy remains constant, the amount of entropy increases with the passage of time. This means that in a closed system, less energy is available to do work as time passes. But work is required to make things more complex and to maintain them at a high level of complexity. If the universe is a closed system, as physicists on the basis of their observations believe it to be, then on the whole things must be getting less complex rather than more complex. In other words, the overall amount of order must be decreasing rather than increasing.

Neglect of Social Issues

Another criticism of the emphasis of humanistic psychologists on self-actualization is that this focus leads to neglect of broad social issues such as the problems of poverty and the environment. This criticism is particularly relevant in schools and classes that follow humanistic approaches to education. For example, Weinstein (1975) noted:

> Humanistic education, to be fully humanistic, must address itself to the social injustice prevalent in our society. As long as any person's right to develop full human potential is denied through the systems we support and in which we participate, the potential for our own development is diminished. No matter how much self-understanding one acquires—unless that self-understanding is used to change systems which prevent others from developing their full humanness—the notion that humanistic education fosters "self-absorbed," "egocentric" and "politically illiterate" persons is warranted. (Weinstein, 1975, p. 10)

It can of course be pointed out that this is only a political problem, and that a political problem cannot show that a theory is false (or true) unless the claim of the theory is that implementing the theory would solve political problems. Although many humanistic psychologists are politically active (generally as nonsecular humanists tending to promote liberal causes), there is nothing in humanistic psychological theory *per se* that requires such an approach.

PSYCHODYNAMIC APPROACH

According to traditional psychoanalysis, a person behaves in such a way as to release tensions arising from the basic drives (i.e., libido and thanatos) stemming from the id, much as the valves in a hydraulic machine open and close to reduce the water pressure operating on them.

The Hydraulic Model

Psychoanalytic theory has therefore been described as a *hydraulic model*; as such, it is clearly nonteleological. Tension pressuring for release is, in Aristotle's terminology, an efficient cause, not a final cause. According to psychoanalytic theorists, a person will be mentally healthy if his or her ego has managed to release tensions in ways that meet with the approval of society, so that punishment from society and from the superego is avoided. While a humanistic psychologist might say that someone who has a highly creative job from which he or she derives immense satisfaction has achieved self-actualization, a Freudian would say that that person has sublimated his or her sexual and aggressive drives in a highly successful manner.

Psychodynamic Opposition to the Hydraulic Model

Many psychodynamic theorists disagree with Freud's hydraulic model. Among those who disagree with it are Kohut, Adler, and Jung.

Heinz Kohut

Heinz Kohut (1913–1981), the founder of an approach called psychoanalytic self psychology, revised or amended Freud's view of the overriding effect of drives. As Kohut put it:

> The theory of sublimation . . . is tied to the concept of the primacy of drives and to the theory of drive processing; it is in principle incapable of telling us anything about the meaningfulness and fulfillment or emptiness and sterility of a person's life. Conflicts, furthermore, are, again in principle, seen as having a deleterious impact on creative-productive activity as long as we remain within the confines of conceptualizations that explain man in terms of a mental apparatus fueled by the drives. Self psychology, on the other hand, while fully acknowledging the value of the traditional conceptualizations with regard to certain delimited experiences of man—temporarily paralyzing guilt feel-

ings, for example, or even unconscious guilt that hampers performance throughout life—is able to show that, in the presence of a firm self, conflict per se is by no means deleterious, not even the largely unconscious conflict to which traditional analysis assigns the causative role in the psychogenesis of psychopathology. (Kohut, 1984, pp. 44–45)

According to Kohut (1984, pp. 188–191), a person is "functioning in accordance with his [or her] design" if he or she has or is developing a whole, nonfractured, or "nondefective" self. Kohut's appeal to *design* in his theory may appear to be teleological. Similar to the way humanistic psychologists describe the growth of the individual toward self-actualization, psychoanalytic self psychologists believe that the individual moves naturally toward preserving, maintaining, or expanding his or her self structure (Tobin, 1991).

Adler and Jung

For Adlerians the goal is to belong and contribute to the community, whereas for Jungians it is the integration of the personality. It has been argued that the main reason for the break between Freud and Jung was their disagreement over teleology rather than their differing concepts of libido (Horne, Sowa, & Isenman, 2000). For classical Adlerians and Jungians, individuals move toward their respective goals in a clearly purposive manner, although they sometimes need therapeutic help in order to do so effectively. It should be noted, however, that there is a group of Jungians, called developmentalists, who are in opposition to classical Jungians. One of the differences between the classical and developmentalist Jungians is that the latter reject teleology (Horne, 2002); that is, although they accept the integration of the personality as an important objective, developmentalists do not believe that there is some overriding principle that inevitably guides the individual toward this integration.

COGNITIVE APPROACH

Aristotle's efficient cause suffices for cognitive science, as it does for most of science. After all, computers know nothing about the future; they respond simply on the basis of past input. Thus, if we are considering the mind as a computer, we do not need to be concerned with inputs into the mind from the future. This raises the question of how devices such as computers can seem to anticipate the future.

Nonteleological Aspects of Cognitivism

Consider the common thermostat. This device keeps the room at a certain temperature by turning on the furnace when the temperature falls below that level and turning it off when the temperature rises above that level. The thermostat is thus acting as though it has a goal or purpose, namely, to maintain the room at a certain temperature. Although the thermostat appears to be showing purposive behavior, however, it operates the way it does because of its construction which involves only known physical principles. A thermostat is so constructed that an increase in the temperature above the set value acts as an efficient cause for the furnace to turn off, while a decrease in the temperature below the set value acts as an efficient cause for the furnace to turn on.

The above example may seem to be too simple to be relevant to the issue of purpose. However, it is not difficult to increase its complexity considerably without having to resort to teleology. For example, we could install a device that senses when someone is home, and program a computer to adjust the thermostat higher when there is someone home than when there isn't. To add further complexity to the example, the computer could be programmed to analyze the comings and goings of people in the house, and to adjust the thermostat in anticipation of the house being occupied or unoccupied. The computer would then appear to have the purpose or goal of keeping people in the house comfortable while minimizing energy expenditure. The computer as described even seems to be engaging in planning to achieve this goal (i.e., by anticipating when the house is going to be occupied or unoccupied). In other words, it seems possible in principle to increase the complexity of the computer's behavior to that approaching the human level, without having to appeal to teleology. This suggests that teleological explanations may not be necessary to account for human purposive behavior.

The Intentional Stance

The philosopher Daniel Dennett (1983, 1987) has argued for a teleological approach to cognitive science that he calls the *intentional stance*. According to this approach, there are certain systems for which it makes sense and gives us explanatory and predictive power to assume that these systems have beliefs, desires, and purposes or goals. The word processor in my computer, for example, may be considered to be an intentional system. When I type a word that is unfamiliar to it, it changes the word to a familiar one. Taking the intentional stance, this is because it has the goal of correcting my spelling errors and believes that I have made one, even if I have not. Knowing that my word processor has this kind of intentionality helps me to predict its behavior.

According to Dennett, the intentional stance may be taken profitably with very simple machines and organisms, as well as with more complex ones. Dennett sees no fundamental difference in principle between the intentionality of a machine and that of humans. In the case of humans, as in the cases of machines and lower organisms, the intentional stance does not imply that intentionality really exists. It is simply an assumption that allows us to make better predictions. An implication that many cognitivists take from this is that since speaking of beliefs, desires, purposes, and goals has predictive power when considering even simple machines and organisms, it must per force be scientifically useful when talking about human behavior.

In disagreement with Dennett, the philosopher John Searle (1983) believes that machines cannot show real intentionality. Instead, he calls the intentionality machines appear to show *derived intentionality* because it is derived from the intentionality of those who designed the machine and those who use it. All my word processor is doing when it changes the words I type is changing patterns of electricity. Any intentionality in the system, according to Searle (e.g., 2004), derives from my beliefs and goals regarding whatever it is that I am typing about. Left unexplained by Searle, however, is the origin of original intentionality—that is, where does it come from and why should it be present in the electrochemical patterns of human neurons but not in the electrical patterns of computers?

Other cognitivists (e.g., Churchland, P. M., 1988; Churchland, P. S., 1983) believe that to take an intentional stance is to speak in the language of folk psychology, which they believe, as behavioral neuroscience progresses, will be and should be replaced by more scientific terminology, specifically that of neurology.

BEHAVIORAL APPROACH

Like psychoanalytic and cognitive theorists, behaviorists are nonteleological in the sense of teleology referring to backward causation. They believe that the function of science is to predict and (where possible) control events in the future on the basis of current states and events. In addition, radical behaviorists would agree with those cognitivists who argue that teleological language smacks of folk psychology and should be replaced by more scientific terminology. However, unlike these cognitivists, radical behaviorists believe that behavioral, rather than neurological, language provides the scientific terminology that is needed.

Nonteleological Aspects of Behaviorism

Some methodological behaviorists have adopted a view similar to that of Freudians with regard to drives. These behaviorists believe that organisms respond in such a way as to reduce internal tensions called *drives* which are produced by deficits or excesses of certain substances in the body. For example, a deficit of food in the body produces hunger, which causes food and stimuli associated with food to be reinforcing to the organism.

Radical behaviorists, as pointed out in chapter 7, do not believe that the concept of drive is useful in furthering a scientific understanding of behavior. They even more forcefully reject the concept of an actualizing tendency or drive existing in humans or other animals. Radical behaviorists would say that through the process of evolution certain stimuli (e.g., food, water, sexual contact) have become primary reinforcers for members of each species because these stimuli lead to the survival of that species. But there is no general drive for survival per se. Other members of our culture present us with conditioned and primary reinforcers for behaving in ways that might be said to show self-actualization; but there is no general drive to engage in such behavior.

Although there is no drive for self-actualization according to radical behaviorists, they nevertheless would not disagree that reaching one's fullest potential—however that might be defined—is a worthy goal, and in fact one that behaviorism can help to achieve. As he recalled in the third volume of his autobiography, Skinner made this point at the 1972 meeting of the American Humanist Association, where he was named Humanist of the Year: "Where existentialism, phenomenology, and structuralism seek to discover what a person *is*, I thought we should more effectively 'actualize the human potential' if we examined what people do and why they do it. Behaviorism was simply effective Humanism" (Skinner, 1983, pp. 342–343; emphasis in original).

A question that is often asked of behaviorists is how it is possible, according to their theory, for someone to appear to work for purposes that seem not to provide primary reinforcement, and may actually deprive the individual of primary reinforcement. An example is the case of altruistic and caring behavior, which humanistic psychologists maintain is characteristic of self-actualized people. One possibility is that we might have altruistic primary reinforcers; that is, we might be programmed genetically to be reinforced by seeing others receiving reinforcement or being freed from aversive stimulation. Such altruistic primary reinforcers might have evolved because they would promote the survival of individuals who had similar genes.

The Concept of Purpose in Behaviorism

That behaviorism is nonteleological does not mean that it totally disregards the concept of purpose. In fact, Skinner (1974, p. 55) stated that "[o]perant behavior is the very field of purpose and intention." He was very clear, however, that he did not mean this in a teleological sense. He believed that the principle of reinforcement moves the purpose of a response from the future into the past, just as Darwin's principle of natural selection did this for an organ or inherited trait. For example, Skinner stated:

> Before Darwin, the purpose of a well-developed eye might have been said to permit the organism to see better. The principle of natural selection moved "seeing better" from the future into the past: organisms with well-developed eyes were descended from those which had been able to see better and had therefore produced more descendants. (Skinner, 1966a, p. 13)

Typically, however, radical behaviorists avoid the word *purpose* when speaking in technical behavioral language. From a behavioral point of view, the word is problematic because it appears to refer to something that has not yet occurred. For example, in the statement that a rat presses a lever for the purpose of getting food, the word *purpose* appears to refer to future food, which suggests that something in the future can be the cause of present behavior. Actually, however, it can only refer to the food which *in the past* has reinforced the rat's lever pressing. It cannot refer to the future food that the rat will get when it presses the lever, for there may not be any.

Now, the fact that humans have verbal behavior enables us to describe our reinforcers or *purposes*—e.g., "My purpose in opening the window was to let in some fresh air." But possessing verbal behavior also permits us to describe events we have never experienced as though they were reinforcers for our behavior—for example, "My purpose in going to college is to get a BA degree," where the speaker has never been reinforced by receiving a BA degree. Hence, in addition to describing past reinforcers, the word *purpose* can also refer to events one has never experienced. However, it is not these events which are determining the individual's behavior; rather, it is past events, including the conditioning of the complex verbal behavior describing events not yet experienced, that determine the individual's subsequent behavior.

Relational Frame Theory

Some humanistic psychologists have argued that our ability to respond to and talk about situations we are not experiencing (and may never have experienced) causes a problem for behaviorists, because talking about something we are not experiencing cannot be caused by prior stimuli (e.g., Rychlak, 2003, pp. 56–57). A radical behaviorist would point out that this argument fails to consider that once a person has acquired a complex verbal repertoire, a number of variables can cause verbal responses to combine in a variety of ways (Skinner, 1957). For example, storytellers of ancient times related experiences they had not had, such as seeing unicorns. Verbal behavior describing unicorns might be produced by encounters with horses and horned creatures in combination with a verbal community that does not strongly reinforce accuracy.

But this does not provide a complete answer to the question of how we are able to discuss and plan for events that have never occurred. Relational frame theory, which was discussed in chapter 8, attempts to provide a more detailed behavioral explanation (e.g., Barnes-Holmes et al., 2001, pp. 113–114). Essentially, this explanation is that we first learn many relational frames involving events we have experienced. We learn, for example, "If you eat too much candy you will get sick"; "If you go out in the rain without an umbrella you will get wet"; "If you do your homework you will be allowed to watch TV." Eventually, some of us can sometimes respond appropriately to "If you smoke cigarettes you will get cancer," "If you eat your vegetables you will have a healthy life," "If you go to church regularly you will go to Heaven," and so on.

Teleological Behaviorism

As mentioned in chapter 7, Howard Rachlin (1992) has proposed a form of radical behaviorism called *teleological behaviorism* that deals with the future in a way that is compatible with (although not dependent on) relational frame theory. To understand Rachlin's theory, we begin by noting that he agrees with philosophers who believe that Aristotle's four causes (especially his final cause) have been misunderstood.

If one were to ask why a chip flew out of a block of marble, for example, one might answer with any of the following, depending on the context of the question or the information the asker is lacking:

- because a sculptor hit the block with a hammer (efficient cause)
- because marble is a substance that breaks when hit with a forceful blow (material cause)
- because a drawing or plan required knocking out that particular chunk (formal cause)
- because a sculptor is making a sculpture (final cause).

Note that in this interpretation, the finished sculpture did not cause the piece to fly out of the block of marble; that is, the future does not act on the present. In addition, note that the fourth (final) (be)cause provides more information about the behavior of the sculptor than do any of the other (be)causes. The first (efficient) (be)cause tells us only that the sculptor has swung a hammer. He or she might have done this randomly, might have been having a tantrum, might be a fake pretending to be a sculptor, and so on. Teleological behaviorism maintains that only by observing an individual's behavior patterns over an interval of time can we make psychologically meaningful statements about that behavior.

Rachlin would agree that the study of operant behavior is the field of purposive behavior. According to Rachlin, Skinner took a very important step when he focused on studying patterns of behavior over time—

which Skinner did with his concept of rate of responding. However, according to Rachlin, Skinner took a wrong step when he defined reinforcement as the increased probability of a response by a stimulus that followed it. Instead of focusing on individual responses and reinforcers, Skinner should have directed his attention to patterns-of-responses under the control of patterns-of-reinforcers over time. Another wrong step Skinner made, according to Rachlin, was the acceptance of the idea that private stimuli can cause overt behavior. According to Rachlin, there are no truly private stimuli that cause behavior. He maintains that to postulate private stimuli as causes of behavior is to make the same mistake methodological behaviorists and cognitive psychologists make, which is to postulate inner efficient causes as opposed to final or teleological causes of behavior. The individual is a privileged observer of the causes of his or her own behavior only by virtue of typically having a larger sample of his or her own behavior over time. Given the same sample size of an individual's behavior, another observer would know as much about that individual as the individual does. Indeed, the other observer would know more because he or she can observe more by being at some distance from the individual being observed. This would (in agreement with Freudian psychology on this one particular point) include the individual's motives.

In a book chapter in which Rachlin was a commentator on Skinner's writings, Rachlin asserted that "in a (truly) Skinnerian science of psychology," even a toothache cannot be considered to be a private event. He made the point that to be consistent with Skinner's psychology, a toothache must be respondent behavior, operant behavior, or some combination of both. If it is respondent behavior, then it must be elicited by the diseased tooth (which is publicly observable, e.g., by a dentist). (Efficient causation is appropriate for reflexive behavior.) To the extent that it is operant behavior, there is no inner stimulus to be observed because operant behavior is (according to Rachlin) controlled by its consequences, not by prior stimuli. Rachlin also maintains that other events or states that methodological behaviorists and cognitive psychologists have postulated as private are, in fact, fully public when an individual's behavior is observed over a long interval of time. For example, in his commentary, Rachlin stated:

> In the case of thoughts, feelings, and other mental events, there is usually no apparent objective cause like a tooth that may be alternately considered inside or outside the organism. There is (usually) no apparent external antecedent stimulus that can be said (by the laws of the reflex) to elicit these mental events. Such events are thus operants—overt actions controlled by their consequences. Nothing . . . Skinner has written, and nothing in nature contradicts this idea. The main difference between a rat's hope and a rat's bar press is not that one is private and internal (even partially) and the other is public and external. Both are wholly

external and (at least potentially) public, but one takes longer to occur than the other. (Rachlin, 1988, p. 201)

Skinner replied in part as follows:

> I found Rachlin's paper puzzling. He evidently uses the term "tooth-ache" for all the behavior elicited or evoked by a carious tooth, where I was using it to mean only the stimulation arising from such a tooth. He also speaks of thoughts, feelings, and other mental events and argues that they must be operants because they have "no apparent external antecedent stimulus." But one point of [the article Rachlin was commenting on] was that a substantial amount of behavior that would be called operant was indeed under the control of private stimuli; that was the problem I was discussing. I can't imagine what Rachlin means by a rat's hope or how he knows that it takes longer than a bar press. (Skinner, 1988b, p. 201)

In giving equal status to the concepts of hope and toothache, Rachlin may have committed what the philosopher Gilbert Ryle (1949/1990) called a category mistake. For example, a hypothetical person who visits a university and asks, "I see all the buildings but where is the university?" is making a category error by placing a university in the same category as a building. A university is a concept at a higher level of abstraction (hence in a different category) than a building. Similarly, although the concepts of hope and toothache may appear to refer to similar sorts of inner things, hope may be at a higher level of abstraction than a toothache (even one that is simply due to a sensitive tooth with no sign of decay). Hope may refer to hopeful behavior, which in a rat may be repeatedly sniffing at an empty feeder that used to provide food. Thus, Rachlin may be right in arguing that hope takes longer to occur (or at least to be observed) than a bar press. Skinner may be right in arguing that a toothache is a private stimulus—that is, a stimulus that is observable to only one person given current technology.

Rachlin has extended teleological behaviorism to self-control (Rachlin, 2000). Problems in self-control involve not giving sufficient weight to long-term consequences. The alcoholic continues to drink, the heavy smoker continues to smoke, the obese person continues to overeat, despite the long-term negative health and social consequences. Following economic value theory, Rachlin conceptualizes the values of the problem behavior and the alternative desirable behavior as two lines with a negative slope on a graph. The line representing the value of the problem behavior is always above the line representing the value of the desirable alternative behavior. At any given point in time, the individual can move from one line to the other. Each movement from one line to the other represents an up or down movement with regard to the value of the behavior. Each time the individual engages in the problem behavior, he or she moves to the right, thus in the downward direction (which Rachlin calls the primrose path). Each time the individual abstains from the problem behavior by engaging in the desirable alternative behavior, he or she moves to the left, thus in the upward direction. Thus, at any given point in time, being on the upper line (the one representing the problem behavior) has a higher value than being on the lower line (the one representing the desirable alternative behavior). Over the long run, however, more value accrues to the desirable alternative than to the problem behavior. Self-control, then, becomes a matter of, in effect, coming under the control of the net value accruing to one's self over a larger portion of this value graph than is currently the case.

Rachlin's theory suggests some potentially useful behavior control techniques. Consistent with relational frame theory, rules that indicate some time period over which a negative effect will occur (e.g., "smoking will shorten your life," "consuming alcohol can harm your fetus," "drugs will ruin your future career prospects") can be effective, although their effectiveness varies considerably. According to Rachlin, anything that draws one's attention to the frequency of the problem behavior over time can also be effective. Thus, recording the number of instances of the problem behavior has been shown to be effective. Interestingly, instructing individuals to decrease the variability of the problem behavior can reduce it even more than simply recording it. Specifically, smokers who are instructed to smoke exactly the same number of cigarettes on each day of each week that they smoked on the first day of the week decrease the number of cigarettes they smoke more than smokers who simply record the number of cigarettes they smoke. The reason according to teleological behaviorism is that for smokers who decrease the variability of the number of cigarettes they smoke, each cigarette smoked on the first day of each week represents not just another cigarette but seven cigarettes spread across the whole week.

Interestingly, Rachlin has extended teleological behaviorism further to account for altruistic behavior. Lack of self-control can be thought of as having a sense of one's own self-interest that encompasses only a very short interval of time. Through self-control one expands one's concept of self-interest to include the interests of one's future self. Similarly, through altruism one expands one's sense of self-interest to include the interests of other people.

SUMMARY

Aristotle postulated four different types of causes for each thing or event: (1) its material cause; (2) its formal cause; (3) its efficient cause; and (4) its final cause. The material cause of a statue is the block of marble with which the sculptor begins; the formal cause is the plan or blueprint of the finished form; the efficient cause is the force the sculptor applies to the chisel with the hammer to shape the block; and the final cause is the purpose or goal of the sculptor in creating the statue. The fourth cause is teleological, where teleology is the view that there are intentions, purposes, or goals in inanimate nature as well as in animal and human behavior. It was efficient cause that came to be most productive of all Aristotle's causes in the development of science. However, this does not necessarily mean that it will prove to be the most productive cause in psychology.

Humanistic psychology emphasizes self-actualization (realization of one's full potential), which is a teleological cause—a goal that pulls the individual toward it. According to Rogers, the self-actualizing tendency is the only motive that exists; all other motives are simply manifestations of it. Abraham Maslow provided what is probably the most systematically developed and best known theory regarding the actualizing tendency: a needs hierarchy. According to Maslow, needs lower on the hierarchy must be satisfied before the higher needs (the drive toward self-actualization is the highest) can express themselves.

Freud adopted a hydraulic model: Tension pressuring for release is, in Aristotle's terminology, an efficient cause, not a final cause. Heinz Kohut, the founder of an approach called psychoanalytic self psychology, revised or amended Freud's view of the overriding effect of drives. Similar to the way humanistic psychologists assume the growth of the individual toward self-actualization, psychoanalytic self psychologists believe that the individual moves naturally toward preserving, maintaining, or expanding his or her self structure. Other psychodynamic psychologists are also teleological in the sense that the individual strives for some deep psychological goal.

Aristotle's efficient and material causes suffice for most cognitivists. Although a thermostat appears to be showing purposive behavior, for example, it operates the way it does because of its construction (a material cause, in Aristotle's terminology), which involves only known physical principles describing how the present affects the future (not the other way around). The efficient cause is a feedback mechanism—although it is worth pointing out that a human had to program the feedback mechanism to achieve a specific purpose. Although cognitivists in general reject teleology, some of them maintain that it is theoretically and practically useful to act as though some machines and simple organisms, as well as humans, have beliefs, desires, intentions, purposes, and goals—that is, to take what Dennett calls an intentional stance.

Like psychoanalytic and cognitive theorists, most behaviorists are non-teleological in the sense that they believe that the function of science is to predict and control events in the future on the basis of current states and events. Radical behaviorists do not believe that the concept of *drive* is useful in furthering a scientific understanding of behavior. They even more forcefully reject the concept of an actualizing tendency. Other members of our culture present us with conditioned and primary reinforcers for behaving in ways that might be said to show self-actualization; but there is no general drive to engage in such behavior.

Howard Rachlin, however, is an exception to the exclusive emphasis of radical behaviorists on efficient causes. He has proposed a behavioral theory, called teleological behaviorism, based on future goals determining current behavior.

Discussion Questions

1. Discuss which of Aristotle's four causes appear to have been the most useful to the older sciences (e.g., physics, chemistry), and which have been the least useful. Why do you suppose this is, and do you think this need be the case for the newer sciences such as psychology?

2. In what sense is humanistic psychology teleological? Discuss whether it is nonteleological in any sense.

3. Discuss whether there is a dark side to humanistic psychology's emphasis on self-actualization.

4. Discuss which of the psychodynamic theories is most teleological, and which is least teleological.

5. Discuss which aspects of cognitivism are nonteleological, and which are teleological. Is a completely teleological cognitivism conceivable? Explain.

6. Discuss the merits and demerits of taking an intentional stance with regard to (a) machines, (b) simple organisms, (c) people.

7. Is there a relationship between Rachlin's teleological behaviorism and the self-other dichotomy as described in chapter 9? Discuss.

8. Discuss the similarities and differences between Rachlin's teleological behaviorism and the intentional stance.

9. Discuss "purpose" in two of the systems presented that disagree on how they view this issue.

10. Discuss the similarities and differences between the teleological aspects of humanistic psychology, psychodynamics, cognitive psychology, and behavioral psychology.

CHAPTER 11

The Issue of Free Will: Determinism vs. Indeterminism

*T*he issue of determinism versus indeterminism or free will arose early in philosophy. The deterministic view is apparent in the philosophy of Democritus, as seen in chapter 1 of this book. Recall that Democritus believed that everything, including the human soul, is composed of atoms that move in an orderly or lawful way. Hence, a person's behavior is determined completely by the lawful movements in the atoms in his or her body. This view did not sit well with Plato and Aristotle, who greatly emphasized the importance of human reasoning powers in guiding people to choose to do good rather than evil. Recall also from chapter 1 that Epicurus adopted Democritus' idea of atoms, with one significant modification. He believed that human soul atoms could execute a *swerve,* by which he meant that they could depart from their determined course. This indeterminacy allowed for a certain amount of free will in humans, which in Epicurus' belief justified punishing people for their misdeeds.

As also seen from chapter 1, the teachings of Aristotle rather than those of Epicurus had a great effect on early Christian theology (e.g., O'Daly, 1999, pp. 403–405). According to Augustine, for example, it is the God-given gift of reason that allows individuals to choose good over evil. Many Christian theologians following Augustine, however, were greatly perplexed by what appeared to be a logical contradiction in the teachings of the Roman Catholic Church. On the one hand, the Church maintained that each person possesses free will—that is, each person is free to choose good or evil. Therefore each person can be held accountable for his or her choices, and may be punished in hell or purgatory for making the wrong choices. On the other hand, the Church maintained that God is omniscient (i.e., all-knowing). However, if God is omniscient, God knows what choices we are going to make before we make them. This seems to imply that the choices we are going to make must be predetermined; but if they are predetermined, we are not free to choose differently as the doctrine of free will would imply.

This quandary led Martin Luther (1483–1546) and John Calvin (1509–1564) to embrace a doctrine known as *predestination*. This doctrine, which was emphasized more by Calvin than by Luther (although it followed logically from both of their positions), stated that whether a person would be good or evil and whether the person was destined to go to heaven or to hell was determined before the universe started, and was not under the person's control. Although this philosophy might seem strange and harsh, Weber pointed out that according to Calvinists:

> For the damned to complain of their lot would be much the same as for animals to bemoan the fact that they were not born as men. . . . [Calvinists] know only that a part of humanity is saved, the rest damned. To assume that human merit or guilt play a part in determining this destiny would be to think God's absolutely free decrees, which have been settled from eternity, as subject to change by human influence, an impossible contradiction. (Weber, 1958, p. 103)

Calvinists assumed that the saved were predetermined to behave in a manner befitting their chosen status—that is, in ways that would be considered to be good.

Perhaps influenced by their reading of Greek philosophers such as Epicurus, European philosophers began to debate the presence or absence of free will. Descartes and Kant, for example, accepted it. Other philosophers, called *compatibalists*—examples being Hobbes and Hume—rejected indeterminism but believed that free will is compatible with determinism. Another name for compatibalism is *soft determinism*—a term coined by William James who favored this position. Although many arguments have been advanced, however, no one has convincingly demonstrated how determinism and free will can be compatible.

As science began to account for more and more of the variability in nature, indeterminism seemed to become less and less tenable. The discovery in the nineteenth century that human statistical data followed a normal distribution across the board (e.g., crime rates, marriages) followed a normal distribution (see chapter 3) led many to seriously question indeterminism and, with it, the notion of free will. Others argued that because statistics predicts only averages it thus leaves room for indeterminacy—and thus possibly free will—at the level of the individual (Porter, 1986, pp. 162–171). Another blow against indeterminism was the rise of

Darwinian evolutionary theory, which implied that humans are subject to the laws of nature just as other, simpler organisms are assumed to be.

Each of the four systems has taken a fairly consistent stand with regard to the issue of determinism versus indeterminism.

HUMANISTIC APPROACH

Humanistic psychologists generally adopt an indeterministic or compatibalistic position. This position appears to leave room for free will or *personal freedom*, as humanistic psychologists tend to call it. They prefer the latter term because the former suggests philosophical division of the mind into components in which will is one component (intellect and emotion being two other components). This goes against the holistic emphasis of humanistic psychology. According to humanistic psychologists, personal freedom refers to our ability to determine our own behavior apart from the environmental and genetic variables operating on us. It is therefore also called *self-determination*.

Evidence and Implications

The major evidence that humanistic psychologists provide for the existence of self-determination is phenomenological. We have the conscious experience of being able to choose freely; therefore we are able to choose freely. The experience is not an illusion. Self-determination exists, is good, and should be developed to the fullest extent possible. Developing it is important in the process of self-actualization. This belief in the importance of personal freedom is a key element in the approach of humanistic psychologists to practical issues.

For example, some humanistic psychologists in clinical practice adopt a *nondirective* form of therapy. In nondirective therapy, the therapist acts as a catalyst in the presence of which the client works through his or her own problems. This consists mainly of repeating back in a slightly modified form whatever the client says. Thus, if the client says, "I'm feeling depressed," the therapist may reply, "So you're feeling depressed"; or if the client says, "My father never liked me," the therapist may reply, "Tell me more about your father." In this way the therapist acts as a sort of mirror for the client to observe his or her own behavior. Throughout treatment the therapist attempts to exert as little control over the client's behavior as possible.

In the humanistic approach to education, teachers attempt to provide a nonpunitive environment in which students are free to learn as they choose. Teachers do not attempt to force the student to learn or to control what the student learns. There are few or no specific times when a student is required to know specific information, as when tests are scheduled. Students are not forced to progress at the same rate. Teachers tend to use small group discussions rather than lectures to focus on specific themes that the teacher would like the student to consider and study, but the student is not obliged to do so.

Carl Rogers' views against the traditional system of education are reflected in his criticism of the manner in which psychology graduate students were being trained. Rogers (1969) stated: "The theme of my statement is that we are doing an unintelligent, ineffectual and wasteful job of preparing psychologists, to the detriment of our discipline and society" (p. 170).

He attacked what he saw as erroneous implicit assumptions of graduate training in psychology, some of which were: (1) "The student cannot be trusted to pursue his own scientific and professional learning." (2) "Evaluation is education; education is evaluation." (3) "Presentation equals learning: What is presented in the lecture is what the student learns." (4) "The truths of psychology are known." (5) "Creative scientists develop from passive learners" (pp. 169–187). Elsewhere he criticized the lack of emphasis on feelings in university courses, stating: "Yet, if we are truly aware, we can hear the 'silent screams' of denied feelings echoing off of every classroom wall and university corridor. And if we are sensitive enough, we can hear the creative thoughts and ideas that often emerge during and from the open expression of our feelings" (1973, p. 385).

Humanistic psychologists also favor a minimal amount of control of the individual by society. They support the freedom of the individual to self-actualize in his or her own way, and oppose all attempts to force people to conform to the arbitrary norms of society. They are against all forms of oppression within society, including the oppression of the poor by the rich, oppression of minorities by the majority, and oppression of those with unpopular political views by the dominant political group.

Freedom is important to existential psychotherapists in several ways. First, there is the phenomenological experience of freedom—that is, we are conscious of, or capable of being conscious of, a feeling of freedom. This can be a frightening experience, leading people to want to (as Erich Fromm, 1965, put it) "escape from freedom." This is why people often seem so eager to put dictators in high political office and to rely so heavily for their opinions on authority figures. Existential therapists try to help the client move toward freedom instead of away from it. As Norcross put it:

> One goal of existential treatment is to assist individuals in loosening their deterministic shackles and to choose freedom. The essence of existential therapy is the client's movement from feeling unfree and controlled by others toward the frightening but rewarding sense of freedom to map out a new "identity" or being. (Norcross, 1987, pp. 48–49)

Second, in addition to heightening the positive phenomenological sense of freedom, existential psychotherapists strive to help the client exercise that freedom in a fulfilling manner through the making of responsible choices. The client is helped to learn to recognize both his or her power to choose and the consequences of those choices, and to take responsibility for his or her choices and their consequences.

Difficulties with the Humanistic Approach

There are some philosophical difficulties with the humanistic position on the issue of determinism. For example, it is not valid to use our feeling of personal freedom to argue that our behavior is not determined. There are many things that we may feel to be true yet are not. We feel that the earth is stationary although careful scientific study has revealed that it is actually rotating and speeding around the sun at a rate of several thousand kilometers per hour. Moreover, there are instances in which a person's behavior is clearly under the control of the environment even though he or she feels perfectly free. For example, a person who is able to spend time with a loved one can safely be predicted to do so; thus, his or her behavior in this case is clearly determined or caused, although the person will almost certainly feel free rather than controlled. Moreover, we have no reason to think that we would have any way of feeling the difference between being free and being determined.

A question of importance for humanistic psychology is whether it is possible to have a science based so strongly on indeterminism. Many of science's most successful achievements occurred when determinism was emphasized, especially in the early stages of a given science. For example, consider the law of gravity. An object that is dropped from a certain height always falls with a specific acceleration that can be calculated in advance and strikes the ground at a specific time that can also be calculated in advance. It is not free to go up instead of down or to suddenly stop in mid-fall for a few seconds. Out of highly reliable results such as these, scientists have formulated laws and principles that have made science into the highly effective enterprise it is today. In latter stages of some sciences, random processes became important. However, these processes were assumed to following well-established statistical laws (see chapter 3).

PSYCHODYNAMIC APPROACH

The traditional psychoanalytic approach adopts a strict deterministic position. All of our behavior is caused by the competition of the id and superego for control over the ego, and the manner in which the ego has been shaped by the environment to resolve these conflicts. Despite the fact that our behavior is determined, we feel free (psychoanalytic theorists maintain) because most of this drama is played out in the unconscious.

Psychoanalytic theory concerning determinism has definite practical implications. Unlike humanistic psychologists, psychoanalysts take a directive role in conducting therapy. At times the therapist may have to push the client very hard to delve into his or her unconscious to bring forth repressed material, for this material is often very painful. Nevertheless, like a physician lancing a boil, psychoanalysts persist in their probing so that the repressed material can be dealt with by the client's ego. Psychoanalysts are also directive in helping the client interpret the material that comes up from the unconscious during sessions and in dreams that are discussed during sessions.

The Control-Freedom Paradox

Psychoanalysts are sensitive to the paradox involved in the view that behavior is determined on the one hand and that on the other the goal of psychotherapy is to help individuals become freer. Miller (1992) described this paradox as follows: "[T]he goal of psychoanalysis is to give people freedom to make choices rationally, to be free of irrational forces dominating their lives. Freud's clinical theory seems to be going in the direction of free will, whereas his metapsychology is clearly deterministic" (Miller, 1992, p. 343).

It might be pointed out, however, that making a rational choice is compatible with determinism. The goal of therapy, on this interpretation of the Freudian view, should be to cause people to stop being deterministic systems that make many irrational choices and to start being deterministic systems that make only rational choices.

Practical Implications

Although psychoanalytic theory has not been applied in any systematic practical way other than therapy, it does have some practical implications.

Education

Psychoanalysts would see education as a socialization process in which the libido and thanatos are redirected from socially unacceptable to socially acceptable activities and objects. Teachers would be encouraged to help the student in this sublimation process by providing material with appropriate symbolic content.

Improvement of Society

Psychoanalytic theory has had little or nothing to say about the improvement of society. Freud was very pessimistic about the possibility of any significant improvement. According to Freud, the id is always in conflict with society and there is no fully satisfactory way to resolve this conflict. An illustration of Freud's pessimism is provided by an exchange of letters between Einstein and him. As a strong pacifist, Einstein wrote to Freud proposing that the two of them (as the best-known physicist and psychiatrist) engage in regular correspondence concerning how the threat of war might be eliminated. Freud wrote back saying, essentially, that such correspondence could serve no useful purpose because the problem is with humanity's aggressive nature which cannot be eliminated.

COGNITIVE APPROACH

If we take the computer as a model of the human mind, as cognitivists tend to do, the only way that free will can be operating in a computer would seem to be as a random or pseudo-random number generator. We first consider both of these starting with the latter.

Pseudo-Randomness

Many computers have built-in random-number generators, and one can also buy programs that are said to generate random numbers. However, although they serve well in most applications calling for random numbers, these numbers are not truly random and are more accurately called *pseudo-random* numbers. They use algorithms, such as computing the digits in an irrational number such as pi or any so-called chaotic function, or by making calls on the computer's internal clock and using the last digit in the reading to generate the pseudo-random number. Such numbers are deterministic in principle, although they effectively mimic randomness for most purposes.

True Randomness

The physicist Frank Tipler (1994) has suggested that it should be possible to build a computer that is genuinely random by tapping into the randomness inherent in elementary physical particles, such as electrons and the constituents of the atomic nucleus. He suggests further that the human brain may actually be doing this (the physicist Roger Penrose, 1994, makes a similar suggestion, which we will return to in the next chapter), and that this gives us free will. Tipler defines free will as follows: An agent would have exercised free will in making a decision if (1) "the agent felt himself/herself to be acting freely" in making the decision, and (2) "the decision was in fact indeterministic at the most basic physical level" (1994, p. 204). However, there are problems with attempting to relate free will to randomness in a cognitive system, as discussed in the following section.

Evidence for and against Free Will in Cognitivism

Aside from discussion of whether or not free will could be built into a computer, there are two major lines of evidence of particular interest to cognitivists regarding the possibility of free will in humans—evidence from physics and evidence from neuropsychology.

Evidence from Physics

Prior to 1925, physics had seemed to be the very model of a deterministic science. In 1925, however, the physicist Werner Heisenberg published a paper on the atom that proved that one cannot in principle precisely measure both the position and velocity (or more specifically, the momentum) of an elementary particle such as an electron. The more exactly one measures position, the more probabilistically one is forced to measure velocity; and conversely, the more exactly one measures velocity, the more probabilistically one is forced to measure position. As one increases the precision of the measurement of the position of the particle, one necessarily decreases the precision of the measurement of the velocity of the particle; and, conversely, as one increases the accuracy of the measurement of the velocity of the particle, one necessarily decreases the accuracy of the measurement of the position of the particle. This is indeterminism, in that certain properties in physics can as a matter of principle be determined only in a probabilistic (or statistical) manner rather than in an absolute manner. Physicists have named this important principle Heisenberg's Uncertainty Principle, after its discoverer.

Physicists have looked at a number of different ways of interpreting this result. One way to look at it is as follows. Although one needs only one measurement to determine position, one needs two measurements to determine velocity (i.e., to determine the velocity of something, one must record the time at which it is at one point and the time that it is at another point, and compute the time required to travel between the two points). Each measurement requires hitting the particle with a photon (i.e., a particle of light), which disrupts the particle since it is so small. The position measurement can be made as accurate as desired simply by increasing the energy of the photon. But the more energetic the photon, the more it disrupts the particle so that the second measurement less accurately reflects the original velocity; the less energetic the photon, the more accurate the velocity measurement but the less accurate the position measurement.

From the above description, Heisenberg's Uncertainty Principle may seem merely technical, and thus one that with enough ingenuity could be overcome. This, however, is not the case. The principle is extremely general, and shows up in many different situations. For example, it is possible to predict an instance of radioactive decay in an atom (i.e., an instance in which a subatomic particle is emitted from the nucleus of a given atom) probabilistically, but not exactly.

Heisenberg's Uncertainty Principle should not be confused with chaos theory. The latter theory shows that in certain situations, when measuring certain types of complex phenomena (such as weather patterns) a small but inevitable measurement error can accumulate so that over time any prediction is likely to be grossly in error. Such errors are inevitable because infinitely many more numbers are irrational (meaning that they occur between the calibration marks on any measuring scale) than are rational. Thus, almost all measurements must contain a certain amount of rounding error. Hence, perfect prediction is impossible even in what is assumed to be a perfectly deterministic system (e.g., the weather), if rounding error leads to chaos in that system (i.e., if small errors accumulate and become magnified over time). However, probabilistic prediction is still possible—although the degree of certainty decreases over time (e.g., the one-day weather forecast is fairly accurate, but the five-day forecast is not).

Either an uncertainty principle or chaos may apply to psychological phenomena. That is, it is possible that behavior is not completely determined by environmental and genetic variables, in the same sense that the position and velocity of an elementary particle are not completely determined. It is also possible that human behavior is chaotic, in the sense that it shows regular deterministic patterns although specific instances cannot be predicted. It has been argued that either of these possibilities, or both acting in combination, allow for the possibility of free will or self-determination (e.g., Garson, 1995). If so, however, it is not clear that this lack of determinism or unpredictability would enable us to be self-determined in the sense that humanistic psychologists seem to think we are. Consider that to the extent that behavior is unpredictable it must be random (or at least pseudo random; i.e., it must at least mimic a random system). Yet random behavior does not seem to be the type of behavior that is supposed to typify the self-actualized person. If anything, it would seem more likely to characterize someone we would label psychotic or disturbed, because random or unpredictable behavior is generally irrational. In addition, if Heisenberg's Uncertainty Principle or chaos theory results in self-determination, then it would seem to follow logically that subatomic particles or chaotic systems such as the weather are self-determined (i.e., have free will). Most humanistic psychologists, however, would probably not be willing to accept the notion that inanimate objects can be self-determined in the sense that humans are supposed to be self-determined.

Evidence from Neuropsychology

There is a famous experiment in psychology that seems to challenge the notion of free will, at least as traditionally conceived (Libet, Curtis, Wright, & Pearl, 1983). In this experiment, brain activity is measured from a human subject while he or she views a simple clock-like device in which a dot on a TV screen moves at a constant rate along the circumference of a circle marked off in small intervals. The subject is told to flex his or her index finger some time during this process, but exactly when is left to the subject to decide. At the end of each trial, the experimenter asks the subject to indicate the position of the dot at the moment he or she decided to flex the finger. The result that is consistently obtained from this experiment is that brain activity predicting the finger flexion occurs on average a fraction of a second before the subject is aware of making a decision to flex the finger. It appears therefore that the subjects could not have been consciously deciding to flex their fingers, and therefore could not have been doing so of their free wills (or in a "self-determined" manner), despite having the phenomenological feeling of doing so. In other words, so the argument goes, because the actual decision—as measured neurologically—to flex the finger occurred before a subject was conscious of making the decision, the decision could not have been made through free choice or free will. If we can generalize this result to all decisions that people think they make of their free will, we would have to conclude that all decisions people make are determined.

There are at least three criticisms of this conclusion that proponents of free will (or self-determination) might make. One is that the subjects' perceptions of the position of the dot tended to be delayed (for some reason that is not yet known), so that the conscious decision to flex the finger occurred earlier than indicated by the experiment. The second possible answer is that although perhaps not able to consciously determine when he or she would flex the finger, the subject might still have been able to freely "veto" the finger flexion before it occurred. That is, even if we don't have free will, we might still have "free won't"—as one commentator (Holmes, 1998, p. 35) suggested, undoubtedly with tongue at least partly in cheek. Daniel Dennett (2003) provides the third criticism that, not surprisingly, is consistent with his views on consciousness (see chapter 9). He suggests that a decision seeming to be made before we are aware of making it appears paradoxical only because of the way we tend to define ourselves. Most of us are still Cartesians in that we think of ourselves as a single (unextended) point somewhere in our heads. Dennett suggests that we recognize that we are actually spread out over space and time.

Presumably this space is still somewhere in our brain, which is still under the control of variables outside of it. So Dennett is not an indeterminist. Rather, he has argued that the physical world is the only source of cause and effect, so it is up to physics to tell us whether or not the world is determined. Either way, according to Dennett, we have free will (most of the time) in the only sense in which it is "worth wanting" or in which we could reasonably ask for it—namely, in the sense that our actions are controlled (most of the time) by what we want and what we think is true. This, according to Dennett (1986, 2003) should suffice for free will.

BEHAVIORAL APPROACH

Behaviorists assume that behavior is determined by the environment and genetics. In this they are no different than most other psychologists. However, they tend to place a greater emphasis on actively investigating the environmental variables that control behavior and a lesser emphasis on possible internal mechanisms that mediate the environmental variables.

The Search for Laws of Behavior

If behavior is determined by the environment and genetics, it should be possible to discover laws of behavior that would allow us to predict it with a high degree of accuracy. As mentioned previously, methodological behaviorists believe that in the attempt to discover such laws it is useful to postulate drives and other nonbehavioral processes, whereas radical behaviorists believe that postulating such processes is counter-productive. Methodological and radical behaviorists agree, however, that the goal of psychology is to predict responses that individuals will make at any given time as function of the stimuli present at that time and past conditioning. Behaviorists generally admit that this goal may not be perfectly achievable—that is, strict determinism may be no truer in psychology than it is in physics.

However, according to most behaviorists, the objective of their science is to come as close to this goal as possible, and one does not do that by assuming indeterminism at the outset. There is an apparent exception to this statement in the case of Skinner. Early in the development of operant theory, Skinner appears to have abandoned any attempt to systematically explain the spontaneous emission of an operant response prior to any reinforcement of that response (e.g., Skinner, 1966a). In some of his writings he suggested that it was a random occurrence that has the same status in operant theory that a mutation does in evolutionary theory (e.g.,

Skinner, 1966b). However, given this random occurrence, a strict determinism is assumed.

Skinner maintained that behaviorists eventually might have to accept some degree of indeterminism in their science, just as physicists have to do in theirs. He believed, however, that this should be done only when data and a well-established theory rule out strict determinism (as was the case in physics).

The Illusion of Freedom

If our behavior is determined by environmental and genetic variables, then the feeling we have of being free from these factors is an illusion. Behaviorists, like psychoanalysts, are obligated to explain why we have this illusion of freedom. It should be pointed out that they have not done so yet; however, they (mainly Skinner) have made some simplified efforts to do so. The following should be read more as work in progress rather than complete explanations, which will require a great deal more empirical research and theoretical development.

Unverbalized Variables

One behavioral explanation for the feeling of freedom is essentially the same one that psychoanalysts give: we are not able to verbalize—that is, we are unconscious of—many of the variables that are controlling our behavior. Reasons for this could range from ones similar to those given by psychoanalysts—for example, the verbal behavior has been punished—to a simple lack of learning—for example, we have not been conditioned to respond verbally to certain variables that control our behavior. However, it does not seem that this can be the full explanation for the illusion of freedom.

Type of Control: Positive Reinforcement vs. Aversive Control

Our feeling that we are free seems to occur most often when our behavior is controlled by positive reinforcement rather than aversively (i.e., by negative reinforcement or punishment), regardless of whether we can verbalize the variables controlling our behavior. Consider, for example, the following two cases.

Case 1. *A thief points a gun at your head and says, "Hand over your wallet!"*
Case 2. You learn that you own a winning lottery ticket.

Now, in **Case 1** you would probably give the thief your wallet and feel controlled. In **Case 2** you would probably collect your winnings and not feel controlled. Note that in both cases your behavior is equally predictable and therefore equally determined; however, you feel controlled in the case in which it is controlled by aversive stimulation (i.e., the threat of violence) and you feel free in the case in which it is controlled by positive reinforcement (i.e., money). From a radical behaviorist point of view, apparently we have been conditioned to describe the feelings correlated with positive reinforcement as feelings of *freedom*, and the feelings correlated with aversive control as feelings of *being controlled*.

Dual Connotations of Control

Much of the disagreement about whether or not it is desirable to control behavior may stem from the dual connotations of the word *control* indicated above. Many humanistic psychologists may be opposed to behavioral control because the word *control* subjectively implies aversive control—i.e., the word *control* elicits aversive feelings—even though technically the word also implies positive reinforcement. In any case, humanistic psychologists are in fundamental disagreement with behavioral psychologists about the use of behavioral techniques to control human behavior. Humanistic psychologists say personal liberation, not control, is the principal aim of their endeavors. In reply to this, a behaviorist might point out that it is impossible to free behavior from control by the environment (and even if one could, one would simply end up with random behavior, as explained earlier, which is probably not what humanistic psychologists mean by *liberation*). What we should do, according to behaviorists, is to try to ensure that people are controlled in desirable ways—that is, in ways that maximize positive reinforcement and minimize aversive stimuli for each individual. A case of undesirable control would be control in which one person benefits inordinately at the expense of another, e.g., a master-slave relationship. A desirable type of control would be one in which both parties benefit about equally, such as people engaging in a cooperative task. Note that although this is an example of mutual control—that is, Person A controls Person B, who in turn controls Person A—it is no more so than the master-slave relationship. The slave controls the master's behavior—for example, reinforcing the master for beating him by complying with the master's demands when the master beats him—as much as the master controls the slave's behavior. What makes the master-slave relationship undesirable is that the slave is being controlled aversively.

Practical Implications

Just as the assumptions about determinism of humanistic psychologists and of psychoanalytic theorists have influenced practical applications of their theories, behavioristic assumptions about determinism have influenced applications of behavioral theory.

Self-Control

Behavioral theory has been applied in psychotherapy and education, as well as other areas, and its application to society as a whole has been advocated. To humanistic psychologists, helping people achieve self-control, which they see as synonymous with self-determination, is the major goal of therapy and counseling. Behaviorists agree with this goal; however, they do not equate self-control with self-determination. According to behaviorists, self-control simply means one behavior of an individual controls another behavior of that same individual (e.g., when a person arranges the environment to make it more likely that he or she will stay home and study rather than go out with friends). But the behavior controlling other behavior is under the control of the environment. Therefore, even when a person exercises self-control, the ultimate control of the behavior still rests with the environment. Using this basic assumption, behaviorists have designed various self-control programs which have proved to be very effective, and which even many humanistic psychologists apparently have come to feel are valuable. Thus, much of behavior therapy is concerned with developing self-control in the client.

Education

Behaviorists approach education by operationally defining education as the modification of behavior (especially verbal behavior). They begin by precisely specifying the behavior to be modified, and then design a program to modify that behavior. For example, in teaching a given subject matter a behavioral educator would design a program that develops the behavior of writing and talking intelligently about the subject. The program would progress sequentially through the material in steps sufficiently small that the student continually experiences success in learning the material, and therefore receives frequent positive reinforcement. As in all behavior modification programs, punishment is kept to a minimum. If the student does not learn, the behavior modifier attempts to correct the problem by making changes in the teaching program. Failure of the student to learn is defined as failure of the teacher to teach.

Improvement of Society

Skinner has strongly advocated the widespread adoption of behavioral techniques by society as a whole. He has presented these arguments most forcefully in his controversial books *Walden Two* (1948) and *Beyond Freedom and Dignity* (1971). The former describes a fictional society based on behavioral principles. Because of the strong emphasis on control in Skinner's fictional society, humanistic psychologists generally consider it to be the antithesis of what they would regard as the ideal society. However, it appears that the goals that Skinner set forth in his book are in agreement with humanistic values, even if the means are not. Although he wrote the book in the 1940s when such views were not popular, Skinner argued that the ideal society should ensure the equality of women with men on every level and in every aspect of the society, should forego the use of any kind of aversive control, should provide adequate health care for everyone, should be concerned with the conservation of the natural environment, should ensure that everyone shares equally in the resources of the society, and should enable everyone to develop to his or her fullest potential according to his or her own interests. It appears that many of the critics of the book may have been so distressed by the fact that Skinner argued for the use of behavioral techniques to achieve these ends that they overlooked the strongly humanistic nature of the book. *Beyond Freedom and Dignity* has also not found favor with most humanistic psychologists. Its title alone seems to attack two of the human attributes that are most cherished by humanistic psychologists. However, it appears that the title of the book is at least somewhat misleading. Skinner was not arguing against freedom (in the sense of political freedom, for example), but against the concept that our behavior is free in the sense of not being controlled by the environment. This concept, according to Skinner, prevents us not only from applying behavioral technology to our problems, but also from realizing how our behavior is being controlled (e.g., by politicians, by advertisers) in ways that are harmful to us. It is important to go "beyond" the concept of freedom (which has been very useful in getting rid of various forms of tyranny in the past) so that we can learn to counteract harmful types of control through the use of what Skinner called *countercontrol*. The concept of dignity that Skinner was arguing against is the notion that some people deserve more dignity or respect than others because of their achievements or social position. If all behavior is determined by genetic and environmental variables, Skinner argued, then we are not responsible for our achievements or social position; therefore, no one deserves any special measure of credit, respect, or dignity. This seems in agreement with humanistic psychology's "person-centeredness" position, which maintains that each person should be valued as a person without regard for his or her achievements or social position; in other words, everyone should be accorded equal respect and dignity.

The chief difference between Skinner and humanistic psychologists is that Skinner—ironically, it might seem for someone who did not believe in self-determination in the sense that humanistic psychologists think of it—argued that we need to take matters into our own hands and use behavioral principles to engage in cultural design rather than depending on cultural improvements to occur naturally or spontaneously. As Skinner (1984, p. 480) put it: "Must we wait for selection to solve the problems of over-population, exhaustion of resources, pollution of the environment, and a nuclear holocaust, or can we take explicit steps to make our future more secure?" As in other areas, Skinner believed that humanistic psychologists have the right goals but not the means to achieve them. This is why, as we saw earlier, he described behaviorism as "effective humanism" (1983, p. 343).

Importance of the Concept of Free Will for the Person

Although behaviorists do not consider the concept of free will to be valid, there is some question about whether and how behaviorists should refer to it in applied situations. According to Hayes, Strosahl, and Wilson (1999), it is important for clients to believe that they are able to choose and are responsible for the choices they make. When a client asks, "Am I responsible for these problems [i.e., the problems that brought the client to the therapist]?" Hayes et al. recommend replying in the following way:

> Responsibility is recognizing the relationship between what we do and what we get. Did you know that originally the word responsible was written response able? To be responsible is simply to be able to respond. So, yes, you are able to respond. And, yes, your actions put you in the hole and your actions can take you out. Response-ability is acknowledging that you are able to respond and that were you to do so, the outcome would be different. If you try to avoid responsibility, there is a painful cost: If you cannot respond, then truly nothing will ever work. . . . So don't back up from responsibility—if you have an ability to respond, then there are things you can do. Your life can work. (Hayes, Strosahl, & Wilson, 1999, p. 103)

The above reply is part of the strategy used in acceptance-and-commitment therapy, which is discussed in more detail in chapter 14.

Response Variability: Can Free Will be Conditioned?

As we have seen, some individuals have opposed the concept of determinism because the predictability of behavior seems incompatible with freedom. If my behavior could have been predicted, then I could not have acted other than I did, and so could not have been free to do as I chose (otherwise the prediction might have been incorrect and so my behavior could not have been predicted). Since the theory of operant conditioning implies that operant conditioning effectively controls behavior, it appears that behavior cannot be unpredictable if the theory is correct. However, it turns out that it is possible to develop apparently unpredictable behavior in both animals and humans by reinforcing variability in behavior (e.g., Grunow & Neuringer, 2002; Neuringer, 1992; Neuringer, Deiss, &

Olson, 2000; Page & Neuringer, 1985; Pryor, Haag, & O'Reilly, 1969). This is done by reinforcing responses when they differ (e.g., in topography or form of the behavior, or its location) from previous responses or previous sequences of responses. In addition to being of theoretical and philosophical interest, the phenomenon has practical implications. For example, it has been used to reduce stereotypy in individuals with autism (Miller & Neuringer, 2000) and has potential for increasing creativity. However, although the behavior developed appears to be random, it may actually be merely pseudo random—that is, predictable in principle—as discussed with regard to cognitive psychology. If the behavior is truly random and can be shown to be such, this would provide an interesting philosophical puzzle. However, this may provide no support for free will or the humanistic position of indeterminacy, as we have already discussed. In addition, to the extent that it does support free will or indeterminacy in humans, it does so for animals as well—which may go against some views of free will as a purely human attribute.

SUMMARY

Humanistic psychologists generally adopt a compatibalistic or an indeterministic position. According to humanistic psychologists, personal freedom refers to our ability to determine our own behavior apart from the environmental and genetic variables operating on us. It is therefore also called self-determination. The major evidence that humanistic psychologists provide for the existence of self-determination is phenomenological. Developing it is important in the process of self-actualization. For example, some humanistic psychologists in clinical practice adopt a *nondirective* form of therapy. Throughout treatment the therapist attempts to exert as little control over the client's behavior as possible. There are some philosophical difficulties with the humanistic position on the issue of determinism, such as that the alternative to strict determinism appears to be randomness or chaos—neither of which is a kind of free will "worth wanting" (as the philosopher Daniel Dennett put it).

Cognitive psychology appears to be deterministic because its goals are to discover the principles by which the mind operates. If lawful principles exist, they would seem to be deterministic. Physics has shown that there are indeterminate laws (e.g., Heisenberg's Uncertainty Principle). However, a similar principle in psychology would seem to imply randomness—which (again in Dennett's phrase) is not a type of free will worth wanting.

The traditional psychoanalytic approach adopts a strict deterministic position. Freud was clearly a strict determinist because he claimed that the mechanisms he postulated had total control over the individual. Other psychodynamic theories are also at least implicitly strictly deterministic.

Clearly unconscious factors are (by definition) outside of the individual's conscious control. However, once material is brought into consciousness, the ego deals with it in a lawful way (depending on the particular psychodynamic principles assumed to be operating). This has definite practical implications. Unlike humanistic psychologists, psychodynamic therapists tend to take a directive role in conducting therapy. According to the psychodynamic approach, the feeling of freedom is an illusion caused by our not being aware of all the forces causing our thoughts and behavior (particularly, by definition, those that are unconscious).

The behavioral approach is extremely explicit regarding determinism versus indeterminism. Almost by definition, behaviorism is the search for laws of behavior, which to the extent they are found imply determinism. Behaviorists account for the feeling of freedom two ways. One way is similar to the way in which psychodynamic theorists account for it. We are not aware of (i.e., cannot verbalize) all the variables controlling our behavior. The second way is that control by positive reinforcement and by aversive stimuli produce qualitatively different feelings. We feel free when we are controlled by positive reinforcement as opposed to punishment or negative reinforcement.

Discussion Questions

1. The Christian tenets that God is all knowing and that humans have free will have perplexed Christian theologians throughout history. Explain why these two tenets appear to be contradictory, and discuss possible solutions to this apparent contradiction.

2. Compare and contrast the concepts of free will, indeterminacy, and self-determination. Which of these concepts is most favored by humanistic psychologists to describe the human condition, and which is least favored, and why?

3. Criticize the humanistic approach to self-determination. How might a humanistic psychologist answer these criticisms?

4. Discuss whether the psychodynamic approach encounters a paradox with regard to control and freedom similar to the one humanistic psychologists face.

5. Discuss whether the concept of self-determination is compatible with the cognitive approach.

6. Discuss whether the behavioral approach encounters a paradox with regard to control and freedom similar to the one humanistic psychologists face.

7. Discuss similarities and differences between Dennett and Skinner regarding free will.

8. Under what conditions do you feel controlled, and under what conditions do you feel free? Do these conditions accord with the behavioral interpretation of the "illusion of freedom" as described in the text?

9. Compare and contrast the ways in which all four approaches explain the feeling (or illusion) of freedom.

10. Discuss the practical implications of each of the four systems' approach to the issue of determinism vs. indeterminism.

CHAPTER 12

The Problem of Values

onsider the following statements:

- Sunsets are beautiful.
- We should be kind to others.
- It is good to be self-actualized.

Are the above statements true? If you said yes or no, how do you know? The above statements are *value* statements, and although we have strong tendencies to attach truth-values to them—that is, to label them as true or false—philosophers and logicians have long recognized that there is a problem in saying that they are true or false in the same sense that statements of fact are. For example, consider the following statements:

- The sun is composed of hot gases.
- Two plus two is four.
- Humans are mortal.

These are statements of fact, and they differ from value statements in at least one important way: we have clear-cut means of verifying them.

The distinction between factual statements and value statements coincides with the distinction between means and ends. Although Aristotle apparently recognized this distinction when he said that deliberation is always about means rather than ends, David Hume appears to have been the first to have clearly made the distinction between facts and values. In one of his most famous statements, he asserted:

- Reason is, and ought only to be, the slave of the passions, and can never pretend to any other office than to serve and obey them. (Hume, 1978, p. 415)

He went on to make similar statements that seemed to go against all previous philosophy stretching as far back as Plato who, it will be recalled, maintained that reason tells us what is good:

> 'Tis not contrary to reason to prefer the destruction of the whole world to the scratching of my finger. 'Tis not contrary to reason for me to chuse my total ruin, to prevent the least uneasiness of [a] person wholly unknown to me. 'Tis as little contrary to reason to prefer even my own acknowledg'd lesser good to my greater, and to have a more ardent affection for the former than the latter. (Hume, 1978, p. 416)

The more recent British philosopher Bertrand Russell made the same point as follows: "Reason has a perfectly clear and concise meaning. It signifies the choice of the right means to an end that you wish to achieve. It has nothing whatever to do with the choice of ends" (Russell, 1954, p. viii).

In the heyday of logical positivism in the early part of the twentieth century, an ethical theory called *emotivism* was prevalent. Recall that logical positivists held that—except for strictly logical sentences and their derivations—only statements whose truth can be verified or refuted by sense data are meaningful. Ethical statements fail this test and are therefore meaningless. According to emotivism, however, they have emotive value: they can express emotion and exhort others to engage or not engage in particular actions. Another name for emotivism is the *boo hurrah theory*—so called because, according to emotivists, to say, for example, "Stealing is wrong," is equivalent to saying, "Stealing—boo!" Similarly, to say, "We should be kind to others," is equivalent to saying, "Kindness to others—hurrah!"

Throughout the centuries philosophers have devised various ethical theories, most holding that values exist independently from people and are discoverable through reason. These views were eclipsed by those of Hume, Russell, and the logical positivists. More recently, however, the view that values can be determined through reason similar to the way that factual knowledge can be has made a comeback (e.g., Hare, 1981; Rachels, 1993; Yardy & Grosch, 1993). One supporting observation is that most people have a sense of right and wrong or good and bad that is comparable in strength to (although of course not the same as) sense data. Of course there are disagreements about values, but this does not (so it is argued) distinguish them from sense data, about which there are also disagreements. In addition, people debate values in a manner similar to that in which they debate facts, and hold values to the same standard of logical reasoning as that to which they hold arguments about facts. For example, consider the premise, "I am morally obligated to keep my promises." From this it follows by logic that I am morally obligated to keep my promise to Sue. If I break my promise to Sue, it then follows by logic that I have done something wrong. However, logic is not defined over sentences that have no truth-value; therefore, it is argued, moral claims have truth-values.

With the above brief introduction to values, we consider now the approaches of each of the four systems to the problem of values.

HUMANISTIC APPROACH

To humanistic psychologists, the best functioning or mentally healthiest people are *authentic* individuals.

Authenticity as a Value

An authentic person is perhaps best defined as one who follows Socrates' advice, "know thyself," and the maxim (spoken by Polonius in Shakespeare's *Hamlet*), "to thine own self be true." An authentic person does not pretend, either covertly or overtly, to be someone or something he or she is not. Humanistic psychologists assume that within each individual there is a norm that one must live up to in order to be authentic.

Maslow's View

According to Maslow, an authentic person is one who lives up to his or her own inner norm, as opposed to arbitrarily conforming to the norms of society. As Maslow (1971) stated, "One cannot choose wisely for a life unless he dares to listen to himself, *his own self*, at each moment in life" (p. 47).

Rogers' View

For Carl Rogers, authenticity is related to the concept of *congruence*, defined as the correspondence between experience, communication, and awareness. *Incongruence* is the lack of agreement between these things. The essence of congruence is captured by the Zen Buddhist saying, "When I am hungry, I eat; when I am tired, I sit; when I am sleepy, I sleep." In other words, the Zen Buddhist does not deny feelings either to him/herself or to others, and is not embarrassed or ashamed to act on those feelings, nor does he/she permit society to dictate when he/she should experience those feelings. To the extent that a person is congruent, that person is said to be authentic.

Existentialist View

Existential therapists see it as their function to help the client become an authentic person, which Norcross (1987) defined as follows: "Authentic people are aware of themselves, their relationships, and their world;

recognize and accept choices and decisions; and take responsibility for their decisions, including full recognition of the consequences" (p. 52).

The ideal of authenticity is based on humanistic themes discussed previously.

Bases of Humanistic Position on Authenticity

Authenticity is based on consciousness (i.e., self-awareness) because in order to be true to one's inner norm, one has to be clearly aware of what that norm is. It is based on holism because in order to be true to one's self, that self must be an integrated whole. It is based on self-actualization because the actualizing tendency provides the sense of direction by which the individual grows toward greater authenticity. Finally, it is based on self-determination because a person can be authentic only if he or she freely chooses to be authentic. Holding authenticity as an ideal consti-tutes a *value judgment*; that is, one is saying that it is better or more valu-able to be authentic than not to be authentic.

Limitations of Science in Prescribing Values

This raises the question of whether or not science can provide us with the means of determining what our values should be. It has been held by philosophers of science that science cannot do this; science can only provide statements of empirical fact, and (as discussed at the beginning of this chapter) values are not included among these. The classic illustra-tion of this point is the observation that the principles of physics can tell us how to make a bomb, but there are no principles in physics (or pre-sumably any other science) that can tell us whether or not we should make a bomb. Similarly, biology can tell us what is necessary for a given organism to stay alive and healthy, but there are no principles in biology that can tell us whether we should keep it alive and healthy. If the pre-ceding is true, the question arises as to whether humanistic psychology can tell us that we should be authentic. Humanistic psychologists have not provided a clear answer to this question. One possible answer is that humanistic psychology only claims that authenticity is healthy, and that whether we should pursue mental health is open to moral argument.

Applied vs. Basic Sciences

Another possibility is to point to the distinction between basic and applied sciences. Physics and biology are both basic sciences, and so can-not provide us with values. Perhaps, however, applied sciences such as engineering and medicine can do so. If this is true, then humanistic psy-chology as an applied science should also be able to provide us with val-ues. However, this does not appear to the way applied sciences function. Applied sciences act on values supplied to them from outside the science (e.g., society). Medicine, for example, is an applied science whose function is to promote and maintain human life because this is a value society has imposed on medicine. This value is not intrinsic to medicine, since it can also be used for the opposite purpose. An example is the controversy over abortion, where there are some who believe that abortion is wrong under all circumstances and others who believe that it is justifiable in at least certain cases.

The Health Analogy

The position that some humanistic psychologists take on this issue is that authenticity is something that nearly everyone agrees is desirable in the same sense that nearly everyone agrees that physical health is better than sickness. However, it is not clear that this is true for at least two reasons: (1) authenticity seems to be a more difficult concept to define operationally than physical health is; and (2) most people seem to value conformity to social norms more than they value the nonconformity that is often entailed by authenticity.

The concept of *authentic self, real self,* or *true self* is related to self-actualization theory in the sense that self-actualization is seen as expressing, realizing, or following the dictates of this real self. Maslow stated this as follows:

> Humans no longer have instincts in the animal sense, powerful, inner voices that tell them unequivocally what to do. . . . All that we have left are instinct-remnants. And furthermore, these are weak, subtle and delicate, very easily drawn out by learning, by cultural expectations, by fear, by disapproval, etc. . . . Authentic selfhood can be defined in part as being able to hear these impulse voices within oneself, i.e., to know what one really wants or doesn't want, what one is fit for and what one is *not* fit for, etc. (Maslow, 1968, p. 191; emphasis in original)

> [M]ost psychopathology results from the denial or the frustration or the twisting of man's essential nature. By this concept what is good? Anything that conduces to this desirable development in the direction of actualization of the inner nature of man. What is bad or abnormal? Anything that frustrates or blocks or denies the essential nature of man. (Maslow, 1970, pp. 269–270)

> Recovering the self *must*, as *sine qua non*, include the recovery of the ability to have and to cognize these inner signals, to know what and whom one likes and dislikes, what is enjoyable and what is not, when to eat and when not to, when to sleep, when to urinate, when to rest. (Maslow, 1971, p. 33; emphasis in original).

Criticism of Authenticity as a Value

Maslow's view of the real self has been criticized for ignoring the social or cultural factors involved in self-development (Geller, 1982, 1984; Wilson,

1988). Moreover, like self-actualization theories, the concept of real self has been criticized as not being capable of being tested scientifically, since it does not seem to be possible to define it operationally. Despite the scientific problems with the concept, it has been argued that (as has been argued in favor of self-actualization) it provides a good myth or metaphor for aiding people in their development (Daniels, 1988; Wilson, 1988).

PSYCHODYNAMIC APPROACH

To traditional psychoanalysts, mental health is directly related to the extent to which the ego is able to resolve conflicts between the id and superego in a socially acceptable manner.

Ego Strength as a Value

A person whose id and superego are too strong relative to the ego has a psychological problem. If the id is too strong relative to the superego, the person will constantly be seeking gratification of his or her desires, which would be disruptive to society and bring negative consequences to the individual. If the superego is too strong relative to the id, the person will be unable to function due to punishment from the superego for quite ordinary and harmless thoughts and actions. Hence, psychoanalysts see one of their functions to be that of helping the client develop *ego strength*. By this they mean helping the individual develop an ego that is strong enough to resist the demands of the id and the superego. The psychoanalytic concept of ego strength may be close to the humanistic concept of authenticity, in that a person whose ego lacks strength relative to the superego may tend to deny certain essential things about him- or herself because of punishment that would occur from the superego if the individual did recognize those things. This could cause the person to be inauthentic from the humanistic point of view. An example might be a person who denies his or her sexual feelings because of the guilt those feelings evoke from the superego. An authentic person would freely admit that he or she is a sexual being with normal sexual feelings.

Kohut's "Cohesive Self" as a Value

Kohut's self psychology, which (as we saw in chapter 10) is a modified form of psychoanalysis, is most in accord with Freud's theory with regard to the development of ego strength as essential to mental health (Kohut, 1984, p. 95). But the *self* that Kohut conceptualizes goes beyond that of simply being a mediator between the id and the superego (Kohut, 1984,

p. 41). According to Kohut, people with "essentially cohesive" selves will realize a set of axiomatic values that give them the experience of leading or—at the end of life—having led "meaningful, joyful, fulfilling lives despite the absence of pleasure and despite the presence of physical and psychological (including psychoneurotic) suffering" (p. 211).

Humanistic psychologists see traditional psychoanalytic theory as counter to authenticity in its apparent emphasis on the adjustment of the individual to the norms of society as a goal of therapy. Kohut's values are more in line with their emphasis on authenticity as an ideal. Making adjustment or the development of a cohesive self as a value has the same problem of philosophical justification for psychoanalysis and self psychology that taking authenticity as a value has for humanistic psychology, namely, the question of how a science can determine a value. People who have what Kohut would consider cohesive selves probably would generally appear well adjusted, and adjustment seems easier to define operationally than authenticity. It is, moreover, a goal that might be agreed upon more readily by more people. That would seem, however, to depend on the society or culture in which one finds oneself, since not all societies or cultures have the same values. This raises the question of whether it is meaningful to speak of a "sick" society or culture.

Possible Relativity of Values

Nazi Germany is the prototypical example of a sick society. Would the mentally healthy thing for non-Jews in that society to have done been to become a Nazi and persecute Jews? Most people would give a definite "no" to this question; but if that answer is correct, then the question becomes what standard does one use to judge whether a society is mentally healthy, and from what is this standard derived? Neither humanistic psychologists nor psychoanalysts have provided a completely satisfactory answer to these questions, although they have attempted to address them in various ways. For example, regarding psychoanalysis and the Nazis, Kohut wrote:

> Psychoanalysis lacked, I submit, an understanding of the pathology of the self, both in the individual and in the group. Both were seen in terms of a mental apparatus that had to be helped in the task of taming the drives. Freud's applications of the drive-defense theory to history were limited in value, to say the least. It is no wonder that analysis felt helpless and that, in the final general theory of a death-instinct that remained untamable, it could do no more than offer proud resignation to the inevitable. It failed, as Christianity had failed, because in the end, after the aggressive drive had been made conscious, it could do no more than apply moral pressure and appeal for inner controls. One of the most telling anecdotes about Freud's attitude concerns his reply to a question

about the source of anti-Semitism. He said, with touching openness, that here his understanding stopped; here he could only hate. (Kohut, 1985, pp. 93–94)

COGNITIVE APPROACH

A computer can be programmed (with some exceptions, as we shall see in a moment) to determine whether given statements of fact are true. However, whether it is possible to program a computer to determine the truth of value statements (unless it does so by deduction from other value statements whose truth it cannot be programmed to determine) is questionable.

Can a Computer be Programmed to Make Moral Judgments?

The issue this raises for cognitivists is: if the mind is a computer program, how is it possible for it to determine true value statements, and thus to give us our sense of values? A possible cognitive scientific response to this is as follows: There is no problem with a computer making moral judgments, if it is trained the way children are trained, or simply given the background beliefs of a person competent in moral judgments. The problem the cognitive approach faces with regard to morality is not explaining how computational systems might represent the world as being morally good or bad; it is a problem of explaining what the ideas of moral goodness or badness refer to, which has nothing to do with computation itself. That is, the problem is where does our sense of values come from?

Penrose's View on Intuitive Knowledge from a Cognitive Perspective

Basing his arguments on mathematical proofs by Gödel and Turing, as discussed in chapter 8, the physicist Roger Penrose (1994) has made an interesting suggestion about where our sense of values comes from.

Gödel

Penrose begins with the mathematician Gödel's (1931) famous proof that any mathematical system that is at least as complex as modern arithmetic must either be inconsistent or must contain statements that are true but cannot be proved to be true. The proof is extremely complex, but, to give a very general idea of it, the trick is to create a sentence of arithmetic such that its truth conditions are the same as the truth conditions for the following sentence: "This sentence cannot be proved to be true."

Note that this sentence cannot be false without producing a contradiction, because if it's false then it must also be true. So it must be true; but then it cannot be possible to prove that it's true, because it's true and that's what it says. It is impossible to know all the Gödel sentences in a given deductive system, because there is no algorithmic procedure for generating them. However, it is possible to know that particular sentences are Gödel sentences: one constructs the sentences following the procedure Gödel outlined. These sentences can be then be proved to be Gödel sentences by using a "strengthened" theory of arithmetic. However, new Gödel sentences then emerge in this "strengthened" theory, so that another "strengthening" needs to occur to prove those sentences; and so on, ad infinitum.

Turing

Another version of Gödel's theorem was discovered independently by Turing (1936), who showed that there are certain problems that cannot in principle be computed—that is, no algorithm can be constructed that will solve them—even though a correct solution does exist. As with Gödel's unprovable true statements, it is impossible to know for certain which problems are not computable (because then we would know the solution and so could design an algorithm that could compute them).

A New Physical Principle?

Although we don't know what statements are unprovable or what problems are not computable in any deductive system, we do know that humans cannot prove those statements or solve those problems by following any kind of general step-by-step procedure or algorithm any more than a computer can. However, Penrose points out that often we do get ideas or come to conclusions that we recognize intuitively to be true or correct, even though we cannot prove them in a logical manner. He suggests that we may have some way or ways of establishing truth that is outside the realm of logic and computation, and that perhaps this is how we come to recognize the truth or falsity of value statements (among other types of statements). As Penrose has put it,

> We have seen . . . that the judgement of what is or is not true cannot be reduced to pure computation. The same (perhaps more obviously) applies to the beautiful, or to the good. These are matters which require awareness and are thus inaccessible to entirely computer-controlled robots. There must always be a continuing controlling input from a sensitive, outside, conscious—presumably human—presence. (Penrose, 1994, pp. 400–401)

And again more succinctly: "There are some types of words which would seem to involve non-computable elements—for example, judgement, common sense, insight, aesthetic sensibility, compassion, morality. . . . These seem to me to be things which are not just features of computation" (Penrose, 1997, p. 125)

Penrose does not suggest that the brain is not a computer. What he proposes instead is that the brain may somehow be tapping into some as yet undiscovered physical principle operating at the level of the fundamental particles of matter. In Penrose's theory, the brain makes use of information it receives from this level in producing our intuitive judgments (and, perhaps as a by-product, the subjective experience of consciousness), including those involving values. Of course, we must recognize that Penrose's theory is highly speculative, and by no means accepted by other cognitivists—especially given its reliance on a physical principle that has yet to be discovered. (We return to this point in chapter 13.)

BEHAVIORAL APPROACH

In a sense, the behavioral approach can be said to be value free in that it does not tell us what our values should be; it simply tells us how to achieve goals consistent with those values.

The Behavioral Approach as Value Free

Referring to the technology of the behavioral approach, behavior modification, Kazin expressed this as follows: "In one sense, behavior modification has no inherent goal. It consists of a series of principles and techniques and a methodological approach toward therapeutic change. It does not necessarily dictate how life should be led" (Kazdin, 1977, p. 257).

Like the applied science of engineering which can tell us how to build a bridge but not whether we should build a particular bridge, behavior modification can tell us how to increase or decrease a particular behavior but not whether it should be increased or decreased. In other words, it does not specify whether a behavior is desirable or undesirable; that decision is left to those who apply behavioral theory, to their clients, or to society as a whole. To illustrate this point, contrast the positions of humanistic psychology, psychoanalytic theory, and behaviorism regarding whether it is mentally healthy or desirable for a given person to be homosexual. A humanistic psychologist would probably encourage the person to look within himself or herself to discover whether homosexuality represents that person's authentic or true self as he or she views that self; if it does, then homosexuality is right for that person. The psychoanalyst (if following the traditional approach of Freud) would see homosexuality as due to inadequate sexual development: the person identified with the parent of the opposite sex rather than with the person of the same sex during the phallic stage. Accordingly, the psychoanalyst (again, if following in the tradition of Freud) would adopt the goal of eliminating the person's homosexuality by causing normal psychosexual development to progress. In contrast, the behavior modifier cannot say *on the basis of behaviorism* whether or not the person's homosexuality should be eliminated. The behavior modifier can only say that if the person wants to change his or her sexual preference, there may be behavioral techniques for that. Perhaps the person has come to the behavior modifier in order to become bisexual, rather than to have his or her homosexuality eliminated. Again, the behavior modifier cannot say *as a behavior modifier* whether this goal is desirable or undesirable. Note that the same is logically true for any other condition, such as schizophrenia or manic depression. Thus, behaviorism lacks a theory of mental disorder.

Reinforcement as a Value

Behaviorism may, however, contain a theory of values from which desirable and undesirable behavior may be inferred. Most behaviorists would probably say that desirable behavior is behavior that results in the most reinforcement for an individual in the long run, without causing harm to others. Concerning authenticity, the behaviorist would likely note that people who are said to be authentic appear to be controlled less by reinforcement from others than by reinforcement from the nonsocial environment. An example would be a bright young person whose parents want him or her to become a medical doctor, but who becomes a carpenter instead because he or she is more highly reinforced by working with wood. People who are not authentic tend to do and say exactly what others reinforce them for doing and saying, regardless of what other reinforcers may be available. Most behaviorists would probably agree that it is better for people to be authentic than to be nonauthentic (or *artificial*), since this probably results in more reinforcement for the individual in the long run. Society also benefits more from authentic people—for example, a person who is more highly reinforced by working with wood than by interacting with sick people will probably benefit society more as a carpenter than as a doctor.

Behaviorists in general try to determine their clients' values in order to help them work toward goals that are consistent with those values. A type of behavioral therapy called *acceptance-and-commitment therapy* (ACT), for example, uses a number of exercises to help clients determine their values (Hayes et al., 1999, pp. 204–234). In an exercise called, "What Do You Want Your Life to Stand For?" for example, the client is asked to consider what kinds of funeral eulogies and tombstone inscription he or she would want. In a homework exercise, to take another example, clients are asked to write out all their values in a comprehensive set of categories, including intimate relations, family relations, career, education, recreation, spirituality, citizenship, and health. ACT therapists emphasize to clients that values do not come from a rational process, but are choices that individuals make freely. The idea of free choice (or free will) is stressed not because it is scientifically correct but in order to ensure the authenticity of the values that the individual chooses (see chapter 11). It is important that the therapist not influence the client's choice of values, even indirectly. If the client's values are such that the therapist cannot work with the client, it is recommended that the therapist refer the client elsewhere (ACT is discussed further in chapter 14.)

Skinner's Theory of Absolute Values

The view that only *relative values* exist (i.e., right and wrong are relative to a given culture), called cultural relativism, used to be prevalent in ethical philosophy until about the 1970s or so. Earlier than that, however, Skinner proposed that absolute values exist and, more strikingly, that these values can be determined by behavioral science. If Skinner's reasoning regarding this is valid, then contrary to what was stated earlier, it appears that scientists can, at least in principle, derive values from science. In a famous debate Skinner had with Carl Rogers, he argued that while other sciences cannot tell us what our values should be, this restriction does not apply to psychology as the science of behavior. He capped his argument with the following statement: "This is where, it seems to me, science can help—not in choosing a goal, but in enabling us to predict the survival value of cultural practices" (Rogers & Skinner, 1956, p. 1065).

By "survival value of cultural practices," Skinner was alluding to his view that cultures evolve in a way that is similar to the way in which species evolve. According to the theory of evolution, a random mutation in the genes of a member of a particular species results in a new characteristic, giving rise to three possibilities: (1) the new characteristic has no effect on the survival or reproductive success of the individual possessing it; (2) the new characteristic is detrimental to survival or reproductive success, in which case individuals who possess it will tend not to pass it on; or (3) the new characteristic is favorable to survival and reproductive success, in which case individuals that have it will tend to survive and pass it on to their offspring so that eventually many, or even all, members of the species will possess it. Such changes in the characteristics of a species are usually very small; but many such changes over thousands of years can result in a totally new species. In Skinner's account of the evolution of cultures, the mutations that occur are changes in the values or practices that various cultures reinforce or punish. Now, some values promote a culture's survival and others do not. For example, a culture that values fighting among its members may be vulnerable to extinction for several reasons. One reason is that its members may spend so much time in mutual antagonisms that they do not produce enough food and other resources to keep the culture thriving. Another reason the culture may be vulnerable to extinction is that the constant bickering makes the culture so nonreinforcing or punishing to its members that they eventually defect to other cultures.

This does not mean that a culture with maladaptive values will immediately become extinct. On the contrary, it may survive for hundreds or even thousands of years. But in the long run it will be extinguished, and this process will be speeded up as it comes into contact with other cultures whose values are more adaptive. Values that lead to the extinction of a culture die with that culture. Values that lead to the survival of a culture tend to survive. Thus, absolute values are those that promote the survival of a culture, since in the long run those are the only values that will survive.

SUMMARY

To humanistic psychologists, the best functioning or mentally healthiest people are authentic individuals. The concept of *authentic self, real self,* or *true self* is related to self-actualization theory in the sense that self-actualization is seen as expressing, realizing, or following the dictates of this real self. A humanistic psychologist would probably encourage the person to look within himself or herself to discover whether a particular behavior represents that person's authentic or true self as he or she views that self; if it does, then that behavior is right for that person.

Psychodynamic theories have built-in values that are determined by how the theory depicts the well-functioning individual. The psychoanalytic concept of ego strength may be close to the humanistic concept of authenticity, in that a person whose ego lacks strength relative to the superego may tend to deny certain essential things about him- or herself because of punishment that would occur from the superego if the individual did recognize those things.

The question that the problem of values raises for cognitivists is this: if the mind is a computer program (i.e., information-processing system), how is it possible for it to determine true value statements, and thus to give us our sense of values? One possibility is that evolution, or society, or a combination of both can be thought of as having programmed our values in us. This, however, implies that there are no absolute values or moral standards, which many people find to be problematic.

In a sense, the behavioral approach can be said to be value free in that it does not tell us what our values should be; it simply tells us how to achieve goals consistent with those values. The behavior modifier cannot say *as a behavior modifier* whether a goal is desirable or undesirable. Skinner, however, proposed that absolute values that apply to all cultures do exist, and that these values can be determined by behavioral science. A value that is valid for a given culture, according to Skinner, is a cultural practice that promotes the survival of that culture. Thus, according to Skinner, authenticity is a value if in the long run it enhances cultural survival.

Discussion Questions

1. Discuss what Hume meant by his statement, "Reason is, and ought only to be, the slave of the passions." Is this a statement with a truth-value, a value statement, or both?

2. Discuss whether values can be established empirically or logically. That is, can we discover through experiment or some logical procedure what our values should be?

3. Critically discuss the basic value or set of values according to each of the four systems.

4. Compare and contrast the values across any two of the systems (e.g., humanistic and behavioral psychology).

5. Is there any system for which the issue of values is especially problematic? If so, discuss why the problem of values is particularly problematic for that approach. If not, discuss why not.

6. Discuss the similarities and differences between the humanistic approach to values and ACT.

7. Discuss whether Skinner purports to discover values through logical reasoning, through science, or both.

8. Some claim that science is, or should be, value free. Discuss whether it is possible to have a value free science. Discuss whether it is possible to have a value free system of psychology.

9. Critically discuss the analogy between physical health and psychological health as values.

10. Relate the approaches of Plato, Hume, Kant, and Russell to those of Maslow and Skinner with regard to values.

CHAPTER 13

Spirituality

ost of us—whatever our religion or lack thereof—have feelings that would be labeled as *spiritual*. The deeply religious might describe these feelings as being closer to God, while the atheist might simply describe them as being closer to nature. But however we might describe them, they are a significant part of the lives of most people and need to be looked at psychologically. Along with these feelings, or independent of them, are beliefs about the universe and our place in it. These beliefs also are part of the issue of spirituality.

In the Western world, during the Middle Ages (usually dated from the late 400s to about the mid–1300s—see chapter 1), spirituality was the domain of the Church. The Church, however, gradually lost much of its influence in this area as a result of two intellectual movements that succeeded each other: (1) the Renaissance (from about the mid–1300s into the 1500s—see chapter 2) and (2) the Enlightenment (the period from the 1600s well into the 1800s—see chapters 2 and 3). Among the leaders of the Enlightenment were Descartes, Locke, Newton, and Darwin.

The Renaissance resulted to a large extent from the rediscovery by Europeans of the art, science, and philosophy of the ancient Greeks and Romans, while the Enlightenment was characterized by a tendency to reject supernatural explanations of phenomena. Out of these two intellectual movements arose the philosophies of rationalism and empiricism. Rationalism held that truth could be discovered primarily or entirely through logical reasoning as opposed to either faith or the senses; the rationalist Descartes is noteworthy in this regard for being one of the first philosophers to take the stance that he would not believe in God if forced to believe on faith alone, but would insist on evidence coming from his own intellect. Empiricism is the view that the senses are the ultimate source of our concepts and knowledge. In general, philosophers of the Enlightenment believed that nature is orderly and that its laws could be discovered through reason, observation, and experiment (although not necessarily in that order). Modern science stems from the underpinning philosophy of the Enlightenment, which is called Modernism. As Polkinghorne (1990) stated,

> At the core of modernism or Enlightenment discourse was the belief that a method for uncovering the laws of nature had been discovered, and that the use of this method would eventually accumulate enough knowledge to build "the heavenly kingdom on earth." The modernist idea was that formal reasoning applied to sense data provided a foundation for certain knowledge. (p. 92)

Religion still held sway among many intellectuals of that time period. But many adopted a view known as Deism, which was the belief that God had set up the universe to run like a giant machine (e.g., analogous to a clock), and did not wish to interfere with his handiwork (see Slife, Hope, & Nebeker, 1999, pp. 54–55; Slife & Williams, 1995, pp. 134–136). This has led to our present-day dilemma of reconciling science and religion. In this chapter we examine how the four systems have dealt with this issue.

HUMANISTIC APPROACH

Many humanistic psychologists believe that in some sense it is possible to transcend (i.e., go beyond) one's limited self, and that this ability is a very important aspect of each person. This self-transcendent ability is said to give meaning to life. Biela and Tobacyk (1987) distinguish between *transcendence* and *self-transcendence*. Following Kozielecki (1983), they maintain that transcendence refers to such activities (which they say "go beyond established properties of the mind") as: (a) self-realization and self-development; (b) altruistic behavior and the formation of new relationships; (c) activities directed toward the natural environment, such as territorial expansion and technological achievement; and (d) the creation of new symbolic productions through art, science, and literature. Self-transcendence, according to Biela and Tobacyk, is a "process by which the person exceeds normative experiential boundaries and experiences [him- or herself] as part of a greater whole" (p. 393). The goal of self-transcendence is "the experience of unification with an absolute level of meaning [which] may be variously experienced or conceptualized as God, Being, truth, other values, or as mystical or peak experiences" (p. 393). According to Biela and Tobacyk (1987), there are two methods of achieving self-transcendence: *vertical* and *horizontal*—vertical self-transcendence involves going directly to unification with the absolute, whereas in horizontal self-transcendence one first experiences unification with others (in the form of deep identification or empathy) before achieving unification with the absolute.

The possibility of self-transcendence—that is, being able in some sense to "go beyond" or transcend one's self—is the primary topic of interest in the field of transpersonal psychology. This field was formally established in 1967 by some of the same people, such as Maslow and Sutich, who founded humanistic psychology. The *Journal of Transpersonal Psychology* began publishing in 1969.

According to Miles Vich, who was involved in the founding and early development of transpersonal psychology:

> Many of us who helped launch the humanistic orientation in psychology . . . were excited by the prospects for the development of the individual self, the healthy human personality, the fully actualizing person. . . . After a number of years of identification with humanistic psychology, a spontaneous shift of interest occurred for many of us. Put simply, the focus on ego development, the self, and the actualizing personality began to seem incomplete. (Vich, 1990, p. 48)

The new field was needed, he stated, because "there was insufficient attention paid to what lay beyond the self, such as the relationship of the individual to a greater sense of consciousness or awareness, including mystical, religious or spiritual experience" (quoted by Sanders, 1989, p. 401).

A number of humanistic psychologists, especially those who are strongly influenced by existentialism, are strongly critical of transpersonal psychology (e.g., Schneider, 1989). For example, May (1989) points to the tendency of "the transpersonal side" of humanistic psychology to imply "it is the 'higher,' having surpassed 'the ego' while other therapists still wallow around in 'the ego'" (p. 247).

Among psychotherapists perhaps those practicing existential psychotherapy come closest to transpersonal psychology in their stress on the importance of the loss of meaning in the manifestation of a number of problems, such as depression, apathy, and anxiety. Anxiety is a particularly evident outcome of the loss of meaning in one's life. According to Norcross:

> This anxiety must be distinguished from the anxiety we all possess that serves as a motivating force in confronting life and our potentialities. The existential vacuum, in its most extreme form, refers to a crippling existential anxiety in which the person feels empty, void, and extremely bored. Individuals feel that they are ailing, possessed by a sickness that is neither physical nor mental, but rather a malaise of spirit, a sickness of alienation. (Norcross, 1987, p. 47)

The existential psychotherapist approaches this problem by helping people learn to create their own meaning—which all fully functioning people do—from their relationship with others and the world.

Modern science seems have been an important factor in the loss of meaning that many people feel. To review some history regarding science's role in this (see chapters 1 and 2), Christian theologians of the late Middle Ages adopted the view of the ancient Greek philosopher Aristotle who taught that the earth is the center of the universe and that the sun, planets, stars, and other heavenly bodies all revolve around it in complex cycles. This view gave the earth, and hence its human inhabitants, a special status in the universe, which seemed consistent with the special status for humanity implied in the Bible. Early Christian theologians also accepted a literal interpretation of the Biblical account of the creation of the earth and of humans and other living things. The account of creation in the Book of Genesis gave humans a unique role in the overall plan of an infinitely powerful Creator.

Cracks in this view of the universe appeared with mounting evidence, provided by Copernicus, Galileo, and ultimately a host of other scientists, that the earth and other planets revolve around the sun (see chapter 2). Today it is widely recognized on the basis of overwhelming scientific evidence that, far from having any special status in terms of its location, the earth revolves around a rather ordinary star (the sun) located on the outer fringes of a rather ordinary galaxy in an unimaginably immense universe.

Additional cracks in the early Western view of the universe appeared with discoveries of the fossilized remains of numerous types of ancient animals that no longer existed (e.g., dinosaurs) and that were not mentioned in the Bible. Interestingly, these discoveries were typically made by scientific members of the clergy who were looking for evidence confirming the occurrence of an ancient worldwide flood and other geological events described in the Bible. At first they thought that the fossilized animal remains they had discovered were from animals that had not been fortunate enough to escape the flood in Noah's ark. One problem with this interpretation, however, was that the Bible made no mention of any kind of animal not surviving the flood. Another problem concerned the level in the ground at which the remains were found. For example, it was not clear why simpler animals were found at lower levels in the ground than were more complex animals, since a flood of the magnitude described in the Bible should have resulted in considerable mixing of animals irrespective of their complexity. Charles Darwin solved this mystery to the satisfaction of most scientists by piecing together the evidence from both extinct and living species to show that there has been a gradual evolution of all life forms from a common ancestor over a period of millions and millions of years (see chapter 3). His theory of evolution consists of two parts: (1) that evolution of complex life forms (including humans) from simpler life forms has occurred, and (2) that new species have appeared gradually through the selection by the environment of characteristics that were more adaptive than others to survival. Although there is some controversy among evolutionary biologists concerning some of the details of evolution, there is no doubting that it occurred. This clearly contradicts a strictly literal reading of the Biblical version of the creation of living things.

Operating on the traces of evidence left by events that occurred long ago, and using ingenious "detective work" to reconstruct those events, scientists have pieced together an account of our origin that is quite different from the Biblical account. It now appears that somewhere between 15 to 20 billion years ago our universe sprang into existence in an event, which cosmologists call the *big bang*, that sent matter and energy hurtling outward at an incredible speed. Created in this event were bits of positively and negatively charged matter called, respectively, protons and electrons, which came together to form the element hydrogen. Clouds of hydrogen gas then coalesced, and were compressed by gravity until they ignited in nuclear reactions to produce stars. All naturally occurring elements other than hydrogen were produced from hydrogen, helium, and probably a bit of lithium in the nuclear furnaces of these stars. Stars eventually run out of efficient fuel and begin burning heavier elements, which do less to sustain the stars from gravitational collapse. When gravitational collapse begins, we get a tension between renewed fusion activity and gravitational collapse. In cases in which enough fusionable material remains (i.e., the star is massive enough), collapse leads to runaway reactions and novas and supernovas are produced—that is, the stars explode, scattering the elements created in them far and wide. Our solar system began to be formed from the debris from an exploded star and hydrogen about 10 billion years ago. The earth and other planets came into being about five billion years ago. The first fossilized life forms are from bacteria dating back to 4.5 billion years ago, whose microscopic imprints have been found in ancient rocks. These were descended from an even simpler organism that gave rise to all life forms through the process of evolution.

Most humanistic psychologists attempt to find meaning in life in a manner that is consistent with the scientific view of the universe described above. This involves either (1) adopting a nonreligious approach, or (2) adopting a religious or transpersonal approach that typically differs from the traditional Judeo-Christian belief of Western culture. Maslow provides a good example of the second way, for toward the end of his life he became more interested in the transpersonal realm of experience. He wrote:

> I should say also that I consider Humanistic, Third Force Psychology to be transitional, a preparation for a still "higher" Fourth Psychology, transpersonal, transhuman, centered in the cosmos rather than in human needs and interests, going beyond humanism, identity, self-actualization and the like. . . . We need something "bigger than we are" to be awed by and to commit ourselves to in a new, naturalistic, empirical, non-churchy sense, perhaps as Thoreau and Whitman, William James and John Dewey did. (Maslow, 1968, pp. iii–iv)

Others, however, find the modern scientific view to be too limited to deal appropriately with spirituality. For example, Slife, Hope, and Nebeker (1999) suggest that all methods have embedded within them assumptions about the phenomena they are designed to study, and that the assumptions embedded within the methods of modern science are inimical to the study of spirituality. According to Slife et al. (1999) there are three hidden assumptions within modern scientific method: universalism, materialism, and atomism. The first is that the laws of nature apply everywhere and always; the second is that only what is visible and tangible is real; and the third is that what is real can be divided into parts that, when fully understood, can be used to explain and predict the whole. However, God—the object of spirituality—does not conform to these assumptions. Slife et al. do not, however, offer any method that they feel would be more appropriate for studying spirituality. Instead, they suggest that the appropriate method(s) may emerge through discussions among those who wish to study spirituality scientifically.

Secular Humanistic Psychology

In chapter 7 we distinguished between humanists and humanistic psychologists. The term *secular* means nonreligious, or outside of religion. The term *secular humanist* is therefore somewhat redundant, although it is commonly used to emphasize that humanists do not believe that a strong sense of morality necessarily depends on religion. According to secular humanists, meaning is to be found in becoming involved with the problems of the world—for example, poverty, pollution, injustice, the threat of nuclear war. As M. Brewster Smith (1986) expressed it:

> I continue to hope without much optimism that aspects of our almost physical plight—the prospects of nuclear Armageddon and planetary depletion and pollution—may conceivably provide humankind with the challenge to transcend its historical shortsightedness and collective stupidity. In this very realistic context, one wholly without historical precedent, I fear that the meanings of being human that have served us so long and so well—the mythic and religious ones handed down to us by tradition—no longer give us good guidance or dependable support, even though they symbolize important truths of human life. The problems of the real world can surely make our lives meaningful, if our imaginations can only be sufficiently aroused to get us involved. (pp. 22–23)

In this quote, Smith speaks of meaning as being derived directly from becoming involved with the problems of the world. There is a close similarity between secular humanists and nonreligious, or secular, humanistic psychologists. Many secular humanistic psychologists, however, emphasize the subjective experience of self-transcendence as being the critical ingredient in creating meaning. Maslow's "peak experience" is one way in which self-transcendence may be experienced. More grandiosely, perhaps, self-transcendence may be experienced as a feeling of one's consciousness expanding to encompass the universe. This feeling may be evoked in various ways.

Many types of experiences can give rise to the feeling of oneness with the universe. For example, Duhl (1986) mentions several experiences that evoked it in him, including "walking along a Pacific beach at night, sensing waves, sand, rocks, and sky and at one moment kicking a pine cone and making a decision to change both my place and kind of work" (p. 50). According to Duhl,

> Such experiences, carrying as they do the internal and external environments, carry meaning, knowledge, and health. During these timeless moments, there is no barrier between inner and outer space; in fact, time and space melt away and reveal themselves to be the mental constructions they really are. With this harmony come awe and an overwhelming sense of well-being, one that nurtures and heals. The sense of interconnection and relationship that such events carry can be overpowering. Their peace and playfulness evoke visions of the womb and remind us of our wistful imaginings that this was how human life was long ago—timeless, capacious, without boundaries or separation, and without the need to control. (pp. 50–51)

As the similarity of their names suggests, secular humanistic psychology and secular humanism (as discussed in chapter 7) are similar. If we can draw a distinction, however, secular humanism probably places more emphasis on traditional science and less on self-transcendence (or feelings of spirituality) than secular humanistic psychology does.

Transpersonal and Religious Humanistic Psychology

Transpersonal and religious humanistic psychologists believe that self-transcendence is not merely a subjective state, but rather that in experiencing it one is coming into contact with something deep that permeates life and even inanimate matter. Carl Jung's view of the existence of a kind of *group mind* which contains collective memories of all humans, termed the *collective unconscious*, is accepted by some transpersonal and religious humanistic psychologists. The collective unconscious can be thought of as a self beyond the personal self, which may be tapped into during self-transcendence.

Humanistic Psychology and Eastern Religions

Transpersonal and religious humanistic psychologists are generally more impressed with Eastern religions, such as Buddhism and Taoism, than with Christianity or Judaism. In Eastern religions God is not described in a personal way as in the Bible. Rather, God is more of an amorphous force, perhaps the universe itself. The object of life is not to get into heaven as conceived of in Christianity, but to unite with the God-force in a blessed state called *Nirvana*. This is typically obtained only by living and dying many times (Eastern religions believe in reincarnation or rebirth) until one obtains through righteous living the wisdom necessary to enter Nirvana. Glimpses of this blessed state, and the wisdom needed to achieve it, are obtained through meditation. Transpersonal and religious humanistic psychologists see these glimpses as a form of self- transcendence, which is another reason they are impressed with Eastern religions.

Eastern religions value such experiences highly, and have developed techniques for evoking them. For example, the lama Tarthang Tulku, Rinpoche, of the Nyingma School of Tibetan Buddhism, describes a series of exercises designed to bring about this experience of oneness with the universe. One of the exercises, to be conducted on a mountain top or high hill, directs the reader to breathe the blue sky in and out, so that space becomes "literally a food that you are eating or grazing on" (Tulku, 1977).

Humanistic psychologists who are less religiously inclined may still find Buddhism attractive. Drawing on the work of a British scholar of Indian philosophy writing around 1900 (Davids, 1912), Hutcheon (1997) pointed out that the Buddha may have taught a position very close to that of modern secular humanists.

Humanistic Psychology and the Judeo-Christian Tradition

There are, of course, Christian and Jewish humanistic psychologists also. Typically they are not bothered by the apparent contradictions between science and the Christian or Jewish Bible because many do not believe that the stories in the Bible are to be taken literally. Rather, they are myths that encapsulate important truths for humanity. In addition, they believe that if one studies the true meaning of the Bible one finds that it is quite compatible with humanistic psychology. For example, ap Iorwerth (1985) wrote:

> The question of the nature of the Ultimate in life is central to humanistic psychology, and whether we use the term "God" or not, the problem still remains. Personally, I think that the term should be abandoned, as it has become meaningless for many in the West. . . . The term "God," however,

does stand for something or someone (or, nothing) no matter how distorted our perception of that something has been over the centuries. Many who are struggling with what it means to become fully human would gain, I believe, from encountering this "something" in as honest and open a way as possible. Biblical experiences witness to encounters with That Which declares 'ehyeh'aser'ehyeh—"I-am-who-I-am," or "I-will-be-there-as-whoever-I-will-be-there," or "I-will-be-who-I-will-be"—all of them equally valid interpretations of the tetragrammaton YHWH. The Bible claims to record these happenings, these breakthroughs, these invasions of a person's private world, by an ultimate Freedom that is at once the ground and source of a person's being, the center of history, and the guide of human destinies. (ap Iowerth, pp. 23–24)

It may seem strange to think that the stories in the New Testament, for example, were not meant to be taken literally. Surely, it might seem, those who first wrote down the stories of the miracles surrounding Jesus' birth, his life, his death, and his resurrection believed that they were writing the literal truth. But this is not necessarily the case. There is evidence that there were early Christians who interpreted the myth of God becoming a man through a virgin birth (a myth that, incidentally, was popular in many ancient religions), for example, to mean that the spirit of God could enter any person open to receiving it. Recently discovered writings from the first and second centuries indicate that many individuals calling themselves Christians shortly after the time of Jesus emphasized using Scripture to focus on "the Christ within." There is also evidence, however, of a systematic and very effective effort to destroy the writings of these early Christians because their view that one need only look inward to find Christ tended to undermine the authority of the early Church, which maintained that one could approach Christ only through it. (See, for example, Harpur, 2004).

Parapsychology

More or less closely related (depending on one's point of view) to the topic of self-transcendence or spirituality is the question of the existence of *parapsychological abilities*, which are abilities outside of the normal realms of psychology and physics. Two major types of parapsychological abilities have been proposed: *extrasensory perception* (*ESP*) and *psychokinesis* (*PK*). ESP is the ability to sense by means other than the scientifically recognized senses. Three types of ESP are generally distinguished: *clairvoyance, precognition*, and *telepathy*. Clairvoyance is the ability to experience the occurrence of an event without physically perceiving it in any way consistent with the laws of physics that are known today; precognition is the ability to predict a future event, again without recourse to methods that are known to present-day physics; telepathy is the ability to tell what someone else is thinking at a covert or private level. PK is the ability to move objects without being in contact with them in any manner consistent with the known laws of physics.

Although a considerable amount of parapsychological research has been carried out and dramatic findings are sometimes reported, the existence of parapsychological phenomena is not accepted by most scientists. The problem is that the phenomena do not seem to be replicable; that is, when experiments reporting positive results are repeated (usually under more tightly controlled conditions) the results are generally negative. It seems that one must conclude either that (1) parapsychological phenomena are not real, or that (2) there is some law of nature that prevents these phenomena from occurring under scientifically controlled conditions. If the latter is the case, however, we could never (by definition) establish that fact using good evidence. Certainly from a scientific point of view, it seems more reasonable to account for reports of these phenomena in terms of phenomena that are already known to occur and that are consistent with established scientific laws.

Distortion and the desire to believe are often involved in reports of parapsychological phenomena. Consider, for example, the case of the so-called Hundredth Monkey Phenomenon. The story begins with some observational research done on the macaque monkeys living on Koshima Island in the 1950s (Kawai, 1962, 1965; Kawamura, 1963; Southwick, 1963). As a result of humans introducing new foods to the monkeys, they acquired a number of new food-related behaviors, including sweet potato washing, wheat washing, begging food from tourists, and candy eating. The manner in which sweet potato washing was acquired was particularly interesting. A juvenile monkey, called Imo, invented it, and from her it was passed on to other monkeys over a period of about five years (from 1953 to 1958). After that it rapidly became universal (except for adults born before 1950 who never learned it). O'Hara (1985) explained this as follows: "What happened was that the juvenile females reached menarche and began to have babies, and whereas friend to friend, child to parent transmission is slow and not automatic, mother-infant transmission is rapid and 100%. The monkeys born after 1958 all learned it, but not by some magical process. They learned it from their mothers" (pp. 65–66).

This, however, was not how the rapid transmission of the behavior was explained by Lyall Watson, who discussed it in his book entitled *Lifetide: A Biology of the Unconscious* (1979). Watson wrote:

> Then something extraordinary took place—the details up to this point in the study are clear, but one has to gather the rest of the story from personal anecdotes and bits of folklore among primate researchers, because

most of them are still not quite sure what happened. And those who do suspect the truth are reluctant to publish it for fear of ridicule. So I am forced to improvise the details, but as near as I can tell, this is what seems to have happened. In the autumn of that year an unspecified number of monkeys were washing sweet potatoes in the sea, because Imo had made a further discovery that salt water not only cleaned the food but also gave it an interesting new flavor. Let us say, for arguments sake, that the number [of potato washers] was 99 and that at 11 o'clock on a Tuesday morning, one further convert was added to the fold in the usual way. But the addition of the hundredth monkey apparently carried the number across some sort of threshold, pushing it through a kind of critical mass, because by that evening almost everyone in the colony was doing it. Not only that, but the habit seems to have jumped natural barriers and to have appeared spontaneously, like glycerine crystals in sealed jars, in colonies on other islands and on the mainland in a troop at Takaskiyama. (pp. 147–148)

Watson presented no data to back up his speculation that the behavior became universal in just a few hours after the hundredth monkey had acquired it. Moreover, he presented no data to support his claim that monkeys on other islands and the mainland acquired the behavior. Even if they had, however, it would not be appropriate to say that the behavior appeared "spontaneously" in them. Watson's analogy of the islands being like "sealed jars" is inaccurate because at least one monkey had been observed to have swum from Koshima Island to another shore (Kawai, 1965).

Despite the weakness of Watson's position, it was very influential among some humanistic psychologists. One reason for this is probably that it seems to support Jung's theory of a collective unconscious toward which, as already mentioned, humanistic psychologists are favorably disposed because of its transpersonal implications. Noting that many humanistic psychologists were willing to abandon critical scientific thinking to accept the myth of the hundredth monkey phenomenon, O'Hara (1985), a scientifically oriented humanistic psychologist, criticized

the rejection of training in science and logical thinking by some would-be humanistic psychologists and other aspiring agents of change. Without such training these people, regardless of their heart-felt commitment to transformation, have practically no basis on which to evaluate claims made in the name of science. Anyone—crackpot, charlatan, genius, or sage—must be dealt with in the same way (believed or disbelieved) solely on the basis of personal opinion. Personal opinion then becomes equated with knowledge and can be asserted without embarrassment. (pp. 72–73)

O'Hara went on to say:

This is not to say that all confusion in humanistic thinking is a result of sloppiness or irresponsibility. Some of it is the inevitable consequence of daring to break new scientific ground. Humanistic science, like most human science, is definable not in terms of methodologies (which may be various), but in terms of subject matter—human beings (Polkinghorne, 1982). Potentially relevant knowledge of the human predicament may be found in literature, mythology, anthropology, biology, psychotherapy, and personal experience (although probably not in physics). All these fields have evolved their own methodologies, rules of evidence, and standards of validity. This renders neophytes (and adepts) in a multidisciplinary field such as ours especially vulnerable to having the wool pulled over their eyes. It makes us easy marks for those who offer comforting explanations of perplexing human dilemmas: be they scientists, pseudoscientists, gurus, psychics, psychotherapists, charismatic speakers, revolutionary leaders, priests, technocrats, or new-age conartists. (pp. 73–74)

Near-Death Experiences

A minority of individuals who have been very close to death (e.g., by being involved in a near-fatal accident or having certain vital signs cease temporarily during surgery or illness) report having had strange experiences, called *near-death experiences* (*NDEs*), that appear to be similar in some respects to transcendental experiences of Eastern religions. Although NDEs have been noted throughout history, both popular and scientific interest in them was sparked by Raymond Moody's book entitled *Life After Life* (1975). According to Moody, although there are differences between the NDEs of different people, there are also some remarkable similarities in many cases. Following Moody's book which described 150 cases, others have carried out more systematic research (e.g., see Baruŝs, 2003, pp. 215–224; Fox, 2002; Groth-Marnat & Schumaker, 1989; Kellehear, 1996). NDEs have a number of different components, and not everyone who has an NDE has all of the components—in fact, most have only one or a few. Some of the component experiences that have been reported, and the range of percentages of individuals who had them among those who reported NDEs in various studies, are: (1) a feeling of calm or peace (37%–100%); (2) a feeling of leaving one's body (42%–100%); (3) darkness or entering a tunnel (23%); (4) seeing a bright light (23%–58%); and, (5) undergoing a review of one's life (3%–6%). Different people may have different types of experiences in each of these categories. For example, sometimes the light is described simply as a bright light that one is attracted toward, and sometimes it is described as a "being of light" that leads one through a review of one's life.

NDEs can have powerful aftereffects, such as increased concern for others, reduced death anxiety, a strengthened belief in an afterlife, reduced interest in material possessions, and increased self-esteem (Groth-Marnat, 1998).

A number of people have taken NDEs as evidence for an afterlife—that is, as evidence for the survival of some part of the individual after the death of the body. One problem with this view is that of course individuals who have reported NDEs have not, by definition, actually died. Therefore, it is impossible to say what experiences (if any) they would have had if all life processes (especially those of the brain) had ceased.

Other arguments against the view that NDEs provide evidence for an afterlife are as follows:

- Less than 40% of individuals who have had a close (but nonfatal) encounter with death report NDEs. Why doesn't everyone who comes close to death have an NDE? It does not seem reasonable to suppose that an afterlife exists for some people but not others (Groth-Marnat & Schumaker, 1989).

- Although it has been claimed that most NDEs are similar, the fact is that different people experience different components and those who do experience the same components often do not do so in the same way. If NDEs represent an afterlife, why are they different for different people?

- The stress of being near death may cause a release of endorphins or enkephalins which are chemically similar to opiates and therefore could produce the feelings of peacefulness and well being in NDEs (Carr, 1981, 1989).

- Some of the components of NDEs could be due to anesthetics and other medical drugs given to the individual prior to the NDE. For example, the anesthetic ketamine produces some of the components of NDEs (Jansen, 2004).

- Extreme activity in the brain arousal system during sleep, as indicated by rapid eye movement (REM), is associated with some components of NDEs. Therefore, NDEs could be due (at least in part) to brain arousal in individuals especially prone to REM during sleep (Nelson, Mattingly, Lee, & Schmitt, 2006).

- It has been found that neurological stimulation of the brain can produce effects similar to components of NDEs, such as hallucinations, joy, detachment, and vivid recollections of previous happenings in one's life (Penfield, 1958). Thus, NDEs could be due to trauma to the brain that produces similar stimulation.

- NDEs may be due to suggestions instilled by one's culture, since one may be particularly suggestible when his or her brain functions are impaired, as would often be the case when death is imminent.

Arguments in support of the view that NDEs provide evidence for an afterlife include the following:

- NDEs are typically felt as having been very real to people who report them. They differ in this respect from dreams, many kinds of hallucinations, and states induced by drugs or trauma to the brain.

- It is difficult to account for some of the aftereffects of NDEs on the basis of our knowledge of the brain. Although some of the effects during the NDE can be accounted for on the basis of known brain processes, there are no known types of brain trauma or drugs that can produce the apparently highly positive aftereffects often reported following NDEs.

- While NDEs are influenced by one's culture or religion, these influences appear to be small (Moody, 1975; Ring, 1980). For example, atheists are just as likely to have NDEs as churchgoers are (Ring, 1980).
- Some individuals who have been blind from birth report having an out-of-body experience during an NDE in which they appear to see (Ring & Cooper, 1999).

Susan Blackmore (1993) has developed a theory that addresses the above points. According to her theory, as the brain begins to die due to lack of oxygen when a person is near death, inhibitory nerve cells in the visual cortex are the first to be affected. This results in the release of inhibition on other nerve cells in the visual cortex. The firing of increasing numbers of these cells, as greater numbers of inhibitory cells stop firing, is seen as a white light growing increasingly larger, which may give the near-death experiencer the feeling of rushing toward a white light at the end of a tunnel. This experience feels real because the appearance of the "tunnel" is extremely stable compared to externally based sensory stimulation—which may be minimal or nonexistent—and our brains are strongly disposed to interpret stable experiences as real (as opposed to imaginary or hallucinated ones, which tend to be less stable than real experiences). The view that NDEs are produced by physiological effects in the brain, given that the brain differs very little or not at all across cultures, explains why NDEs are similar across cultures. Blackmore acknowledges that people are often changed dramatically as a result of having an NDE, frequently becoming much more selfless (or less selfish). She believes that this is due to the breakdown of the model each person's brain has of that person's self. As the death of the brain proceeds, that model can no longer be sustained in the brain, and so the person experiences a dissolving of the self into nature (or the universe, or God)—much the same as the enlightenment practitioners of Eastern religions strive for. And, like the Buddhists or followers of other Eastern religions who have achieved enlightenment, the near-death experiencer whose model of self has broken down has come to believe—at some level—that the notion of *self* is an illusion, and hence becomes kinder to others and more giving.

Allan Kellehear (1996) argued for a sociological explanation as opposed to a physiological one such as Blackmore's. He noted that traumatic events that do not bring the individual close to death can produce NDE-like effects. Moreover, he pointed to cultural differences (e.g., the absence of a tunnel and a life review in some cultures) as indicating a limitation of any purely physiological explanation.

PSYCHODYNAMIC APPROACH

Psychodynamics and Religion

Regarding religious belief, the traditional psychoanalytic approach in general is nonreligious (there are, of course, individual psychoanalysts who may subscribe to various religions). The psychoanalytic approach accounts for feelings of spirituality in several ways.

According to the psychoanalytic approach, the elements that make up self-transcendental experiences can arise from several sources. One of these, according to Freud, is the survival of a portion of the ego that, at least in some people, is still undifferentiated from the external world.

> [O]riginally the ego includes everything, later it separates off an external world for itself. Our present ego-feeling is, therefore, only a shrunken residue of a much more inclusive—indeed, an all-embracing—feeling which corresponds to a more intimate bond between the ego and the world about it. If we may assume that there are many people in whose mental life this primary ego-feeling has persisted to a greater or less degree, it would exist in them side by side with the narrower and more sharply demarcated ego-feeling of maturity, like a kind of counterpart to it. In that case, the ideational contents appropriate to it would be precisely those of limitlessness and of a bond with the universe." (Freud, 1961, p. 68)

It is consistent with the psychoanalytic approach to hypothesize that various sorts of meditative techniques, such as those used by practitioners of Eastern religions, facilitate this "oceanic feeling," as Freud termed it (see, for example, Epstein, 1995, pp. 33). (They may also bring it about in another way, as will be indicated later in this section.)

According to Freud, God is a product of the mind invented to provide a father substitute. The popularity of myths and religions in which a god assumes human form and is then killed (represented today most notably in Christianity) reflects the ambivalence of the id toward the father—needing him for love and support, but also viewing him with jealousy and wanting to kill him.

Another source of the experience of self-transcendence is the collective unconscious, which, as already mentioned, consists of memory traces of those who lived before us, and which supposedly exists in every human being. The collective unconscious was a relatively minor aspect of Freud's theory; he invoked this concept mainly to explain why orphans have Oedipus complexes even though they have no mothers and fathers. However, Carl Jung made it central to his theory. As mentioned earlier, Jung disagreed with Freud about many things, including the importance of sexual motivation in determining the personality. In fact, Jung thought that Freud's idea of sexuality actually contained a spiritual component that Freud, due to his psychological makeup, could not acknowledge. For example, writing in his memoirs about Freud, Jung stated:

> Basically, he wanted to teach—or so at least it seemed to me—that, regarded from within, sexuality included spirituality, and had an intrinsic meaning. But his concretistic terminology was too narrow to express this idea. He gave me the impression that he was working against his own goal and against himself. . .
>
> Freud never asked himself why he was compelled to talk continually of sex, why this idea had taken such possession of him. He remained unaware that his "monotony of interpretation" expressed a flight from himself, or from that other side of him which might perhaps be called mystical. So long as he refused to acknowledge that side, he could never be reconciled with himself. He was blind toward the paradox and ambiguity of the contents of the unconscious, and did not know that everything which arises out of the unconscious has a top and a bottom, an inside and an outside. When we speak of the outside—and that is what Freud did—we are considering only half of the whole, with the result that a countereffect arises out of the unconscious. (Jung, 1961, p. 154)

According to Jung, personality is composed of a number of subsystems, and the goal of personality development is to unify these parts into an integrated whole. These parts are represented in the collective unconscious by psychic structures called *archetypes*. These archetypes are represented by certain symbols that appear to be universal, in that they appear in many different cultures even though those cultures presumably had no contact with each other. One of the best-known archetypes is the yin-yang symbol of Eastern religions. According to Jungian psychology these symbols are used in various religions because they represent the striving for unification of the different parts of the personality, and as such stimulate contact with this universal goal. This contact with the collective unconscious is experienced as self-transcendence. Although humanistic psychologists eschew Freudian psychoanalysis, as indicated earlier they are typically more favorably disposed toward Jung's theory of the collective unconscious. This may be due to Jung's theory seeming to imply a self that exists independent of the personal self, and which therefore apparently makes self-transcendence a real possibility.

The preceding discussion of Jung should not be taken to imply that he regarded the Eastern ways of thinking and spirituality to be superior to those of the West. On the contrary, stressing the importance of a balance between the intuitive and the intellectual sides of the personality, he believed that Eastern thinkers tended to favor the former too much whereas the opposite was the case with Western thinkers. The ideal, presumably, would be a harmonious blend of both approaches.

In one crucial respect, however, the Eastern approach to spirituality—especially that of Buddhism—appears to be diametrically opposed to the psychodynamic approach. All the major psychodynamic theories maintain that psychological health depends on a strong sense of self. Jung even postulated that there exists an inner "divinity" that he called the "self," which he considered to be an archetype of completeness or of the completely integrated self. This archetype guides the individual toward integration of the self or self-realization (Jung, 1916/1969). The process also results in individuation, which is the differentiation of the self from the social collective (and is held to occur rather late in life). If this self is divine, however, then it exists in everyone and is not the isolated self of mere ego. Concerning this, Jung wrote:

> . . . Indian philosophy, which developed the idea of the self, Atman or Purusha, to the highest degree, makes no distinction in principle between the human essence and the divine. Correspondingly, in the Western mandala, the scintilla or soul-spark, the innermost divine essence of man, is characterized by symbols which can just as well express a God-image, namely the image of Deity unfolding in the world, in nature, and in man. (Jung, 1955/1983, p. 238)

In Freudian theory self-realization is achieved by strengthening the ego, while in Jungian theory it is achieved through proper balancing of the components of the personality. In contrast, Buddhism stresses the importance of eliminating suffering through the dissolution of the self. Despite these apparently opposite objectives, some psychoanalysts have proposed that Buddhism and psychoanalysis are compatible. Engler (1984), for example, suggests that dissolution of the self is a higher stage of development after the achievement of a strong sense of self. This view can perhaps best be summed up by the phrase, "You have to be somebody before you can be nobody" (Engler, 1984, p. 24). Another approach is that of Rubin (1993, 1996), who proposes that a sense of self and no-self are equally valid alternative ways of viewing one's state of being, similar to the way in which physicists may view light as composed of particles or of waves depending on the situation or context. Illustrating this approach by describing the successful treatment of a specific client, Rubin stated that the client came to recognize

> that states of self-centeredness and unselfconsciousness were both part of his attempts to live a full and meaningful life. The former was necessary to help him fixate the self and view it as a concrete, substantial entity. This helped him to reflect on his life and conduct, delineate what he felt and valued, assess situations, formulate plans and goals and choose among potential courses of action. . . . Sensitivity to states of non-self-consciousness enabled him to live less self-centeredly, more fluidly

and gracefully. The view of the self as a process facilitated his appreciation of art, his capacity to listen to his students, play music, and experience love. (Rubin, 1996, p. 186)

Mark Epstein, in his book *Thoughts Without a Thinker* (1995, pp. 154–
155), provides yet another way to look at how Buddhism is compatible
with developing ego strength. According to Epstein, the idea of self is a
concept for describing how we know and think. However, it is an illusion. Through Buddhist meditation, we do not dissolve or eliminate the
self; that would be impossible, because the self does not really exist in the
first place—except as a concept. What happens is that we come to recognize that the self is an illusion, so that it may appear that we have eliminated or dissolved it. With this recognition comes a higher, different,
sense of self—one that recognizes that the self is not a real thing, not an
entity, but a process of thinking and knowing. According to Epstein
(1995, p. 155), "this requires not the obliteration of ego but the development of mental faculties beyond those that are conventionally accepted
as adequate for 'normal' functioning." This, according to Epstein, appears to be what Freud was trying to get at through the concept of ego
strength (although he probably did not realize it or think of it in exactly
that way).

Psychodynamics and the Paranormal

Parapsychological phenomena are neither implied nor denied by psychoanalytic theory. Being a materialist, Freud would have denied the possibility of life after death. However, although at first rejecting paranormal
phenomena out of hand, he eventually became interested in the possibility of mental telepathy and other ESP phenomena that did not necessarily
imply a nonmaterial or spiritual world.

Concerning Freud's views on paranormal phenomena, Jung wrote:

> When I visited him [Freud] in Vienna in 1909 I asked him what he
> thought of these matters. Because of his materialistic prejudice, he
> rejected this entire complex of questions as nonsensical, and did so in
> terms of so shallow a positivism that I had difficulty in checking the
> sharp retort on the tip of my tongue. It was some years before he recog-
> nized the seriousness of parapsychology and acknowledged the factu-
> ality of "occult" phenomena. (Jung, 1961, p. 155)

Jung's theory, which holds that at a deep level we are all connected to
a timeless universal consciousness (the collective unconscious) is consistent with paranormal phenomena, especially telepathy.

Criticisms of the Psychodynamic Approach

Wilber's "Pre/Trans Fallacy"

Recall from chapter 8 that Ken Wilber postulated a number of levels of consciousness. Some of these levels are at the rational stage, others are at the prerational stage, and still others are at the transrational, transpersonal, or spiritual stage. Wilber (1982) argued that psychoanalytic theory commits what he calls the *pre/trans fallacy*. He takes the humanistic position that there is a developmental progression or evolution from lower levels of consciousness to higher levels. Freud, according to Wilber, was essentially correct in outlining an evolution from the primitive id to the development of ego. However, he failed to recognize the further development of ego to a transpersonal state of consciousness. Instead, he committed a pre/trans fallacy by confusing the higher form—the transrational stage—with the lower form—the prerational stage. That is, according to Wilber, Freud mistook the tendency to evolve to the higher, transpersonal level for a tendency to regress back to the lower level or id (as Freud called it).

Jung, who emphasized the transpersonal stage, does not escape Wilber's critique. Wilber regards Jung as having committed a pre/trans fallacy in the opposite direction to that of Freud. The archetypes that Jung regarded as belonging to the spiritual realm were actually at a primitive, prerational level. Wilber believes that many who adopt a mystical or spiritual viewpoint, including many humanistic psychologists, have committed a similar pre/trans fallacy.

Jung's Theory of Archetypes

Jung's theory of archetypes is also vulnerable to criticism (Neher, 1996). A major criticism is that he never adequately explained how the archetypes originated. It is difficult to see, for example, what survival value many of his archetypes would have had, and therefore why they would have evolved. Another major criticism is that most of the evidence he presented for the archetypes—such as similarities between mythical or religious images of different cultures and between the mythical or religious images of specific cultures and the dream images of his patients—can be explained in other, simpler ways. For example, coincidence (or chance, as statisticians would say) could explain these similarities, as could cross-influences between cultures and access of Jung's patients to information about various cultural practices. That human activities necessarily are similar across cultures would also tend to restrict the variability that can exist in the images humans use to symbolize those activities, which also would tend to result in similar mythical and religious images across cultures. Moreover, there have been no controlled studies that clearly support Jung's theory of archetypes.

The "Jung Cult"

Noll (1994) has likened Jungian analytical psychology to a religious movement in a destructive sense. He calls it a "cult" or "secret church." For example, he stated:

> Starting in the late 1910s, it was clear that to become a member of the secret church one must undergo a subterranean initiation in the mystery grotto of the collective unconscious in Switzerland—and for a fee. Individuation—then as now—was primarily developed through a fee-paying arrangement with Jung or one of his approved analysts. Analyst status within this subculture meant that one was an exemplar of individuation and therefore also a charismatic spark derived from Jung. The fantasy of individuation is based upon the fantasy of being a Jungian analyst and quickly became the driving source of new income for the Jungian analytic elite. It remains so today, and with the manufactured pseudocharisma of Jung widely distributed in the mass media, many in today's society are attracted to the idea of becoming closer to Jung or to becoming like him in a spiritually charismatic way. Within the Jungian subculture the only objective standard by which one can recognize such a vague quality as individuation in another is by the "charisma of office"; i.e., the title "Jungian analyst." To be individuated is to be like Jung and add his name as the "cult totem" to one's own identity. Today, one must pay for several years of analysis (usually one hundred hours at a cost of perhaps $10,000 to $15,000) before even applying to an approved Jungian training institute, which then requires six to ten more years of training (analysis, readings in the Jungian literature, and, in some institutes, instruction in the occult sciences such as astrology, palmistry, the *I Ching*, and other intuitive methods), which can cost up to another $100,000 or so. (p. 281)

COGNITIVE APPROACH

It might be thought that cognitive science could have nothing to say about spirituality, since nothing seems (at least to many people) less spiritual than a computer. There is evidence that the feelings that we regard as spiritual are due to brain processes; and, if the brain is a computer, then these feelings can be accounted for as due to the physical properties of the brain and its computational processes.

Spirituality as a Cognitive or Brain Process

Most cognitivists assume that the capacity for spirituality and religiosity, like other mental properties or structures, evolved. Unlike humanistic psychologists, many cognitivists see little value in religion in modern society. An example is Stephen Pinker, Director of the Center for Cognitive Neuroscience at the Massachusetts Institute of Technology, who has written a number of popular books on cognitive psychology. In *How the Mind Works* (1997), Pinker addresses the question of why religion evolved and why it persists. To understand Pinker's answer, we need to understand how he views the mind. He writes, "The mind is a system of organs of computation, designed by natural selection to solve the kinds of problems our ancestors faced in their foraging ways of life, in particular understanding and outmaneuvering objects, animals, plants, and other people" (Pinker, 1997, p. 21).

One might think that if the capacity for religion evolved, then religion must have served a survival function. However, this is not necessarily the case. The mental computational organs that enable religion to exist might be analogous to the human vertebral column, which evolved to permit us to walk upright but is not well adapted for lifting heavy objects. Thus, many people severely injure their vertebrae by using their backs to do heavy lifting. Analogously, according to Pinker, we encounter problems when we use our mental apparatus inappropriately. He writes:

> Religion, like philosophy, involves a futile effort to understand that which we are innately incapable of understanding. . . . [R]eligion and philosophy are in part the application of mental tools to problems they were not designed to solve. (p. 525)
>
> Our thoroughgoing perplexity about the enigmas of consciousness, self, will, and knowledge may come from a mismatch between the very nature of these problems and the computational apparatus that natural selection has fitted us with. (p. 565)

The harm that this misuse of our intellect does, according to Pinker, is that it prevents us from using our minds in productive ways. For example, he writes: "For anyone with a persistent intellectual curiosity, religious explanations are not worth knowing because they pile equally baffling enigmas on top of the original ones" (p. 560).

Some cognitivists are interested in studying the mental and neurological components involved in spirituality and religion. Barret, Patock-Peckham, Hutchinson, and Nagoshi (2005), for example, found a correlation between certain cognitive styles and attitudes of religious people. Religious people who, as indicated by questionnaire data, have a "need for structure" thinking style, will tend to adhere uncritically to religious dogma and disapprove of those who disagree, while religious people with a "need for cognition" will be less judgmental and approach religion like a puzzle that needs to be solved. Borg, Andree, Soderstrom, and Farde (2003) found a positive correlation between the density of receptors for serotonin (a neurotransmitter) in the brain and self-transcendence, as measured on a self-report questionnaire. The most striking findings, however, have been with regard to the involvement of certain brain areas—especially the temporal lobes of the brain—in spirituality and religiosity.

A growing body of evidence implicates abnormalities in the temporal lobes in feelings of spirituality and religiosity. Damage to the temporal lobes can create a heightened sense of religiosity and spirituality. Sometimes extensive damage, such as might occur from traumatic brain injury, epilepsy, or a brain tumor, is correlated with abnormal religious behavior involving hallucinations and delusions. For example, a person might hallucinate that he or she is talking to Jesus, or harbor the delusional belief of being Jesus or God. Epileptic seizures in the temporal lobes can also cause extreme feelings of spirituality and religiosity (e.g., Ramachandran & Blakeslee, 1998).

Involvement of the temporal lobes in religious experiences is not limited to persons with grossly abnormal brain functioning. Michael A. Persinger (e.g., 1983, 1987, 1993, 1999; Makarec & Persinger, 1985; Persinger & Makarec, 1987; Persinger, Bureau, Peredery & Richards, 1994) and his colleagues, for example, have accumulated evidence indicating that a sense of spirituality and various spiritual experiences can result from temporal lobe activity. Much of this evidence comes from questionnaire data taken from individuals who exhibit behavior correlated to varying degrees with neurological disturbances in the temporal lobes. In addition, Persinger and his colleagues have actually generated various spiritual and mystical feelings—the "God Experience" as Persinger describes it—by mildly stimulating the temporal lobes of volunteers with a computer-modulated electromagnetic field. Persinger (1994) has also postulated that NDEs may result from temporal-lobe activity caused by the process of brain death. Studies of the brains of praying Franciscan nuns and meditating Buddhists have found specific effects of these activities in the frontal lobes (Newberg, d'Aquili, & Rause, 2001).

The view that abnormal behavior is due to brain abnormalities has been present since neurology began to emerge as a science in the late 1700s. As scientific thinking began to encroach on religious belief, it was but a short step to conclude that religious belief in general is due to neurological or mental abnormality. An often-cited example—but there are many others—is the epileptic-seizure-like experience that the apostle Paul had while he was on the road to Damascus to persecute Christians, which resulted in his conversion to that faith, with profound effects on its development. As we have seen, Freud clearly viewed all religiosity as a form of psychopathology.

Not surprisingly, religiously inclined people, and others, oppose the tendency to discredit all religious experience as being due to neurological abnormality. In his classic book *The Varieties of Religious Experience*, first published in 1902, William James (2003) pointed out that (a) abnormal brain states are not easily definable as distinct from normal brain states, and (b) although many individuals of great genius appear to be mentally afflicted, we do not therefore discredit their artistic, scientific, and other nonreligious contributions. Therefore, according to James, we should not reject religious practices or beliefs simply because they appear to be the product of a disordered brain or mind. The crucial test of a particular practice or belief, according to James, is not the brain state that produced it, but whether it leads to good consequences in the long run.

While disagreeing on the specifics of James' pragmatic view, cognitivists with religious interests have tended to agree that simply because activity in certain brain areas is associated with religiosity or spirituality in no way discredits religious experience. Some Christian cognitivists have argued that this indeed is exactly what one would expect from a properly understood Christian point of view. These writers reject the idea of an immaterial soul as being a valid Christian concept. Early Christians did not believe in an immaterial soul, but this was an idea that came in through the Greeks and was refined later by Descartes and other Western philosophers (see chapters 1 and 2). According to Christian cognitivists, God created the body, including the brain, and just as the brain is involved in receiving input from the physical environment, so—if Christianity is correct—the brain must also be involved in receiving input from God. Thus, the fact that certain brain areas are particularly involved in religious experience should be no more surprising than the fact that particular brain areas are involved in receiving particular information from God. The fact that certain mental abnormalities can develop from damage to these areas should be no more surprising than the fact that abnormalities of sensation and perception can develop from damage to areas involved in these functions.

Most cognitive psychologists would probably not be impressed with attempts to provide a cognitive-science justification of religion. Some Christian cognitive theorists, however, have proposed cognitive mechanisms that are consistent with the current state of cognitive psychology and with Christianity. Since these mechanisms have not been tested empirically, they will not be described in detail here (details may be found in d'Aquili & Newberg, 1998; Watts, 1999). Suffice it to say that the hypothesized mechanisms involve an intuitive component and a propositional component. The intuitive component is hypothesized to be the part of the cognitive apparatus that directly senses or receives input from God; the propositional component is hypothesized to be connected to the intuitive component and to the language function. The intuitive component communicates with the propositional component, which translates its information directly into spoken or written language. However, because the intuitive function is nonlinguistic its fit with the propositional functions is imprecise, which is why religious or spiritual insights are ineffable or difficult to express in words. It should also be noted that these mechanism are not limited to religious functions—otherwise, presumably there would not be any reason for them to evolve. Thus, any empirical test of them would never be able to conclusively establish their function as a receptor of God's input, which is consistent with the view that religious belief must be based on faith rather than empirical evidence.

Another religiously oriented cognitivist is Vilayanur S. Ramachandran, Director of the Center for Brain and Cognition at the University of California, San Diego, who was raised as a Hindu in India. In a book called *Phantoms in the Brain*, cowritten with Sandra Blakeslee, a science writer for *The New York Times* (Ramachandran & Blakeslee, 1998), on the basis of his research, Ramachandran, like others, concludes that there are brain circuits involved in religious experiences and that these can be activated during epileptic seizures. According to him, however, this does not negate or detract from genuine religious experiences. Similarly, Andrew Newberg and the late Eugene d'Aquili, a radiologist and psychiatrist, respectively, found what they considered to be similarities in the brain activation of praying nuns and meditating Buddhists, and concluded that there is one ultimate religious state that they termed *absolute unity*, which may be interpreted in different ways according to one's upbringing and other environmental factors (Newberg, d'Aquili, & Rause, 2001).

Hence, it appears that religiously oriented and nonreligiously oriented cognitivists take a similar nondualistic stance in agreement that brain processes are involved in religious experiences. Both religiously and nonreligiously oriented cognitivists also appear to agree, overall, that the existence of the brain processes can neither prove nor disprove the truth of any particular religious viewpoint.

Cognitivism and the Paranormal

Because cognitive science is based squarely on principles of physics, and physics admits only of natural phenomena, there is scant room for the paranormal within cognitivism. According to conventional physics, occurrence of clairvoyance, precognition, and telepathy, if they are possible at all, would require far more energy than can be generated by the brain. Moreover, the requisite energy would be so great as to totally destroy any brain that outputted it, assuming that were even possible. Of course, the discovery of a new principle of physics that would allow paranormal phenomena to occur can never be absolutely ruled out. In the past a new physics paradigm has overthrown an old one (Kuhn, 1962), and this could happen again. However, the amount of confirmation that has taken place with current physical theory makes this extremely unlikely. Even at the level of elementary particles, where very strange things happen—such as one particle having an instantaneous effect on another regardless of the distance separating the two particles—information cannot be communicated instantaneously from one location to another, as required by the descriptions of certain paranormal events. Alleged paranormal events must therefore, according to current cognitive scientific thinking, be due to coincidences, misperceptions, faulty memories, unreliable reporting, hoaxes, or some combination of any of these.

BEHAVIORAL APPROACH

Nothing could seem to be further apart than behaviorism, with its physicalistic view, and spirituality. However, it cannot be denied that feelings of spirituality exist, and, from a radical behaviorist point of view, feelings are behavior. Therefore, there must be a behavioral account of feelings of spirituality as well as of spiritual beliefs.

Behavioral Explanations of Feelings of Self-Transcendence

Among the strongest of spiritual feelings are those of self-transcendence. Aside from the possibility that experiences of self-transcendence are spontaneously produced responses, there are several possible ways to explain them from a behavioral point of view.

Discrimination of Self and Non-Self

From early childhood we are taught to discriminate verbally ourselves from other people and other things. That is, we are conditioned to respond verbally to our own bodies and behavior. This verbal discriminative behavior is our consciousness or self-awareness. Under certain conditions, such as when one takes certain drugs or meditates, this discriminative behavior may tend to break down. *Self-transcendence* is one name for this effect. This might explain why *koans* are used in Zen meditation exercises. A koan is a type of riddle or thought-provoking question on which the individual is to meditate, and which is very difficult or impossible to answer—that is, to respond to verbally. Two well-known examples are, "Show me your face before your mother and father met," and "What is the sound of one hand clapping?" The function of the koan may be to help break down verbal discriminations, or to cause the individual through extinction or mild punishment temporarily to stop responding verbally altogether. This can also have a beneficial effect in getting us to respond to our environment more directly rather than indirectly through our verbalizations. For example, when I see a flower my conditioning history is such that I almost automatically respond either overtly or covertly with the word *flower*. The word *flower* then becomes part of my environment, affecting to some extent my subsequent response to the flower, thereby detracting to a certain extent from my experience of (or ability to respond directly to) the flower itself (see Williams, 1986).

Relational Frame Theory

Complementary to the above, another way to view self-transcendence from the behavioral approach utilizes relational frame theory (which we encountered in chapters 8 and 10). Relational frames are organized groups of symbols into which more elementary symbols (e.g., words) may be placed, and which function both as discriminative stimuli and as operant responses. Humans, much more than any other species, are extremely adept at learning relational frames in appropriate contexts.

To take a simplified example, consider the relational frame "_____ is here now." As a result of many experiences with different words inserted in the blank in this frame, individuals learn in various contexts to insert appropriate lower-order symbols into this frame and to respond appropriately to the contents of this frame. Thus individuals can appropriately respond to and say, "Bob is here now," "Daddy is here now," "Sue is here now," and so on, in the appropriate contexts (e.g., when the indicated individuals are in fact present). It is important to note that a person learns many different frames at about the same time, and that they interact with each other. The frame "_____ is here now" is not learned independently of the substitutability of *there* and *here* (i.e., depending on the location of various objects, events, etc.), or independently of tense (i.e., dependence on the time at which an event occurs).

Another example of a relational frame is "_____ is the same as _____." Thus, in various contexts individuals learn to substitute whatever is in the first blank in the frame with whatever is in the second blank, and vice versa. For example, individuals learn the relation "*am* is the same as *is*" when in the context of the word *I* at the beginning of a frame. Thus, individuals learn to say and respond appropriately to relations such as "Bob is tall," "Mary is running," and "I am sleepy." Of course, as indicated here, these frames are learned in conjunction with many other frames describing contrasting situations. Eventually, it becomes possible for an individual to say, appropriately, "I am here now." Notice, however, that unlike most statements we can make, this statement is always true in the context of oneself. Wherever I go, there I am. I have never experienced a situation in which I am not present. It is the ability to emit frames of this sort that leads to a feeling of oneness with the universe (i.e., I am my universe), which is a feeling of self-transcendence (Barnes-Holmes, Hayes, & Dymond, 2001).

Relational frames also potentially provide a feeling of self-transcendence in another way. Emotional effects conditioned to words in relational frames transfer readily to other words in the frames. Since many words are paired with aversive events, we are constantly presenting ourselves with aversive stimuli in our internal dialogues. These internal dialogues are typically incessant and practically unstoppable; however, acceptance-and-commitment therapy (ACT), which as mentioned earlier in this book is a form of behavior therapy that is based on relational frame theory, takes an approach to this problem that is similar to Zen Buddhism. As in Zen Buddhism, our propensity for language is seen as being the problem. In fact, in all forms of Buddhism, human suffering is a result of our cravings, our desires, and our fears. Our verbal behavior seems to be capable of intensifying these—as when, for example, we tell ourselves that we absolutely must have something that is beyond our reach or that we absolutely cannot stand a particular situation that is unavoidable. As part of its overall strategy, therefore, ACT involves making oneself a dispassionate observer of one's inner dialogue (see chapter 8). It does this by transforming the frame "I have [a specific thought or emotional reaction] here and now" to "I had [a specific thought or emotional reaction] there and then." In this way, one's thoughts and emotions are objectified (Barnes-Holmes, Hayes, & Gregg, 2001, pp. 241–249). ACT is discussed in more detail in chapter 14.

Like psychoanalysts and cognitivists, behaviorists tend to take a materialistic view of the universe. From a behavioral point of view, it is difficult to see how there can be a "spiritual essence" which continues after the death of the body. Behaviorists view all so-called "mental" and "spiritual" processes as behavior. Behavior is a product of the body, and cannot exist apart from the body; therefore, when the body dies all so-called "mental" or "spiritual" functioning must cease. Note that the cognitive approach to the mind as a computer program does not dispute the behavioral position on this. What cognitivists regard to be a computer program in the brain are to the behaviorist patterns of behavior, and thus cannot exist apart from the body that engages in them.

Behaviorism and the Paranormal

Behaviorists assume that stimuli and responses are consistent with the laws of physics. It is not difficult to see in theory, however, how parapsychological phenomena could be possible from a behavioral point of view. It could conceivably be discovered that we have supplementary sense modalities that can only be explained after substantially revising the laws of physics. If that were to happen, the concepts of stimulus and response might have to be redefined in such as way as to be compatible with the current definitions of parapsychological phenomena (e.g., it may be necessary to assume that an event in a distant location or even a covert response of another person can be a stimulus for an individual). However, most physicists agree that the possibility of such forces or laws being discovered is remote—as discussed earlier in the section on cognitivism and the paranormal.

Behaviorism and Religion

From these ideas just discussed, it might seem that within behaviorism there could be no room for religion or spirituality in any form. This, however, is not the case. As with adherents of other systems of psychology, there are behaviorists who practice various traditional faiths. Psychologists in general, however, tend to be less religious (at least in the traditional sense) than the general population (see Jones, 1994); and this may be particularly true of behaviorists.

Dualistic religions appear to go strongly against the grain of behaviorism because of its emphasis on the nondualistic nature of humans. Although most Western behaviorists (like most other Westerners) have little knowledge of Eastern religions, the nondualistic nature of some Eastern religions might appeal to some behaviorists as it does to some humanistic psychologists.

SUMMARY

Most humanistic psychologists attempt to find meaning in life in a manner that is consistent with the scientific view of the universe. This involves either (1) adopting a nonreligious approach, or (2) adopting a religious or transpersonal approach that typically differs from the traditional Judeo-Christian belief of Western culture. There is a close similarity between secular humanists and nonreligious, or secular, humanistic psychologists. Transpersonal and religious humanistic psychologists believe that self-transcendence is not merely a subjective state, but rather that in experiencing it one comes into contact with something deep that permeates life and even inanimate matter. Transpersonal and religious humanistic psychologists are typically more impressed with Eastern religions, such as Buddhism and Taoism, than with Christianity or Judaism.

Psychodynamic theories tend to be nonspiritual. Jungian theory is an exception, as according to Jung religious symbolism is an extremely important part of the collective unconscious. The traditional psychoanalytic approach in general is nonreligious (there are, of course, individual psychoanalysts who may subscribe to various theistic religions). According to the psychoanalytic approach, God is a father substitute. The elements that make up self-transcendental experiences arise largely from the oceanic feeling that stems from the primordial memory of being an undifferentiated infant. In Jungian theory, contact with the collective unconscious is experienced as self-transcendence. In one crucial respect, however, the Eastern approach to spirituality—especially that of Buddhism—appears to be diametrically opposed to the psychodynamic approach. All the major psychodynamic theories maintain that psychological health depends on a strong sense of self.

The mainstream cognitive approach has not directly addressed the issue of spirituality. This is not surprising, as it is difficult to imagine a computer with feelings of spirituality. In fact, the area of feeling and emotion in general has been largely neglected by cognitive psychology. There are correlations between disturbances in the temporal lobes of the brain and religiosity or spirituality, suggesting a neurological basis for transpersonal experiences. Less mainstream cognitive views of religion postulate undiscovered laws in physics to account for religion.

Like psychoanalysts and mainstream cognitive psychologists, behaviorists tend to take a materialistic view of the universe. Behaviorists view all so-called mental and spiritual processes as behavior. Behavior is a product of the body, and cannot exist apart from the body; therefore, when the body dies, all so-called mental or spiritual functioning must cease. The reason is that stimuli and responses are assumed to be physical in the sense of known laws of physics. There are several ways to explain the experience of self-transcendence from a behavioral point of view. One involves verbal discriminative behavior, which is our consciousness or self-awareness. Another way to view self-transcendence from a behavioral approach utilizes relational frame theory. Humans, much more than any other species, are extremely adept at learning relational frames in appropriate contexts. As a result of many experiences with different words inserted in the blank of a frame, individuals learn in various contexts to insert particular words into the frame and to respond appropriately to the contents of the frame. Relational frames also provide a feeling of self-transcendence in another way. Emotional effects conditioned to words in relational frames transfer readily to other words in the frames.

Discussion Questions

1. It is often said that there is a conflict between science and religion. Discuss whether this is true, and if so, whether this conflict can be resolved (and if so, how).

2. Which of the four approaches has been most concerned with resolving the conflict (or apparent conflict) between science and religion? How has this approach attempted to resolve the conflict?

3. What are the different possible meanings of self-transcendence according to humanistic psychologists? Discuss which of these meanings are compatible with the other approaches.

4. Discuss whether true spirituality requires a belief in a personal God.

5. Discuss whether the evidence for or against paranormal phenomena supports a spiritual or nonspiritual belief.

6. Discuss whether near-death experiences have a naturalistic explanation or provide evidence for an afterlife.

7. Discuss how each of the nonhumanistic approaches can accommodate a spiritualistic position.

8. Describe Wilber's pre/trans fallacy. Discuss whether it applies to approaches other than the psychodynamic approach.

9. Discuss how each of the four approaches might accommodate paranormal phenomena if strong evidence supporting such phenomena were to develop.

10. Discuss which religion appears to be most compatible with each of the four broad systems.

CHAPTER 14

Therapy

Psychotherapy is one of the main ways in which the four systems differ. This is particularly important not only because of the great potential of therapy for doing good, but also because of its potential to do harm. An often-quoted dictum commonly attributed to the famous Hippocratic Oath that the physicians of ancient Greece swore to abide by is: "Do no harm." This admonition may be traceable to ancient Greece, but it was not part of the oath, which consisted of concrete, enforceable rules. As Miles (2004, p. 144) pointed out, all therapy involves some risk; thus, the injunction never to do harm may be impossible to adhere to absolutely. Nevertheless, it is an important caution for therapists to keep uppermost in mind, because it reminds them when choosing a particular procedure to always carefully weigh its potential benefits against its risks, and to refrain from using it if the latter outweigh the former. This chapter therefore considers not only how the four approaches attempt to do good, but also how they try to avoid doing harm.

HUMANISTIC APPROACH

Humanistic psychologists adopt a *person-centered* approach to therapy and counseling. By this they mean that they treat their clients as people rather than as objects to be manipulated and controlled.

Assumptions of the Person-Centered Approach

The emphasis on person-centeredness seems to underscore two strong views held by humanistic psychologists: (1) the view that each person is a unique individual who cannot be described by any set of principles in the manner that the laws of physics describe the behavior of physical objects; (2) the view that humans are not to be controlled in the same sense that physical objects can be controlled by applying the laws of physics.

Rogers devoted his life to developing the person-centered approach. He wrote:

> What do I mean by a person-centered approach? It expresses the primary theme of my whole professional life, as that theme has become clarified through experience, interaction with others, and research. I smile as I think of the various labels I have given to this theme during the course of my career—nondirective counseling, client-centered therapy, student-centered teaching, group-centered leadership. (1980, p. 114)

"Non-Techniques" of Humanistic Psychotherapy

Although humanistic psychologists reject the use of *techniques* as described in other approaches, humanistic psychology is sometimes characterized as using two major techniques.

Reflection of Feeling

One technique is known as *reflection of feeling*, or simply, *reflection*. This involves restating or reiterating statements the client makes about his or her feelings with respect to a given situation, so that the client's feelings are, as it were, "reflected back" to him or her. For example, if during the course of therapy a client says, "I wish I could die," the therapist might respond: "You wish you could die, don't you? M-hm. You feel so awful, you wish you could perish." Reflection appears to accomplish at least two things: (1) it communicates the interest and concern of the therapist for the client; (2) it enables the client to recognize feelings in himself or herself that the client might otherwise not recognize or acknowledge.

Questioning

The other major technique that humanistic therapists are sometimes said to use is *questioning* (or *probing*). This involves asking for more information, often in a nonspecific manner, about something the client has said or alluded to. For example, if the client mentions his or her mother, the therapist might say, "Tell me more about your mother." Questioning and reflecting are used together; the former is used to get the client to express his/her feelings about significant things in his/her life, and the latter to reflect those feelings back to the client.

A Humanistic Psychotherapy Computer Program

Ironically for an approach that eschews techniques, and whose advocates claim it cannot by its very nature be formalized into any sort of algorithm, the first psychotherapy computer program was modeled after the humanistic approach to psychotherapy. The program, called *ELIZA* after Eliza Doolittle in George Bernard Shaw's play *Pygmalion*, was written by a computer scientist in an effort to develop a computer program that can converse with a human. The author of the program, Weizenbaum (1966), wished to use it to study natural language communication between humans and machines. In one version of the program, called DOCTOR (Weizenbaum, 1966, 1976), the program assumes the role of a Rogerian psychotherapist. It has been argued that the program shows promise as a therapeutic tool. Kleinmuntz (1969), for example, supported this suggestion with the following excerpt from a "conversation" between a person and a computer programmed with DOCTOR and acting as a therapist:

> PATIENT: Men are all alike.
> THERAPIST: In what way?
> PT: They're always bugging us about something or other.
> TH: Can you think of a specific example?
> PT: Well, my boyfriend made me come here.
> TH: Your boyfriend made you come here?
> PT: He says I'm depressed much of the time.
> TH: I am sorry to hear you are depressed.
> PT: It's true. I am unhappy.
> TH: Do you think coming here will help you not to be unhappy?
> PT: I need some help. That much seems certain.
> (Kleinmuntz, 1969, pp. 153–154)

Weizenbaum was shocked at the view being entertained by a number of psychiatrists that his creation could be made to substitute for a real therapist on the assumption that a human therapist can be viewed as an "information processor and decision maker with a set of decision rules which are closely linked to short-range and long-range goals" (Weizenbaum, 1976, p. 6). For example, he asked: "What can the psychiatrist's image of his patient be when he sees himself, as therapist, not as a human being acting as a healer, but as an information processor following rules, etc.?" (Weizenbaum, 1976, p. 6; see also Weiszenbaum, 1995).

Although Eliza may appear to understand what a client is saying, in reality it is following only a few simple linguistic rules. For example, Eliza is programmed to respond, "In what way?" when it finds the word *alike* in a sentence, and to ask for a specific example when it finds the word *always* in a sentence. Clearly, if the program cannot really understand the client, it cannot empathize with him or her—and, according to humanistic psychologists, both understanding and empathy are essential in order for psychotherapy to have any value. Of course, more sophisticated programs could be written; however, according to many humanistic psychologists, the problem would still remain. Thus, according to J. W. Murphy and Pardeck (1988), the main problem with computer-mediated psychotherapy is that "[s]uperficial qualities are assumed to be representative of a person's soul, while the dimension of the interhuman is transformed into a nexus of logic and calculation" (p. 131).

Psychotherapy as a Growth Process

As already indicated, humanistic psychologists are generally opposed to the idea that their methods can be characterized as *techniques* or specified by a set of rules that can be programmed into a computer or even taught—at least as a cognitive or intellectual skill. They believe that what is important is the attitude of empathy for the client that lies behind the techniques. For example, Rogers stated:

> I . . . wince at the phrase *reflection of feeling*. It does not describe what I am trying to do when I work with a client. My responses are attempts to check my understanding with the client's internal world. I wish to keep an accurate, up-to-the minute sensitivity to his or her inner searchings, and the [reflection-of-feeling] response is an endeavor to find out if I am on course with my client. I regret that the phrase *reflection of feeling* has come to be used to describe this complex type of interaction. (Rogers, 1987, p. 39; italics in original)

Rogers arrived at his person-centered position through carrying out therapy, as indicated by the following statement: "It began to occur to me that unless I had a need to demonstrate my own cleverness and learning, I would be better to rely upon the client for the direction of movement in the process" (1967, p. 359).

Rogers began developing his person-centered approach, which he initially called client-centered therapy (Rogers, 1951), in the 1930s. The following is a quote from a 1940 speech in which he first described the approach:

1. This newer approach relies much more heavily on the individual drive toward growth, health, and adjustment. [Therapy] is a matter of freeing [the client] for normal growth and development.
2. This therapy places greater stress upon the feeling aspects of the situation than upon the intellectual aspects.
3. This newer therapy places greater stress upon the immediate situation than upon the individual's past.
4. This approach lays stress upon the therapeutic relationship itself as a growth experience. (Rogers, 1970, p.12)

Rogers' person-centered approach emphasizes therapy as a growth experience for the therapist as well as for the client. He stated:

> . . . [T]he more the therapist is able to listen acceptantly to what is going on within himself, and the more he is able to be the complexity of his feelings, without fear, the higher the degree of his congruence. (1961, p. 61)

and

> The important thing is that two unique persons are in tune with each other in an astonishing moment of growth and change. Both of us are changed, although the growth might be greater in the client. (Rogers, 1987, p. 39)

Humanistic psychologists emphasize the *growth* of the individual—even where that growth does not conform to the norms of society. By growth, humanistic psychologists mean the process of *self-actualization* (as discussed in previous chapters).

Criticisms of the Non-Directive Approach

Concerning humanistic psychologists' procedures, there are two logical possibilities: either (1) the procedures are effective, or (2) they are ineffective. Now, in order to be effective, the procedures must produce a desirable change in the client's behavior. But if the procedures used by humanistic psychologists produce a change in the client's behavior, then humanistic psychologists are controlling behavior (at least as the word *control* is used by behaviorists). Conversely, if humanistic psychologists do not control behavior, their procedures are ineffective and clients are wasting their time and money subjecting themselves to those procedures. At least this is what a non-humanistic therapist, especially a behaviorist, would argue.

Even within humanistic psychology there is some controversy about the extent to which therapists should be nondirective. For example, Kahn (1999, 2002) argued that occasional intervention by the therapist, such as by making suggestions, may be beneficial in the therapeutic process and need not contravene the person-centered approach. He further argued that it is impossible for a therapist to be completely nondirective (in the "pure" sense) because the therapist's subjective and theoretical biases are bound to affect the way he or she interacts with the client. He suggested that rather than striving to be nondirective, the person-centered therapist should strive for humility in the sense of acknowledging that he or she might be fallible—that is, might not always select the best way of intervening with a particular client. These criticisms of nondirective therapy prompted vigorous replies from several client-centered therapists (Bozarth, 2002; Merry & Brodley, 2002; Sommerbeck, 2002).

Kahn's critics argued that he had misunderstood the meaning of *nondirectivity* in the person-centered approach. They asserted that nondirectivity does not mean that the therapist does not influence the client. Rather, it simply means that the therapist (1) does not seek to influence the client in any way whatsoever, (2) maintains an attitude of nondirectivity, (3) works within the client's framework rather than within that of the therapist, (4) provides the conditions under which the actualizing tendency can work and promote the growth of the client, and (5) trusts in the power of the actualizing tendency to do just that. Perhaps this was most forcefully stated by Sommerbeck (2002, p. 86) as follows:

> Nondirectivity is about abstinence from trying to be helpful; that is, the therapist does not try to be immediately and directly helpful in any systematic or goal-directed way. Nondirectivity is about the (empathic) interpretation that is not made, the connection that is not drawn, the probing question that is not asked, the good idea that is not shared, and so forth, because the therapist's whole attention is on understanding, not on trying to be helpful. The consequence is that the therapist does not even notice opportunities for making such interventions and does not even think of them. Nondirectivity is also about the client directing the therapist's frame of reference with a search or request for directivity, which the therapist accommodates, if he or she will and can, not primarily to be helpful but to remain fundamentally nondirective.

Humanistic psychologists' procedures are probably at least somewhat effective with at least some people. In fact, there are data indicating that clients in humanistic therapies generally show the same amounts of change as clients in nonhumanistic therapies do (Elliott, 2002). Thus, whether it is their intent or not, humanistic psychologists likely do control behavior to some extent. For example, it is possible that Rogers reinforced (with verbalizations indicating interest, understanding, empathy) certain classes of verbal responses and that, in at least some cases, the verbal responses in the reinforced classes increased in frequency (e.g., Greenspoon, 1955). However, both Rogers and his clients would probably have been unaware that this type of control was occurring in the sessions.

Relationship Between Client and Therapist

As indicated above, humanistic psychologists put a great deal of emphasis on the equality of the relationship between the therapist and the client as a means of promoting growth in the client. That such equality is possible, however, has been questioned. For example, consider the following interchange between Carl Rogers and Martin Buber:

> Carl Rogers: . . . I do feel there's a real sense of equality between us [therapist and client].
>
>   Martin Buber: No doubt about it. But I am not speaking now about your feelings but about a real situation. I mean you two look, as you just said, on *his* experience. Neither he nor you look on *your* experience. . . . He cannot in the course of, let's say, a talk with you . . . change his position and ask you, "Oh, Doctor, where were you yesterday? Oh, you were

in the movies? What was it and how were you impressed?" He *cannot* do it. So, I see and feel very well your feeling, your attitude, your taking his part. But you cannot change the given situation. There is something objectively real that confronts you, the person, but also the situation. . . .

Carl Rogers: . . . But it has been my experience that that is a reality when viewed from the outside, and that that really has *nothing* to do with therapy. That is something immediate, equal, a meeting of two people on an equal basis. . . . (Buber, Rogers, & Friedman, 1965, pp. 173; emphasis in original)

Burstow (1988), an existential psychotherapist, enumerated several areas in which she feels the relationship between the humanistic psychotherapist and client are equal and several in which she feels the relationship cannot be one of equality. On the one hand, according to Burstow, the client and therapist are (1) equally meaning-making human beings, (2) equal in worth, and (3) equally capable of realizing their own unique potential (although that potential may not be equal). On the other hand, the client and therapist may not be equal (1) in coping skills or (2) in their comfort with the world. In addition, they are necessarily unequal in one significant respect: "They are not in the same position in relation to each other; and they are not in an equal position. One is help*er* and the other is help*ee*. [emphasis in original]" (Burstow, 1977, p. 15). Burstow was answered by Bink (1987)—a humanistic psychologist—and by Rogers (1987). Both stressed that "equality," like other humanistic precepts, cannot be imposed as a rule to be followed rigidly in therapy. The important thing is the attitude of the therapist toward the client. Presumably the therapist should respect the client as an equal, and feel that the relationship is one of equality whether or not the reality is otherwise, as Rogers stated to Martin Buber in the above quotation.

In any case, humanistic psychologists attach a great deal of importance to the relationship between the client and the therapist. The extent to which the client and therapist work together in the therapy is termed the therapeutic alliance, and many psychotherapists (not just humanistic ones) consider it critical for a successful therapeutic outcome.

Extensions to Non-Therapy Situations

The humanistic approach has been extended to other applications in addition to therapy. Research suggests that workers whose employers adopt a person-centered attitude have less stress (Ikemi & Kubota, 1996). A training program to develop a person-centered attitude in employers involves teaching them to listen more genuinely to their employees without trying to impose their own views on them.

PSYCHODYNAMIC APPROACH

The psychoanalytic approach has undergone considerable change since Freud's death in 1939.

Traditional Psychoanalytic Approach

In the traditional psychoanalytic approach, the analyst takes a neutral, nonjudgmental, and nondirective stance in the sense that the he or she does not try to influence how the client (also called the patient or analysand) conducts his or her life. However, the therapist does attempt to elicit certain material (e.g., dreams, memories of childhood incidents) from the client. Much of this material that the client brings into the session is assumed to come from the unconscious, although usually in a disguised form that the therapist must interpret for the client or try to help the client interpret. When the client arrives at the correct interpretation, insight is said to occur which, according to psychoanalytic theory, should help the client overcome the problems that brought him or her into therapy. Overall, however, the therapist is aloof from the therapeutic process. That is, the therapist maintains an objective or neutral, nonjudgmental position. Because of the aloofness of the therapist the traditional psychoanalytic approach has been called a *one-person* therapy (meaning that all the focus is on the client).

Moves Toward a More Interactional Approach

Psychodynamic therapists who broke with Freud focused on the interaction between the therapist and the client. More recently, therapists who remain psychoanalysts have modified psychoanalysis to become more interactional.

Adler's Approach

In contrast to Freud and other pioneering psychodynamic therapists, Alfred Adler stressed a more egalitarian relationship between the therapist and client. In fact, Adler has been compared to Martin Buber in that, among other similarities, both emphasized an I-Thou relationship between individuals (Jääskeläinen, 2000). Moreover, Cain (2002, p. 15) noted that Adler's ideas influenced several of the founders of humanistic psychology (e.g., May, Rogers, and Maslow), and expressed surprise "that Adler has not had more direct influence on the development of humanistic therapies because he anticipated many of the ideas, attitudes, and therapeutic response that would later be embraced by them."

Emphasis on Relationships in Psychoanalysis

Recently, there has been a trend within mainstream psychoanalysis to conceptualize psychoanalysis as an interaction between two individuals—that is, to conceptualize it as a two-person process. In this view, it is theoretically acceptable for the analyst to express emotions that he or she may be experience in the session. In this regard, psychoanalysis may be moving closer to humanistic psychotherapy (Portnoy, 1999).

Decreased emphasis on certain traditional psychoanalytic concepts. In general, there has been a strong trend in psychoanalysis away from emphasis on sexuality and more on relationships. As Drew Westen put it:

> Contemporary psychoanalysts and psychodynamic therapists no longer write much about ids and egos, nor do they conceive of treatment for psychological disorders as an archaeological expedition in search of lost memories. . . . People do sometimes describe feelings or behaviors in therapy that conform remarkably to aspects of Freud's psychosexual theories (such as a patient of mine with erectile problems whose associations to a sexual encounter led to an image of having sex with his mother, followed by some unpleasant anal imagery). Nevertheless, psychotherapists who rely on theories derived from Freud do not typically spend their time lying in wait for phallic symbols. They pay attention to sexuality, because it is an important part of human life and intimate relationships and one that is often filled with conflict. Today, however, most psychodynamic theorists and therapists spend much of their time helping people with problematic interpersonal patterns, such as difficulty getting emotionally intimate or repeatedly getting intimate with the wrong kind of person (see Greenberg & Mitchell, 1983). (Westen, 1998, p. 333)

Increased emphasis on transference. Freud saw the relationship between the client and the therapist (or therapeutic alliance) as important within his particular theoretical framework (Freud, 1961). There has been an increasing trend among psychoanalysts to put more and more emphasis on this aspect of Freud's theory.

Freud's Theory of Transference and Countertransference

Two aspects of therapy that Freud considered extremely important were transference and countertransference. Transference refers to an emotion or set of emotions (either positive or negative) that, early in therapy, an analysand—that is, the client or person undergoing psychoanalysis—transfers from a parent to the therapist. In other words, the therapist becomes a father or a mother figure for the client, although the client generally is unaware of this feeling. It is, in other words, confined to the client's unconscious. One of the therapist's tasks is to bring the client's transference to his or her consciousness, thereby resulting in insight that helps the client understand past and present relations with and feelings toward the parent who was the source of the transference. Hence, Freud considered the occurrence of transference to be a positive sign in therapy, provided the therapist handles it correctly. If not handled correctly, it could be dangerous. For example, the client could develop an excessive dependence on the therapist, like that of a child on its mother or father. While the transference was a desirable although risky part of therapy, Freud saw the countertransference as generally undesirable. It referred to strong unconscious feelings the therapist might develop toward the client, perhaps as a result of the transference. Freud wrote: "We have become aware of 'the countertransference,' which arises in him [the psychoanalyst] as a result of the patient's influence on his unconscious feelings, and we are almost inclined to insist that he shall recognize this countertransference in himself and overcome it" (Freud, 1910/1957, pp. 144–145).

For example, the therapist might begin to have maternal or paternal feelings toward the analysand. In traditional psychoanalytic therapy the therapist was to suppress these feelings, as they tended to interfere with the neutral stance the therapist was supposed to take and could detract from the therapeutic process (e.g., by inhibiting insight).

Kohut's Psychoanalytic Self Psychology

Transference is important in Kohut's psychoanalytic self psychology. This is because strengthening the self requires the presence of individuals whom Kohut called selfobjects. Although self-object may be better English, Kohut wants to make it clear that the selfobject is seen as part of the self and different from the self simultaneously. In infancy and childhood, these individuals would most likely be a parent or parents. In adulthood they are close friends and significant others. A damaged or fractured self is not relating well to selfobjects, or may have none with which to relate. In the transference, the therapist becomes a selfobject to the analysand or client. The desired result is a healing of the client's self, in which the individual is then able to find and relate to other selfobjects who further sustain the self (Kohut, 1984, pp. 198–207).

Psychoanalytic self psychology places more emphasis than humanistic psychology on the use of medical terms and the expertise of the therapist. However, it draws on a number of humanistic concepts such as the idea that empathy (in the sense of thoroughly communicating the therapist's understanding of the client) is important in the healing process. Moreover, since people naturally tend to heal themselves, psychoanalytic self psychology maintains that the therapist should not try overly to influence the direction in which the client is moving (Kahn, 1999; Tobin, 1991). (a or b?) According to psychoanalytic self psychology, however, the therapist may still provide some interpretations and directivity, as this is considered to be part of being empathetic.

Frank's Enactments

Kenneth A. Frank (1999, 2002) further developed Freud's approach to the relationship between client and therapist. Frank begins with the psychoanalytic concept of *enactment*, which refers to the interactions between the analysand and therapist stemming from the transference and countertransference. However, he then broadens the concept of enactment to include much more. He stated: "When analysts speak of enactments, they usually refer very specifically to automatic, preconscious interaction patterns involving patients' and analysts' unique, interlocking, personal psychodynamic systems, which structure the psychoanalytic relationship in ways that inhibit progress" (Frank, 2002, p. 279).

More succinctly, he defined patients' enactments as "their reflexive attempts to influence interpersonal interactions in personal ways based on their psychodynamics, both with the therapist and with others outside the therapy setting" (Frank, 2002, p. 267).

To simplify, we might think of an enactment as a significant social interaction. Frank recommends focusing on enactments within the therapy session, and outside of it as well. Thus, therapy becomes open to discussion with the client regarding not only the transference, but also the countertransference, and the current relationships of the client with others. This change in psychoanalytic therapy is so radical that it has been regarded as a paradigm shift. Traditionally, psychoanalysts frowned on drawing attention to their personal feelings toward their clients. They also de-emphasized their clients' current social interactions because they believed that much earlier social interactions—especially those that occurred in infancy and childhood with the parents—had much more important effects on clients' current psychodynamics and hence on the problems that necessitated therapy.

The concept of enactment suggests that the therapist can work with the client on his or her current social relations within a consistent psychodynamic framework. In addition, transference and countertransference can be used, not only as a catalyst for insight, but also as a way for the client to practice and learn positive social interactions. In effect, as Frank points out, this provides a bridge for the integration of psychoanalysis with behavior therapy. It should be noted that this represents quite a dramatic shift in traditional psychoanalysis. As Frank stated, "Until recently, psychoanalytic theorizing, based on the monadic [i.e., one-person] model and a view of the psychoanalytic situation as somehow separate from the rest of the patient's life, emphasized that experiential insight into the transference alone was the key to change" (Frank, 2002, p. 274).

In commenting on Frank's extension of Freud's concept of transference and countertransference, Anchin (2002, p. 341) considers the relational psychoanalytic paradigm to represent a radical transformation in psychoanalytic theory and practice that is, nevertheless, firmly anchored in the Freudian school of thought. Interestingly, while relational psychoanalysis is growing, recent information gleaned from autobiographies and letters of Freud's analysands and Freud's own correspondence shows that he did not follow some of his own strict recommendations for relating to his clients (Lynn & Vaillant, 1998). For example, he frequently revealed aspects of his private life to many of his clients. Further, on occasion he made strong suggestions to his clients regarding how they should handle their private lives. In fact, some of his behavior would be considered extremely unethical today. Particularly egregious lapses were conducting analysis on friends and a family member (his daughter, Anna Freud) and revealing confidences of his clients to other clients and to friends. Although these lapses occurred long ago and may seem to have little relevance today, they could call his theory into question if the procedures he used to obtain results in support of the theory were at odds with those required by the theory.

Relationship to the Other Therapies

Often a neglected component of psychoanalysis, the countertransference has been picked up as an important and useful concept by some psychotherapists of other orientations—perhaps especially those who subscribe to a movement called psychotherapy integration that, as its names implies, seeks to integrate the various forms of psychotherapy. For example, Marcus and Buffington-Vollum (2005) see a potential benefit to psychotherapy from the study of the countertransference as a social phenomenon.

By beginning to focus on current social relationships, as indicated above, Freudian psychoanalysts have moved closer to both humanistic and behavioral psychotherapies. Psychoanalysts have also moved closer to cognitive psychotherapies. As we shall explain in more detail, cognitive psychotherapy focuses on changing maladaptive schemata or schemas—that is, "stable structures derived from emotionally significant past experiences that function as profoundly held beliefs about living" (Frank, 2002, p. 273). From a psychoanalytic point of view, schemas distorted early in childhood through particular types of family interactions can be maladaptive, if the interactions were not ideal. These maladaptive schemas lead to automatic (i.e., unconscious) self-defeating thinking (or cognitions) and behavior. The task of psychotherapy from a psychoanalytic point of view, then, is to change these maladaptive schemas. In psychoanalysis the major tool for doing this is insight (i.e., inducing the client to recognize, that is, become aware of, the maladaptive schemas). Cognitive psychotherapists take a somewhat different approach, as we shall see.

COGNITIVE APPROACH

There are several streams leading into the cognitive approach to therapy. One comes directly from cognitive psychology, and is manifested by the attempt to develop a computer model of mind. A second stream comes from a conception of psychological problems as chiefly due to maladaptive thinking or a failure to think rationally. This stream views psychotherapy largely as a teaching process—that is, teaching rational or adaptive thinking. A third stream comes from a merger of behavioral approaches with cognitive approaches to therapy.

Computer Simulations

Most cognitivists probably have little or no problem with the notion that a computer (in principle) could be programmed to carry out psychotherapy. From the point of view of cognitive psychology, it should be possible to simulate the mind of any expert—or the "composite mind" of all the experts—on any particular type of therapy. Such a program, which would be a type of program called an expert system or a production system, should be particularly feasible for therapies the procedures of which are well-specified, such as most cognitive therapies.

There has been some promising research on programming computers to carry out at least some aspects of cognitive psychotherapy (e.g., Stuart & LaRue, 1996). In addition, just as there have been attempts to simulate normal minds using artificial intelligence, there have also been attempts to simulate psychological disorders in the hope of understanding them better (e.g., Cohen & Servan-Schreiber, 1992; Siegel, 1997, 1999). There have also been attempts to use information-processing approaches (e.g., Hamilton, 1979, 1980; Ingram & Hollon, 1986; Ingram & Kendall, 1986; Neufeld & Mothersill, 1980) and neural networks approaches (e.g. Tryon, 1993a,b) to understand psychopathologies.

Cognitive Restructuring: Changing Maladaptive Thoughts

In general, cognitivists have been more theoretically than practically oriented. They have not focused on developing therapies for individuals with psychological problems. However, a number of psychotherapists developed cognitive psychotherapies based to a greater or lesser extent (depending on the specific therapy) on concepts, data, and theory current in cognitivism. In these psychotherapies, psychological problems are assumed to be the result of faulty or maladaptive thoughts or beliefs—that is, schemata or schemas (to use the cognitive term)—relating to the self. For example, if a client is pathologically depressed the therapist will look for some pattern of thinking that may be causing the depression. The client may, for example, be depressed because of a belief that she is a failure because (a) her grade-point average is below "A," or (b) she is unattractive. Or, to take another example, (c) the client may be depressed because he believes that others are constantly laughing at him. In (a) and (b) the depression is caused by an erroneous value statement, namely, that one must get straight "A's" or be extremely attractive to the opposite sex to be a worthwhile person. In (c), the depression is caused by a tendency to misinterpret factual information regarding the laughter of others—who probably are not laughing at the client—as well as an erroneous value statement that it is terrible to be laughed at. Cognitive therapists treat clients by first helping them to recognize their maladaptive thoughts and beliefs, and then helping them to replace maladaptive thoughts and beliefs with more productive ways of thinking. This process, called *cognitive restructuring*, is perhaps in some ways analogous to debugging a computer program.

There are two broad types of cognitive psychotherapies, which are generally called *cognitive therapy* and *cognitive-behavioral therapy* (also known as cognitive behavior modification). As the name suggests, cognitive-behavioral therapy is a merger between cognitive and behavioral therapies. One reason for the development of these approaches was dissatisfaction with the prevailing psychoanalytic approach combined with an unwillingness fully to adopt either humanistic or behavioristic approaches. Cognitive and cognitive-behavioristic therapists found the humanistic approach too non-directive (or not focused enough on specific techniques), while the behavioristic approach seemed to ignore cognitive variables that they regarded as important. Three major developers of cognitive and cognitive-behavioral therapies are Albert Ellis, Aaron Beck, and Donald Meichenbaum.

Albert Ellis. Ellis' approach has undergone several name changes. It was first called rational psychotherapy, because of its emphasis on helping clients rid themselves of irrational thinking, which Ellis regarded as the cause of many psychological problems. The name was then changed to rational-emotive therapy (RET) because of the criticism that it neglected clients' emotional side. Finally, the name was changed to rational emotive behavior therapy (REBT) because of the criticism that it neglected clients' behaviors. These name changes did not reflect changes in the therapy itself; Ellis designed each new name to represent the therapy more accurately.

Influences on REBT

Ellis acknowledged a wide variety of influences on the development of REBT, including the eighteenth-century philosopher Immanuel Kant (especially his work *Critique of Pure Reason*), the secular humanistic philosopher Bertrand Russell, the theologian Paul Tillich, existentialists (e.g., Heidegger), the general semanticist A. Korzybsky, the psychodynamic therapists Karen Horney and Alfred Adler, and the early behaviorists John B. Watson, Mary Cover Jones, and Knight Dunlap (Dryden & Ellis, 2001). The influences were their emphases on the following:

- Kant: power and limitations of cognition and ideation.
- Russell: power of logical thinking.
- Existentialists: centrality of humans (as opposed to a supernatural deity) and the ability of humans to exercise will or choice.
- Korzybsky: the deleterious effect careless language has on our thinking.
- Horney: the "tyranny of the shoulds" (i.e., the things we tell ourselves we should or must do when there is no rational reason for these particular shoulds).
- Adler: the important role feelings of inferiority play in psychological disturbance, the importance of goals, values, and meanings, and the use of persuasion.
- Behaviorists: systematic methods to encourage clients to practice and engage in behaviors that help overcome their problems.

Rationale and Procedure

The basic premise of REBT is that people tend to be irrational, and this irrationality leads to psychological problems. Ellis' approach attempts to teach clients to overcome psychological problems by learning to think rationally, where rational "means that which is true, is logical, and aids people in achieving their basic goals and purposes" (Dryden & Ellis, 2001, p. 298).

Aaron Beck. Beck started out as a psychoanalytic therapist, but soon found that psychoanalysis was ineffective when he attempted to use it to treat severe depression.

It seemed to Beck that the problem stemmed from an incorrect view of depression in psychoanalytic theory. From his observations Beck concluded that depression is caused not by inward-directed hostility, as psychoanalysts believed, but by erroneous or maladaptive thinking (Beck, 1976). According to Beck and Emery (1985), "the primary pathology or dysfunction during a depression or an anxiety disorder is the cognitive apparatus" (p. 85). Beck enumerates a number of types of thinking errors that can lead to depression. These include all-or-nothing thinking (e.g., if one's work is not flawless it is defective), overgeneralization (e.g., if I lose my temper occasionally I can't control my temper), discounting positives (e.g., if I do well on some project it couldn't have been important), mind reading (e.g., people think I'm incompetent), fortune telling (e.g., things will not turn out well), magnifying/minimizing (overestimating/underestimating the importance of negative/positive events), making "should" statements (telling oneself what one should have done or not done), labeling (applying an unflattering label to oneself inappropriately), and inappropriate blaming (using the 20:20 feature of hindsight to reproach oneself for what one "should" have or have not done).

Beck's cognitive therapy attempts to cure clients' depression by replacing dysfunctional thinking with functional thinking.

Donald Meichenbaum. While conducting his doctoral research on operant conditioning of mental patients, Meichenbaum (1969) made the serendipitous discovery that patients who instructed themselves to "talk healthy" showed more gains on a variety of measures than patients who did not engage in this behavior.

Meichenbaum was influenced by the Soviet psychologists Alexander Luria (1961) and Lev Vygotsky (1962), who studied the role of language in the thought disorders of mental illness. These influences and the serendipitous finding he made led Meichenbaum and his associates to explore the use of self-instructional therapy, whereby clients are instructed in methods for self-instructing their own appropriate behavior, in a variety of areas: impulsivity in children, schizophrenia, speech anxiety, test anxiety, and phobias (Mahoney, 1974; Meichenbaum, 1973, 1977).

Another cognitive-behavioral procedure Meichenbaum developed is called stress-inoculation therapy. This involves exposing clients to relatively small, graduated amounts of stress (possibly just in imagination) in order to teach them how to cope with large amounts of stress. In theory this inoculates a person against the debilitating effects of stress in a manner analogous to the way in which one is inoculated against a disease by being injected with a relatively weak form of the germ that causes the disease.

Differences Between Cognitive and Cognitive-Behavioral Approaches

Cognitive and cognitive-behavioral therapists emphasize the role of cognitions (i.e., thinking) in determining behavior. Hence, most cognitive and cognitive-behavioral therapists focus on changing cognitions (e.g., faulty thinking) in order to change an individual's psychological problems and problem behavior. The difference between cognitive and cognitive-behavioral therapy is one of degree. Cognitive-behavioral therapists place more emphasis on (1) using behavioral measures to assess change and (2) using behavioral techniques (e.g., "homework" assignments in which clients practice desired behaviors), in addition to cognitive techniques, to bring about behavioral change. Most therapists who use cognitive methods today likely would describe themselves as cognitive-behavioral therapists.

Cognitive Therapy and Constructivism

The cognitive sciences focus on how the mind processes information from the environment in order to deal with the environment. In this processing, the mind (in the cognitive view) builds up some sort of representation of the environment. But what assurance do we have that this representation, in any particular case, is the correct one? In other words, what assurance do we have that there is a direct, one-to-one correspondence between any particular representation of reality and reality itself? We know that different people have different views of reality, so who is to say that one person's view is right and the other is wrong—and on what basis? To continue this line of questioning to its logical conclusion: what if there is no one correct view of reality? What if any logically consistent view is as correct as another? In short, what if reality exists not "out there" somewhere, but is constructed in the mind? This philosophical position is called (appropriately enough) *constructivism*. It is part of an approach called postmodernism, which is a movement away from authoritative edicts in art and science.

Constructivism has had an influence on psychotherapies in all four approaches discussed in this book. But its effect on the cognitive and cognitive behavioral therapies has been particularly strong. This is because, as indicated previously, the mind is seen as interpreting reality but not presenting a complete or perfect representation of it. If everyone's view of reality is correct, why is therapy needed to change it? The reason is that, sometimes, a person's view of reality may be causing him or her problems. In those cases a therapist may be needed to help that person change his or her view of reality in order to alleviate those problems.

The opposite of constructivism—the view that there is an ultimate, knowable reality—is called rationalism. It appears that there may be no rationalist-cognitive or cognitive-behavioral therapists. Even Albert Ellis, whose therapeutic approach has the word *rational* in its title, adheres to a form of constructivism. There are, however, different types and degrees of constructivism.

Rational-emotive behavior therapy and constructivism. Writing with W. Dryden, Ellis stated:

> REBT is a constructivist approach to psychotherapy, in that it holds that while people's preferences are influenced by their upbringing and their culture, they disturb themselves when their desires are not met by constructing irrational beliefs about such situations. However, REBT disagrees with constructivistic approaches that argue that all constructions are equally viable. By contrast, REBT theory holds that some constructions (i.e., rational beliefs) are more consistent with reality, more logical, and more functional than other constructions (i.e., irrational beliefs). Consequently, a major goal of REBT is to encourage clients to make rational constructions about average situations rather than irrational constructions. (Dryden & Ellis, 2001, p. 301).

From this quotation, one might question whether REBT is truly constructivism as it is usually defined, since Dryden and Ellis appears to refer to an external reality to which beliefs may be consistent or inconsistent. REBT does, however, have the characteristic of constructivism that beliefs are constructions of the individuals holding them.

Narrative psychology. Meichenbaum (1993) has also adopted a type of constructivism called narrative psychology. This is the view that each of us has a narrative or story that we tell ourselves about ourselves. These personal stories are not just a set of self-statements; they are more complex than that. They are an interwoven set of self-statements about our lives, what kind of people we are, and how the daily events in our lives fit in with our perceptions of ourselves. These stories or narratives are different for different individuals. Some narratives help us cope better with the stresses in our lives than others do. The job of the therapist, in this view, is to help the client repair a narrative that has become debilitating (e.g., interpreting events as confirming how hopeless one's situation is) to make it more effective in coping with the environment (e.g., interpreting events as challenging one to find inner sources of strength and resourcefulness).

Constructivism and humanistic psychotherapy. Constructivism contains a strong element of subjectivity (since it is, essentially, the view that everyone constructs his or her own reality). One might therefore think it to be more in line with humanistic than cognitive psychology. However, as we have seen, it is quite consistent with the cognitive approach because, taken to its logical conclusion, it implies that the only way we can know reality is through computations performed by the mind on the data supplied to us by (presumably) reality—and no two minds (or even the same mind at different times) need perform exactly the same computations on the same data to construct a representation of reality that can be interacted with effectively.

Constructivism and psychodynamic therapy. Constructivism appears also to be having an impact on psychoanalysis. Safran (2002) notes that the relational approach that psychoanalysis appears to be moving toward is compatible with constructivism. In fact, he appears to believe that in some ways the new relational psychoanalysis is more consistent with constructivism than current cognitive psychotherapies are. He states that cognitive constructivists "tend to speak as though they can stand more or less outside of the relational field in which they are participating. By focusing almost exclusively on the patient's construction of reality, they tend to ignore the way patient and therapist are always influencing one another at both conscious and unconscious levels" (Safran, 2002, p. 300).

Cognitive therapy and Buddhism. Another approach that we might think of as being more associated with humanistic psychology than cognitive psychology is Buddhism. Nevertheless, it appears that Buddhism may be beginning to exert an influence on cognitive psychotherapy. This was highlighted in a special issue of the journal *Cognitive and Behavioral Practice* (2002, Vol. 9, pp. 38–78). Buddhism is relevant to cognitive psychotherapy because both maintain that human suffering is due to incorrect (or dysfunctional) thinking. Both therefore attempt to alleviate human suffering by changing how individuals think. Unlike standard cognitive therapy where the usual way to change thinking is through logical argument, the primary technique Buddhism uses for changing thinking (i.e., to establish *right mindfulness*) is meditation. There are various types of meditation, but all involve an individual quietly observing his or her thoughts, perceptions, etc. in a detached or unemotional manner. Through meditation the individual discovers or comes to feel that we are all interconnected, and attains a sense of inner peace and compassion. Early results on using meditation in cognitive psychotherapy have been particularly promising with regard to rehabilitation of criminals (Bleick & Abrams, 1987) and the treatment of alcoholism and other addictions (Marlatt, 1994, 2002).

Mindfulness-Based Cognitive Therapy

A final cognitive approach to be mentioned is similar to the meditative approach described previously. This approach is called *mindfulness-based cognitive therapy* (*MBCT*). The idea behind this approach is that in depression, which is the main focus of the approach, the client views negative thoughts as reflective of reality or of the self. The client is therefore encouraged, through mindfulness training, to view negative thoughts as separate from the self and not necessarily reflective of reality. This strengthens the client's *metacognitive awareness,* which this approach equates with consciousness (Segal, Williams, & Teasdale, 2002). Similar to humanistic therapists, mindfulness-based cognitive therapists are fairly nondirective. They are encouraged to "think of your instructor role as planting seeds. You do not know how long they will take to germinate, and, in a real sense, that is not under your control. As best you can, cultivate instead an openness, a sense of discovery" (Segal, Williams, & Teasdale, 2002, p. 90).

Mindfulness-based cognitive therapists are, however, more directive than humanistic therapists, as is indicated by the reference to the "instructor role" in the above.

BEHAVIORAL APPROACH

Behavioral therapy is widely applied in areas that were once the province of more traditional forms of psychotherapy. Methodological behaviorism fits in very well with cognitive-behavioral therapy. In methodological behaviorism, behavior is seen as a way of studying the mind (as an intervening variable or set of intervening variables, operationally defined, of course). In cognitive-behavioral therapy, operating on the mind is seen as a way of changing behavior. Not surprisingly, however, the behavioral approach to therapy is similar to the cognitive-behavioral approach.

Differences Between Behavioral and Cognitive Behavioral Therapy

The main difference is that the cognitive-behavioral approach, like the cognitive approach, tends to be dualistic in the sense that it generally holds that cognitions (e.g., thoughts, images, beliefs) are something other than behavior. In the behavioral approach, cognitions are behavior that is difficult or impossible to observe directly. Thinking, as we have seen, is behavior—private behavior (except when one is "thinking out loud," as the saying goes), but otherwise no different from any other behavior. Thinking may be composed of verbal behavior emitted privately to oneself; or images, which, assuming that sensations are private responses to external stimuli, can be described as *conditioned seeing* (or *conditioned hearing*, *conditioned smelling*, etc., in the cases of nonvisual images). Beliefs may be described behaviorally as dispositions to behave as though certain things are true; for example, behaviorists translate the belief that it will rain today as the tendency to take an umbrella when going out, to advise others to do so, and so on.

Because the behavior that clients wish to change is often public behavior, behaviorists tend not to work with private behavior the way that cognitive psychologists and cognitive behavior therapists attempt to do. Cognitions (i.e., private behavior) may sometimes cause public behavior (since cognitions from a behaviorist point of view are behavior and behavior can produce stimuli that elicit or evoke other behavior); but private behavior need not cause public behavior and public behavior need not be caused by private behavior. Behaviorists therefore tend to work directly with problem behavior, whether it is public or private.

Developmental Disabilities and Autism

Because, unlike the other major approaches, the behavioral approach does not depend on verbal behavior, it has been effective in working with individuals whose verbal behavior is limited or nonexistent. It is, for example, the treatment of choice for individuals with developmental disabilities and autism. In fact, one of the greatest success stories of the behavioral approach is in the area of development disabilities and autism, where the approach is known as applied behavior analysis or ABA.

Because of a large body of supporting evidence, the Surgeon General of the United States has pronounced ABA to be the treatment of choice for children with autism (U. S. Department of Health and Human Services, 1999). A similar recommendation has been made by the New York State Department of Health (1999), which has provided an early intervention ABA program for the treatment of children with developmental disabilities and autism.

One of the main targets of treatment is verbal behavior. Viewing verbal behavior as behavior to be conditioned, the applied behavior analysts use reinforcement in combination with other procedures to establish simple requesting, naming, sentence construction, and academic tasks, as well as self-care and interpersonal skills that enable individuals with developmental disabilities and autism to function more fully in society (see Martin & Pear, 2007, pp. 246–247).

Working Directly with Behavior

Language is used effectively in behavior therapy with individuals who have verbal behavior. Nevertheless, individuals with verbal behavior are treated using behavioral principles rather than attempting to change their cognitions through rational argument. Behavioral therapists use a number of techniques that involve working directly with the behavior of interest. One of these, for example, is *role playing*, in which participants act out behaviors (e.g., being assertive) that enable them to function more effectively in social situations. Homework assignments are frequently given, for example, asking married couples to engage in behaviors together that will enable them to overcome sexual inhibitions.

Systematic Desensitization

Joseph Wolpe developed a conditioning approach called *systematic desensitization* to help clients overcome phobias and generalized anxiety. To illustrate, consider a person who has a debilitating fear of flying. A cognitive therapist might search for some deep-seated erroneous belief that the client has about the risks of flying and attempt to change that belief through rational argument. A behavioral therapist using systematic desensitization, however, would treat the problem as one involving an undesirable conditioned response—anxiety—to stimuli paired with airplanes. The therapist using systematic desensitization to treat this problem attempts to condition to these stimuli a desirable behavior—specifically, relaxation—that would compete with the undesirable anxiety response. This would be done (as the name of the procedure implies) in a systematic way in which the stimuli associated with flying are introduced gradually while the client remains in a relaxed state. In the early part of the procedure the stimuli associated with flying would be introduced by asking the client to imagine them (since from a behavioral point of view, mental images are responses that have stimulus properties that are similar to the things they represent).

Systematic desensitization might be confused with cognitive procedures because it involves the use of images, which cognitive psychotherapists regard as cognitions. However, in systematic desensitization images serve as convenient substitutes for stimuli that the individual would be likely to encounter in the natural environment, because they are similar to those stimuli and images and are convenient to use in an office treatment setting. In addition, it is often useful to start with images because they elicit weaker fear responses than stimuli in the natural environment; however, behavioral therapists generally move to in-vivo desensitization or guided exposure—that is, exposure to anxiety-producing stimuli in the natural environment, or an environment resembling the natural environment as much as possible—as soon as possible so that the anxiety has a better chance of extinguishing to stimuli more like those that the client is likely to encounter.

Treating Cognitions as Behavior

Clients often expect a behavior therapist to work directly on their cognitions and emotions to change them, and it is not inconsistent for behavior therapists to do this. In fact, a behavior therapist might do this in a manner that is indistinguishable from that of a cognitive therapist. The difference is that the behavior therapist will more clearly identify the so-called cognitions and emotions as behavior (albeit private or covert behavior), and thus subject to the same laws or principles as other behavior.

Acceptance and Commitment Therapy

A type of behavior therapy called *acceptance-and-commitment therapy* (ACT), takes a quite different approach (e.g., Hayes, Strosahl, & Wilson, 1999). Unlike cognitive psychotherapy, ACT does not attempt to change cognitions—thoughts, images—or internal emotional reactions, at least not directly. This is the *acceptance* part of ACT; that is, the client is encouraged to accept these inner cognitions and emotions rather than trying to change them. The commitment part of ACT involves encouraging the client to commit to changing aspects of his or her overt behavior pertaining to the presenting problem. There are two major reasons for the acceptance part of ACT: First, trying to change the client's cognitions or emotional reactions, in the view of ACT, risks making them worse (as will be explained in more detail below). Second, according to ACT, the client's thoughts and emotional reactions are not the problem, nor the causes of the problem, except insofar as the client reacts to them as though they were the problem or causes of it. For example, a client may say, "I didn't go to the party because I was depressed." To an ACT therapist, however, depression is not a *cause* of behavior in the sense of necessitating it (in the way that, for example, kicking a ball causes it to move). It would be more accurate for the client to say, "I was depressed *and* I didn't go to the party." The therapist would therefore attempt to get the client to (1) accept the feeling of depression and (2) commit to engaging in desirable social activities regardless of the feeling. After all, many people engage competently in activities that elicit negative emotions (e.g., famous actors who experience stage fright).

ACT is based on research in relational frame theory (e.g., Hayes, Barnes-Holmes, & Roche, 2001), which has been touched on earlier in this book (chapters 8, 10, and 13). Research in this area has tended to show that humans differ in a very striking way from other animals: emotional responses condition readily to arbitrary stimuli, and their effects transfer readily to other arbitrary stimuli in a bi-directional manner. There are numerous experiments documenting this effect, but advertising provides a convenient example. If I see on TV an attractive movie star drinking from a bottle of a particular soft drink, that soft drink will now take on positive emotional effects for me. This is not a rational process; it occurs in all humans, which is why advertisers pay for such images. Now suppose that in a news program I see a politician, about whom I have no particular feeling one way or the other, drinking that same soft drink. Some of the positive feelings previously conditioned to the soft drink will now transfer to the politician. Note that this is not a rational or conscious process; research shows that probably none of us are exempt from it. The bi-directionality of the effect is illustrated by the fact that if the feelings toward the politician were negative, some of this negativity would transfer via the soft drink back to the movie star. Because verbal stimuli (such as words) are constantly being paired with other verbal stimuli and with positive and negative events, vast networks of associations in which positive and negative emotions may be triggered by a large variety of verbal stimuli and events are built up in all of us.

Positive and negative effects travel through these networks with lightning speed; and the effects are not always what one might expect. The advertising example may not work on me if the commercial offends me in some way, thus transferring a negative rather than a positive emotion to the soft drink. Things that one might expect to be positive can readily take on a negative quality. For example, you might feel depressed upon seeing a beautiful sunset because of an unpleasant breakup with a former lover who was paired with similar beautiful experiences. Even the word *happy*, for example, can tend to elicit sad feelings because it has been paired with the word *sad*, which has been paired with unhappy events.

As already mentioned, one rationale for the acceptance part of ACT is that the client's thoughts and emotional reactions to them are not the problem, nor the causes of the problem, except insofar as the client reacts to them as though they were the problem or causes of it. In addition, because of the powerful associations implied by relational frame theory, any attempts to control the client's internal thoughts and emotional reactions directly will likely only make them worse, because it will result in a paradox similar to that of telling someone not to think of a white tiger. By its very nature, the instruction not to think of a white tiger (or any other specific thing) is impossible to obey. Similarly, a client told by his or her therapist not to be anxious will become anxious about the possibility of becoming anxious; a client who is told not to worry will worry about worrying; a client who is told to stop thinking obsessive thoughts will obsess about his or her obsessive thoughts; and so on. Likewise, rational argument is not considered effective in trying to get the client to accept his or her problematic thoughts and emotions. In fact, the therapist takes great care not to overly explain the rationale of the therapy or argue about it with the client. Instead, the therapist uses various exercises and metaphors that are unlikely to have strong emotional reactions conditioned to them.

An example of a metaphor that an ACT therapist might use is that the client is a bus driver with a number of unruly, obnoxious passengers who are demanding that the destination be changed. Another metaphor involves a disgusting bum who shows up at a party hosted by the client to which "everyone is invited!" The obnoxious passengers in the first metaphor and the disgusting bum in the second represent, of course, the client's undesirable thoughts and emotional reactions, which the metaphors encourage the client to accept. The bus driver cannot throw the passengers off the bus, but nevertheless must continue on his or her designated route; the host has invited everyone, and it would be rude and disruptive to the party to try to force the bum to leave.

An example of an exercise used in ACT is to have the client, in a perfectly relaxed state, imagine sitting by a river with leaves from a tree falling into the river and being carried downstream. On each leaf the client is to put whatever thought or image occurs to him or her at that particular instant. The object of the exercise is to teach the client to observe his or her own thought processes without trying to change them. As mentioned in chapter 13, it does this by transforming the frame "I have [a specific thought or emotion] here and now" to "I had [a specific thought or emotion] there and then" (Barnes-Holmes, Hayes, & Gregg, 2001, pp. 241–249). There are some similarities of this exercise with Buddhist meditation, although Buddhism had no explicit influence on the development of ACT (Hayes, 2002). In that it induces the client to observe his or her thoughts in a detached manner, the exercise is also consistent with mindfulness-based cognitive therapy, as described in the previous section.

Once the client has learned to accept his or her undesirable cognitions and emotions, and has committed to changing his or her overt behavior, other behavioral techniques—such as role playing and graduated exposure—may be used to help the client carry through with the overt behavior change. Perhaps it is not too much of an oversimplification of ACT to sum it up with the well-known prayer, "Lord grant me the patience to accept the things I cannot change, the strength to change the things I can, and the wisdom to know the difference!"

Behavioral Approach Compared and Contrasted with Humanistic Approach

Although behavioral psychology is often considered to be the antithesis of humanistic psychology, there are some interesting similarities as well as differences between the behavioral and humanistic approaches. The behavioral approach is similar to the humanistic approach in several ways with respect to humanistic psychologists' concept of person-centeredness. First, the behavioral approach does not emphasize rigid conformity to the norms of society. Skinner pointed out that variety in behavior contributes to the survival of a culture, and that variety rather than conformity should therefore be promoted within the culture. As to how much variety should be present in a culture, Skinner advocated as much as possible so long as obviously harmful forms of behavior are excluded. Second, behavioral psychologists, like humanistic psychologists, do not take an authoritarian approach to their clients. Instead, they see themselves in a consulting or collaborative role with their clients. Before therapy begins, for example, the behavior therapist helps the client specify his or her goals for therapy in behavioral terms—that is, in terms of exactly what behavior change the client would like to have occur as a result of the therapy. The goals therefore come from the client; they are not imposed on the client by the therapist. The therapist simply helps the client clarify his or her goals, and then helps the client develop and carry out a program for achieving those goals.

Despite such similarities between the humanistic and behavioral approaches to therapy, there are two very important differences that should be pointed out. First, unlike most humanistic psychologists, behaviorists do not regard the client's values or goals as being generated from within the client. Rather, they are conditioned reinforcers that have been established by the client's social environment. As long as the client's values or goals are not obviously harmful, however, the behaviorist accepts them just as the humanistic psychologist does. Second, the behavior change that occurs under behavior therapy might be characterized as *growth* or *self-actualization*—certainly it involves developing the client's potential in some way—but behaviorists typically find these terms to be too vague to suit their purpose. Instead, they simply try to specify as precisely as possible the actual behavior changes to be produced by their procedures.

Humanistic psychologists stress the importance of developing the client's self-determination. To the extent that *self-determination* means *self-control*, behaviorists are in full agreement with this emphasis. Behavior modifiers have developed effective methods for teaching clients to achieve control over their own behavior. Behaviorists, however, believe that the ultimate control lies in the client's environment. A significant part of that environment is the therapist, and hence the therapist has a significant amount of control over the client's behavior. Nevertheless, as already pointed out, control is not absent in humanistic psychotherapy according to behaviorists; it is merely hidden. Skinner and other behaviorists have frequently argued that such hidden control is dangerous because of the difficulty of applying countercontrol to it. In contrast, the goals and procedures in a behavior modification or behavior therapy program are clearly spelled out to the client so that the client is clearly aware of exactly how his or her behavior is being controlled, and therefore can presumably alter or terminate that control at any time.

RELATIVE THERAPEUTIC EFFECTIVENESS OF THE FOUR APPROACHES

From a strictly practical point of view it is natural to inquire which of the four systems works the best in psychotherapy. The competition among the four approaches to generate the most effective psychotherapy has been compared to a strange race organized by a dodo bird in Lewis Carroll's *Alice's Adventures in Wonderland*:

> First [the Dodo] marked out a race-course, in a sort of circle, ("the exact shape doesn't matter," it said), and then all the party were placed along the course, here and there. There was no "One, two, three, and away," but they began running when they liked, and left off when they liked, so that it was not easy to know when the race was over. However, when they had been running half an hour or so, . . . , the Dodo suddenly called out "The race is over!" and they all crowded round it, panting, and asking "But who has won?"
>
> This question the Dodo could not answer without a great deal of thought, and it stood for a long time with one finger pressed upon its

forehead (the position in which you usually see Shakespeare, in the pictures of him), while the rest waited in silence. At last the Dodo said,
"*Everybody* has won, and all must have prizes." (Carroll, 1898, pp. 30–31)

In 1936, behavioral, cognitive, and humanistic psychotherapies had
not yet emerged, and there were few competitors to psychoanalysis. But
there were some. Saul Rosenzweig, a psychiatrist at Worcester State Hospital in Massachusetts, speculated that the common factors inherent in
these different psychotherapeutic approaches would outweigh their differences and that they would all be found to be beneficial, but none more
so than any other. In other words, all would win. On the analogy of the
race in Lewis Carroll's story, Rosewzweig (1936) called his insight the
Dodo-bird effect.

Beginning in the 1950s, a number of studies began to challenge the effectiveness of psychoanalysis in comparison with other procedures. There is
now a large amount of data indicating that people with psychological problems are helped as much by seeing untrained helpers, in what is called
placebo therapy (analogous to the nonmedicinal sugar pills used in drug
studies), than by trained psychoanalysts (Berman & Norton, 1985; Durlak,
1979; Eysenck, 1952; Hattie, Sharpley, & Rogers, 1984; Rachman, 1971).

Then Luborsky, Singer, and Luborsky (1975) compared the proportions
of patients who improved under different types of therapy as reported
in the literature. Echoing Rosenzweig, Luborsky et al. concluded that
while all the treatments studied tend to be effective, there is little difference between them in overall effectiveness. Like Rosenzweig, they suggested that common factors outweigh the differences between the therapies. Over the decades, in ever increasing numbers, studies have tended
to find that while psychotherapy in general is highly effective when compared to no treatment at all, there is little or no difference between the
therapies in terms of their overall effectiveness (e.g., Lambert & Bergin,
1994; Luborsky et al., 1999; Luborsky et al., 2002; Smith & Glass, 1977;
Wampold, 2001).

The competition about which treatments produce the demonstrably
most effective psychotherapy resembles Lewis Carroll's race not only in
outcome, but also in the manner in which it is conducted. In studies that
compare the approaches it is often unclear exactly what is being compared. Typically, the comparison is done using a technique known as
meta-analysis, in which the results of a number of published studies are
combined statistically. In typical comparisons many different types of disorders are lumped together—for example, phobias, depression, obsessive-compulsive disorder, unresolved bereavement, eating disorders, and
marital distress. Sometimes data from different types of treatments are
also combined in ways that are not necessarily the most appropriate. For
example, in one study, cognitive therapies were lumped with humanis-

tic and psychodynamic therapies on the basis that all are verbal (or *talk*) therapies (Smith, Glass, & Miller, 1980), whereas it would seem to make more sense from a theoretical perspective to combine data from cognitive therapies with data from behavioral and cognitive-behavioral therapies. As another example, pharmacotherapy has been combined with psychodynamic therapy, thus confounding the effects of the latter when compared with other psychotherapies (Luborsky et al., 1999). In another study, treatments were considered different—namely, two types of cognitive behavioral therapy—that were actually quite similar (Wampold et al., 1997), so that it is not particularly surprising that differences in the results did not reach statistical significance.

It seems to be true that when you combine data from different psychotherapies as used with a number of different problems, little difference is found between the treatments. Imagine an experiment in which the effects of penicillin, aspirin, a laxative, and blood pressure medication are compared on a wide variety of physical complaints, without distinguishing between those complaints in the data analysis. Even though each of these drugs is effective for certain specific conditions (e.g., aspirin generally helps to relieve headaches but does nothing for constipation, whereas the reverse is the case for laxatives), no one would be surprised if none of these drugs showed superiority over the others overall. This analogy suggests that what is needed is not a broad comparison of general therapeutic approaches used on an undifferentiated collection of problems, but rather specific tests and comparisons of well-defined procedures on well-defined problems. Of course, theoretical considerations should help guide the different treatments that are tested, and the results should be used to inform further theoretical development.

The behavioral and cognitive-behavioral approaches have led the way with the above strategy because from their beginnings they have been oriented toward technique and outcome. Thus, these approaches have developed techniques that have been demonstrated to be effective, relative to no treatment, for specific problems—for example, obsessive-compulsive disorder, phobias, panic attack, depression—and have also done well in comparison with other psychotherapeutic procedures on these specific problems (see Chambless & Ollendick, 2001; Deacon & Abramowitz, 2004; Fedoroff & Taylor, 2001; Martin & Pear, 2007, pp. 373–387). In addition, the behavioral and cognitive-behavioral approaches have taken on challenging problems that other approaches have been reluctant or unable to treat, such as schizophrenia (Dickerson, 2000) and severe childhood problems such as autism and developmental disabilities—as mentioned earlier in this chapter. Some of the challenging problems behavioral and cognitive-behavioral therapists have taken on may be inherently more difficult to treat than problems that other approaches take on, which, if included in a general overall comparison of procedures, could make behavioral and cognitive-behavioral procedures appear to be less effective than they actually are.

Third-party payers, such as insurance companies, HMOs, governments, and employers who have to pay for psychological treatments, have emphasized the importance of using only empirically supported treatments (ESTs) in psychotherapy. This emphasis is echoed by professional organizations, such as the American Psychological Association (Task Force on Promotion and Dissemination of Psychological Procedures, 1995; Task Force on Psychological Intervention Guidelines, 1995). In response to this emphasis on ESTs, proponents of various approaches may accelerate their efforts to produce and test specific procedures on specific problems, and to compare those procedures with procedures that proponents of other approaches designed to treat the same type of problem. Some have cautioned against a potential oversimplification inherent in this approach. For example, Westen and Bradley (2005) argued that while there is much to be said for ESTs, care should be taken to avoid examining only therapies that can be tested relatively easily on specific problems in a short time period with designs using randomized controlled trials, while ignoring treatments that do not fit neatly into this methodology but that may be better for dealing with more complex cases in natural settings.

SUMMARY

Humanistic psychology adopts a person-centered approach to therapy that tries not to control the client. An important technique (although many humanistic psychologists do not like the term *technique*) of humanistic psychology is reflection of feeling. Reflection appears to accomplish at least two things: (1) it communicates the interest and concern of the therapist for the client; (2) it enables the client to recognize feelings in himself or herself that the client might otherwise not recognize or acknowledge. Humanistic psychologists put a strong emphasis on the self-determination of the client. A criticism of this nondirective approach is that if the procedures used by humanistic psychologists produce a change in the client's behavior, then humanistic psychologists are controlling behavior. Conversely, if humanistic psychologists do not control behavior, their procedures are ineffective and clients are wasting their time and money subjecting themselves to those procedures.

The psychoanalytic approach has undergone considerable change since Freud's death in 1939. Psychodynamic therapists who broke with Freud and neo-Freudians focused on the interaction between the therapist and the client. Traditionally, psychoanalysts frowned on drawing attention to their personal feelings toward their clients. More emphasis has now been placed on the transference as a way of developing the client's social behavior. The concept of enactment suggests that the therapist can work with the client on his or her current social relations within a consistent psychodynamic framework.

There are several streams leading into the cognitive approach to therapy. One stream comes from a merger of behavioral approaches with cognitive approaches to therapy. In general, cognitive therapists attempt to change their clients' maladaptive thinking. For example, if a client is pathologically depressed the therapist will look for some pattern of thinking that may be causing the depression. Cognitive therapists treat clients by first helping them to recognize their maladaptive thoughts and beliefs, and then helping them to replace maladaptive thoughts and beliefs with more productive ways of thinking. This process, called cognitive restructuring, is perhaps analogous to debugging a computer program. There are two broad types of cognitive psychotherapies, which are generally called cognitive therapy and cognitive-behavioral therapy (also known as cognitive behavior modification). Cognitive and cognitive-behavioristic therapists found the humanistic approach too nondirective (or not focused enough on specific techniques), while the behavioristic approach seemed to ignore cognitive variables that they regarded as important. Three major developers of cognitive and cognitive-behavioral therapies are Albert Ellis, Aaron Beck, and Donald Meichenbaum.

Methodological behaviorism fits in very well with cognitive-behavioral therapy. In cognitive-behavioral therapy, operating on the mind is seen as a way of changing behavior. Radical behaviorists maintain that cognitions (i.e., private behavior) may sometimes cause public behavior (since behavior can produce stimuli that elicit or evoke other behavior); but private behavior need not cause public behavior. Because, unlike the other major approaches, the behavioral approach does not depend on verbal behavior—either private or public—it has been effective in working with individuals whose verbal behavior is limited or nonexistent. Language is used effectively in behavior therapy with individuals who have verbal behavior. Nevertheless, individuals with verbal behavior are treated using behavioral principles rather than attempting to change their cognitions through rational argument. Behavior therapists use a number of techniques that involve working directly with the behavior of interest. Specific behavioral techniques include systematic desensitization and acceptance-and-commitment therapy. The behavioral approach is similar to the humanistic approach in taking a non-authoritarian stance and attempting to develop self-control (self-determination)—although behaviorists believe that ultimate control always resides in the environment.

In what is known as the Dodo-bird effect, studies have tended to find little or no differences in the effectiveness of therapies derived from the four systems. However, when comparisons are made between specific treatments on specific problems, techniques derived from behavioral and cognitive-behavioral psychotherapies tend to perform better than techniques derived from other theoretical positions. This may change as other approaches begin to develop specific techniques to treat specific problems.

Discussion Questions

1. Discuss the pros and cons of the nondirective approach to therapy as espoused by humanistic psychologists.

2. Discuss whether it is possible, or desirable, for client and therapist to have a completely equal relationship as advocated by Rogers.

3. Describe how the psychodynamic approach to therapy has become similar to the humanistic approach, by (a) stressing some psychodynamic factors and (b) down-playing others.

4. Cognitive therapy is more indirectly than directly related to cognitive psychology. Discuss the somewhat complex history of cognitive therapy.

5. Discuss the similarities between cognitive and behavioral therapy that resulted in a merger between the two types of therapy.

6. Discuss the relationship between cognitive therapy and constructivism, and whether the other types of psychotherapy are also compatible with constructivism.

7. Discuss the similarities and differences between constructivism in cognitive therapy as described by Ellis and pragmatism as formulated by William James (as discussed in chapters 4 and 10).

8. Discuss the similarity between cognitive therapy and Buddhism.

9. Acceptance and commitment therapy does not fit what people usually think of as behavioral therapy. Discuss what makes it a behavior therapy as opposed to, say, a humanistic therapy (other than the fact that behaviorists developed it).

10. By maintaining that cognitions are simply private behavior, have radical behaviorists contributed anything more than a mere semantic suggestion to the issue of studying and treating cognitions? That is, to resolve the differences between cognitivists and radical behaviorists, would it be sufficient for the two sides to simply agree to use the words *private behavior* and *cognition* interchangeably? Discuss.

CHAPTER 15

Scientific Research

E ver since the founding of psychology as an experimental science in the latter part of the nineteenth century, the question of exactly how scientific research in psychology should be done has been in contention. One question, for example, is whether psychology should use the same methods that are used by other sciences, such as physics, chemistry, and biology. And for those psychologists who believe that it should, the question then arises: What exactly are the methods used in other sciences and how, exactly, should we apply them in psychology?

In essence, we are talking here about research designs. There are two major types or categories of research designs in psychology: quantitative and qualitative. The former, which are the ones that enjoy more standard use in psychology, involve three things: (1) specification of a dependent variable; (2) specification of an independent variable; and (3) manipulation of the independent variable to determine how the dependent variable is functionally related to it. Generally, this means that we have to measure—that is, quantify or assign numbers to—the dependent variable. The independent variable is often quantitative as well, but may also be categorical instead (e.g., experimental condition versus control condition, or treatment condition versus no-treatment condition). Typically, some form of inferential statistics with appropriate controls is employed to ensure the reliability of the results.

This type of design applies to both causal and correlation studies. For example, in a study in which the dependent variable is a score on an intelligence test and the independent variable is race, the data might indicate that members of one race score lower than do members of another race. It cannot be concluded from these data, however, that race (or the genetic factors that determine race) bears a causal relationship to intelligence (as measured by a particular test). All that can be concluded is that there appears to be a correlation between race and intelligence. If such a correlation exists, however, then it is assumed that a causal relationship exists and can be found. For example, it might be that members of one race do not have the same educational opportunities that members of the other race have, and that education level has a causal effect on intelligence-test score. Whether this is the case could be determined in a subsequent study in which education level is varied across members of both races. There are various methods for determining causal factors as well as correlation. For example, if rats in an impoverished environment perform significantly worse (according to number of trials to learn or some other measure) on a maze-learning test than rats raised in an enriched environment, and if all other factors except richness of the environment have been held constant, we might conclude that environment can have an effect on intelligence (as measured by a maze-learning task). Sometimes an experiment cannot ethically be performed on humans, of course, but in combination with human correlational data, animal study can provide important corroborating evidence.

Research designs in the less standard category—qualitative research designs—are more descriptive and are less (if at all) concerned with prediction and control than quantitative designs are. Basically, these designs consist of highly systematic methods of describing particular psychological phenomena, especially subjective phenomena.

HUMANISTIC APPROACH

In addition to being one of the founders of humanistic psychology, Carl Rogers was the initiator of quantitative research in psychotherapy. Indeed, in 1954 Rogers co-edited a book quantitatively documenting positive personality changes resulting from client-centered psychotherapy (Rogers & Dymond, 1954). Because of his research studies, Rogers received a Distinguished Scientific Contribution Award from the American Psychological Association in 1956 (Cain, 2002). Rogers clearly believed that outcome research—research quantitatively demonstrating the effects of therapy—would support his client-centered approach. As he put it, "The facts are friendly" (Rogers, 1961, p. 25).

Nevertheless, some humanistic psychologists have found reliance on standard research designs to be problematic (e.g., Giorgi, 2005). The quantitative approach to research design causes problems for humanistic psychology particularly with regard to the themes of holism, self-determination, and person-centeredness. Standard experimental designs cause problems for holism because each independent variable represents only a part of the totality of influences affecting a person and each dependent variable represents only a part of the individual's totality of actions (and whatever perceptions, motivations, attitudes, etc. may be involved) with regard to those influences.

Standard experimental designs cause problems for self-determination because to whatever extent a dependent variable is shown to be functionally related to an independent variable, it logically follows that the dependent variable is controlled or determined to at least that extent. Thus, if a study is successful in demonstrating a functional relationship between an independent and a dependent variable, some degree of self-determination is removed. Moreover, if a study fails to demonstrate a functional relationship between an independent and a dependent variable, logically all one can say is that possible determining or controlling factors for that dependent variable have not been identified in the study—one cannot logically say that self-determination has been demonstrated. Thus, standard experimental designs are a "no-win situation" for anyone desiring to make a case for self-determination.

Giorgi (2005) put the humanistic psychology case against designs in which the researchers exercise their personal freedom to attempt to make predictions about their experimental participants as follows:

> If we genuinely posit freedom for humans, can prediction be used in the same way (as in the natural sciences such as physics)? Are we not then tempted to try to control and manipulate conditions unduly, so that our predictions become more sound? Are we not then using certain human capacities that we deny to our participants? As researchers, we are free to vary, but our participants' expressiveness is constrained. But in a genuine nonreductionistic science, no interpretive characteristic can be denied our participants that we are not willing to deny ourselves. (Giorgi, 2005, p. 213)

Standard experimental designs cause problems for person-centeredness because they often require that the person being studied (the participant or subject) follow instructions set down according to a rigorously specified procedure, with little or no ability to alter the course of the experiment. This is an unequal relationship in which the experimenter has more power than does the participant. Moreover, typically the experimenter is more interested in the data generated by the participant than in the participant as a person. (It should be noted that although it follows from this that there is a moral downside to experimental research, according to humanistic psychology, it does not follow that there is any actual scientific challenge in testing humanistic psychology claims.)

Standard experimental designs also cause problems for the other themes of humanistic psychology—phenomenology, actualizing tendency, authenticity, and self-transcendence—with regard to operational definitions, which are required by standard designs in order for specification of independent and dependent variables. For example, how does one operationally define being *aware* or *conscious* of a particular object, event, or process? One solution is to use a person's verbal report, but there may be difficulty in obtaining general agreement on what kind of verbal report is necessary to indicate awareness or consciousness of the object, event, or process in question. There are even greater difficulties involved in obtaining agreement concerning operational definitions of self-actualization, authentic or true self, and self-transcendence.

In addition, many humanistic psychologists see standard experimental designs as dehumanizing. Although the American Psychological Association has changed the term for the individuals studied in experimental research from *subjects* to *participants,* and now ethically requires experimenters to ensure that their participants are uncoerced volunteers and to inform them fully of the purpose and results of the research in a timely fashion after its completion, some humanistic psychologists see this as simply an expedient political move. Standard research designs have not changed their general manner of treating the individuals under investigation. They are still, in the eyes of many humanistic psychologists, treated as objects rather than as truly equal participants in the research enterprise.

No science can advance without research, because that is the only way in which assumptions and theories can be tested and that new knowledge can be added to the field. To hold that research is not necessary is tantamount to claiming that we already know everything that we need to know or that we can know about a particular topic, and that everything else about that topic should or must remain mysterious. To take this position is to take more of a religious stance than a scientific one. Since most humanistic psychologists—at least most academic humanistic psychologists—believe that humanistic psychology is or should be scientific, there have been a number of exhortations from humanistic psychologists for others within their field to become more involved in research. For example, Norcross (1987) called for more research on the effects of existential psychotherapy. He cited the difficulties involved in operational definitions and specification of variables—"Such outcome studies would necessitate hard and creative work, including the development of sensitive measures that tap more than symptom relief, such as the primacy of the subjective, an enlarged sense of identity, change in life experiences, and in-therapy outcomes" (Norcross, 1987, p. 63)—but he expressed the belief that these difficulties are not insurmountable. However, he did not discuss the other difficulties mentioned above, such as the one involving self-determination; i.e., if existential therapy can be shown to lead to a particular type of change in a person, then it follows logically that existential therapy has exerted control over that individual.

Humanistic Research Designs

Humanistic psychologists have introduced or adopted several kinds of qualitative research designs that they find more suitable than standard quantitative research designs (see, for example, Eckartsberg, 1986; Tesch, 1990). A major difference between these designs and the standard designs is that the humanistic research designs are not aimed at predicting or controlling behavior; instead, they are directed toward enhancing *understanding* in the everyday sense of understanding the meaning behind a person's words or actions. For example, if we hear someone exclaim, "I am famished!" or if we see someone gobbling down a large quantity of food, we understand that person's hunger on the basis of our own experience of hunger, even if we do not know how that person came to be so hungry and cannot predict when he or she will again be extremely hungry. We might surmise, of course, that the person is extremely hungry as a result of having gone a long time without food, but this is not necessary to our understanding of the person's hunger. In fact, it may not even be correct, since the person may have a disorder that causes extreme hunger even when one has just had a meal that would be fully satisfying to a physically healthy person. It should be pointed out that the example of hunger is used here to provide a simplified illustration of what humanistic psychologists mean by *understanding*. Hunger is such an obvious biological urge that it is typically of less interest to humanistic psychologists than the more socially relevant feelings such as anxiety, fear, anger, and love.

Humanistic psychologists advocate flexibility in research, as opposed to the use of rigid experimental designs. However, it is possible to identify six general research designs that they tend to favor: the *experiential*, *hermeneutical*, *grounded theory*, *perceptual psychological*, *phenomenological*, and *heuristic methods*. Each of these will be considered in turn. Before doing this, it should be pointed out that because each of these methods must be considered as a whole, and does not consist of specific rules to be followed, it is not possible to describe these methods adequately in a few words. Therefore, this will not be attempted. What will be attempted is simply to provide the reader with the flavor of these methods as opposed to the manner in which they are actually carried out.

Experiential Method

The purpose of the experiential method is to discover the common factors in specific emotions in the belief that these represent the *structure* or *essence* of the experience of that emotion. In order to do this, one or more investigators imagine themselves to be in situations that are likely to lead to the emotion being studied. After imagining each situation, each investigator writes a set of statements descriptive of the situation and the emotion. After doing this for a number of situations, the investigator compares the lists for all situations and notes what factors in the statements seem to be common across situations. For the emotion of anxiety, for example, one factor common to all situations might be: "I feel uncertain about the outcome of a situation." To validate the list consensually, a group of investigators get together and discuss their lists of common factors until they arrive at a consensus regarding the common factors (Barrell, Medeiros, Barrell & Price, 1985). These common factors are then said to constitute the structure of the experience, or to indicate what it is like to be *in* the experience. Advocates of this method maintain that, in addition to providing useful information for further study and theorizing, it has practical value in helping people to understand how they *create* certain emotions within themselves. Through this understanding, people can promote in themselves those emotions they consider desirable and avoid those they do not wish to experience.

Hermeneutical Method

The hermeneutical method, or hermeneutics, is an ancient scholarly tool. Possibly named after Hermes, the Greek god who not only transmitted messages but who also could unlock their meaning, the method was originally used to find hidden or underlying meanings (or *messages*) in religious texts. Essentially the method involves studying the words in the text and their relation to other words; e.g., one might use hermeneutics to investigate why the expression *great fish* (as opposed to, for example, *large sea animal*) is used to describe the creature that swallowed Jonah in the Biblical account of that event. To do this, one would investigate all possible meanings and connotations of the words *great* and *fish* as those words are used elsewhere in the Bible and in other texts written in Biblical times (of course, this would be done with respect to the language of the original text, i.e., ancient Hebrew in the case of the Bible).

In the nineteenth century, hermeneutics was extended to all forms of historical, literary, and artistic works. By the end of that century it was also being applied to the human sciences as well (Palmer, 1969). Any student who has been assigned to write a paper exploring the meanings in a poem or novel, for example, has engaged in hermeneutics.

A psychologist applying hermeneutics to an experience such as *anxiety* might begin by consulting various texts to determine how the word *anxiety* is related to other words and expressions in those texts (Barrell, Aanstoos, Richards & Arons, 1987). As the psychologist proceeds in this manner, one word or expression leads to other words and expressions in a manner similar to that of following a long, twisted thread. Eventually the process leads back to the original word in what is called the *hermeneutic circle*. The purpose is to enhance understanding rather than to arrive at particular conclusions: "The process does not attempt to end somewhere or conclude; it simply continues to broaden and deepen one's understanding of the topic being explored" (Barrell et al., 1987).

Packer (1985) described the use of hermeneutics to study meanings in speech communications. He observed individuals playing a game called Prisoner's dilemma, which critically depends on teamwork, negotiations, and trust. One aspect of the game Packer found interesting was the manner in which opposing team members communicated in resolving the conflicts produced by the game. His observations were hermeneutic in that they focused on the shifts in interpretations that occurred as the participants struggled to get their meanings across to opposing players. Packer stated: "I ended up unable to predict the precise form future conflicts might take (the conflicts differed in ways I did not see causes for) and unable to 'model' such conflicts with a computer program. I had, however, a greatly increased and differentiated sensitivity to the concerns at work in such conflicts" (Packer, 1985, p. 1091).

Hermeneutics has been used with statements individuals make in structured interviews. A psychologist might, for example, interview a number of individuals on some topic. Then he or she would abstract certain themes from the interviews, similar to the way in which a literary reviewer might extract themes from a novel. For example, Shantall (1999) interviewed seven holocaust survivors. Her research question was whether life can "still be experienced as meaningful in the face of tragedy, grief, and suffering, or is such suffering only a soul-destroying experience from which nothing positive can emerge" (p. 97). Over a period of 2 years, Shantall conducted interviews which included questions to the survivors such as, What happened to them during the holocaust? How did they feel and cope at the time? How did they come to terms with what happened to them? From these interviews, a number of themes emerged. The main theme was that individuals are able to find great meaning in humiliation and suffering, if they make morally correct choices in the face of these affronts. These results were similar to the conclusion reached by the famed existential psychologist Victor Frankl (1968) in his analysis of experiences he suffered as an inmate of Auschwitz.

As another example of the use of hermeneutics with interview data, Widera-Wysoczañska (1999) investigated the experience of death awareness in 12 healthy women who had not yet experienced the death of anyone close to them. The women were asked questions about when they first become aware of the possibility of their own death or that of someone close to them. Several different ways of reacting to the death awareness experience were found, depending on the type of support obtained in childhood. If parents were very supportive the effects could be positive (the individual may develop greater independence and personal freedom), but unsupportive parents could lead to negative effects (unconscious fear of death, feeling of powerlessness with regard to death, loss of free expression of feelings).

Grounded Theory Design

Grounded theory design, like some forms of hermeneutics, also uses interviews to obtain data. However, in grounded theory design the interviews are less structured; and rather than looking for *themes* and *units of meaning*, one sorts the material obtained into a large number of exhaustive categories (see Glaser, 1992). Working from the ground up (as the name of the approach implies), these categories are organized into clusters, which are then grouped into areas of content. For example, Levitt (1999) used grounded theory in studying the development of wisdom as experienced by Tibetan monks. As a result of interviewing 13 monks, she extracted 95 categories from which she obtained a number of clusters that grouped themselves into the following areas of content: definition, facilitative conditions, the teaching process, methods, and personal experiences. Under these areas of content were the clusters; for example, the clusters under the teaching process were teachings, the teaching relationship, and individuality of the teaching process. Through the exposition of what the monks had to say on each of these topics, an understanding of the development of wisdom, as they experienced it, emerges.

Perceptual Psychological Method

In the perceptual psychological method, it is assumed that behavior is caused by perceptions and meanings, organized as a *field of personal meanings*, within the individual. This field of personal meanings consists of the perception of self, including one's purposes, goals, attitudes, beliefs, values, and general orientation, and of one's perceptions of other people and things. In what is called *reading behavior backwards* (Combs, Richards, & Richards, 1976, p. 377), the method uses raters to assess a person's field of meanings on various dimensions (e.g., perception of self as adequate or inadequate) from written self-descriptions of that person's behavior. Because the raters perform their assessment largely by putting themselves in the place of the person whose personal field of meanings is being assessed, they are typically selected on the basis of possessing a high degree of empathy. In addition, prior to conducting the research, they are trained on practice samples of behavior to ensure a high degree of interrater reliability. Typically, reliability during the study is above .80—the minimum level considered acceptable. Advocates of the method maintain that in addition to the understanding it can provide to the researcher seeking to understand the personal field of meanings, it can be useful in helping to identify people in need of counseling (Barrell et al., 1987).

Phenomenological Method

As discussed in chapter 4, Edmund Husserl developed the phenomenological method in an attempt to objectify the study of conscious experience to the greatest extent possible (Husserl, 1970). The researcher using the phenomenological method attempts to go directly to the experience itself, unimpeded by any prior conceptions of the experience. Constructs—that is, the categories into which we tend to place things, or the labels we tend to give them—are to be avoided as much as possible, as it is assumed that they distort the experience and keep us from understanding it as it really is. Suppose, for example, that the research topic is anxiety (e.g., Fischer, 1982). The first thing the researcher does is to note that anxiety is a concept that is far removed from the actual experience from which it is abstracted. One does not have anxiety as a thing, in the sense that one might possess an object; one *is* anxious. The experience of anxiety is more accurately referred to as *being anxious* because this is closer to what the experience is at the preconceptual level, prior to its being reified as *anxiety*.

After the phenomenon has been identified at the preconceptual level as being anxious rather than anxiety, the next step in the phenomenological method is to ask someone to describe in writing or into a tape recorder situations in which he or she was anxious and, as accurately as possible, the experience of being anxious. The researcher first studies the written or tape-recorded description, and then interviews the participant to obtain clarification and amplification of the description of the experience. The researcher then applies the following three techniques to the description: *bracketing*, *intuiting*, and *describing*. In bracketing the researcher reads through the description in a totally empathetic manner, as free as possible of all prior assumptions, without judging or questioning it or applying any constructs to it. In intuiting the researcher attempts to determine, through empathy or imagination, the essential constituents of the experience. For example, if the participant reports being anxious when his or her work is being inspected by a supervisor, the researcher might try to intuit whether inspection by someone in a position of authority is essential to the experience of being anxious when the participant's work is being inspected. A list of these essential aspects of the experience, similar to the list obtained through the experiential method, is thus obtained through the process of intuiting. The items on the list are called the *essential psychological meanings* of the experience. In the third technique, describing, these essential psychological meanings are related to each other to form a single *psychological structure*, which is tested (usually through imagination by the researcher) for its generality across situations. The resulting psychological structure has been summarized as follows:

> The general structure is the researcher's attempt to articulate descriptively the essential coherence of psychological meaning as it is lived. The test of a structure's validity is the extent to which it explicates the sense of the subject's original description without imposing any sense that cannot be grounded in that original description. Phenomenological research is an inexhaustible task of explication: of making explicit that which was lived implicitly, of reflecting upon the prereflective. (Barrell et al., 1987, pp. 451–452)

Heuristic Method

The word *heuristic* comes from the Greek word for *invent, discover*, or *find*. It has the same root as *Eureka*! Heuristics usually refers to the use of *rules of thumb* or informal, intuitive rules in solving problems. Humanistic psychologists use it to refer to a particular method or set of methods for seeking out "meaning and essence in significant human experience" (Douglass & Moustakas, 1985, p. 40). The object of the heuristic approach, according to Douglass and Moustakas, "is not to prove or disprove the influence of one thing or another, but rather to discover the nature of the problem or phenomenon itself and to explicate it as it exists in human experience" (p. 42). Heuristics differs from phenomenology in that it emphasizes the relation of the person to the phenomenon, whereas phenomenology involves detachment from the phenomenon. "Phenomenology ends with the essence of experience; heuristics retains the essence of the person in the experience" (Douglass & Moustakas, 1985, p. 43).

Douglass and Moustakas list three steps in heuristic inquiry: *immersion, acquisition*, and *realization.*

In immersion the person becomes so totally involved or absorbed in a problem that it seems to contain the whole world. Acquisition is considered to be a kind of data collection, although not in the sense of standard scientific procedures. It involves focusing on and differentiating different aspects of the phenomenon, and following a path (much like a hermeneutic circle) that uncovers more and more interrelated meanings. In realization the essences and meanings uncovered during acquisition are assembled into a unified whole. The resulting synthesis is "a new reality, a new monolithic significance that embodies the essence of the heuristic truth" (Douglass & Moustakas, 1985, p. 43). Moustakas (1961, 1975) used the method to produce several treatises on loneliness.

The research methods recommended by humanistic psychologists are difficult to describe and difficult to learn. This should not be surprising. New scientific methods are always difficult to learn if for no other reason than that they require us to think in ways that are unfamiliar to us. It should not be assumed, however, that these methods must be scientific just because they are difficult to learn. Painting, sculpting, composing music, and writing stories and poems are also difficult to learn—at least, they are difficult to learn to do well—but we do not call these creative activities science.

Humanistic Psychology and Subjectivity in Science

The importance of subjectivity in science is a theme that runs strongly throughout the arguments humanistic psychologists give for the research methods they advocate. It might seem strange to think of subjectivity as an important aspect of science, since it is the objectivity of science that is usually stressed by scientists and philosophers of science. Nevertheless, advocates of humanistic research methods quote scientists and philosophers of science liberally to support their arguments. For example, Douglass and Moustakas (1985) use the following quotation from Bridgman to punctuate their point that the heuristic investigator must look to his or her own intuition for guidance as opposed to following rigidly formulated rules of discovery:

> The process that I want to call scientific is a process that involves the continual apprehension of meaning, the constant appraisal of significance, accompanied by a running act of checking to be sure that I am doing what I want to do, and of judging correctness or incorrectness. This checking and judging and accepting that together constitute understanding, are done by me and can be done for me by no one else. They are as private as my toothache, and without them science is dead. (Bridgman, 1955, p. 50)

Humanistic psychologists are correct in noting that subjectivity is an important factor in science. If good science were simply a matter of rigorously following rigid rules, all scientists who can follow rules conscientiously should be equally good. This, however, is not the case. Some scientists seem to have a remarkable knack for making important discoveries. It is as though when confronted with a scientific problem to solve, they make an intuitive leap to the correct solution in a manner that has little or nothing to do with any known rules of science. Moreover, when asked how they achieve their creative problem-solving insights, they are usually unable to provide a coherent explanation. In this regard, they are like poets and other creative artists, who also cannot explain the source of their inspirations. This similarity between scientists and creative artists has led some scientists and philosophers to speak of the "art of science" (e.g., Beveridge, 1957).

Despite the similarity between science and art with regard to subjectivity, there is an important difference in the final product. Artists strive to create a work that has a particular emotional effect on those toward whom it is directed, whereas scientists usually attempt to formulate concise statements that accurately describe nature with little or no concern for any emotional effects those statements might produce. Whether the statements of science are obtained from experiment or theory, it is important that they can be confirmed or verified by other scientists. No matter how inspired and brilliant an experiment or how gifted its author, the results of that experiment will be discarded if they cannot be reproduced when the experiment is replicated by other scientists. Likewise, no matter how inspired a scientific theory is, it will not be accepted by scientists unless and until the statements derived from it are supported by experiments whose results are reproducible by other scientists in the field. Thus, while the creative aspects of science are indeed subjective, the process of testing the products of science is objective.

The question arises as to whether the research methods described above can be considered to be scientific. Clearly their purpose does not seem to be to produce concise and accurate statements about nature—as do other sciences—but rather to generate a holistic *understanding* of humans and their emotions. Whether such a purpose is consistent with science would seem to depend on one's definition of science. Perhaps a more serious issue is that of whether the methods give rise to reproducible results, since replication is widely regarded by scientists to be a cornerstone of science. It is not clear, however, whether replication applies to the humanistic research methods. That is, do these methods lead to the same results—the same *understanding*—when carried out by different researchers in the same way that generally accepted scientific methods do? Unless this question can be answered in the affirmative, it is difficult to see how these research designs can be regarded as scientific.

While the research methods recommended by many humanistic psychologists tend to discourage manipulation of independent variables, it is often possible to make such manipulations when using these methods. For example, Osborne (1987) used the phenomenological method to show that graduate students shifted their views about learning toward a more humanistic perspective as a function of being in a graduate course in learning taught by a humanistic psychologist.

There are humanistic psychologists who argue that far from being incompatible with the humanistic approach, quantitative methods can complement the qualitative methods used by humanistic psychologists. For example, Sheldon and Kasser (2001) showed that quantitative methods can be used to verify a number of humanistic postulates, such as that orienting toward intrinsic values leads to greater feelings of well-being than orienting toward extrinsic values.

In general, then, there is ambivalence about the use of standard quantitative research by humanistic psychologists. Elliott (2002), pointing out that Carl Rogers was one of the pioneers in outcome research in humanistic psychology, asserted that:

> Client centered therapists in North America largely lost interest in outcome research in the early 1960s. Furthermore, the other two major strands of humanistic therapy, Gestalt therapy and existential therapy, never developed research traditions of their own. As a result, from the late 1970s on, it became increasingly easy for mainstream psychologists and advocates of cognitive and behavioral therapies to dismiss humanistic therapies as irrelevant and lacking in empirical support. (p. 57)

Elliott provided a meta-analysis (i.e., a statistical analysis combining the published statistical summary results of a large number of studies) indicating that humanistic therapy can be at least as effective as other forms of therapy. In a somewhat different vein, Stiles (2002) recognized, but appears to begrudge, the need for outcome research in humanistic psychology for what he calls "political reasons" (pp. 607–608). These political reasons would include the fact that, increasingly, clinical training programs and insurance companies that reimburse clients for treatment favor therapies that are backed up by data indicating that they are effective. However, Stiles believes that traditional outcome measures are flawed and prefers the less traditional types of research, such as discussed herein.

PSYCHODYNAMIC APPROACH

Freud and the other founders of the psychodynamic approach were physicians, and the approach thus borrowed heavily from a medical tradition at that time, which involved noting what appeared to work and what appeared not to work in treating patients. The theory that Freud developed was therefore based largely on his clinical observations, and, interestingly, his extensive reading of classical literature. Other early psychodynamic practitioners accepted Freud's theory, in its entirety or at least in large measure. The latter, such as Jung and Adler, even though they accepted much of psychoanalysis, were—as we have seen—forced to found their own psychodynamic schools of thought. The following focuses mainly on Freudian theory, although much of what is said also applies to other psychodynamic theories.

Observation

When conducting psychoanalysis, Freud took extensive notes on the verbalizations of his patients. These were the data on which he largely based his theories. For Freud, therefore, psychoanalysis was the major research method for testing his theory of the mind and generating new knowledge about the mind.

Problems with Replicability

A question concerning psychoanalysis as a research method is whether the procedure is specified clearly enough that different researchers following it can obtain the same scientific findings. This, of course, is the question of replicability that was discussed previously in connection with humanistic research methods. Historically, replicability does not seem to be a feature of the psychoanalytic method as a scientific tool. Many of Freud's early followers broke with him to found their own competing theories (e.g., Adler, Jung—see chapter 7), which were quite different from his, even though they began by using the psychoanalytic method.

Problems with Falsifiability

The philosopher of science Karl Popper (1959, 1962) famously maintained that only theories that are falsifiable—that is, capable of being proved wrong—are worthy of scientific consideration. Regarding psychoanalysis, Popper (1962, pp. 37–38) wrote skeptically of "those 'clinical observations' which analysts naively believe confirm their theory cannot do this any more than the daily confirmations which astrologers find in their practice." Like astrological signs, psychoanalytic theory incorporates symbols that may be interpreted in many different ways. If one interpretation does not fit the facts, one can simply change to another interpretation without invalidating the theory. In addition, built into the theory are factors that allow both a given result and its opposite to be taken as support for the theory. For example, suppose that during the course of therapy a patient relates a dream in which she placed her father's necktie in a dresser drawer. Freud might interpret this to mean that she wishes to have sex with her father (the Electra complex). If she accepts this interpretation, this indicates that the meanings behind the dream have been, or are being, admitted into consciousness and she is well on the way to resolving her Electra complex and other psychological problems she may have. Suppose, however, that she denies vehemently that she has any wish to have sex with her father. Far from disproving the Freudian interpretation of her dream, this is taken as confirming evidence. According to Freud, her denial is simply a way of keeping her superego from recognizing the presence of the forbidden wish and administering punishment in the form of guilt. Even the fact that a number of Freud's early followers eventually rejected the theory was used in support of it. Freud interpreted their rejection to be due to repression of their unconscious sexual urges whose existence was forced on them by the theory. For their part, they had comparable explanations for Freud's inability to accept their theories.

There are criticisms of Popper's theory of science. One criticism is that Popper based his theory on physics and chemistry. In these sciences, which deal with relatively simple quantifiable variables, there typically are explicit tests that can falsify theories. In sciences such as biology, however, theories are less easily falsified. It would be difficult to think of a critical test of, for example, the theory of evolution. However, the falsifiability criterion may be unrealistic even in a science such as physics. Kuhn (1962), focusing on physics, argued that tests of a scientific theory—or *paradigm*, to use Kuhn's term—rarely result in its overthrow (i.e., *falsification* in Popper's terms). According to Kuhn, as long as a paradigm continues to be successful in solving scientific puzzles and problems, adherents to it either ignore data that disagree with the paradigm or modify it just enough to accommodate the discrepant data. Thus, a paradigm is never falsified. Eventually, however, a competing paradigm will replace one that, due to the build up of anomalous data, is less successful in solving scientific puzzles and problems.

Apart from arguments again Popper's theory in general, such as those of Kuhn, a specific argument against Popper's critique of Freud is that psychoanalysis is indeed falsifiable through direct experimentation. Evidence for this argument is considered in the next section.

Experimental Tests of Psychoanalytic Theory

As mentioned earlier, Freud did not use the experimental method, nor is it completely clear whether he even endorsed it as a means of verifying his theory. However, his theory should be susceptible to tests with those methods because of its deterministic nature.

Experimenters interested in psychoanalytic concepts have developed various procedures to study the tenability of those concepts. For example, psychological tests using incomplete, subliminal (i.e., below threshold), or ambiguous (e.g., projective tests such as the Rorschach) stimuli are used to explore personality and unconscious defense mechanisms (e.g., Kline, 1987). There have been some experiments using standard experimental designs that support some of Freud's concepts. Examples are as follows:

- Lazarus and McCleary (1951) found that if certain words were followed by a shock, and then presented so briefly that the individual could not report detecting them, those words nevertheless elicited a stronger emotional response (as measured by change in skin conductance) than words that had not been paired with shock.
- McGinnies (1949) found that individuals tended to perceive taboo words less readily than nontaboo words when the words were flashed briefly on a screen.
- Morokoff (1985) showed that women high in self-reported sexual guilt report less arousal but show greater physiological arousal as measured by an instrument (called a plethysmograph) that measures blood flow to the genitals.
- Watson & Getz (1990) found that children, as reported by parents, tend to show more affection toward the parent of the opposite sex and more aggression toward the parent of the same sex, and that these tendencies are strongest at about 4 years of age and begin to decline before about 5 years of age.

The first three studies provide some support for Freud's view of the unconscious (or unconscious processes) and repression, while the last study appears to support Freud's theory of the Oedipus complex. However, the results of the first three studies are also consistent with behaviorism, as they are the predicted effects of aversive conditioning or punishment. Moreover, in the fourth study, the behavior of the child might be explained by parents tending to lavish more attention on their offspring who are of the opposite sex from themselves when the children are very young. In addition, there is no evidence that these results are due to sexual motivation, since there are numerous possible nonsexual reasons for a child to behave more favorably toward the parent of the opposite sex.

In addition, data supporting a number of other Freudian concepts such as projection, repression, castration complex, penis envy, and the psychosexual stages of development are weak at best.

Thus, it appears that there are no experimental data in support of psychoanalytic theory that are not subject to other, possibly more plausible, interpretations. In addition, there is some strong disconfirming evidence regarding at least one Freudian prediction. According to traditional psychoanalytic theory, behavior modification should not work because it only treats symptoms (i.e., deviant behavior) rather than the underlying psychodynamic causes of those symptoms. Although psychoanalysts concede that symptoms might be removed through the use of behavioral techniques, new symptoms should appear because the underlying problem has not been eliminated. However, although numerous studies confirming the effectiveness of behavior modification have been carried out, this phenomenon of symptom substitution that psychoanalysts warned about has failed to materialize (e.g., Bandura, 1969; Franks, 1969).

Effectiveness of Psychoanalysis

Staunch psychoanalysts maintain that "clinical benefits of analytically oriented therapies are indeed borne out over the course of one's professional experience in using these approaches" (Anchin, 2002, p. 315). However, there is some recognition that more standard forms of research are necessary to develop psychoanalysis further and to convince nonpsychoanalytical therapists of its effectiveness. For example, writing for a psychoanalytic audience, McWilliams (1999, p. 3) stated: "we need to invest in the very expensive, complex, and creative research that psychoanalysis requires to establish its empirical status." Nevertheless, the relevance of standard research designs to testing the effectiveness of psychoanalysis is still controversial among psychoanalysts (e.g., see Kernberg, 2006; Perron, 2006).

COGNITIVE APPROACH

Following the lead of Newell and Simon (1956, 1972), some cognitive researchers write computer programs that attempt to simulate cognitive processes. The success of the computer simulation is judged according to how realistically it mimics the major aspects of the process being simulated. Thus, a simulation is used in the same way that a theory is to make specific predictions about behavior. As in testing a theory, standard experimental procedures are typically used to determine whether individuals behave in the manner predicted by the simulation.

Often simulations consist of production rules, which are the presumed rules that individuals follow in solving specific problems (e.g., Anderson & Lebiere, 1998; Rosenbloom, Laird, & Newell, 1993). A fairly simple production rule, for example, would be the steps an individual follows in solving a problem in long division. Hypothesized production rules are incorporated into proposed simulations of various cognitive processes.

In order to obtain information about the cognitive processes to be simulated, Simon and his colleagues developed a technique called *protocol analysis* (Ericsson & Simon, 1993; Newell and Simon, 1972). This involves having individuals verbalize aloud their thought processes while they are actively solving logical and other types of problems. The researchers analyze the recorded verbalizations, called protocols, to obtain insights into the cognitive processes involved in specific types of problem solving. These analyses give rise to what are called production rules.

Simulations form a minority of the research by cognitive psychologists. However, most cognitive research is based on hypotheses that appeal to a computer metaphor. In addition, harking back to Frans Donders, who in the 1860s used reaction time to study the time taken by higher mental processes in discrimination tasks (see chapter 3), cognitive psychologists often use reaction time to study the processing times involved in various complex tasks—for example, the cognitive processing of different types of sentences or the mental rotations of different objects. In addition to reaction-time measures, cognitive psychologists have incorporated other types of instrumentation. These include eye-movement measurements and brain-imaging techniques while individuals are carrying out various cognitive tasks. The fixations of the eyes on certain words or letters in a reading task, for example, can indicate which parts of the task require the most processing; the activation of certain brain regions can indicate which parts of the brain are most involved in processing the information needed to successfully carry out the task.

BEHAVIORAL APPROACH

As in physics and other natural sciences, behaviorists have the goal of obtaining quantitative laws; however, they generally believe that at this stage in behavioral science the best that can usually be obtained is simply the general shape of the function, or even merely greater-than/less-than relationships. For example, an experiment considered informative might simply show that one teaching method produces higher test scores than another teaching method, where teaching method is the independent variable and test score is the dependent variable.

Standard Research Designs

Within the behavioral approach there has been considerable controversy regarding two different types of standard designs that seem to be based largely on two different philosophical approaches to the study of behavior as a function of the environment: (1) the *inferential-statistics approach*, and (2) the *individual-organism approach*.

Inferential-Statistics Approach

The inferential-statistical approach typically involves using the mean of a group of individuals to estimate each value of a dependent variable corresponding to values of an independent variable. Inferential statistical techniques are used to determine the accuracy of the estimation and whether statistically different values of the dependent variable correspond to different values or levels of the independent variable. If the values of the dependent variable at different values or levels of the independent variable show differences greater than what would be expected simply on the basis of random fluctuations in the values of the dependent variable, the independent variable is said to have been shown to have a statistically significant effect on the dependent variable, and the effect is considered to have been demonstrated scientifically.

Individual-Organism Approach

The individual-organism approach takes data from individuals rather than data averaged across individuals (i.e., group averages) as the primary data of interest. Despite the word *individual* in the name of the method, it is rarely the case that data are obtained from only one individual in an individual-organism study. Such studies usually do collect data from fewer individuals than typically participate in inferential-statistical studies; in addition, individual-organism studies usually collect the data over longer time periods, thus obtaining more data from each individual than is typically the case in inferential-statistics studies. For individual-organism studies, the criterion for positive results is not statistical significance, but rather replication of the result across the individuals participating in the study. In other words, in general, each individual in the study must show the same relationship between the dependent and the independent variable in order for the result to be considered reliable. In addition, other researchers must also be able to replicate the result with the same procedure in order for the finding to be firmly accepted by the scientific community (or at least those members who subscribe to the individual organism methodology). The functional relationship need not be quantitatively identical across individuals, for different individuals clearly differ quantitatively in a number of ways; however, the form of the functional relationship must be the same in order for a scientist using the individual-organism approach to claim to have made a definite finding.

Differences Between Methodological and Radical Behaviorists

Methodological behaviorists tend to favor the inferential-statistical approach, whereas radical behaviorists tend to favor the individual-organism approach. The reasons for these different preferences among methodological and radical behaviorists may to at least some extent be historical, since the leading radical behaviorist, B. F. Skinner, was a strong advocate of the individual-organism approach. Skinner argued that methodological behaviorists prefer the inferential-statistical approach because group averages seem to them to be closer than the data of individuals to processes that are going on in the mind. Skinner believed that such averaging obscures behavioral processes, which should be the real focus of attention in psychological studies. Murray Sidman (1960), in his classic text on individual-organism research methodology, argued that the focus on replicability in this approach is more in keeping with the approach adopted by other sciences, which demands that results can be shown to be reproducible in order to be admitted as scientifically valid. Sidman pointed out that statistical significance does not insure replicability. In addition, both Skinner and Sidman, as well as other radical behaviorists, have noted that since psychology is usually considered to be a science of the individual, psychological research should focus on the behavior of individuals rather than group averages.

Because both the inferential-statistical approach and the individual-organism approach are based on determinism, neither is popular among humanistic psychologists. It might seem that they would consider the inferential-statistical approach to be the "lesser of two evils" because it appears to allow for a degree of indeterminacy—that is, chance or random fluctuations within groups. However, the emphasis of the approach is on predictability, not unpredictability. In addition, we have already seen that chance or random fluctuation does not provide a good argument for the type of freedom that humanistic psychologists advocate.

Some Points of Contact Between the Research Approaches of the Four Systems

The behavioristic use of individual-organism research is similar to the psychodynamic approach's use of case studies. In both cases, the focus is on individuals in specific situations, as opposed to group averages. Since one cannot rely on a statistical criterion to indicate whether a reliable finding has been made, keen scientific judgment is required. Because this involves some subjectivity, it is sometimes criticized as unscientific. Case studies are defended in psychodynamic and to some extent in behavioristic individual-organism research when they seem to shed light (either negative or positive) on current theory. In addition, a rigorous standard has evolved for the single-organism approach that sets it apart from the case-study approach; specifically, in order for the results to be admitted into the compendium of factual information, they must be replicable both within and across experiments. Any failure to replicate must be accounted for, or the results are cast into doubt (see Sidman, 1960).

The uncompromising determinism of the individual-organism approach, which does not admit to *chance* or *randomness* (preferring to apply the label *uncontrolled variation,* implying that fluctuations in the data that cannot be shown to be produced by the independent variable are controllable in principle once the relevant independent variables have been identified), clearly does not endear itself to humanistic psychologists. Particularly disturbing to humanistic psychologists are the assumptions of the approach that (1) given sufficient knowledge, the behavior of any given individual can be predicted precisely; and (2) there are laws of behavior, analogous to the laws in the naturalistic sciences, which are the same for all individuals. The first assumption seems to take away the individual's freedom, while the second seems to take away his or her individuality.

Nevertheless, the individual-organism research approach shares two important similarities with humanistic psychology that are not shared by the inferential-statistical approach: focus on the individual, and a genuine concern for individual differences. With regard to this point, although the emphasis is on similarities, differences are taken into account in order to arrive at those similarities. For example, in order for the principle of reinforcement to work, an effective reinforcer must be found for each individual, and the individual-organism approach recognizes that different things may be reinforcing to different individuals.

There also may be a stronger tendency to recognize the importance of subjectivity by at least some advocates of the individual-organism approach than by the inferential-statistics approach, perhaps because the individual-organism approach does not follow the rigidly prescribed hypothesis-testing rules that frequently are associated with the inferential-statistics approach. For example, Sidman (1960) wrote:

> [B]oth scientists and poets—at least, the best of each—know more things than the rules of logic would permit them to derive from the available evidence. Discovery has nearly always preceded proof, and the two functions are not always performed by the same person. Yet the discoverer is often given credit even when the formally convincing evidence has been supplied by someone else. Scientists may talk grandly about the bloodless objectivity of their pursuit, but their other behavior is evidence that they really know better. (Sidman, 1960, p. 130)

Of course, the work of the scientist may begin with subjectivity, but (according to behaviorists, at least) it cannot be allowed to end there. A discovery cannot be accepted by the scientific community until "formally convincing evidence has been supplied," whether by the discoverer or by someone else. Nevertheless, the statement that the knowledge of good poets and scientists transcends the rules of logic (i.e., that there is much poetic and scientific behavior that is not rule-governed) is a sentiment that humanistic psychologists can express just as readily as behaviorists.

Moreover, at least one cognitive scientist would tend to agree with the focus on individuals and the inevitability of some subjectivity in research. Speaking of his studies involving single individuals solving problems over long periods of time, Herbert A. Simon wrote:

> If the methodology troubles us, it may be comforting to recall that detailed longitudinal analysis of the behavior of a single solar system was the foundation stone for Kepler's laws, and ultimately for Newton's. Perhaps it is not our methodology that needs revising so much as the standard textbooks on methodology, which perversely warn us against running an experiment until precise hypotheses have been formulated and experimental and control conditions defined. Perhaps we need to add to the textbooks a chapter, or several chapters, describing how basic scientific discoveries can be made by observing the world intently, in the laboratory or outside it, with controls or without them, heavy with hypotheses or innocent of them. (Simon, 1991, p. 385)

SUMMARY

Although humanistic psychologists are increasingly favoring qualitative research designs, Rogers clearly believed that outcome research—research quantitatively demonstrating the effects of therapy—would support the client-centered approach. However, standard experimental designs cause problems for self-determination because to whatever extent a dependent variable is shown to be functionally related to an independent variable, it logically follows that to at least that extent the dependent variable is controlled or determined. Thus, if a study is successful in demonstrating a functional relationship between a dependent and an independent variable, some degree of self-determination is removed. Moreover, if a study fails to demonstrate a functional relationship between a dependent and an independent variable, logically all one can say is that possible determining or controlling factors for that dependent variable have not been identified in the study—one cannot logically say that self-determination has been demonstrated. Since most humanistic psychologists, at least most academic humanistic psychologists, believe that humanistic psychology is or should be scientific, there have been a number of exhortations from humanistic psychologists for others within their field to become more involved in research.

The importance of subjectivity in science is a theme that runs strongly throughout the arguments humanistic psychologists give for the research methods they advocate. Humanistic psychologists are correct in noting that subjectivity is an important factor in science. If good science were simply a matter of rigorously following rigid rules, all scientists who can follow rules conscientiously should be equally good. Whether the statements of science are obtained from experiment or theory, it is important that they can be confirmed or verified by other scientists. Likewise, no matter how inspired a scientific theory is, it will not be accepted by scientists unless and until the statements derived from it are supported by studies the results of which are reproducible by other scientists in the field.

For Freud psychoanalysis was the major research method for testing his theory of the mind and generating new knowledge about the mind. A question concerning psychoanalysis as a research method is whether the procedure is specified clearly enough that different researchers following it can obtain the same scientific findings. This is the question of replicability. Scientists interested in psychoanalytic concepts have developed various procedures outside of therapy to study the tenability of those concepts.

The cognitive approach uses traditional experimental designs and modern statistical methods. Some cognitive research is done by writing computer programs in an attempt to simulate some cognitive process, as well as or in combination with standard experimental methodology. The success of the simulation is judged according to how realistically it mimics the major aspects of the process being simulated. Sometimes the simulation is used in the same way that a theory is to make specific predictions about behavior. As in testing a theory, an experiment is then conducted with humans to determine whether they behave in the manner predicted by the simulation.

Behavioral psychology makes use of two different types of standard designs that seem to be based largely on two different philosophical approaches to the study of behavior as a function of the environment: (1) the inferential-statistics approach, and (2) the individual-organism approach. The inferential-statistical approach typically involves using the mean of a group of individuals to estimate each value of a dependent variable corresponding to values of an independent variable. For individual-organism studies, the aim is replication of the result across the individuals participating in the study. Methodological behaviorists tend to favor the inferential-statistical approach, whereas radical behaviorists tend to favor the individual-organism approach. The individual-organism approach shares two important similarities with humanistic psychology that are not shared by the inferential-statistical approach: focus on the individual, and a genuine concern for individual differences. There also may be a stronger tendency to recognize the importance of subjectivity by at least some advocates of the individual-organism approach than by adherents of the inferential-statistics approach, perhaps because the individual-organism approach does not follow the rigidly prescribed hypothesis testing rules that frequently are associated with the inferential-statistics approach.

Discussion Questions

1. Discuss the pros and cons of the move by humanistic psychologists toward nonstandard (qualitative) research designs.

2. Compare and contrast the different qualitative designs. Discuss whether some qualitative techniques are likely to be more informative than others.

3. Discuss whether the nonhumanistic approaches might benefit by incorporating qualitative techniques.

4. One might argue that it is more incumbent on the psychodynamic theories of the mind and/or behavior than on the other approaches to test their theoretical validity by proving to be therapeutically effective. Discuss whether such an argument would have merit.

5. Discuss the relative advantages of the traditional research method of psychodynamic therapists and standard research designs for studying the effects of psychodynamic therapy.

6. Discuss the use of computer simulations in cognitive research. Discuss whether other approaches could benefit from the use of computer simulations.

7. Discuss the similarities between radical behaviorists and humanistic psychologists in their approach to research.

8. Discuss the advantages and disadvantages of the individual-organism research approach with respect to the inferential-statistics approach.

9. Discuss whether psychology should attempt to emulate the research methods of sciences such as physics and chemistry.

10. Discuss whether protocol analysis, as used by Simon and his colleagues, is a reversion to introspection as practiced in the late 1800s and early 1900s.

CHAPTER 16

Conclusion

he history of psychology traces back to the concept of the soul (psuchè or psyche) as this concept developed in the Mediterranean region. The soul was originally conceptualized as a very weak entity—a pale reflection of the body. For the ancient Greek philosophers, however, the soul gradually took on more of a controlling function over the body. Socrates and Plato emphasized its moral aspect in controlling our impulses that tend to make us act in ways that are immoral or that Christians were later to call "sinful."

Plato's most influential student, Aristotle, took issue with his mentor's teaching about the soul. According to Aristotle, the soul is not an entity within the body that controls the body and that, possibly, lives on after the death of the body. The soul, according to Aristotle, is the "form of the body"—by which he seemed to mean that the soul is the functioning of the body. This includes the vegetative functioning (e.g., digestion and other functions that maintain life), sensing (i.e., our conscious awareness of the world around us), and thinking and behaving (i.e., the rational functions of the body). Thus, even in those early times, we have the beginning of a controversy that is similar to the philosophical controversy that was to occur in more recent times between mentalists and behaviorists. This is the question of whether the mind is a real entity or whether the term *mind* is just a term that, in the final analysis, simply refers to the behavior of the body.

Early Christian thinkers incorporated much of Plato and Aristotle's thinking, as filtered through the Neoplatonists, into the Christian philosophy that predominated in the West. To the ancient Greeks the soul was made of a finer type of substance than the rest of the body, but it was nonetheless composed of a physical substance. With Plato the concept of the soul began to undergo a metamorphosis into the present concept of it. According to Plato there exists a world of ideal forms that are nonphysical.

365

The soul strives to reach its ideal form, which is God. This view was picked up and elaborated on by the Neoplatonists and eventually, as mentioned previously, influenced early Christian thinkers.

The French philosopher René Descartes was very important in preparing the way for psychology in two respects. The first was that he specified that the body is a machine. This implied that it can be studied in the same way that a machine can be studied, which can give rise to mechanical principles describing the functioning of the body. Descartes further helped this process along by being the first to postulate reflexes—automatic responses to stimuli. Descartes' concept of the reflex, traveling down through the centuries and combining with discoveries in physiology, eventually impacted on the Russian reflexologists (in particular, Pavlov and Bekhterev) who were to have a profound effect on American behaviorists (e.g., Watson and Skinner). The second respect in which Descartes paved the way for psychology was by postulating that the soul is made up of an entirely different substance from that which makes up the body. Although Descartes did not speculate on how the soul can be studied, his philosophy implies that the techniques for studying it—if such exist—differ from those in which the body can be studied. This separate treatment of soul and body has been called Cartesian dualism. Although it seems to answer the question of how it is that we can experience consciousness and feel that we have free will, it raises another question: how is it possible for a nonmaterial substance (the soul) to interact with a material substance? This is a question that has plagued philosophy from the time of Descartes to the present day.

For Plato and Aristotle the soul has nonrational as well as rational aspects. Western philosophers, however, stressed the rational aspects. The English language has a word that refers to the rational aspects of the soul; that word is *mind*. Although most other major European languages use the words for spirit or ghost to refer to the mind, it is generally clear from context what they are referring to. A group of philosophers known as the British empiricists were among the first to start using the term *mind* to refer to what previously had been called the rational soul. To the British empiricists, the mind starts out largely as a blank slate, and almost all ideas and concepts are learned through associations.

In strong disagreement with the British empiricists, a group of philosophers known as the German idealists believed that innate ideas and emotions, particularly the will, are major ingredients of the mind. Reason alone—at least the straightforward, linear type of reason adhered to by the British Associationists—cannot, according to the German idealists, lead to the truth about the universe and the place of humans in it. Far from being the result of a straightforward, orderly process acquired through associations that include chains of reasoning, true knowledge (insofar as it is obtainable) comes about through willful confrontations with the contradictions inherent in the universe.

Speculation about the mind eventually gave way to attempts to subject it to the methods that had been successful in physics and other sciences. In Germany Wundt developed an experimental method for analyzing the components of the mind; in Austria Brentano developed a method for studying the actions of the mind; in America William James studied consciousness as a stream, and focused on the function of the mind in the adaptation of the individual to the environment.

An Austrian medical doctor named Sigmund Freud made a different kind of attempt to apply scientific methodology to the study of the mind. Using a free-association method he attempted to analyze the minds of his neurotic patients to uncover the causes of their symptoms, and in so doing to discover the dynamic principles by which the mind operates. He ended up disagreeing with many of his initial followers, the most prominent of whom were Alfred Adler and Carl Jung, who developed their own psychodynamic systems.

Titchener became the leading advocate of Wundt's introspection method in America, where functionalists and structuralists debated whether the mind's function or its structure should be the first object of study. Under the leadership of John B. Watson, the behaviorists argued that psychology should be an objective science, like the other natural sciences, and that therefore behavior—not the mind—is its proper object of study. Incorporating the conditioned reflex terminology of Pavlov and the association-reflex methodology of Bekhterev, Watson made the conditioned reflex the basic unit of analysis. Later B. F. Skinner, who assumed the mantle of the leading spokesperson for radical behaviorism after Watson's departure from psychology, added the concept of the operant.

At this point psychology contained two major approaches: behaviorism and Freudian psychoanalysis. Two reactions to this state of affairs occurred. First, a movement called third-force psychology, also known as humanistic psychology, arose under the leadership of Abraham Maslow, Carl Rogers, and others. This movement was largely influenced by existential philosophy stemming from the German idealists and phenomenological philosophy stemming from the teachings of Brentano and his student Husserl. Essentially, humanistic psychologists object to what they perceived as the over-simplified and mechanistic approaches of behaviorism and Freudian psychoanalysis. Humanistic psychologists are somewhat more favorably disposed toward other psychodynamic approaches—especially those of Jung and Adler. Cognitive psychology, stemming mainly from advances in computer science, constitutes another reaction to behaviorism. Cognitive psychologists believe that the mind can be studied as objectively as one can study a computer program.

Thus, there are currently four broad systems within psychology: the psychodynamic, the cognitive, the behavioral, and the humanistic. In the second part of this book we have compared these four approaches with respect to the issues that, in one form or another, have been important throughout the history of psychology. These issues are: (a) the importance of consciousness and how best to study it; (b) the extent to which we can understand the whole individual by analyzing the person into units or elements; (c) the role the future plays in influencing present behavior; (d) whether we are merely the product of our genes and environments or something more; (e) the role of values in the science of psychology; (f) how psychology should approach or study spirituality; (g) how clients should be treated both therapeutically and as individuals; and (h) how psychological research should be conducted to best advance psychological knowledge.

All four approaches recognize consciousness, in the sense of self-awareness, as an important topic of investigation. The behavioral point of view that consciousness is a social product that depends on language seems to have agreement from humanistic psychologists. It is also not inconsistent with cognitive psychology, although this approach may tend to look more for either an algorithmic or neurological explanation of consciousness. The psychodynamic point of view tends to look at consciousness as a given, whose further explanation depends on neurological work rather than psychodynamic research. In addition, unlike the other approaches, the psychodynamic approach tends to reify consciousness as the counterpart of the unconscious. Specifically, the psychodynamic approach views consciousness as a receptacle for material from the unconscious. This, however, may be regarded simply as a convenient metaphor rather than something that should be taken literally. Regardless of how consciousness is looked at by the approaches, all approaches seem to concur that, depending on their respective definitions of consciousness, the expansion or augmenting of consciousness is desirable.

There are a number of types of reductionism. All approaches are reductionistic in the sense that it is impossible to talk about any phenomenon without focusing on some aspects or facets of that phenomenon while at least temporally ignoring others. The question is whether the most natural or effective reduction has been made in any particular instance. There is consensus among the approaches that distinguishing between material and nonmaterial substances (such as matter vs. mind) is not useful. There appears to be no consensus, however, on what the natural fracture points are—for example, stimuli and responses, modules of computer code, or facets of the personality.

Aristotle's efficient cause worked well for physics, but this does not mean that it is the most appropriate or the only way to investigate psychological processes. Humanistic psychology is more teleological than the other approaches. Within the behavioral approach, Rachlin has developed teleological behaviorism, which provides a way to look at potential future events controlling present behavior. However, the underlying assumption of the behavioral approach is that all behavioral phenomena may be explained in terms of efficient causes. Both the psychodynamic and cognitive approaches are nonteleological in that they explain phenomena on the basis of efficient causes.

The humanistic approach has emphasized the importance of the phenomenological experience of freedom. The behavioral approach has emphasized that control is always present. The phenomenological experience of freedom is dependent not on whether behavior is controlled, but on the type of control. Behaviorism stresses that the phenomenological experience of freedom depends on control by positive reinforcement. For the psychodynamic approach, the feeling of freedom is enhanced by material from the unconscious being made conscious. The more control is given over to consciousness, the greater the feeling of freedom. This is not incompatible with the behavioral approach. Increasing consciousness is perhaps another way of saying that more options are provided, which translates into more control by positive reinforcement and less by aversive events. None of this is inconsistent with the cognitive approach, although it may tend to look for algorithmic or neurological explanations for the feeling of freedom.

The standard view of most scientists is that science cannot provide values. Both humanistic and behavioral psychology question whether this applies to the science of psychology. The reason why it might not is that values are a component of the human psyche or behavior. From a humanistic point of view, humans seek to self-actualize. To behaviorists, humans seek to maximize reinforcement, which may be the same thing as self-actualization given a definition of reinforcement broad enough to include social factors. Rachlin's teleological behaviorism has tried to explain altruism, which is an important social value, by relating it to people's concern for their own individual futures. To the psychodynamic approach, what is most valued is the movement toward enhanced consciousness. The cognitive approach appears not to have directly addressed the issue of values; however, none of the preceding is necessarily incompatible with it.

Spirituality is an important aspect of humans that, except for humanistic psychology, has been largely neglected. To the extent that other approaches have addressed it, they have tended to provide naturalistic explanations. Both Freudian and Jungian theory have explained it from their respective perspectives. The similarity of behavioral psychology to the nonagentic (i.e., no-soul) views of Eastern religions has been pointed out, which accords well with the humanistic predilection toward Eastern religions. In discussions of psychology and spirituality, there is some blurring of the distinction between using psychology as a tool to study spirituality and using a particular system of psychology to promote a particular religious point of view. This is cause for concern. The separation between science and religion may be just as important as the separation between church and state. Science may inform us about religion, but probably should not be used to promote any particular religion.

With regard to psychotherapy, there seems to be a strongly converging trend that the emphasis should generally be on helping clients to improve their social relationships. Each approach has attempted to justify this emphasis on the basis of its own particular theoretical perspective. While all four approaches have produced effective therapies, there is no clear evidence that one has produced a general therapy that is more effective than any of the others.

The four systems are perhaps farthest apart in the way in which they advocate research be done. The humanistic approach has increasingly focused on qualitative research; the psychodynamic approach still focuses on the individual case study; the behavioral approach tends to advocate individual-organism research design; and the cognitive approach tends to rely on inferential statistics. Having a variety of research designs, however, is better than having too few. Coming at an objective from more than one direction is probably a good strategy.

Discussion Questions

1. Discuss the similarities between the split between Plato and Aristotle's views and contemporary differences among the four systems discussed in this book.

2. Discuss the influence Descartes seems to have had on each of the four systems.

3. Discuss how the differences between the British empiricists and the German idealists are possibly reflected in the differences among the four systems discussed in this book.

4. Discuss how the differences among Wundt, Brentano, and James are possibly reflected in the four systems discussed in this book.

5. Discuss how Freud's experience as a practicing physician may have influenced the methodological approach he developed, as opposed to the approaches of Wundt, Brentano, and James.

6. Of the issues discussed in the second part of this book, choose four that you think are particularly important and state similarities among the approaches with regard to those issues.

7. Of the issues discussed in the second part of this book, choose four that you think are particularly important and state differences among the approaches with regard to those issues.

8. In your opinion, do the four systems seem to be converging, diverging, or staying about the same with regard to critical issues in psychology? That is, does the amount of agreement among the approaches seem to be increasing, decreasing, or staying the same? State the reasons for your opinion.

9. Speculate on the fate in the next 50 years of each of the four systems.

10. Speculate on the fate in the next 50 years of each of the eight topics—consciousness, holism or reductionism, teleology, determinism, values, spirituality, psychotherapy, and research—discussed in the second part of this book.

References

Adams, F., & Aizawa, K. (2001). The bounds of consciousness. *Philosophical Psychology, 14*, 43–64.

Allport, G. W. (1968). *The person in psychology: Selected essays.* Boston: Beacon.

Anchin, J. C. (2002). Relational psychoanalytic enactments and psychotherapy integration: Dualities, dialectics, and directions: Comments on Frank (2002). *Journal of Psychotherapy Integration, 12*, 302–346.

Anderson, J. R., & Lebiere, C. (1998). The atomic components of thought. Mahwah, NJ: Lawrence Erlbaum Associates.

Ansbacher, H. L., & Ansbacher, R. R. (1956): *The Individual Psychology of Alfred Adler: A systematic presentation in selections from his writings.* New York: Harper & Row.

ap Iorwerth, G. (1985). Humanistic psychology and the Judeo-Christian heritage. *Journal of Humanistic Psychology, 25*(2), 13–34.

Arkin, R. C. (1998). *Behavior-based robotics.* Cambridge, MA: MIT Press.

Aspinwall, L. G., & Staudinger, U. M. (Eds.). (2003). *A psychology of human strengths: Fundamental questions and future directions for a positive psychology.* Washington, DC: American Psychological Association.

Bandura, A. (1969). *Principles of behavior modification.* New York: Holt, Rinehart and Winston.

Bandura, A. (1978). The self-system in reciprocal determinism. *American Psychologist, 33*, 344–358.

Barnes-Holmes, D., Hayes, S. C., & Dymond, S. (2001). Self and self-directed rules. In S. C. Hayes, D. Barnes-Holmes, & B. Roche, (Eds.), *Relational frame theory: A post-Skinnerian account of human language and cognition.* (pp. 119–139). New York: Plenum.

Barnes-Holmes, D., Hayes, S. C., & Gregg, J. (2001). Religion, spirituality, and transcendence. In S. C. Hayes, D. Barnes-Holmes, & B. Roche, (Eds.), *Relational frame theory: A post-Skinnerian account of human language and cognition.* (pp. 239–251). New York: Plenum.

Barnes-Holmes, D., O'Hora, D., Roche, B., Hayes, S. C., Bissett, R. T., & Lyddy, F. (2001). Understanding and verbal regulation. In S. C. Hayes, D. Barnes-

Holmes, & B. Roche, (Eds.), *Relational frame theory: A post-Skinnerian account of human language and cognition.* (pp. 103–117). New York: Plenum.

Baruš, I. (2003). *Alterations of consciousness: An empirical analysis for social scientists.* Washington, DC: American Psychological Association.

Barrell, J. J., Aanstoos, C., Richards, A. C., & Arons, M. (1987). Human science research methods. *Journal of Humanistic Psychology, 27*(4), 424–457.

Barrell, J. J., Medeiros, D., Barrell, J. E., & Price, D. (1985). The causes and treatment of performance anxiety: An experiential approach. *Journal of Humanistic Psychology, 25*(2), 106–122.

Barret, D. W., Patock-Peckham, J. A., Hutchinson, G. T., & Nagoshi, C. T. (2005). Cognitive motivation and religious orientation. *Personality and Individual differences, 38,* 461–474.

Beahrs, J. O. (1982). *Unity and multiplicity: Multilevel consciousness of self in hypnosis, psychiatric disorder and mental health.* New York: Brunner/Mazel.

Bechtel, W. (2005). The challenge of characterizing operations in the mechanisms underlying behavior. *Journal of the Experimental Analysis of Behavior, 84,* 313–325.

Beck, A. T. (1976). *Cognitive therapy and the emotional disorders.* Connecticut: International Universities Press.

Beck, A. T., & Emery, G. (1985). *Anxiety disorders and phobias: A cognitive perspective.* New York: Basic Books.

Beer, R. (1995). A dynamical systems perspective on agent-environment interaction. *Artificial Intelligence, 72,* 173–215.

Bennett, M. R., & Hacker, P. M. S. (2003). *Philosophical foundations of neuroscience.* Malden, MA: Blackwell Publishing.

Berman, J., & Norton, N. (1985). Does professional training make a therapist more effective? *Psychological Bulletin, 98,* 401–407.

Beveridge, W. I. B. (1957). *The art of scientific investigation.* New York: Vintage Books.

Biela, A., & Tobacyk, J. J. (1987). Self-transcendence in the agoral gathering: A case study of Pope John Paul II's 1979 visit to Poland. *Journal of Humanistic Psychology, 27*(4), 390–405.

Blackmore, S. (1993). *Dying to live: Science and the near-death experience.* London: Grafton.

Bleick, C. R., & Abrams, A. I. (1987). The Transcendental Meditation program and criminal recidivism in California. *Journal of Criminal Justice, 15*(3), 211–230.

Borg, J., Andree, B., Soderstrom, H., & Farde, L. (2003). The serotonin system and spiritual experiences. *American Journal of Psychiatry, 160,* 1965–1969.

Bourguignon, E. (Ed.). (1973). *Religion, altered states of consciousness, and social change.* Columbus: Ohio State University Press.

Bozarth, J. D. (2002). Nondirectivity in the person-centered approach: Critique of Kahn's critique. *Journal of Humanistic Psychology, 42*(2), 78–83.

Bridgman, P. W. (1928). *The logic of modern physics.* New York: The Macmillan Company.

Bridgman, P. W. (1955). *Reflections of a physicist.* New York: Philosophical Library.

Brookes, R. (1991). Intelligence without representation. *Artificial Intelligence, 47,* 139–159.

Brookes, R. (1999). *Cambrian intelligence: The early history of the new AI.* Cambridge, MA: The MIT Press.

Buber, M., Rogers, C., & Friedman, M. (1965). Dialogue between Martin Buber and Carl Rogers. In M. Friedman (Ed.), *M. Buber, The knowledge of man: Selected essays* (pp. 166–184). New York: Harper & Row.

Buckley, K. W. (1989). *Mechanical man: John Broadus Watson and the beginnings of behaviorism.* New York: Guilford.

Budge, E. A. W. (1997). *Egyptian religion.* New York: Citadel Press.

Bulbrook, M. E. (1932). An experimental inquiry into the nature and existence of "insight." *American Journal of Psychology, 44,* 409–453.

Burstow, B. (1987). Humanistic psychotherapy and the issue of equality. *Journal of Humanistic Psychology, 27*(1), 9–25.

Buss, D. M. (1995). Evolutionary psychology: A new paradigm for psychological science. *Psychological Inquiry, 6,* 1–30.

Butterfield, H. (1957). *The origins of modern science: 1300–1800* (Rev. ed.). New York: Macmillan.

Cain, D. J. (2002). Defining characteristics, history, and evolution of humanistic psychotherapies. In D. J. Cain & J. Seeman (Eds.), *Humanistic psychotherapies: Handbook of research and practice* (pp. 3–54). Washington, DC: American Psychological Association.

Carr, D. B. (1981). Endorphins at the approach of death. *Lancet, 1,* 390.

Carr, D. B. (1989). On the evolving neurobiology of the near-death experience. *Journal of Near-Death Studies, 7,* 251–254.

Carroll, L. (1898). *Alice's adventures in Wonderland.* London: Macmillan.

Casti, J. L. (2000). *Paradigms regained: A further exploration of the mysteries of modern science.* New York: Harper Collins.

Chambless, D. L. & Ollendick, T. H. (2001). Empirically supported psychological intervention: Controversies and evidence. *Annual Review of Psychology, 52,* 685–716.

Cheney, D. L., & Seyfarth, R. M. (1990). *How monkeys see the world: Inside the mind of another species.* Chicago: University of Chicago Press.

Chomsky, N. (1957). *Syntactic structures.* The Hague, Netherlands: Mouton.

Chomsky, N. (1959). *Verbal Behavior* by B. F. Skinner. *Language, 35,* 26–58.

Chomsky, N. (1963). Formal properties of grammars. In R. D. Luce, R. R. Bush, & E. Galanter (Eds.), *Handbook of mathematical psychology* (Vol. 3, pp. 323–418). New York: Wiley.

Churchland, P. M. (1988). The ontological status of intentional states: Nailing folk psychology to its perch, *Behavioral & Brain Science, 11,* 507–508.

Churchland, P. S. (1983). Dennett's instrumentalism: A frog at the bottom of the drug. *Behavioral & Brain Science, 6,* 358–359.

Cliff, D., & Noble, J. (1997). Knowledge-based vision and simple visual machines. *Philosophical Transactions of the Royal Society: Biological Science, 352,* 1165–1175.

Cohen, J. D., & Servan-Schreiber, D. (1992). Introduction to neural network models in psychiatry. *Psychiatric Annals, 22,* 113–118.

Combs, A. W., Richards, A. C., & Richards, F. (1976). *Perceptual psychology: A humanistic approach to the study of persons.* New York: Harper & Row.

Coyne, J. A. (2003). Of vice and men: A case study in evolutionary psychology. In C. B. Travis (Ed.), *Evolution, gender, and rape.* Cambridge, MA: MIT Press.

Crick, F. (1994). *The astonishing hypothesis.* New York: Scribner.

Cullmann, O. (1958). *Immortality of the soul or resurrection of the dead?* New York: Macmillan.

d'Aquili, E. G., & Newberg, A. B. (1998). The neuropsychology of religion. In F. Watts (Ed.), *Science meets faith* (pp. 73–91). London: SPCK.

Daniels, M. (1988). The myth of self-actualization. *Journal of Humanistic Psychology, 28*(1), 7–38.

Davids, R. (1912). *Buddhism.* London: The London and Norwich Press.

Dawkins, R. (1976). *The selfish gene.* Oxford: Oxford University Press.

Deacon, B. .J., & Abramowitz, J. S. (2004). Cognitive and behavioral treatments for anxiety disorders: A review of meta analytic findings. *Journal of Clinical Psychology, 60,* 421–441.

Decarvalho, R. J. (1991). *The founders of humanistic psychology.* New York: Praeger.

Dennett, D. C. (1983). Intentional systems in cognitive ethology: The "Panglossian paradigm" defended. *Behavioral and Brain Sciences, 6,* 343–390.

Dennett, D. C. (1984). *Elbow room: The varieties of free will worth wanting.* Cambridge, MA: MIT Press/A Bradford Book.

Dennett, D. C. (1987). *The intentional stance.* Cambridge, MA: MIT Press/A Bradford Book.

Dennett, D. C. (1991). *Consciousness explained.* Toronto: Little, Brown and Company.

Dennett, D. C. (1996). *Kinds of minds.* New York: Basic Books.

Dennett, D. C. (2003). *Freedom evolves.* New York: Viking.

Diamond, J. (1997). *Guns, germs, and steel: The fates of human societies.* New York: Norton.

Dickerson, F. B. (2000). Cognitive behavioral psychotherapy for schizophrenia: A review of recent studies. *Schizophrenia Research, 43,* 71–90.

Dieckmann, U., Doebeli, M., Metz, J. A. J., & Tautz, D. (2004). (Eds.). *Adaptive speciation.* Cambridge: Cambridge University Press.

Dijksterhuis, E. J. (1961). *The mechanization of the world picture* (C. Dikshoorn, Trans.) Oxford: Clarendon Press.

Douglass, B. G., & Moustakas, C. (1985). Heuristic inquiry. The internal search to know. *Journal of Humanistic Psychology, 25*(3), 39–55.

Draaisma, D. (2000). *Metaphors of memory: A history of ideas about the mind* (P. Vincent, Trans.) Cambridge: Cambridge University Press.

Dryden, W., & Ellis, A. (2001). Rational emotive behavior therapy. In K. S. Dobson (Ed.), *Handbook of cognitive-behavioral therapies* (pp. 295–348). New York: Guilford.

Duhl, L. J. (1986). Health and the inner and outer sky. *Journal of Humanistic Psychology, 26*(3), 46–61.

Duncker, K. (1926). A qualitative (experimental and theoretical) study of productive thinking (solving of comprehensible problems). *Pedagogical Seminary, 33,* 642–708.

Durlak, J. (1979). Comparative effectiveness of paraprofessional and professional helpers. *Psychological Bulletin, 86,* 80–92.

Eckartsberg, R. (1986). *Life-world experience: Existential-phenomenological research approaches in psychology.* Cambridge, MA: Harvard University Press.

Edge, L. (2001). The spectrum of dissociation: From pathology to self-realization. *Journal of Transpersonal Psychology, 33,* 53–63.

Elliott, R. (2002). The effectiveness of humanistic therapies: A meta-analysis. In D. J. Cain & J. Seeman (Eds.), *Humanistic psychotherapies: Handbook of research and practice* (pp. 57–81). Washington, DC: American Psychological Association.

Emilsson, E. K. (1999). Neo-Platonism. In D. Furley (Ed.), *From Aristotle to Augustine* (pp. 356–387). New York: Routledge.

Engler, J. (1986). Therapeutic aims in psychotherapy and meditation: Developmental stages in the representation of self. In K. Wilber, J. Engler, & D. Brown, (Eds.), *Transformations of consciousness: Conventional and contemplative perspectives on human development* (pp. 17–51). Boston: Shambhala.

Epstein, M. (1995). *Thoughts without a thinker: Psychotherapy from a Buddhist perspective.* New York: Basic Books.

Ericsson, K. A., & Simon, H. A. (1984). *Protocol analysis: Verbal reports as data.* Cambridge, MA: MIT Press.

Ericsson, K. A., & Simon, H. A. (1993). *Protocol analysis: Verbal reports as data* (Rev. ed.). Cambridge, MA: MIT Press.

Eysenck, H. J. (1952). The effects of psychotherapy: An evaluation. *Journal of Consulting and Clinical Psychology, 60,* 659–663.

Fedoroff, I. C., & Taylor, S. (2001). Psychological and pharmacological treatments of social phobia: A meta analysis. *Journal of Clinical Psychopharmacology, 21,* 311–324.

Fischer, W. F. (1982). An empirical-phenomenological approach to the psychology of anxiety. In A. J. de Koning & F. A. Jenner (Eds.), *Duquesne studies in phenomenological psychology.* (Vol. 2, pp. 82–103). Pittsburgh. PA: Duquesne University Press.

Flew, A. (Ed.). (1979). *A dictionary of philosophy.* Aylesbury: Laurence Urdang Associates.

Fox, M. (2002). *Through the valley of the shadow of death: Religion, spirituality, and the near-death experience.* New York: Routledge.

Frank, K. A. (1999). *Psychoanalytic participation: Action, interaction, and integration.* Hillsdale, NJ: Analytic Press.

Frank, K. A. (2002). The "ins and outs" of enactment: A relational bridge for psychotherapy integration. *Journal of Psychotherapy Integration, 12,* 267–286.

Frankl, V. E. (1968). *Man's search for meaning: An introduction to logotherapy.* London: Hodder and Stoughton.

Franks, C. (Ed.) (1969). *Behavioral therapy: Appraisal and status.* New York: McGraw-Hill.

Freud, S. (1901/1914). *Psychopathology of everyday life.* (A. A. Brill, Trans.) London: Fisher Unwin.

Freud, S. (1910/1957). The future prospects of psycho-analytic theory. In J. Strachey (Ed. & Trans.) *The standard edition of the complete psychological works of Sigmund Freud* (Vol. 11, pp. 139–152). London: Hogarth. (Original work published in 1910.)

Freud, S. (1961). *The complete psychological works of Sigmund Freud. Vol. 21: 1927–1931.* (J. Strachey, A. Freud, A. Strachey, & Tyson, A., Trans.) London: Hogarth Press.

Frick, W. B. (1993). Subpersonalities: Who conducts the orchestra? *Journal of Humanistic Psychology, 33*(2), 122–128.

Fromm, E. *Escape from freedom.* New York: Avon Books.

Gallop, D. (1999). Aristotle: Aesthetics and philosophy of mind. In D. Furley (Ed.), *From Aristotle to Augustine* (pp. 76–108). New York: Routledge.

Gardner, H. (2001). The philosophy-science continuum. *The Chronicle of Higher Education (Section 2: The Chronicle Review), 47,* B7–B10.

Garson, J. W. (1995). Chaos and free will. *Philosophical Psychology, 8*, 365–373.

Gazzaniga, M. S. (2002). The split brain revisited. *Scientific American, 12*(1), 26–31.

Gazzaniga, M. S., Borgen, J. E., & Sperry, R. W. (1965). Observations on visual perception after disconnexion of the cerebral hemispheres in man. *Brain, 88*(Part 2), 221–236.

Geller, L. (1982). The failure of self-actualization theory: A critique of Carl Rogers and Abraham Maslow. *Journal of Humanistic Psychology, 22*(2), 56–73.

Geller, L. (1984). Another look at self-actualization. *Journal of Humanistic Psychology, 24*(2), 93–106.

Giorgi, A. (2005). Remaining challenges for humanistic psychology. *Journal of Humanistic Psychology, 45*, 204–216.

Glaser, B. (1992). *Emergence vs. forcing: Basics of grounded theory analysis.* Mill Valley, CA: Sociology Press.

Goodman, F. D. (1986). Body posture and the religious altered state of consciousness. *Journal of Humanistic Psychology, 26* (3), 81–118.

Gould, S. J. (1987). Darwinism defined: The difference between fact and theory. *Discover, 8*(1), 64–70.

Gould, S. J. (1977). *Ever since Darwin: Reflections in natural history.* New York: W. W. Norton.

Grayling, A. C. (2003). *What is good?: The search for the best way to live.* London: Weidenfeld & Nicolson.

Greenberg, J. R. & Mitchell, S. (1983). *Object relations in psychoanalytic theory.* Cambridge, MA: Harvard University Press.

Greening, T. (1985). The origins of the *Journal of Humanistic Psychology* and the Association for Humanistic Psychology. *Journal of Humanistic Psychology, 25* (2), 7–11.

Greenspoon, J. (1955). The reinforcing effect of two spoken words on the frequency of two responses. *American Journal of Psychology, 68*, 409–416.

Grosskurth, P. (1991). *The secret ring: Freud's inner circle and the politics of psychoanalysis.* Reading, MA: Addison-Wesley.

Grosskurth, P. (1998). Psychoanalysis: A dysfunctional family? *Journal of Analytical Psychology, 43*, 87–95.

Groth-Marnat, G. (1998). Altered beliefs, attitudes, and behaviors following near-death experiences. *Journal of Humanistic Psychology, 38*(3), 110–125.

Groth-Marnat, G., & Schumaker, J. F. (1989). The near-death experience: A review and critique. *Journal of Humanistic Psychology, 29*(1), 109–133.

Grunow, A., & Neuringer, A. (2002). Learning to vary and varying to learn. *Psychonomic Bulletin and Review, 9*, 250–258.

Grush, R. (1997). The architecture of representation. *Philosophical Psychology, 10*, 5–25.

Guthrie, E. R., & Horton, G. P. *Cats in a puzzle box.* New York: Rinehart.

Hamilton, V. (1979). An information processing approach to neurotic anxieties and schizophrenias. In V. Hamilton & D. M. Warburton (Eds.), *Human stress and cognition: An information processing approach* (pp. 383–430). Chichester, England: Wiley.

Hamilton, V. (1980). An information processing analysis of environmental stress and life crises.. In I. G. Sarason & C. D. Spielberger (Eds.), *Stress and anxiety* (Vol. 7, pp. 13–30). Washington, DC: Hemisphere.

Hare, R. M. (1981). *Moral thinking: Its levels, method, and point.* Oxford: Clarendon.

Harnad, S. (1990). The symbol grounding problem. *Physica D, 42*, 335–346.

Harpur, T. (2004). The pagan Christ: Recovering the lost light. Toronto: Thomas Allen Publishers.

Haselager, P., de Groot, A., & van Rappard, H. (2003). Representation vs. anti-representation: A debate for the sake of appearance. *Philosophical Psychology, 16*, 5–23.

Hattie, J., Sharpley, C., & Rogers, H. (1984). Comparative effectiveness of professional and paraprofessional helpers. *Psychological Bulletin, 95*, 534–541.

Hayes, S. C. (2002). Buddhism and commitment therapy. *Cognitive and Behavioral Practice, 9*, 58–66.

Hayes, S. C., Barnes-Holmes, D., & Roche, B. (Eds.). (2001). *Relational frame theory: A post-Skinnerian account of human language and cognition.* New York: Plenum.

Hayes, S. C., Strosahl, K. D., & Wilson, K. G. (1999). *Acceptance and commitment therapy: An experimental approach to behavior change.* New York: Guilford.

Hearst, E. (1999). After the puzzle boxes: Thorndike in the 20th century. *Journal of the Experimental Analysis of Behavior, 72*, 441–446.

Held, B. S. (2004). The negative side of positive psychology. *Journal of Humanistic Psychology, 44*, 9–46.

Hillner, K. P. (1984). *History and systems of modern psychology: A conceptual approach.* New York: Gardner.

Hodgson, D. (1991). *The mind matters: Consciousness and choice in a quantum world.* Oxford: Clarendon Press.

Holmes, B. (1998). Irresistible illusions. *New Scientist, 159* (2150), 32–37.

Horne, M. (2002). Aristotle's ontogenesis: A theory of individuation which integrates the classical and developmental perspectives. *Journal of Analytical Psychology, 47*, 613–628.

Horne, M., Sowa, A., & Isenman, D. (2000). Philosophical assumptions in Freud, Jung and Bion: Questions of causality. *Journal of Analytical Psychology, 45*, 109–121.

Hume, D. (1978). *A treatise of human nature* (L. A. Selby-Bigge, Ed.). Oxford: Clarendon.

Hunt, H., Dougan, S., Grant, K., & House, M. (2002). Growth enhancing versus dissociative states of consciousness: A questionnaire study. *Journal of Humanistic Psychology, 42*(1), 90–106.

Husserl, E. (1970). *The crisis of European sciences and transcendental phenomenology.* Evanston, IL: Northwestern University Press.

Hutcheon, P. D. (1997). Was the Buddha the first humanist? *Humanist in Canada, 30*(2), 20–23.

Ikemi, A., & Kubota, S. (1996). Humanistic psychology in Japanese corporations: Listening and the small steps of change. *Journal of Humanistic Psychology, 36*(1), 104–121.

Ingram, R. E., & Hollon, S. D. (1986). Cognitive theory of depression from an information processing perspective. In R. E. Ingram (Ed.), *Information processing approaches to clinical psychology* (pp. 261–284). Orlando, FL: Academic Press.

Ingram, R. E., & Kendall, P. C. (1986). Cognitive clinical psychology: Implications of an information processing perspective. In R. E. Ingram (Ed.), *Information processing approaches to clinical psychology* (pp. 3–21). London: Academic Press.

Jääskeläinen, M. (2000). A comparative study of Adler and Buber: From contact to cooperation. *Journal of Individual Psychology, 56*, 141–154.

James, W. (2003/1902). The varieties of religious experience: A study in human nature. New York: Penguin Putnam.

Jansen, K. L. R. (2004). The ketamine model of the near-death experience: A central role for the *N*-methyl-D-aspartate receptor. *Journal of Near-Death Studies, 16*, 5–26.

Jonçich, G. (1968). *The sane positivist: A biography of Edward L. Thorndike.* Middletown, CT: Wesleyan University Press.

Jones, M. C. (1924). A laboratory study of fear: The case of Peter. *Pedagogical Seminary, 31*, 308–315.

Jones, S. L. (1994). A constructive relationship for religion with the science and profession of psychology. *American Psychologist, 49*, 184–199.

Jung, C. G. (1916/1969). The transcendent function. In H. Read, M. Fordham, & G. Adler (Eds.), R. C. F. Hull (Trans.), *Collected Works, Vol. 8* (2nd ed.; pars. 131–193). Princeton, NJ: University of Princeton Press.

Jung, C. G. (1955/1969/1983). Mandalas. In H. Read, M. Fordham, & G. Adler (Eds.), R. C. F. Hull (Trans.), *Collected Works, Vol. 8* (2nd ed.; pars. 713–718). Princeton, NJ: University of Princeton Press. Reprinted in A. Storr (Ed.), *The essential Jung* (pp. 235–238). Princeton, NJ: Princeton University Press.

Jung, C. G. (1961). *Memories, dreams, reflections.* (R. Winston & C. Winston, Trans.) New York: Random House.

Kahn, E. (1999). A critique of nondirectivity in the person-centered approach. *Journal of Humanistic Psychology, 39*(4), 94–110.

Kahn, E. (2002). A way to help people by holding theory lightly: A response to Bozarth, Merry and Brodley, and Sommerbeck. *Journal of Humanistic Psychology, 42*(2), 88–96.

Kantor, J. R. (1942). Preface to interbehavioral psychology. *Psychological Record, 5*, 173–193.

Kantor, J. R. (1970). An analysis of the experimental analysis of behavior (TEAB). *Journal of the Experimental Analysis of Behavior, 13*, 101–108.

Kawai, M. (1962). On the newly acquired behavior of the natural troop of Japanese monkeys on Koshima Island. *Primates, 5*, 3–4.

Kawai, M. (1965). Newly acquired pre-cultural behavior of the natural troop of Japanese monkeys on Koshima Islet. *Primates, 6*, 1–31.

Kawamura, M. (1963). The process of sub-cultural propagation among Japanese monkeys. In C. H. Southwick (Ed.), *Primate social behavior* (pp. 82–99). Princeton, NJ: Van Nostrand Reinhold.

Kazdin, A. E. (1977). *The token economy.* New York: Plenum Press.

Keijzer, F. (2001). *Representation and behavior.* Cambridge, MA: MIT Press.

Kellehear, A. (1996). *Experiences near death: Beyond medicine and religion.* Oxford: Oxford University Press.

Kernberg, O. F. (2006). The pressing need to increase research in and on psychoanalysis. *International Journal of Psychoanalysis, 87*, 919–926.

Khaleel, K. (2003). *Science in the name of God: How men of God originated the sciences.* Buffalo Grove, IL: Knowledge House.

Killeen, P. R. (2001). Modeling games from the 20th century. *Behavioural Processes, 54*, 33–52.

Kilmartin, C., & Dervin, D. (1997). Inaccurate representation of the Electra Complex in psychology textbooks. *Teaching of Psychology, 24*, 269–270.

Kim, J. (1996). *Philosophy of mind*. Boulder, CO: Westview Press.

Kleinmuntz, B. (1969). *Clinical information processing by computer: An essay and selected readings*. New York: Holt, Rinehart & Winston.

Kline, P. (1987). The experimental study of the psychoanalytic unconscious. *Personality and Social Psychology Bulletin, 13*, 363–378.

Kluft, R. P. (1986). High functioning multiple personality patients. *Journal of Nervous and Mental Disease, 174*, 722–726.

Kohut, H. (1984). *How does analysis cure?* (A. Goldberg & P. Stepansky, Eds.). Chicago: University of Chicago Press.

Kohut, H. (1985). *Self psychology and the humanities: Reflections on a new psychoanalytic approach*. (C. B. Strozier, Ed.). New York: Norton.

Kozielecki, J. (1983). *Dzialania transgracyjne: Przekroczenie granic samego siebie. Przeglad Psychologiczny, 3*, 505–517.

Krebs, J. R., & Dawkins, R. (1984). Animal signals: Mind reading and manipulation. In J. R. Krebs & N. B. Davies (Eds.), *Behavioural ecology* (pp. 380–402). Oxford: Blackwell.

Krippner, S. (Ed.). (1972). The plateau experience: A. H. Maslow and others. *Journal of Transpersonal Psychology, 4*, 107–120.

Krstiç, K. (1964). Marko Maruliç—the author of the term "psychology." *Acta Instituti Psychologici Universitatis Zagrabiensis, 35–48*, 7–13.

Kuhn, T. S. (1962). *The structure of scientific revolutions*. Chicago: University of Chicago Press.

Kurtz, P. (1983). *In defense of secular humanism*. Buffalo, N.Y.: Prometheus Books.

Lambert, M. J., & Bergin, A. E. (1994). The effectiveness of psychotherapy. In A. E. Bergin & S. L. Garfield (Eds.), *Handbook of psychotherapy and behavior change* (4th ed., pp. 143–189). New York: Wiley.

Larson, C. A., & Sullivan, J. J. (1965). Watson's relation to Titchener. *Journal of the History of the Behavioral Sciences, 1*, 338–354.

Laudan, L. (1981). *Science and hypothesis: Historical essays on scientific methodology*. Boston: D. Reidel.

Lazarus, R. S., & McCleary, R. A. (1951). Autonomic discrimination without awareness: A study in subception. *Psychological Review, 58*, 113–122.

Leslie, J. C. (2006). Herbert Spencer's contributions to behavior analysis: A retrospective review of *Principles of Psychology. Journal of the Experimental Analysis of Behavior, 86*, 123–129.

Levitt, H. M. (1999). The development of wisdom: An analysis of Tibetan Buddhist experience. *Journal of Humanistic Psychology, 39*(2), 86–105.

Libet, B., Curtis, A. G., Wright, E. W., & Pearl, D. K. (1983). Time of conscious intention to act in relation to onset of cerebral activity (readiness potential). The unconscious initiation of a freely voluntary act. *Brain, 106*, 640.

Linley, P. A., Joseph, S., Harrington, S., & Wood, A. M. (2006). Positive psychology: Past, present, and (possible) future. *The Journal of Positive Psychology, 1*, 3–16.

Looren de Jong, H. (2002). Levels of explanation in biological psychology. *Philosophical Psychology, 15*, 441–462.

Lowry, R. (1973). *A. H. Maslow: An intellectual portrait*. Monterey, CA: Brooks/Cole.

Luborsky, L., Diguer, L., Seligman, D. A., Rosenthal, R., Krause, E. D., Johnson, S., Halperin, G., Bishop, M., Berman, J. S., & Schweizer, E. (1999). The researcher's own therapy allegiance: A "wild card" in comparisons of treatment efficacy. *Clinical Psychology: Science and Practice, 6*, 95–106.

Luborsky, L, Rosenthal, R., Diguer, L, Andrusyna, T. P., Berman, J. S., Levitt, J. T., & Seligman, D. A. (2002). The Dodo bird verdict is alive and well—mostly. *Clinical Psychology: Science and Practice, 9*, 2–12.

Luborsky, L., Singer, B., & Luborsky, E. (1975). Comparative studies of psychotherapies: Is it true that "Everybody has won and all must have prizes"? *Archives of General Psychiatry, 32*, 995–1008.

Lucas, J. R. (1961). Minds, machines and Gödel. *Philosophy, 36*, 112–127.

Luria, A. R. (1961*). The role of speech in the regulation of normal and abnormal behavior*. New York: Liveright.

Lynn, D. J., & Vaillant, G. E. (1998). Anonymity, neutrality, and confidentiality in the actual methods of Sigmund Freud: A review of 43 cases, 1907–1939. *American Journal of Psychiatry, 155*, 163–171.

MacCorquodale, K. (1970). On Chomsky's review of Skinner's *Verbal Behavior. Journal of the Experimental Analysis of Behavior, 13*, 82–89.

Maguire, E. A., Gadian, D. G., Johnsrude, I. S., Good, C. D., Ashburner, J., Frackowiak, R. S. J., & Frith, C. D. (2000). Navigation-related structural change in the hippocampi of taxi drivers. *Proceedings of the National Academy of Sciences, 97*, 4398–4403.

Mahoney, M. J. (1974). *Cognition and behavior modification*. Cambridge, MA: Ballinger.

Maisels, C. K. (2001). *Early civilizations of the Old World: The formative histories of Egypt, the Levant, Mesopotamia, India, and China*. London: Routledge.

Makarec, K., & Persinger, M. A. (1985). Temporal lobe signs: Electroencephalographic validity and enhanced scores in special populations. *Perceptual and Motor Skills, 60*, 831–842.

Marcus, D. K., & Buffington-Vollum, J. K. (2005). Countertransference: A social relations perspective. *Journal of Psychotherapy Integration, 15*, 254–283.

Marcus, G. F. (2001). *The algebraic mind*. Cambridge, MA: MIT Press.

Marlatt, G. A. (1994). Addiction, mindfulness, and acceptance. In S. C. Hayes, N. S. Jacobson, V, M. Follette, & M. J. Dougher (Eds.), *Acceptance and change: Content and context in psychotherapy* (pp. 175–197). Reno, NV: Context Press.

Marlatt, G. A. (2002). Buddhist philosophy and the treatment of addictive behavior. *Cognitive and Behavioral Practice, 9*, 44–50.

Martin, G., & Pear, J. (2007). *Behavior modification: What it is and how to do it* (8th ed.). Upper Saddle River, NJ: Pearson Prentice Hall.

Maslow, A. (1968). *Toward a psychology of being* (2nd ed.). New York. Van Nostrand Reinhold.

Maslow, A. H. (1970). *Motivation and personality*. (2nd ed.). New York: Harper & Row.

Maslow, A. H. (1971). *The farther reaches of human nature*. New York: Viking Press.

May, R. (1982). The problem of evil: An open letter to Carl Rogers. *Journal of Humanistic Psychology, 22*(3), 10–21.

May, R. (1989). Answers to Ken Wilber and John Rowan. *Journal of Humanistic Psychology, 29*, 244–248.

McDannell, C., & Lang, B. (1988). *Heaven: A history*. New Haven: Yale University Press.

McDougall, I., Brown, F. H., & Fleagle, J. G. (2005). Stratigraphic placement and age of modern humans from Kibish, Ethiopia. *Nature, 433*, 733–736.

McEvilley, T. (2002). *The shape of ancient thought: Comparative studies in Greek and Indian philosophies*. New York: Allworth Press.

McGinnies, E. (1949). Emotionality and perceptual defense. *Psychological Review, 56*, 244–251.

McNeill, D. (1971). Sentences as biological systems. In P. A. Weiss (Ed.), *Hierarchically organized systems in theory and practice* (pp. 59–68). New York: Hafner.

McWilliams, N. (1999). *Psychoanalytic case formulation*. New York: Guilford Press.

Mehlman, B. (1967). Animal research and human psychology. *Journal of Humanistic Psychology, 7*(1), 66–79.

Meichenbaum, D. H. (1969). The effects of instructions and reinforcement on thinking and language behaviours of schizophrenics. *Behaviour Research and Therapy, 7*, 101–104.

Meichenbaum, D. H. (1973). Cognitive factors in behavior modification: Modifying what clients say to themselves. In C. M. Franks & G. T. Wilson (Eds.), *Annual review of behavior therapy: Theory and practice* (pp. 416–432). New York: Brunner/Mazel.

Meichenbaum, D. H. (1977). *Cognitive-behavior modification*. New York: Plenum.

Meichenbaum, D. H. (1993). A constructivist narrative perspective on stress and coping: Stress inoculation applications. In L. Goldberger & S. Breznitz (Eds.), *Handbook of stress* (2nd Ed., pp. 706–723). New York: The Free Press.

Menand, L. (2001). *The metaphysical club: A story of ideas in America*. New York: Farrar, Straus, and Giroux.

Merry, T., & Brodley, B. T. (2002). The nondirective attitude in client-centered therapy: A response to Kahn. *Journal of Humanistic Psychology, 42*(2), 66–77.

Miles, S. H. (2004). *The Hippocratic Oath and the ethics of medicine*. Oxford: Oxford University Press.

Miller, N., & Neuringer, A. (2000). Reinforcing variability in adolescents with autism. *Journal of Applied Behavior Analysis, 33*, 151–165.

Miller, R. B. (1992). Introduction: Philosophical problems of the psychoanalytic approach. In R. B. Miller (Ed.), *The restoration of dialogue: Readings in the philosophy of clinical psychology* (pp. 343–346). Washington, DC: American Psychological Association.

Moody, R. (1975). *Life after life*. Covington, GA: Mockingbird.

Morokoff, P. J. (1985). Effects of sex guilt, repression, sexual "arousability," and sexual experience on female sexual arousal during erotica and fantasy. *Journal of Personality and Social Psychology, 49*, 177–187.

Moustakas, C. (1961). *Loneliness*. Englewood Cliffs, NJ: Prentice-Hall.

Moustakas, C. (1975). *The touch of loneliness*. Englewood Cliffs, NJ: Prentice-Hall.

Moustakas, C. (1985). Humanistic or humanism? *Journal of Humanistic Psychology, 25* (3), 5–12.

Murphy, J. W., & Pardeck, J. T. (1988). Technology and language use: Computer mediated therapy. *Journal of Humanistic Psychology, 28*(1), 120–134.

Murphy, N. (1998). Human nature: Historical, scientific, and religious issues. In W. S. Brown, N. Murphy, & H. N. Malony (Eds.). *Whatever happened to the soul?*

Scientific and theological portraits of human nature (pp. 1–29). Minneapolis: Fortress Press.

Murray, D. (1988). Psychology in Canada one hundred years ago: James Mark Baldwin at the University of Toronto. *Canadian Psychology, 33,* 683–694.

Nagel, E. (1961). *The structure of science.* London: Routledge.

Nagel, T. (1974). What is it like to be a bat? *Philosophical Review, 83,* 435–450.

Neher, A. (1996). Jung's theory of archetypes: A critique. *Journal of Humanistic Psychology, 36,* 61–91.

Neisser, U. (1967). *Cognitive psychology.* New York: Appleton-Century-Crofts.

Nelson, K. R., Mattingly, M., Lee, S. A., & Schmitt, F. A. (2006). Does the arousal system contribute to near death experience? *Neurology, 66,* 1003–1009.

Neufeld, R. W. J., & Mothersill, K. J. (1980). Stress as an irritant of psychopathology. In I. G. Sarason & C. D. Spielberger (Eds.), *Stress and anxiety.* (Vol. 7, pp. 31–56). Washington, DC: Hemisphere.

Neuringer, A. (1992). Choosing to vary and repeat. *Psychological Science, 3,* 246–250.

Neuringer, A., Deiss, C., & Olson, G. (2000). Reinforced variability and operant learning. *Journal of Experimental Psychology: Animal Behavior Processes, 26,* 98–111.

New York State Department of Health Early Intervention Program (1999). *Clinical practice guidelines: Report of the recommendations, autism/pervasive developmental disorders, assessment and intervention for young children.* Publication #4215. Health Education Services, P.O. Box 7126, Albany, NY 12224.

Newberg, A., d'Aquili, E., & Rause, V. (2001). *Why God won't go away: Brain science and the biology of belief.* New York: Ballantine Books.

Newell, A., & Simon, H. A. (1956). The Logic Theory Machine: A complex information processing system. *IRE Transactions on Information Theory* IT–2(3), 61–79.

Newell, A., & Simon, H. A. (1963). General Problem Solver, a program that simulates human thought. In E. A. Feigenbaum & J. Feldman (Eds.), *Computers and thought* (pp. 279–293). New York: McGraw Hill.

Newell, A., & Simon, H. A. (1972). *Human problem solving.* Englewood Cliffs, NJ: Prentice-Hall.

Noll, R. (1994). *The Jung cult: Origins of a charismatic movement.* Princeton, NJ: Princeton University Press.

Norcross, J. C. (1987). A rational and empirical analysis of existential psychotherapy. *Journal of Humanistic Psychology, 27*(1), 41–68.

Norem, J. K. (2001). Defensive pessimism, optimism, and pessimism. In E. C. Chang (Ed.), *Optimism and pessimism: Implications for theory, research, and practice* (pp. 77–100). Washington, DC: American Psychological Association.

Norem, J. K., & Chang, E. C. (2002). The positive power of negative thinking. *Journal of Clinical Psychology, 58,* 993–1001.

Nuttin, J. (1953). *Psychoanalysis and personality: A dynamic theory of normal personality.* New York: Sheed and Ward.

O'Daly, G. (1999). Augustine. In D. Furley (Ed.), *From Aristotle to Augustine* (pp. 388–428). New York: Routledge.

O'Hara, M. (1985). Of myths and monkeys: A critical look at a theory of critical mass. *Journal of Humanistic Psychology, 25* (1), 61–78.

O'Regan, J. K., & Noë, A. (2001). A sensorimotor account of vision and visual consciousness. *Behavioral and Brain Sciences, 24,* 939–1031.

Observer. (1984). *Psychological comments and queries*. Chicago: The Principia Press.

Osborne, J. (1987). A human science study of learning about "learning." *Journal of Humanistic Psychology, 27*(4), 485–500.

Packer, M. J. (1985). Hermeneutic inquiry in the study of human conduct. *American Psychologist, 40*, 1081–1093.

Page, S., & Neuringer, A. (1985). Variability as an operant. *Journal of Experimental Psychology: Animal Behavior Processes, 11*, 429–452.

Palmer, R. (1969). *Hermeneutics*. Evanston, IL: Northwestern University Press.

Palmer, S. E. (1990). Modern theories of Gestalt perception. *Language and Mind, 5*, 289–323.

Parfit, D. (1984). *Reasons and persons*. New York: Oxford University Press.

Paris, J. (2005). *The fall of an icon: Psychoanalysis and academic psychiatry*. Toronto: University of Toronto Press.

Penfield, W. (1958). *The excitable cortex in conscious man*. Springfield, IL.: Charles C. Thomas.

Penrose, R. (1989). *The emperor's new mind: Concerning computers, minds, and the laws of physics*. New York: Oxford University Press.

Penrose, R. (1994). *Shadows of the mind: A search for the missing science of consciousness*. New York: Oxford University Press.

Penrose, R. (1997). *The large, the small and the human mind*. Cambridge, England: Cambridge University Press.

Penrose, R. (2002). Consciousness, computation, and the Chinese room. In J. Preston & M. Bishop (Eds.), *Views into the Chinese room: New essays on Searle and artificial intelligence* (pp. 226–249). Oxford: Clarendon.

Perron, R. (2006). How to do research: Reply to Otto Kernberg. *International Journal of Psychoanalysis, 87*, 927–932.

Perry, J. (Ed.). (1975). *Personal identity*. Berkeley: University of California Press.

Persinger, M. A. (1983). Religious and mystical experiences as artifacts of temporal lobe function: A general hypothesis. *Perceptual and Motor Skills, 57*, 1255–1262.

Persinger, M. A. (1987). *Neuropsychological bases of God beliefs*. Westport, CT: Praeger Publishers.

Persinger, M. A. (1993). Vectorial cerebral hemisphericity as differential sources for the sensed presence: Mystical experiences and religious conversions. *Perceptual and Motor Skills, 76*, 915–930.

Persinger, M. A. (1994). Near death experiences: Determining the neuroanatomical pathways by experiential patterns and simulation in experimental settings. In L. Bessette (Ed.), *Healing: Beyond suffering or death* (pp. 277–285). Beauport, Quebec: Publications MNH.

Persinger, M. A. (1999). *Neuropsychological bases of God beliefs*. New York: Praeger.

Persinger, M. A., & Makarec, K. (1987). Temporal lobe epileptic signs and correlative behaviors displayed by normal populations. *Journal of General Psychology, 114*, 179–195.

Persinger, M. A., Bureau, Y. R. J., Peredery, O. P., & Richards, P. M. (1994). The sensed presence as right hemispheric intrusions into the left hemispheric awareness of self: An illustrative case study. *Perceptual and Motor Skills, 78*, 999–1009.

Pinker, S. (1997). *How the mind works*. New York: W. W. Norton & Company.

Polkinghorne, D. (1982). What makes research humanistic? *Journal of Humanistic Psychology*, 22 (3), 47–54.

Polkinghorne, D. (1990). Psychology after philosophy. In J. Faulconer & R. Williams (Eds.), *Reconsidering psychology: Perspectives from continental philosophy* (pp. 92–115). Pittsburgh, PA: DuQuesne University Press.

Polkinghorne, D. (2003). Franz Brentano's *Psychology from an empirical standpoint*. In R. J. Sternberg (Ed.), *The anatomy of impact: What makes the great works of psychology great* (pp. 43–70). Washington, DC: American Psychological Association.

Poortman, B. (1994). Death and immortality in Greek philosophy: From the Presocratics to the Hellenistic era. In J. M. Bremer, Th. P.J. Van Den Hout, R. Peters (Eds.), *Hidden futures: Death and immortality in Ancient Egypt, Anatolia, the Classical, Biblical, and Arabic-Islamic world* (pp. 197–220). Amsterdam: Amsterdam University Press.

Popper, K. R. (1959). *The logic of scientific discovery*. London: Hutchinson.

Popper, K. R. (1962). *Conjectures and Refutations: The Growth of Scientific Knowledge* New York: Basic Books.

Porter, T. M. (1986). *The rise of statistical thinking: 1820–1900*. Princeton: Princeton University Press.

Portnoy, D. (1999). Relatedness: Where humanistic and psychoanalytic psychotherapy converge. *Journal of Humanistic Psychology*, 39(1), 19–34.

Povinelli, D. J., Nelson, K. E., & Boysen, S. T. (1990). Inferences about guessing and knowing by chimpanzees. *Journal of Comparative Psychology*, 104, 203–210.

Preston, J. (2002). Introduction. In J. Preston & M. Bishop (Eds.), *Views into the Chinese room: New essays on Searle and artificial intelligence* (pp. 1–50). Oxford: Clarendon.

Premack, D., & Woodruff, G. (1978). Does the chimpanzee have a theory of mind. *Behavioral and Brain Sciences*, 4, 515–526.

Pryor, K. W., Haag, R., & O'Reilly, J. (1969). The creative porpoise: Training for novel behavior. *Journal of the Experimental Analysis of Behavior*, 12, 653–661.

Putnam, H. (1988). *Representation and reality*. Cambridge, MA: MIT Press.

Rachels, J. (1993). *The elements of moral philosophy* (Second Edition). New York: McGraw-Hill.

Rachlin, H. (1988). Mental yes; private no. In A. C. Catania & S. Harnad (Eds.), *The selection of behavior: The operant behaviorism of B. F. Skinner* (pp. 200–202). New York: Cambridge University Press.

Rachlin, H. (1992). Teleological behaviorism. *American Psychologist*, 47, 1371–1382.

Rachlin, H. (2000). *The science of self-control*. Cambridge, MA: Harvard University Press.

Rachman, S. (1971). *The effects of psychotherapy*. New York: Pergamon Press.

Ramachandran, V. S., & Blakeslee, S. (1998). *Phantoms in the brain: Probing the mysteries of the human mind*. New York: Quill.

Reisman, J. M. (1966). *The development of clinical psychology*. New York: Appleton-Century-Crofts.

Richards, D. G. (1990). Dissociation and transformation. *Journal of Humanistic Psychology*, 30(3), 54–83.

Ring, K. (1980). *Life at death: A scientific investigation of the near-death experience*. New York: Coward, McCann, and Geoghegan.

Ring, K., & Cooper, S. (1999). *Mindsight: Near-death and out-of-body experiences in the blind*. Palo Alto, CA: William James Center for Consciousness Studies.

Rogers, C. R. (1951). *Client-centered therapy: Its current practice, implications, and theory*. Boston: Houghton-Mifflin.

Rogers, C. R. (1959). A theory of therapy, personality, and interpersonal relationships, as developed in the client-centered framework. In S. Koch (Ed.), *Psychology: A study of a science. Vol. 3. Formulations of the person and the social context* (pp. 184–256). New York: McGraw-Hill.

Rogers, C. R. (1961). *On becoming a person: A therapist's view of psychotherapy*. Boston: Houghton Mifflin.

Rogers, C. R. (1964). Toward a science of the person. In T. W. Wann (Ed.), *Behaviorism and phenomenology: Contrasting bases for modern psychology* (pp. 109–132). Chicago: University of Chicago Press.

Rogers, C. R. (1969). *Freedom to learn: A view of what education might become*. Columbus, Ohio: Merrill.

Rogers, C. R. (1980). *A way of being*. Boston: Houghton Mifflin.

Rogers, C. R. (1982). Reply to Rollo May's letter. *Journal of Humanistic Psychology, 22*(4), 85–89.

Rogers, C. R. (1987). Comments on the issue of equality in psychotherapy. *Journal of Humanistic Psychology, 27*, 38–40.

Rogers, C. R., & Dymond, R. F. (Eds.) (1954). *Psychotherapy and personality change*. Chicago: University of Chicago Press.

Rogers, C. R., & Skinner, B. F. (1956). Some issues concerning the control of human behavior: A symposium. *Science, 124*, 1057–1066.

Rorty, A. O. (1976). *The identities of persons*. Berkeley: University of California Press.

Rosenbloom, P. S., Laird, J. E., & Newell, A. (Eds.). (1993). *The Soar papers: Research on integrated intelligence*. Cambridge, MA: MIT Press.

Rosenzweig, S. (1936). Some implicit common factors in diverse methods of psychotherapy. *American Journal of Orthopsychiatry, 6*, 412–415.

Rotter, J. B. (1954). *Social learning and clinical psychology*. Englewood Cliffs, NJ: Prentice-Hall.

Roughgarden, J. (2004). *Evolution's rainbow: Diversity, gender, and sexuality in nature and people*. Berkeley: University of California Press.

Rubin, J. B. (1993). Psychoanalysis and Buddhism: Toward an integration. In G. Stricker & J. Gold (Eds.), *Comprehensive textbook of psychotherapy integration* (pp. 249–266). New York: Plenum.

Rubin, J. B. (1996). *Psychoanalysis and Buddhism: Toward an integration*. New York: Plenum.

Russell, B. (1946). *A history of Western philosophy*. London: Unwin Hyman Ltd.

Russell, B. (1954). *Human society in ethics and politics*. London: Allen and Unwin.

Rychlak, J. F. (2003). *The human image in postmodern America*. Washington, DC: American Psychological Association.

Ryle, G. (1949/1990). *The concept of mind*. New York: Penguin Books.

Safran, J. D. (2002). Relational theory, constructivism, and psychotherapy integration: Commentary on Frank (2002). *Journal of Psychotherapy Integration, 12*, 294–301.

Sanders, J. (1989). Happy birthday JTP! *Journal of Humanistic Psychology, 29*, 400–405.

Sartre, J.-P. (1948). *Existentialism and humanism*. (P. Mairet, Trans.) London: Methuen.

Schneider, K. J. (1989). Infallibility is so damn appealing: A reply to Ken Wilber. *Journal of Humanistic Psychology, 29*, 470–481.

Schwartz, R. (2006). *Visual versions*. Cambridge, MA: MIT Press.

Searle J. R. (1983). *Intentionality: An essay in the philosophy of mind*. Cambridge: Cambridge University Press.

Searle, J. R. (1980). Minds, brains, and programs. *Behavioral and Brain Sciences, 3*, 417–424.

Searle, J. R. (1992). *The rediscovery of the mind*. Boston: MIT Press.

Searle J. R. (2004). *Mind: A brief introduction*. Oxford: Oxford University Press.

Segal, Z. V., Williams, J. M. G., & Teasdale, J. D. (2002). *Mindfulness-based cognitive therapy for depression*. Guilford Press: New York.

Seligman, M. E. P. (2002). *Authentic happiness: Using the new positive psychology to realize your potential for lasting fulfillment*. New York: Free Press.

Seligman, M. E. P., & Csikszentmihalyi, M. (2000). Positive psychology: An introduction. *American Psychologist, 55*, 5–14.

Shannon, C. E. (1938). A symbolic analysis of relay and switching circuits. *Transactions of the American Institute of Electrical Engineers, 57*, 1–11.

Shantall, T. (1999). The experience of meaning in suffering among holocaust survivors. *Journal of Humanistic Psychology, 39*(3), 96–124.

Sheldon, K. M., & Kasser, T. (2001). Goals, congruence, and positive well-being: New empirical support for humanistic theories. *Journal of Humanistic Psychology, 41*(1), 30–50.

Sheldon, K. M., & King, L. (2001). Why positive psychology is necessary. *American Psychologist, 56*, 216–217.

Shorter, E. (1997). *A history of psychiatry: From the era of the asylum to the age of Prozac*. New York: Wiley.

Sidman, M. (1960). *Tactics of scientific research: Evaluating experimental data in psychology*. New York: Basic Books.

Siegel, G. J. (1997). Why I make models (or what I learned in graduate school about validating clinical causal theories with computational models). *The Behavior Therapist, 20*, 179–184.

Siegel, G. J. (1999). A neural network model of attention biases in depression. In J. Reggia & E. Ruppin (Eds.), *Neural network models of brain and cognitive disorders* (Vol. 2, pp. 415–441). Amsterdam: Elsevier.

Simon, H. A. (1981). *The sciences of the artificial*. Cambridge, MA: MIT Press.

Simon, H. A. (1991). *Models of my life*. New York: Basic Books.

Simons, D. J., & Ambinder, M. S. (2005). Change blindness: Theory and consequences. *Current Directions in Psychological Science, 11*, 44–48.

Simons, D. J., & Levin, D. T. (1998). Failure to detect changes in people in real-world interaction. *Psychonomic Bulletin & Review, 5*, 644–649.

Skinner, B. F. (1945). The operational analysis of psychological terms. *Psychological Review, 42*, 270–277.

Skinner, B. F. (1948). *Walden Two*. New York: Macmillan.

Skinner, B. F. (1950). Are theories of learning necessary? *Psychological Review, 57*, 193–216.

Skinner, B. F. (1953). *Science and human behavior*. New York: Macmillan.

Skinner, B. F. (1957). *Verbal behavior*. New York: Appleton-Century-Crofts.

Skinner, B. F. (1963). Behaviorism at fifty. *Science, 140*, 951–958.

Skinner, B. F. (1966a). Operant behavior. In W. K. Honig (Ed.), *Operant behavior: Areas of research and application* (pp. 12–32). New York: Appleton-Century-Crofts.

Skinner, B. F. (1966b). The phylogeny and ontogeny of behavior. *Science, 153*, 1204–1213.

Skinner, B. F. (1969). *Contingencies of reinforcement: A theoretical analysis.* Englewood Cliffs, NJ: Prentice-Hall.

Skinner, B. F. (1971). *Beyond freedom and dignity.* New York: Knopf.

Skinner, B. F. (1974). *About behaviorism.* New York: Knopf.

Skinner, B. F. (1980). *Notebooks.* (R. Epstein, Ed.) Englewood Cliffs, NJ: Prentice-Hall.

Skinner, B. F. (1983). *A matter of consequences: Part three of an autobiography.* New York: Knopf.

Skinner, B. F. (1984). Selection by consequences. *Behavioral and Brain Sciences, 7*, 502–510.

Skinner, B. F. (1988a). Reply to M. N. Richelle's "Are Skinner's writings still relevant to current psychology." In A. C. Catania & S. Harnad (Eds.), *The selection of behavior: The operant behaviorism of B. F. Skinner* (p. 128). New York: Cambridge University Press.

Skinner, B. F. (1988b). Reply to H. Rachlin's "Mental yes; private no." In A. C. Catania & S. Harnad (Eds.), *The selection of behavior: The operant behaviorism of B. F. Skinner* (pp. 200–202). New York: Cambridge University Press.

Skinner, B. F. (1988c). Reply to G. E. Zuriff's "Radical behaviorism and theoretical entities." In A. C. Catania & S. Harnad (Eds.), *The selection of behavior: The operant behaviorism of B. F. Skinner* (p. 217). New York: Cambridge University Press.

Skinner, B. F. (1988d). Reply to G. G. Gallup's "Consciousness, explanation, and the verbal community." In A. C. Catania & S. Harnad (Eds.), *The selection of behavior: The operant behaviorism of B. F. Skinner* (pp. 305–307). New York: Cambridge University Press.

Slife, B. D., Hope, C., & Nebeker, R. S. (1999). Examining the relationship between religious spirituality and psychological science. *Journal of Humanistic Psychology, 39*(2), 51–85.

Slife, B. D., & Williams, R. N. (1995). *What's behind the research? Discovering hidden assumptions in the behavioral sciences.* Thousand Oaks, CA: Sage.

Smith, H. (1985). The sacred unconscious, with footnotes on self-actualization and evil. *Journal of Humanistic Psychology, 25* (3), 65–80.

Smith, M. B. (1986). Toward a secular humanistic psychology. *Journal of Humanistic Psychology, 26* (1), 7–26.

Smith, M. B. (2003). Positive psychology: Documentation of a burgeoning movement [Review of the book Handbook of Positive Psychology]. *American Journal of Psychology, 116*, 159–163.

Smith, M. L., & Glass, G. V. (1977). Meta-analysis of psychotherapy outcome studies. *American Psychologist, 32*, 752–760.

Smith, M. L., Glass, G. V., & Miller, T. I. (1980). *The benefits of psychotherapy.* Baltimore: Johns Hopkins University Press.

Snyder, C. R., & Lopez, S. J. (2002/2005). *Handbook of positive psychology.* Oxford: Oxford University Press.

Sokal, M. M. (1984). The Gestalt psychologists in behaviorist America. *The American Historical Review, 89*, 1240–1263.

Sommerbeck, L. (2002). Person-centered or eclectic? A response to Kahn. *Journal of Humanistic Psychology, 42*(2), 84–87.

Southwick, C. H. (Ed.), (1963). *Primate social behavior.* Princeton, NJ: Van Nostrand Reinhold.

Sperry, R. W. (1961). Cerebral organization and behavior. *Science, 133,* 1749–1757.

Sperry, R. W. (1980). Mind-brain interaction: Mentalism yes, dualism no. *Neuroscience, 5,* 195–206.

Sperry, R. W. (1995). The riddle of consciousness and the changing scientific worldview. *Journal of Humanistic Psychology, 35*(2), 7–33.

Staats, A. W. (1994). Psychological behaviorism and behaviorizing psychology. *Behavior Analyst, 17,* 93–114.

Staats, A. W. (1996). *Behavior and personality: Psychological behaviorism.* New York: Springer.

Stigler, S. M. (1986). *The history of statistics: The measurement of uncertainty before 1900.* Cambridge, MA: Harvard University Press.

Stiles, W. B.. (2002). Future directions in research on humanistic psychotherapy. In D. J. Cain & J. Seeman (Eds.), *Humanistic psychotherapies: Handbook of research and practice* (pp. 605–616). Washington, DC: American Psychological Association.

Stuart, S., & LaRue, S. (1996). Computerized cognitive therapy: The interface between man and machine. *Journal of Cognitive Psychotherapy, 10,* 181–191.

Tageson, C. W. (1982). *Humanistic psychology: A synthesis.* Homewood, Ill: Dorsey.

Tart, C. T. (1969). Introduction. In C. T. Tart (Ed.), *Altered states of consciousness.* New York: Wiley.

Task Force on Promotion and Dissemination of Psychological Procedures. (1995). Training in and dissemination of empirically validated psychological treatments: Report and recommendation. *Clinical Psychology, 48*(1), 3–23.

Task Force on Psychological Intervention Guidelines. (1995). *Template for developing guidelines: Interventions for mental disorders and psychosocial aspects of physical disorders.* Washington, DC: American Psychological Association.

Taylor, E. (1999). An intellectual Renaissance in humanistic psychology? *Journal of Humanistic Psychology, 39* (2), 7–25.

Taylor, E. (2001). Positive psychology and humanistic psychology: A reply to Seligman. *Journal of Humanistic Psychology, 41,* 13–29.

Tesch, R. (1990). *Qualitative research: Analysis types and software tools.* New York: Falmer.

Tipler, F. J. (1994). *The physics of immortality: Modern cosmology, God and the resurrection of the dead.* New York: Doubleday.

Tobin, S. A. (1991). A comparison of psychoanalytic self psychology and Carl Rogers's person-centered therapy. *Journal of Humanistic Psychology, 31*(1), 9–33.

Tolman, E. C. (1932). *Purposive behavior in animals and men.* New York: Century Psychology Series.

Tolman, E. C. (1938). The determiners of behavior at a choice point. *Psychological Review, 45,* 1–41.

Tryon, W. W. (1993a). Neural networks: I. Theoretical unification through connectionism. *Clinical Psychology Review, 13,* 341–352.

Tryon, W. W. (1993b). Neural networks: II. Unified learning theory and behavioral psychotherapy. *Clinical Psychology Review, 13,* 353–371.

Tulku, T. (1977). *Time, space and knowledge.* Emeryville, CA: Darma Press.

Turing, A. M. (1936). On computable numbers, with an application to the Entscheidungsproblem. *Proceedings of the London Mathematical Society, second series, 42,* 230–265.

Turing, A. M. (1950). Computing machinery and intelligence. *Mind, 59,* 433–450.

U.S. Department of Health and Human Services (1999). *Mental health: A report of the Surgeon General.* U. S. Department of Health and Human Services: Rockville, MD.

Van Gelder, T. (1998). The dynamical hypothesis in cognitive science. *Behavioral and Brain Sciences, 21,* 615–665.

van Uchelen, N. (1994). Death and the after-life in the Hebrew Bible of ancient Israel. In J. M. Bremer, Th. P.J. Van Den Hout, R. Peters (Eds.). *Hidden futures: Death and immortality in Ancient Egypt, Anatolia, the Classical, Biblical, and Arabic-Islamic world* (pp. 77–90). Amsterdam: Amsterdam University Press.

Varela, F. J., Thompson, E., & Rosch, E. (1991). *The embodied mind: Cognitive science and human experience.* Cambridge, MA: MIT Press.

Vassiliades, D. T. (2004). Greeks and Buddhism: Historical contacts in the development of a universal religion. *The Eastern Buddhist, 36*(1, 2), 134–183.

Vich, M. A. (1990). The origins and growth of transpersonal psychology. *Journal of Humanistic Psychology, 30*(2), 47–50.

von Neuman, J. (1958). *The computer and the brain.* New Haven, CT: Yale University Press.

Vygotsky , L. S. (1962). *Thought and language.* Cambridge, MA: MIT Press.

Wampold, B. E. (2001). *The great psychotherapy debate: Models, methods, and findings.* Mahwah, NJ: Lawrence Erlbaum Associates.

Wampold, B. E., Mondin, G. W., Moody, M., Stich, F., Benson, K., & Ahn, H. (1997). A meta-analysis of outcome studies comparing bona fide psychotherapies: Empirically, "All must have prizes." *Psychological Bulletin, 122,* 203–215.

Watson, J. B. (1913). Psychology as the behaviorist views it. *Psychological Review, 20,* 158–177.

Watson, J. B. (1919). *Psychology from the standpoint of a behaviorist.* Philadelphia: J. B. Lippincott & Co.

Watson, J. B. (1920). Is thinking merely the action of language mechanisms? *British Journal of Psychology, 11,* 87–104.

Watson, J. B., & Rayner, R. (1920). Conditioned emotional reactions. *Journal of Psychology, 3,* 1–14.

Watson, L. (1979). *Lifetide: A biology of the unconscious.* New York: Simon & Schuster.

Watson, M. W., & Getz, K. (1990). The relationship between Oedipal behaviors and children's family role concepts. *Merrill-Palmer Quarterly, 36,* 487–505.

Watts, F. (1999). Cognitive neuroscience and religious consciousness. In R. J. Russell, N. Murphy, T. C. Meyering, & M. A. Arbib (Eds.), *Neuroscience and the person: Scientific perspectives on divine action* (pp. 327–346). Vatican City State: Vatican Observatory Publications.

Weber, M. (1958). *Economy and society. Vol. 2.* Indianapolis: Bobbs Merrill.

Weinstein, G. (1975). Humanistic education: What it is and what it isn't. *Meforum: Journal of Educational Diversity and Innovation, 2*(1), 8–11.

Weiss, P. A. (1971). The basic concept of hierarchic systems. In P. A. Weiss (Ed.), *Hierarchically organized systems in theory and practice* (pp. 1–43). New York: Hafner.

Weizenbaum, J. (1966). ELIZA—A computer program for the study of natural language communication between man and machine. *Communications of the ACM, 9,* 36–45.

Weizenbaum, J. (1976). *Computer power and human reason.* San Francisco: W.H. Freeman.

Weizenbaum, J. (1995). The myth of the last metaphor. In P. Baumgartner & S. Payr (Eds.), *Speaking minds: Interviews with twenty eminent scientists* (pp. 249–264). Princeton, N.J.: Princeton University Press.

Wertheimer, M. (1965). Relativity and Gestalt: A note on Albert Einstein and Max Wertheimer. *Journal of the History of the Behavioral Sciences, 1,* 86–87.

Westen, D. (1998). The scientific legacy of Sigmund Freud: Toward a psychodynamically informed psychological science. *Psychological Bulletin, 124,* 333–371.

Westen, D., & Bradley, R. (2005). Empirically supported complexity: Rethinking evidence-based practice in psychology. *Current Directions in Psychological Science, 14,* 266–271.

Whiten, A., & Byrne, R. W. (1991). The emergence of metarepresentation in human ontogony. In A. Whiten (Ed.), *Natural theories of mind: Evolution, development, and simulation of everyday mindreading* (pp. 267–282). Oxford: Blackwell.

Widera-Wysoczańska, A. (1999). Everyday awareness of death: A qualitative investigation. *Journal of Humanistic Psychology, 39*(3), 73–95.

Wiener, N. (1948). *Cybernetics.* New York: Wiley.

Wilber, K. (1982). The pre/trans fallacy. *Journal of Humanistic Psychology, 22,* 5–43.

Wilber, K. (1985). *No boundary: Eastern and Western approaches to personal growth.* Boston: Shambhala.

Williams, B. (1973). *Problems of the self: Philosophical papers 1956–1972.* Cambridge, England: Cambridge University Press.

Williams, J. L. (1986). The behavioral and the mystical: Reflections on behaviorism and Eastern thought. *The Behavior Analyst, 9,* 167–173.

Wilson, S. R. (1988). The "real-self" controversy: Toward an integration of humanistic and interactionist theory. *Journal of Humanistic Psychology, 28*(1), 39–65.

Woodworth, R. S. (1938). Experimental psychology. New York: Holt, Rinehart, & Winston.

Wozniak, R. H. (1993). Conwy Lloyd Morgan, mental evolution, and the *Introduction to Comparative Psychology.* In Morgan, C. L. *An introduction to comparative psychology* (Reprint ed. 1894/1993, pp. vii-xix). London: Routledge/Thommes.

Wright, R. (2004). A short history of progress. Toronto: House of Anansi Press.

Wundt, W. (1896). *Human and animal psychology. Second edition.* (J. R. Creighton & E. B. Titchener, Trans.) London: Swan Sonnenschein & Co.

Wundt, W. (1910). *Principles of physiological psychology. Vol. 1.* (E. B. Titchener, Trans.) London: Swan Sonnenschein.

Wundt, W. (1912). *An introduction to psychology.* (R. Pintner, Trans.) London: George Allen.

Yardy, P., & Grosch, P. (1999). *The puzzle of ethics* (Revised Edition). London: Fount Paperbacks.

Zeilinger, A. (2003). Quantum teleportation. *Scientific American, 13*(1), 34–43.

Zuriff, G. E. (1985). *Behaviorism: A conceptual reconstruction.* New York: Columbia University Press.

Author Index

Subject Index